CLOSE
HARMONY

D0732290

CLOSE HARMONY

A History of Southern Gospel

James R. Goff Jr.

The University of North Carolina Press

Chapel Hill & London

© 2002
The University of North Carolina Press
All rights reserved
Manufactured in the United States of America
Designed by Richard Hendel
Set in Bell and Didot types
by Tseng Information Systems, Inc.
The paper in this book meets the guidelines for
permanence and durability of the Committee on
Production Guidelines for Book Longevity of the
Council on Library Resources.

Library of Congress Cataloging-in-Publication Data
Goff, James R., 1957–
Close harmony : a history of southern gospel /
James R. Goff Jr.
p. cm.
Includes bibliographical references (p.   ) and index.
ISBN 0-8078-2681-2 (cloth : alk. paper)—
ISBN 0-8078-5346-1 (pbk. : alk. paper)
1. Gospel music—History and criticism.
2. Contemporary Christian music—
History and criticism.   I. Title.
ML3187 .G64   2002
782.25'4'0975—dc21   2001043372

Cloth: 06   05   04   03   02   5   4   3   2   1
Paper: 06   05   04   03   02   5   4   3   2   1

For
Mama and Daddy
to whom I owe
the gift of love,
the foundation of faith,
and the music of life

CONTENTS

Preface xi

Introduction 1

FIGURES & ILLUSTRATIONS

PREFACE

"What's your next book going to be about?" my neighbor asked on a picturesque autumn day in the mountains as we walked back from our mailboxes. "It'll be about gospel music," I replied, and then furtively added, "specifically white gospel music." With a stunned look but an amiable smile, this neighbor—herself a northern transplant to the southern Appalachian region—replied, "Oh. Well, that's going to require an awful lot of research, isn't it? I wonder if you'll be able to find anything."

Such was one of the many conversations during the early phase of my research on the quartets of the style today known as southern gospel. At the time, I smiled but did not contradict my neighbor's wisdom—or, in this case, lack of knowledge. It was not the first time I had encountered such skepticism. My colleagues in universities across America were often no less in the dark. They assumed that gospel music must be black gospel and to look specifically at the white roots of gospel would be to find little, if anything, of value. But I knew better. I had grown up with the southern gospel quartets. No Sunday morning passed without the television tuned to the *Gospel Singing Jubilee*, where, among others, the Florida Boys and the Happy Goodmans primed my family for the Sabbath. Names like Blackwood Brothers, LeFevre Trio, Speer Family, Chuck Wagon Gang, Statesmen, and Segos were second nature to us. And individual members of groups . . . James Blackwood, J. D. Sumner, Hovie Lister, Eva Mae LeFevre, Vestal Goodman, Mom and Dad Speer, Les Beasley, Rose Carter Karnes, Naomi Sego . . . we filed those names away in our brains much as we did baseball stars or the casts of our favorite television shows. They just always were because southern gospel always was.

But many Americans did not recognize these names. They eventually heard about Mahalia Jackson, Shirley Caesar, and the Reverend James Cleveland—the great singers of the black gospel tradition—especially as the 1960s brought much deserved attention to these artists who had labored long and hard in relative obscurity. But much less attention came to those who toiled in the white gospel tradition—though they, too, emerged in poverty and fought long odds to sing about a message that stretched deep into their souls.

Southern gospel music might well be the best-kept secret in America. With a fervent following and a century of history, the genre survives today as a vibrant musical style. It has both borrowed from and contributed to the larger musical culture of America in ways that few comprehend or understand. This is the story of four generations of American gospel singers, songwriters, and music promoters. They followed a dream and created a legacy that has endured. Their story deserves to be told.

Many people have shared in the creation of this book. Colleagues on the faculty and in the administration at Appalachian State University expressed an early interest, as did a number of my students. Specifically, I have benefited from the generous support of three department chairs, George Antone, Gale Christianson, and Michael Wade. Longtime colleague and basketball adversary, Tim Silver, also offered invaluable advice and insight. One of my students, Drinda Benge, served faithfully as my research assistant during one of the first years of the project. Former music professor Charles Isley emerged from retirement to share his intimate knowledge of shape notes with me. Through it all, they and numerous others have cheered me on in the true spirit of the academy.

Outside of my own university, old friends and new acquaintances alike helped to hone my instincts about the value of music in American life and culture. Bill Malone, Charles Wolfe, Grant Wacker, Willard Gatewood, Ed Harrell, and Sam Hill provided particular encouragement and advice. Their work and influence, as well as their willingness to offer valuable criticism, have made this a better book.

The staff at the University of North Carolina Press encouraged the project from the beginning. In particular, Elaine Maisner provided regular advice from the time of the initial proposal to the final stages of the manuscript. Along the way, she urged me to write carefully and clearly so that others might understand and appreciate what I knew deep inside. My editor, Mary Caviness, strengthened the manuscript with her insight and a careful eye for how others were likely to read and interpret my words. Like everyone else, they proved to be patient and kept the faith through the inevitable setbacks and delays.

From the start, the southern gospel music industry has been enthusiastic and supportive. The research phase of the book was made possible by a $35,000 grant from the *Singing News Magazine* of Boone,

North Carolina. Owner and publisher Maurice Templeton, editor-in-chief Jerry Kirksey, and the entire staff have been both patient and encouraging. Without their help, the book would simply not exist. Of special note were the efforts of Sharon Kinsey and Mary Aparicio, for relaying messages and helping with the numerous overnight mailings; Ken Kirksey, who read and shared comments on an early manuscript draft; Danny Jones, for reminding me about the pictures; and the late Rick Templeton, who I wish could have lived to read this book.

In addition, I have benefited from the support of the Southern Gospel Music Association. Executive Director Heather Campbell and members of the SGMA board opened doors and cleared the path for me. Listed in the notes at the end of the book are references to the more than sixty interviews I conducted with southern gospel artists and industry executives. Each interviewee proved graceful and most willing to talk openly and honestly about an industry they had helped create. Of particular importance in my understanding of southern gospel were veteran performers James Blackwood and Les Beasley as well as promoter Charles Waller. They each provided the candor and friendship I needed, and, for that, I will always be appreciative. Some individuals I met along the way passed from this life without the opportunity to see the end result of their cooperation, and it is with some regret but fond memories that I note the names of J. D. Sumner, Brock Speer, Ottis Knippers, Roy Carter, Glen Payne, and Rex Nelon.

Historians would be lost without the patient support of good archivists and librarians. In that regard, I am most indebted to Appalachian State librarian and former student Susan Jennings—the finest researcher I know and my lifeline to the new world of computer cataloguing. Others on the Appalachian State library staff have also contributed, especially those in the Appalachian Collection and the Music Library. I am also indebted to staff archivists at the Country Music Foundation in Nashville; the Center for Popular Music in Murfreesboro, Tennessee; the Gospel Music Association in Nashville; the Flower Pentecostal Heritage Center in Springfield, Missouri; the Hal Bernard Dixon Jr. Pentecostal Research Center in Cleveland, Tennessee; and the Performing Arts Reading Room of the Library of Congress in Washington, D.C.

There is also much of one's own experience that goes into a book such as this, and a few honest words might be helpful from the outset. Interspersed between the chapters are personal accounts based on some of the interviews and encounters that fed my own understanding of southern gospel. I included them because I believe they offer insight beyond the realm of names, dates, and events. Southern gospel, like other forms of popular music, affects lives in a profound way—no less the ardent fan than the artist. I too am a product of the music. I grew up with it, left it for a time, only to return and find nourishment in both the music and the community that produces it. Throughout the book, I have tried to convey an understanding of the world of southern gospel—with an eye toward objectivity but also with the empathy that can only come from having lived for some time within the family.

I am grateful for the unfailing support of my wife, Connie. She first suggested the topic and has remained my strongest ally. More than anyone else, she has been at my side for the travel, the long days and nights of research and writing, and the seemingly endless process of proofreading and editing. She read my words first, and her advice served to strengthen the book from start to finish. My kids, Gideon and Kacy, were small when this effort began. They are small no longer, but they, too, have memories of following Daddy to concerts and listening to endless conversations about singing conventions, concert promoters, and quartet singers. They have grown up with the book, and I only hope that this process did not pull too much of me away from them.

My own musical heritage proved invaluable in understanding the people and events portrayed in this book. I understood because, in at least a limited way, I had known the excitement of performing on stage, the euphoria of seeing my picture on an album cover, and the responsibility of singing the gospel message to an audience. And so to my childhood friends who helped make up the Oak Street Youth Choir back in the 1960s and 1970s, I say thank you. I couldn't have done it without you. And dittos to Aunt Carolyn . . . for teaching me to sing.

Finally, I would like to thank my parents, James and Kathryn Goff. It is to them that I respectfully dedicate this book. For more years than I care to mention they have instilled a core set of values that cushioned my transition from childhood to manhood. Though in different ways, they each taught me to love God, to cherish others, and to relish the opportunity that comes with time. Always there was a respect for family and heritage . . . always a recognition of the music that is life.

June 2001

CLOSE
HARMONY

INTRODUCTION

On a warm spring evening in 1997, thirty-eight individuals were inducted as the initial class of the Southern Gospel Music Association's Hall of Fame. For many, this black-tie affair was the symbol of a life-long dream come true. Though all had been honored before in a variety of settings, never had they been honored in such a distinct way—and never had southern gospel been showcased more clearly as a specific musical art form. One industry veteran referred to the evening as a night that "topped any and everything I have ever attended." Reflecting on the two short years since the organization's founding and the imminent construction of a museum and Hall of Fame complex, he editorialized: "The SGMA membership has grown to over 10,000, making the SGMA the largest Gospel Music organization in the world. Anybody see the hand of God at work here?"[1]

Early in the nation's history, gospel music emerged as a central part of the expression of American culture. Practically speaking, it provided a foundation for other styles of music that came to enrich the life of its citizens. More important, it built a bulwark upon which a developing nation and its people could assemble a religious identity. At least since the first few decades of the nineteenth century, Americans have been among the world's most religious people. And even before the rural revivals of the early 1800s turned the cultural landscape of the nation into a bastion of evangelicalism, Americans were comfortable with the tenets of the Judeo-Christian heritage and understood the majority of their values within those boundaries. In that context, gospel music helped mold the culture through which the collective hopes, dreams, and beliefs of most Americans found expression.

Few books have examined the American gospel music tradition. One can search library shelves and find a significant number of works on the evolution and importance of most forms of classical and popular music. On the popular side, a number of impressive efforts have chronicled the rise of blues, jazz, rock 'n' roll, and country music. In recent years, a sizable number of similar works on the role of black gospel have even appeared.[2] Yet almost ignored is the parallel treatment of the white gospel tradition.

An exception has been the charting of the rather limited role of the *Sacred Harp* songbooks and the rural singing conventions that flourished in the late nineteenth and early twentieth centuries.[3] Almost nothing exists on the more important and popular seven-note tradition of shape notes. For more than a century, these seven-note shapes formed the core of a booming songbook industry, located primarily in the South and drawing its strength from the rural and small-town, working class–rooted evangelical churches. Generations of rural southerners learned to sing by these shapes and ultimately identified with a style of music popularized by songwriters who promoted this musical method.

The songbook industry itself provided the spark that, when coupled with the growth of radio and phonograph recordings, forged the success of the white gospel music industry in the South. Developing alongside the black gospel music industry, which was rooted more in the urban centers of both the South and North, the white industry has suffered from a lack of academic attention. Always dwarfed by larger segments of the traditionally white music industry, gospel nonetheless played a primary role in establishing the dominant styles of popular music in America. A few scholarly efforts have come as parallels to a predominant interest in country and folk/bluegrass music.[4] More specialized treatments have most often remained unpublished doctoral dissertations.[5] A handful of efforts have focused specifically on the shape-note tradition with little emphasis on the professional gospel music industry that grew out of that tradition.[6] The result has been a gospel music heritage evaluated almost exclusively by fans and industry insiders.[7]

It is an indictment of American history that black and white gospel developed as separate—and parallel—traditions.[8] A sense of injustice no doubt led many scholars to investigate first the considerable accomplishments of black gospel songwriters and artists. Another reason is perhaps because, though gospel music generated a greater volume of sales among the larger white population, in segregated America, gospel music provided only a small component of the overall musical market for white America while it played a much larger role in the black community. For whatever reason, when the mainstream media and Americans generally outside the tight-knit world of Christian song initially came into contact with the music—and gospel quartets in particular—they came to associate that music with black Americans only. A typical newspaper article from the mid-1990s gave substantial treatment to the subject of gospel music, dividing the genre into traditional and contemporary categories. However, white gospel artists were referred to solely in the contemporary category, which dates back only to the last three decades, and, even then, no southern gospel artist received mention.[9]

Gospel music in America should be understood in a couple of different contexts. The largest context is singing songs with religious lyrical content. This tradition dates back to the Puritans, borrowed heavily from early European hymn singing, and is associated most commonly with the development of nineteenth-century mainline Protestant worship.[10] Within the world of gospel music, the late nineteenth century offered a new variety of sounds and lyrics—so varied that churchmen agonized over the growing divide between hymns and gospel singing.[11] Hymns became associated with congregational singing in Sunday worship services; gospel singing, with a more vibrant (and often controversial) singing of religious lyrics to popular tunes. In the broadest sense, then, gospel singing served as a wellspring of worship within the American music tradition—honoring neither color line nor stylistic limitation.

More limited in scope is the gospel music industry. If we focus only on the ties that developed economically—and stylistically, inasmuch as style dictated the parameters of a given market—a clearer picture comes into view. By the early part of the twentieth century, two separate gospel music industries had developed. Ironically, given the strength of segregation in the nation's northern cities as well as in the South, these industries—drawn along racial lines—crossed paths much more often than is commonly acknowledged. Yet, there was little mixing of audiences until the 1960s, when racial barriers were challenged by the civil rights movement and new approaches to musical style were also more actively encouraged. As contemporary gospel began to emerge, the racial barriers that had defined the previous three generations of American gospel music became blurred, though by then stylistic differences—related to race but only marginally—had dictated separate paths for many individuals associated with the industry.

At first glance, gospel music is still just gospel song—music centered on a Christian theme. As a result, the important differences among the gospel performances of Tennessee Ernie Ford, Elvis Presley, Mahalia Jackson, and James Blackwood might not be recognized. But, for those within the industry, a clear distinction exists. Ford and Presley sang gospel songs but were not gospel singers. Jackson was a gospel singer firmly within the black gospel genre. Blackwood, on the other hand, achieved his reputation as a gospel singer in the tradition of the white gospel quartets.

Gospel as a separate musical art form emerged primarily in the South and, as one music historian has argued, stands alongside jazz, blues, and country music as "the fourth great genre of grass roots music" and "the fourth major type of southern music."[12] Others have characterized the intimate connection between the region and its music by noting that "southern religious life . . . affected both the nature of songs and the manner in which they were performed."[13] Yet, of the four, only gospel—specifically southern gospel—identified itself with the region by name. This has been a recent phenomenon, one that emerged within the white gospel industry in order to designate the older styles of music from the growing contemporary Christian music that, in the 1960s and 1970s, borrowed heavily from sounds associated with the radio strains of rock 'n' roll and pop.

But there is much more to the self-conscious designation of "southern" gospel than a concern for traditional music. More powerful is the degree to which the music has come to identify itself with a marketplace that mirrors the growth of conservative evangelical Christianity. As a result, recent advocates of southern gospel have argued that the real distinction in their music is a concern for theologically correct lyrics and for performers who maintain some semblance of a Christian lifestyle.[14] Though this concern has not always been a primary factor within the industry, it is consistent with the roots of a gospel music tradition whose mission was identified first and foremost as serving the evangelical churches of rural America. Over the last three decades of the twentieth century, America seemed to become more conservative—particularly on issues related to the nation's social policies. Religious conservatives grew in political power, or at least grew more visible via traditional media outlets, and gained much more prominence in the nation's political and social discourse. The growing voice of the nation's social conservatives dovetailed nicely with the aims and aspirations of most southern gospel singers.

Many scholars who have studied gospel music have noted stark differences in the attributes of white and black gospel. The result of this observation has oftentimes been to suppose mistakenly that one simply emerged from the other and, in the case of white gospel, that it is simply a pale imitation. Consequently, many authors have fought a senseless battle over which came first and who influenced whom without a full recognition of the integrated nature of southern life, particularly during the formative years of the eighteenth and nineteenth centuries.[15] White and black southerners lived, worked, and worshiped together even though custom and economic status often sanctioned the firm foundation of white supremacy. Even after segregation laws took effect in the late years of the nineteenth century, southerners of both races continued to influence one another on an almost daily basis.

Ironically, the area of life most divided in 1900 was religious life—segregation by custom rather than by any particular detail of a state's Jim Crow package. In part to experience fully one of the few areas where they had total control, blacks in the decades after the Civil War flocked to churches and denominations that were operated and controlled within the black community.[16] A by-product was an increased separation in the performance of and preference for gospel music. The timing was pivotal, for the late decades of the nineteenth century would be the crucial decades in the development of the shape-note songbook publishing business and also in the formation of early quartet styling. Black and white singers would still listen to and learn, and consciously borrow from each other, but segregation in general would mean that their audiences and the confines of their market would be separate for at least the first six decades of the twentieth century.

Religious affiliation has made an important impact on the southern gospel music industry. By far the strongest denominational ties are to independent Baptists and to the Holiness and Pentecostal organizations that dotted the landscape early in the twentieth century and have enjoyed phenomenal growth ever since. Gauging the impact of denominations is not an easy or exact science. Nevertheless, any analysis of the denominational background of successful artists as well as the churches that have provided the strongest support for the industry since its inception makes such a conclusion inevitable. Many writers have speculated that the Holiness-Pentecostal connection flourished because of an increased openness in worship style that allowed the innovative, often upbeat, performance of commercial gospel music. The influence of these religious groups has also contained a biracial dynamic. Both independent Baptists and Holiness-Pentecostals have survived as strong organizations within white and black communities in the South.[17]

The Holiness-Pentecostal connection to southern gospel is particularly important because it is precisely that wing of the white Protestant world that has generally been overlooked and misunderstood by music historians. Convinced that white Protestants displayed little emotion in their services, writers have stereotyped black gospel as expressive while stereotyping white gospel as staid.[18] The fact is that both white and black Christians affiliated with the Holiness-Pentecostal wing of Protestantism found much to shout about in their worship services and those emotions spilled logically over into their singing. The roots of gospel music are found in the rural churches that routinely failed to conform to the more sophisticated style of their urban counterparts. Students of black gospel music have noted that much of that rural character was transferred to urban areas as a result of the large number of black southerners migrating north in search of economic opportunity during the early decades of the twentieth century. The same migration story was true for whites who, disillusioned with the agricultural setbacks of the Depression years, remained tied to the southern, rural culture of their youth long after they found new homes outside the bounds of the traditional South.[19]

The term "gospel music" first appeared in the late nineteenth century and was used specifically to refer to a more popular genre of songs than the hymns commonly sung in Sunday morning worship services. Likewise, the distinction emerged within black and white communities, spawning slightly different styles depending upon the experiences of performers and the tastes of the audiences that fueled their musical ambitions. In all instances, gospel singing borrowed freely from the musical innovations emanating from other areas of American music, from blues and country music, as well as from the older hymnody and spirituals of the past.

In both black and white communities, gospel singing became associated with the singing of new songs, thus eliminating elements of the new genre from any elevation to the spiritual status of hymns. The result was an important distinction between hymn singing, which focused on tradition, and gospel singing, which created by necessity an ongoing search for talent and artistic creation. The tie here also necessitated a market, an enduring market that would be large enough to sustain the livelihood of performers, publishers, and promoters.

A second distinction was one of degree. Gospel singing, unlike the singing of hymns in church on Sunday, required that some individuals choose the making and performing of gospel music as their primary occupation. This differentiated gospel performers in both white and

Introduction

black communities from two other groups that also sang gospel tunes: 1) secular singers, who invariably chose gospel songs already popular and thus familiar to the audience as a part of a larger repertoire,[20] and 2) church singers, who practiced their craft without benefit of pay and justified their singing as a part of using one's talent for God.[21]

Recognizing southern gospel as a specific art form is important for several reasons. First of all, the music of southern gospel is the music of much of America. From the mid-nineteenth century on, a high percentage of Americans have been influenced from childhood by conservative Protestant Christianity. A vital subset of that influence was the church music—hymns and gospel songs—that became as much a part of Sunday worship as the preacher's sermon, Sunday school classes, and intercessory prayer. The overwhelming success of the Bill Gaither *Homecoming* video series attests to the impact of Sunday morning and evening services on many Americans. Though some songs might be known only to gospel music fans who immediately identify a particular song with a group from the past, the bulk of the tunes in the video presentations include older songs that resonate to a middle-aged audience in search of its roots.[22]

A second reason that southern gospel deserves further recognition is that the songs and the style in which they are sung, though smaller in impact than Protestant hymnody, have stirred a significant subset of Americans. The music is fun, invigorating, and lively. It quite naturally takes something about which many Americans feel deeply, the Christian gospel, and applies it to a variety of musical styles that listeners find appealing. The appeal is particularly strong in the rural South and Midwest; in these parts of the country there has been a core of southern gospel fans since the industry's beginnings in the second decade of the twentieth century. Through the years, those fans have struggled with a peculiar problem unknown to fans of other forms of popular music. Is gospel music a genre to be genuinely enjoyed as entertainment? Or should these songs only be celebrated as a part of worship? Is it possible for both those things to occur simultaneously? Sometimes regarded as less a concern in black gospel circles, the issue clearly impeded the growth of white gospel as a valid extension of the music industry.[23]

Popular singers and promoters quickly learned the perils of becoming embroiled in church politics. Making matters difficult, they needed to appeal to a cross-section of evangelical Protestants, many of whom made an art form of theological debate and dissension. A few church members resolved these questions early and came to regard gospel music as wholesome entertainment, precisely the kind of entertainment that a conservative Christian should enjoy. Most, however, continued to maintain a tenuous alliance, making a firm distinction between music as a form of worship and the market-driven world of the southern gospel quartets. These members and their churches might support the gospel music industry, but they did so cautiously, concerned about the theological content of song lyrics and the degree to which musical style mirrored the popular advances of the secular music industry. Above all, they kept a scrupulous vigil over the personal lives of Christian entertainers. Whether or not a singer had a testimony that, by the account of personal witnesses, matched the specifics of day-to-day living became a constant query faced by gospel performers but not by their secular counterparts. In fact, secular musicians might often profit from the publicity of a scandal in their personal lives. For gospel singers, such publicity could spell the end of their careers. Though many prominent singers acknowledged that their primary purpose was entertainment, their dependence on a conservative Protestant audience prevented them from ever fully escaping life within the confines of the evangelical fish bowl.

A final reason for learning more about the southern gospel genre is that it reveals the influence of gospel music on American music in general. A few southern gospel artists have moved into the secular field with success. The most notable example is the Oak Ridge Boys, who reached the pinnacle of success within the gospel music market by the early 1970s and then turned to a career in country music. Predictably the switch was not an amiable one for many gospel music fans, who interpreted the move as an abandoning of the gospel music family for greener pastures and larger paychecks. A lesser publicized switch came in the late 1950s, when the well-known Jordanaires chose Nashville studio work over the routine gospel music concert circuit. Best known for their work with Elvis Presley, the group was both envied and alienated by those who stayed on the more typical gospel music path. The Statler Brothers, a regional gospel group from the Shenandoah Valley of Virginia, who in the early 1960s achieved success in country music through their association with Johnny Cash, charted a similar trail. Ironically, traditional southern gospel fans have reacted very differently to the success of the Statlers, in large part because their shift into country seemed a natural move rather than an abrupt break. Unlike the Oaks, the Statlers were not very well known at the time of their initial association with Cash. In addition, the

Statlers have been very open about their indebtedness to the southern gospel industry and its giants, in large measure endearing themselves to gospel music advocates by keeping the same rural styling and clean-cut looks of traditional gospel quartets.

Though the thought of moving into more lucrative areas of the music industry has been a constant temptation for some performers, others have made quite a following for themselves with long careers in gospel alone. Names like James Blackwood, Eva Mae LeFevre, J. D. Sumner, Brock Speer, Naomi Sego, and Hovie Lister became household names for anyone with a background in southern gospel.[24] In addition, their influence remained strong enough that they, and many others like them, became a source of inspiration for a number of secular artists who as kids thrilled at the sight and sound of these legends and as adults marveled at their staying power and longevity.

Southern gospel music today is a varied field with styles ranging from the traditional four-part harmony quartet singing that molded its original identity to a blend of country and bluegrass gospel that thrives on the border of country-and-western music.[25] A handful of black gospel groups have even found success within its ranks, offering a blend of traditional black and white gospel that illustrates the degree to which the music remained an interracial phenomenon despite the vestiges of racism and segregation. The most important defining criterion of southern gospel has become its link with the burgeoning evangelical movement, a link that promises financial success even while it forecasts a move away from an entertainment-based industry to one that more deliberately mixes entertainment with ministry.

There are those within the camp who are nervous about the mix. They recognize that high-profile evangelism often suffers from the same media exposure needed to propel it to success and know deep down that the American public has a low tolerance for the gilded sparkle of high-tech spirituality. Even so, those who fear the pitfalls know also that traditional gospel quartet music has always survived at the mercy of conservative American Christianity. Though gospel music and gospel worship have never been precisely the same in American history, neither have they ever been too far apart. Gauging the relationship, as well as the subtle differences, between the two is crucial to understanding the place of southern gospel in modern American life.

I
THE ROOTS OF A MUSICAL GENRE

Alexandria, Indiana, April 3, 1996

The red-and-white-striped tent where we have gathered to eat is big. And the people inside it seem larger than life to me. There's James Blackwood, along with his sons, Jimmy and Billy . . . there's been a Blackwood in the gospel music industry since 1934. There's Hovie Lister, the founder of the Statesmen Quartet, and Howard and Vestal Goodman of the Happy Goodman Family. There's Jake Hess and Rex Nelon. Over in the corner is J. D. Sumner, the lowest singing bass singer on record and probably gospel music's most recognized personality long before he and the Stamps joined Elvis Presley on tour in the early 1970s. The list seems endless . . . Brock and Ben Speer, along with their sisters Rosa Nell and Mary Tom, Lily Fern Weatherford, Glen Payne and George Younce, Naomi Sego, Les Beasley. They're all here . . . along with a younger generation of gospel singers — Terry Blackwood, Jessy Dixon, Sue Dodge, Kirk Talley, Ann Downing, Gerald Wolfe, Kenny Bishop, Janet Paschal, Ivan Parker . . . far more than I can comprehend in one setting. Gospel singers all and each one here as guests of Bill and Gloria Gaither, themselves a part of the gospel music world for more than three decades.

The singers are here to record footage for more of Gaither's *Homecoming* video series. I'm here to observe and meet as many as I can . . . to get their stories, to experience their struggles, to understand their dream. It is insight into a world I have known all my life . . . though only from the outside. Now I am inside . . . inside, under the tent, where the memories flow and the ancient songs are sweet.

1
GOSPEL MUSIC IN THE NINETEENTH CENTURY

Like most successful innovations in twentieth-century America, the gospel music industry emerged from a combination of forces that coalesced in the nineteenth. A revival of religious faith that stressed personal experience, a reform attitude that sparked among other things an interest in improved literacy within the population, a continuous fascination with transportation advances and the resulting ease of communication between one region and the next—all these factors helped define the character of nineteenth-century America and, thereby, contributed to the nation's destiny. Whatever Americans became over the course of that century, they did so with the belief that they were somehow irreparably changing the course of history as they knew it. Despite the awesome nature of this conviction, Americans of a century ago remained remarkably confidant that they would succeed in building a great nation and that descendants would praise their efforts.[1]

Yet before the heady accomplishments of nineteenth-century Americans, earlier American settlers had begun the trends that would set into motion the limits of America's religious music culture. American colonists inherited the worship traditions of Protestant Europe and, as a result, focused much of their energy in the early seventeenth and eighteenth centuries on the proper use of scripture in musical form. The oldest tradition in Christian hymnody was singing the Old Testament Psalms, a heritage that limited creativity among church musicians but that allowed for little debate on the issue of lyrical content. The earliest American Psalters arrived already bound within the Bibles of the Pilgrim colonists in 1620. A similar Psalter arrived with the more numerous Puritans who settled the Massachusetts Bay colony beginning in 1630. In response to some concern over the proper translation of the Psalms, settlers in Massachusetts soon enjoyed the publication of a new Psalter all their own when, in 1640, *The Bay Psalm Book* became "the first book-length product of a printing press in British North America."[2] Even with the presence of the new Psalter, Psalm-tunes were oftentimes "lined out," a method by which the song leader would recite one or two lines and then have the audience chant the same words back in a songlike fashion. The method became even more prominent as rural churches formed in the backcountry and copies of the Psalter were neither easily available nor affordable.[3]

Always conscious—and to some degree self-conscious—of the colonial link to European culture, New England ministers pushed for improved musical ability among their congregations in a movement begun in the 1720s. Advocates of what was known as "the singing school movement," or the "singing school war," feared a loss of musical ability and pointed to the increased and almost exclusive use of "lining out" in some Puritan churches. Others feared the disappearance of good music itself. One New England minister, Thomas Walter, strongly pledged his support of the singing school movement, noting that Sunday singing in area churches produced "an horrid Medly [*sic*] of confused and disorderly noises."[4] The venerable Puritan spokesman Cotton Mather himself endorsed the musical improvements, which focused essentially on teaching a larger percentage of parishioners to read music.[5] Opponents, on the other hand, feared that singing societies would detract from the serious nature of rational worship and accused proponents of being too concerned with frivolous trappings and ornamental aspects of the service. The New England "singing war" had some success in establishing local singing societies and generally seems to have contributed to the earliest elements of popular congregational singing in America.[6] The impact of the singing societies was considerable, and, by the early 1700s, the movement had begun to make its influence felt even in the few Anglican churches of the remote southern colonies.[7]

Americans were also affected by the innovative musical contribution of Isaac Watts (1674–1748), perhaps the most influential of English songwriters. Watts introduced diversity into the English worship service by taking a broad approach in translating the message of the Psalms and, subsequently, broke with the Psalm-only tradition entirely in composing religious hymns for singing. Incredibly varied and abundant, Watts's works became the best loved of the early American hymns and were included subsequently in almost every collection of religious songs published.[8] Other innovative Englishmen, most notably John and Charles Wesley, continued the tradition and wrote songs designed to deepen the spiritual commitment of the earnest believer. By the time of the American Revolution, Americans were quite familiar with the concept of religious hymn singing as a separate part of the weekly worship service.[9]

But Americans would ultimately chart their own course in political and spiritual matters. Within a generation after political independence, a series of revivals erupted initially in scattered New England congregations in the 1790s but, most prominently, in the frontier communities of the trans-Appalachian West in the first few years of the nineteenth century. These revivals, which thrived in some areas until midcentury, ultimately shaped the character of American religion more than any single factor before or since.[10]

The revival spirit of the early nineteenth century occurred alongside perhaps the most creative period in American history. As the Revolutionary generation died out, a new generation of Americans sought meaning in the everyday experiences of building a nation. More than any other generation, they struggled with the definition of America and with what its citizens would aspire to become. As a result, the next half century would be spent redefining the context of democracy and citizenship, inaugurating a dizzying array of reform programs, and—just as important—experimenting with new ways of religious expression.

One of the most significant developments of the religious revivals was the birth of evangelical theology. Consistent with the drift of individualism and democratic government, evangelicalism came to embrace the view that personal salvation was a matter of individual choice, where, regardless of how it might be explained theologically, human beings shared at least some of the responsibility for initiating the process of conversion. In addition, evangelicals were certain that, once personal salvation had been secured, individual Christians would go about the business of changing their world from a den of iniquity into a kingdom of righteousness. Those two major impulses, individual choice in Christian salvation and active participation in social improvement, stood at the root of much of the reform spirit of the early years of the century. It was an exciting time, a moment of unparalleled restlessness.[11]

The Great Revival found its most unique expression in the areas of the

The Roots of a Musical Genre

American landscape least tied to either Europe or the colonial heritage. On the isolated frontier of Kentucky and Tennessee, men and women of all races came together to praise God and worship in an excited frenzy unmatched in American history. By the time revivalism reached a crescendo in midcentury, membership rolls in evangelical-style Protestant denominations had mushroomed and the cultural influence that these churches held over some regions and communities likewise increased. The biggest organizational benefactors were the Methodists, Baptists, and Presbyterians, the overwhelming majority of whom adjusted both their theological views and worship practices to express the message and conform to the method of evangelical revival.[12]

The growth in membership of these Protestant organizations during the nineteenth century, particularly in the formerly unchurched South, was nothing short of amazing. Southern Presbyterians, numbering 20,000 in 1790 doubled in number by 1813 and topped 160,000 by 1835. Baptist churches enjoyed a similar growth pattern, moving from a membership of little more than 40,000 to almost 300,000 over the same period. By the end of the century, members of the Southern Baptist Convention alone would number more than 1,101,000. Methodists experienced the largest organizational growth. Separated from the Anglican Church in the 1780s, the Methodist Church in the South grew in membership from just over 40,000 in 1790 to well over a million by the conclusion of the Civil War. By the 1890s, black and white Methodists and Baptists in the South combined totaled between 4.5 and 5 million adherents.[13]

The center of the revival activity in many rural areas was the camp meeting, an extended festival of religious worship in which most Protestant denominations represented in a given area participated. Coordinated best and most often by Methodists, these four-to seven-day camp meetings became events of considerable social significance quite apart from the measure of religious significance they held. In remote areas where neighbors saw each other infrequently at best, the camp meeting flourished as an annual event held in conjunction with a lull in the agricultural calendar. No camp meeting achieved a greater legacy than the Cane Ridge Camp Meeting begun in 1801 in Bourbon County, Kentucky. Originally planned by area Presbyterians as a communitywide communion service, the meeting tapped into an already brewing revival spirit. Drawing crowds in excess of 10,000 during the earliest years of the century, Cane Ridge became famous for the emotional freedom that many worshipers demonstrated as they shouted and danced under the influence of religious power.[14]

Among the many activities enjoyed in the camp meetings, singing proved to be one of the most influential.[15] Around evening campfires both before and following the preaching service, devout followers gathered to sing their favorite hymns. Especially popular were the choruses, many of which were constructed specifically to adjoin traditional hymns with which worshipers were already familiar.[16] Choruses were popular for several reasons. They tended to be catchy tunes that were easy to sing and thus easy to learn. Not coincidentally, they were often constructed from popular folk melodies that were already well known to many in the audience. In addition, they solved in one step the dual problem of illiteracy and a shortage of songbooks. A handful of individuals with books or with small collections of song lyrics called songsters could sing the verses while the bulk of the participants joined in on the chorus.[17]

Memoirs of the great camp meeting days invariably recall the centrality of music and credit the songs with much of the spiritual atmosphere that the meetings were able to engender. A participant at Cane Ridge remembered that a "serenade of music cheered all their spirits, which never desisted from their first happy coalition, until they decamped, and everyone sung what he pleased, and to the tunes with which he was best acquainted."[18] Within a few years of the eruption at Cane Ridge, many Presbyterians and Baptists grew lukewarm about their participation in the annual camp meetings. Concerned about what many considered emotional excesses and perhaps unsettled by the theological implications of camp meeting–style religion, these rural Calvinists remained no less the supporters of revivalism.[19] Baptists and Presbyterians continued their allegiance by substituting the camp meetings with in-house revival campaigns known as protracted meetings. Methodists, on the other hand, went about the business of organizing and improving the unofficial camp meeting campaigns, in part by building permanent structures at established locations and sponsoring the meetings on an annual basis.[20]

Whether in outdoor brush arbors, camp meeting auditoriums, or local church buildings for a communitywide protracted meeting, music encouraged revival—a fact not lost on evangelicals interested in reaching the lost with the gospel message. By midcentury, revival advocates were unabashedly extolling the merits of religious tunes. In 1850, Methodist Luther Lee's *Revival Manual* urged, "Singing during a revival is an important part of religious exercise. . . . An appropriate verse, well sung, at the right time, will sometimes do more to assist the struggling spirit to take hold on Christ by faith, than a long sermon or a long prayer."[21]

By the last quarter of the century, all evangelicals had accepted the important role that music could play in achieving their religious goal of converting men and women to the gospel. A promotional pamphlet appropriately titled *The Fire and the Hammer: Revivals and How to Promote Them*, published in Boston in 1877, noted with no apology the connection of music's status to the somewhat reduced role now assigned to evangelical preaching: "The singing of appropriate hymns performs a very important part in promoting revivals. I believe there is as much conviction lodged in the mind by singing as by preaching. The melody softens the feelings, and the sentiment of the hymns leaves its stamp upon the melting heart and ripens into fruit. The singing calls out charms, and keeps the people together more than the preaching. The great public attraction of all gatherings is the music. You cannot carry on a dance, a show, a circus, a theatre, or a war, without music."[22]

The evangelical success of revivalism was not limited by race. Worshipers at Cane Ridge commented often on the degree to which black and white southerners participated in the services and were the recipients of God's grace. Some camp meetings, like Cane Ridge, established segregated services with white and black ministers routinely abiding by strict racial guidelines. At other camp meetings, no wall of segregation existed and interracial worship services carried the day. Such was the incongruity of the South, particularly during the antebellum period.[23]

Even on those occasions when segregated services were the rule, blacks and whites in the South did not fail to influence each other. The camp meeting provided a greater degree of unrestrained worship for participants of both races. Whites came to view—stereotypically, of course—blacks as expert singers and years later regaled in the memories of their black counterparts as "the life of the camp meeting." Methodist preacher G. W. Henry ascribed special singing abilities to blacks, noting that "nine out of ten of them would have a melodious voice for singing" and that their melodies could be heard "at a great distance from the campground."[24] Here in the midst of a common worship experience, despite the invariable conflict of racial stereotypes and limits imposed by southern culture, worshipers listened, learned, and shared. Black participants were no less enamored with the lyrical poetry of the English writer Isaac Watts than were their white counterparts. At the same time, whites gained an appreciation for rhythmic variances that many scholars believe originated with previous generations on the African continent and were passed down through adaptations born and preserved in the southern slave community. One of the most widely referred to examples of African retention is the call-and-response style represented in gospel songs sung by a dominant lead singer and punctuated by repetitive lines echoed by the congregation. The method approximates much of the style that emerged out of the Puritan "lining out" process, and thus both traditions mutually enforced the development of repetitive lines in early-nineteenth-century refrains.[25]

The participation of blacks and whites in the frontier camp meeting was instructive in another way. It foreshadowed the cross-fertilization that would thrive in gospel music in the decades after Reconstruction, when southern society moved rapidly toward segregation. Although white gospel and black gospel would emerge as separate industries by the early years of the twentieth century, proponents never ignored the progress and development of their racial counterparts. As a result, divided by race and by the condition of early-twentieth-century American society, they would nonetheless inspire and influence each other even as they remained indebted to a common heritage.[26]

Local American Indians participated in camp meetings as well, where, once again, their contribution to the music was considered unique. James Finley's account of mid-nineteenth-century Methodist camp meetings included the following flowery description sure to capture the imagination of white readers fascinated with what was left of the native tribes once so numerous along the eastern seaboard: "Soon the Christian chiefs and queens and all were formed in a circle, and the voice of praise and prayer made the forest arches ring. After singing one of their Christian songs, as only Indians can sing, they fell on their knees and lifted up their faces toward heaven as if they expected the Great Spirit to descend."[27]

In the midst of such evangelical success, religious singing entered a new era of popularity. Coupled with an increase in literacy brought in part by advances in public education opportunities, the Great Revival was ripe for commercial expansion into the religious music arena. Publishers eager to capitalize on the new interest began publishing compiled volumes of hymns and religious folk songs by the early years of the century. Yet little could be achieved by publishers if the public at large remained virtually ignorant of the rudiments of music. Thus the interests of Puritan ministers a century before came to merge with the interests

The Roots of a Musical Genre

FA SOL LA FA SOL LA MI

Figure 1. The early-nineteenth-century four-note system.

of revivalists and religious music publishers of the early nineteenth century.[28]

Early in the eighteenth century, New England minister John Tufts had struggled with the same concern and, in an effort to simplify musical training, borrowed from a European method of printing music using a system of letters in place of musical notations on the traditional lines and spaces. Tufts used F, S, L, and M to represent the major steps on the scale, corresponding directly to the solmization syllables fa, sol, la, and mi. In addition, he added time values using various punctuation marks. His *Introduction to the Singing of Psalm-Tunes,* published in Boston in 1721, stood as a landmark in the attempt to promote music among the masses.[29] He was concerned with how best to reach a wider audience with musical knowledge, now made easier by his having abbreviated and simplified the very core of musical language. But the system he devised was difficult to adapt to music of significant complexity and, as a result, received little promotion.[30]

The major breakthrough in fine-tuning Tufts's idea came a few decades later with the publication of an instructional booklet appropriately named *The Easy Instructor.* Published first in 1798 by William Little and William Smith,[31] the pathbreaking musical handbook used Tufts's basic concept but, in place of the awkward letter notation, substituted uniquely shaped notes on the traditional scale of lines and spaces (see Figure 1). The immediate advantage was apparent. Nothing would be lost for the student who studied music through traditional methods and yet each solmization syllable would still be instantly recognized by virtue of its own unique shape. Dubbed the character-note, or shape-note, system, the method caught on, particularly in the South, where, in some circles, its advantages would be touted with an almost religiouslike devotion.[32]

Figure 2. Jesse Aikin's seven-note system.

Within a few decades, the shape-note concept introduced by *The Easy Instructor* would undergo one final revision—though this change was adopted by only some members of the shape-note community. With Jesse Aikin's publication of *The Christian Minstrel* in 1846, an additional three character notes were added to the scale complete with distinct shapes of their own. This allowed for all seven notes on the traditional scale to be represented individually to avoid any confusion of musical note and shape. Two of the major advantages of the system were that it allowed the reader to recognize immediately the key of a particular piece (i.e., by virtue of a shape note so indicating) and, given the initial pitch of a particular selection, to sight read the music without concern for key changes (see Figure 2).[33] Supporters of the revised system contended that the added notes were a part of progress and natural reform. One of the new converts viewed the addition as a matter of common sense, asking his contemporaries, "Would any parents having seven children, ever think of calling them by only four names?"[34]

Advocates of the shape-note system came to believe fervently that their method, if integrated into society at large, would finally take musical ability to the common man. Those interested in learning music on a higher, more technical level could receive additional instruction by traditional methods without a disadvantage from having learned originally by character notes. And, on a larger scale, proponents saw the little shapes as a clearly improved teaching technique for the large majority of music students. Like so many reform ideas of the early nineteenth century, the shape-note system brought an air of the revival spirit, launching what many considered to be, in short order, a popular-music renaissance.[35]

The Roots of a Musical Genre

Not all music advocates were so optimistic about the appearance of the little shapes, however. Convinced that such shortcuts were both ill-advised and impractical, hard-liners fought the musical reform movement almost from the beginning. As early as the 1830s, the American music publisher and promoter Thomas Hastings (1784–1872) dubbed the characters "dunce notes" and denounced anyone who favored the reform.[36] Lowell Mason (1792–1872), Hastings's contemporary and probably the most influential music promoter in nineteenth-century America, also refused to accept the new system and was instrumental in determining that traditional methods would be used in early public school curricula.[37] At the root of the conservative reaction against shape notes was their association with the common folk. From the beginning, shape-note promoters were enthusiastic that their method would result in most Americans, regardless of their educational or income level, being able to sing correctly. A class conflict emerged in part because the shape-note movement proposed to eliminate the need for acquiring the traditional training and skills associated with the educated elite. Likewise, shape-note promoters were much more likely than their counterparts to embrace the musical tastes of unlettered Americans and thus to encourage the expansion of folk tunes that had emerged outside traditional music circles. As a result, shape notes became as heralded in rural America as they were irrelevant in urban centers. Almost from their beginning, they were relegated only to those pockets of community activity that steadfastly clung to the new musical vision.[38]

At the forefront of the shape-note euphoria was a handful of publishers who astutely understood that, if the system caught on and transformed the numbers of Americans able to read music, a new market would be created for a host of instructional manuals and songbooks. As early as 1816, collections of songs featuring the four original shapes introduced by Smith and Little began meeting with considerable commercial success. The most popular of the four-note collections, *The Sacred Harp*, published in 1844 by Benjamin Franklin White (1800–1879), created a loyal following that still exists in pockets of the rural South.[39] When the pioneer historian of early shape-note music, George Pullen Jackson, took up the subject of the famous songbook in 1944, he judged that "aside from the Holy Bible, the book found oftenest in the homes of rural southern people is without doubt the big oblong volume of song called *The Sacred Harp*."[40] Other popular collections that emerged in this first wave of shape-note enthusiasm were *Kentucky Harmony*, published by Ananias Davisson (1780–1857) in 1816, *The Southern Harmony*, by William "Singin' Billy" Walker (1809–75) in 1835, and *Genuine Church Music*, which appeared under the auspices of Joseph Funk (1777–1862) in 1832.[41]

By midcentury, shape-note collections using some form of the seven-note system were also popular. Aikin's *Christian Minstrel* was a commercial success from the outset and continued to be printed in subsequent editions into the 1870s. *The New Harp of Columbia*, which appeared shortly thereafter from Marcus Lafayette Swan of Knoxville, was enormously popular in Tennessee and remains in print to the present day. Although Walker initially resisted the additional characters, he soon became an enthusiastic convert himself. His *Christian Harmony*, published in Philadelphia in 1866, adopted the seven-note scheme with Walker touting it "the quickest and most desirable method known."[42] More than a decade earlier, in 1851, Joseph Funk had made a similar switch, renaming the fourth edition of *Genuine Church Music* as *Harmonia Sacra*. Funk's work in the South would prove to be the most influential in the sequence of events that would ultimately inaugurate the professional gospel quartet industry.[43]

Running parallel to the camp meeting enthusiasm of the early nineteenth century was a national campaign to improve literacy. By the 1840s, public-education advocates like Horace Mann in Massachusetts were successfully convincing legislatures to commit larger expenditures to the goal of educating the nation's children and to require a limited school term that all students would be mandated by law to attend. In the South, North Carolina's Calvin H. Wiley, Alabama's William F. Perry, and Virginia's Charles Fenton Mercer and Henry Ruffner worked similar reforms through their states' legislatures in hopes of greater literacy.[44] Though progress in the South clearly lagged behind that of northern states, a growing emphasis on public education ultimately meant a parallel rise in the number of Americans who could read and write. If met, the goal of literacy would also increase the public's leisure activities and, of those activities, music advocates hoped shape-note singing would become a part.[45]

An intense period of revival just before the outbreak of the Civil War rejuvenated many memories of the Great Revival period and the camp meetings at places like Cane Ridge. In the two-year span that would be remembered by participants as the "Great Revival of 1857–58," evangelicals once again enjoyed the enthusiasm of revival, although this time the

The Roots of a Musical Genre

revival was centered in urban rather than rural areas. And once again religious songs became a popular way of expressing spiritual experience. More prepared than a generation earlier to exploit the advantages of music, leaders of this new phase of revival promoted an advanced commercialism with more and more music specifically written for the revival. Given the progress of those pushing for education reform, the commercial spillover of the revival was also greater by midcentury. In the midst of the revival spirit, Joseph Funk established a monthly magazine, *The Southern Musical Advocate and Singer's Friend*, to publicize his increased catalog of music books and to advertise his singing schools.[46] By the time the nation entered the turmoil of the Civil War in early 1861, many evangelicals feared that conflict would upset the revival fires. Nevertheless, both Union and Confederate armies participated in regular revival activities throughout the war years. An important part of those wartime services included singing the songs that had become so associated with the camp meeting–style of revivalism.[47]

By the latter decades of the nineteenth century, revivalism had shifted completely from the rural community gatherings of the camp meetings and small-town protracted meetings to encompass the organized, well-oiled machinery of urban revival campaigns. By far the champion of late-nineteenth-century revivalism was Dwight Lyman Moody, himself a layman most closely identified with the Young Men's Christian Association (YMCA) in Chicago.[48] Moody's campaigns began in earnest with a trip to England in 1873, and they drew much of their defining character from Ira D. Sankey, a songwriter and singer from New Castle, Pennsylvania. After impressing Moody with his singing at a YMCA convention in 1870, Sankey joined the Moody campaign and devoted most of the rest of his life to publicizing the great evangelist's work.[49] Sankey is also generally given credit for linking the term "gospel" to religious music because of his popularity in England during the Moody campaign and as a result of his successful compilation, *Gospel Hymns and Sacred Songs*, published in 1875. The association of religious tunes with the specific message of the gospel linked the music forever with the conversion theology and millennial character of evangelicalism and would stick as a defining point of popular religious music within both black and white communities.[50]

In part because of Moody's success, the newly dubbed "gospel songs" entered a new wave of popularity among evangelicals. The popularity also led to an increase in songwriting with some writers becoming particularly well known to American congregations. Among the most enduring songwriters were Phillip P. Bliss, James Rowe, William B. Bradbury, William Kirkpatrick, and Fanny Crosby.[51]

Phillip P. Bliss was born in Clearfield County, Pennsylvania, on July 9, 1838, and rose to prominence while still a young man. A close friend of Moody, he teamed up with another nineteenth-century evangelist, M. D. W. Whittle, and conducted revival campaigns throughout the country. It was apparently Bliss and his association with another songwriter, Philip Phillips, that convinced Moody to seek the services of a full-time song leader.[52] Given his short lifespan—he died prematurely in a train wreck in December 1876—Bliss authored an extraordinary number of songs, penning such favorites as "I Will Sing of My Redeemer," "Wonderful Words of Life," and "Jesus Loves Even Me," and composing the music to the classic "It Is Well with My Soul."[53]

James Rowe (1865–1933) was perhaps the most prolific of late-nineteenth-century gospel lyricists. His own estimate that he had written the lyrics to more than 20,000 songs is nothing short of remarkable, even if one allows for considerable exaggeration. Among his best-known productions were "I Would Be Like Jesus," "If I Could Hear My Mother Pray Again," and "Love Lifted Me," one of the best-loved of the nineteenth-century gospel songs. Born in England, Rowe lived most of his life in New York State and represented a growing awareness by northern writers of the possibilities of an untapped southern market. Late in life, he relocated for a short time to Lawrenceburg, Tennessee, where he became associated with James D. Vaughan and the Vaughan Music and Publishing Company. Rowe's gift of rhyme—he wrote lyrics but never the musical accompaniment—was nothing short of legendary. In addition to cranking out gospel song lyrics, he supplemented his income by writing poems used by an eastern seaboard–based greeting card company. In fact, so one story goes, he was so delighted with a $63 check he had received from the company for a collection of lyrics that he scribbled off a thank you note to the firm. Shortly thereafter, he received another check for $3 thanking him for the additional selection that would soon find its way into the world of commercial greetings.[54]

William B. Bradbury (1816–68) and William Kirkpatrick (1838–1921) became best known for a host of Sunday school songs written for children in the mid-1870s. Over time, the best or most enduring of the Sunday school songs would come to occupy a place of prominence in the hearts and minds of American evangelicals. Kirkpatrick was most adept at writing the music for some of the best-known lyrics that emerged

The Roots of a Musical Genre

from popular late-nineteenth-century gospel song collections. Among his lasting musical contributions were "The Comforter Has Come," "He Hideth My Soul," "'Tis So Sweet to Trust in Jesus," and "Jesus Saves!" Kirkpatrick also wrote words and music to the stirring "Lord, I'm Coming Home," which he composed at a revival he was helping conduct in the late nineteenth century.[55] Similarly, Bradbury contributed the musical score for a host of favorite numbers, including "Jesus Loves Me, This I Know," "The Solid Rock," "He Leadeth Me, O Blessed Thought," "Just As I Am, without One Plea," "Sweet Hour of Prayer," and "Savior, Like a Shepherd Lead Us."[56]

Of all the late-nineteenth-century gospel songwriters, none achieved the lasting fame and admiration of Mrs. Alexander Van Alstyne, better known to the public as Fanny Crosby (1820–1915). Crosby, who was blinded in an accident that occurred when she was six weeks old, studied at the New York Institute for the Blind. She developed a prodigious talent for songwriting and poetry, writing secular as well as sacred verse. Despite her handicap, and perhaps due in part to her determination and her use of her other senses, she possessed unique insight into the realm of the human heart, and her descriptive powers in her sacred songs touched a responsive chord in evangelical Protestant audiences. For many twentieth-century Protestants, a recounting of her gospel hymns reads like a *Who's Who* list of all-time favorites. By the time of her death, 6,000 of the more than 8,000 songs she had penned had been published, some under the 203 pseudonyms she occasionally used. With selections like "Blessed Assurance," "I Am Thine, O Lord," "To God Be the Glory," "Praise Him! Praise Him!," "Tell Me the Story of Jesus," "Near the Cross," "All the Way My Savior Leads Me," "He Hideth My Soul," "Pass Me Not, O Gentle Savior," "Redeemed," "Rescue the Perishing," and "My Savior First of All," she became one of the most beloved gospel composers of all time.[57] When Crosby died, well-known music teacher B. C. Unseld informed readers of *The Musical Visitor* of her passing by carefully selecting the following segment from an obituary in the *Nashville Tennessean and American:* "It is not too much to say that this blind writer of songs has touched and chastened and cheered more hearts than any other man or woman who ever lived in America, and it is not too much to believe that many a writer would rather have to his credit the achievement of a single song like 'Jesus, Keep Me Near the Cross,' than to have written the whole Encyclopedia Brittanica [*sic*]."[58]

Also important were the contributions of Charles H. Gabriel (1856–

1932), William H. Doane (1832–1915), and Robert Lowry (1826–99). Gabriel wrote the music for such standards as "Pentecostal Power," "His Eye Is on the Sparrow," "Higher Ground," and "Since Jesus Came into My Heart." He also contributed lyrics and music to "My Savior's Love" and "Send the Light." Doane fashioned the music for Fanny Crosby's "To God Be the Glory," "Near the Cross," "I Am Thine, O Lord," "Rescue the Perishing," and "Pass Me Not, O Gentle Savior" as well as that for "Precious Name," written by poet Lydia Baxter. Lowry wrote the music to Crosby's "All the Way My Savior Leads Me" and contributed both words and music to the well-known "Nothing but the Blood," "Christ Arose!," "Shall We Gather at the River," "Marching to Zion" (with Isaac Watts), and "I Need Thee Every Hour" (with Annie S. Hawks).[59]

Two prominent black songwriters deserve mention for their contribution to the collection of gospel hymns with which Protestants came to identify. Charles Albert Tindley (1851–1933), a highly successful Methodist minister from Philadelphia, penned words and music to a handful of songs that found their way into hymnbooks across Protestant America with seemingly no regard to race. Known for his prowess in the pulpit, Tindley was recognized as one of the most accomplished orators of his day, and his congregation in Philadelphia numbered some 7,000 members. Among Tindley's greatest musical compositions were "Nothing Between," "Leave It There," "We'll Understand It Better By and By," and "Stand By Me."[60]

Even more enduring were the compositions of Thomas A. Dorsey (1899–1993), another black songwriter who followed a generation later. Although Dorsey was influenced by Tindley, his background and circumstances hardly could have been more different. Dorsey was a former blues pianist in Chicago who shifted to gospel songwriting during the late 1920s. The tragic loss of his wife and child in 1932 led him to write "Precious Lord, Take My Hand." Dorsey would go on to revolutionize gospel music within the black community, but his songwriting talents, reflected particularly in the song "Peace in the Valley," which he wrote in 1939, would resonate no less in white gospel circles.[61]

Consistent with the popular nature of congregational singing, writers like Crosby and Bliss tended to use unashamedly the influences of popular music.[62] Crosby was especially adept at writing secular music and seems to have had no particular scruples against popular music of any style. Similarly, William Bradbury and another famous northern writer, George Root, excelled at composing secular, patriotic music during the

The Roots of a Musical Genre

height of the Civil War.[63] Early gospel songs also coexisted with tunes associated with nineteenth-century political parties and labor organizations. Phillip Bliss's popular "Hold the Fort" was used widely as a tune for labor parties and farmer organizations like the Grange. During the hotly contested presidential campaign of 1876, proponents of both the Democrat Samuel J. Tilden and Republican Rutherford B. Hayes used the melody in support of their candidate.[64]

Quite naturally, then, religious tunes borrowed directly from secular music in a tradition that stretched all the way back—in spirit at least—to the Protestant reformer Martin Luther, who supposedly justified his use of tavern tunes set to his sacred lyrics by noting, "Why should the devil have all the good music?"[65] This incorporation of popular tunes was a relief for many Americans growing up in churches that expected them to devote a considerable, and perhaps a majority, of their time and efforts to spiritual matters. One North Carolina Methodist woman from the 1860s remembered that church members could be chastised for singing secular tunes. If perchance a church member would "hum a popular air, or sing 'Sweet Barbara Allen' or 'Lord Erins's Daughter' someone would say, 'I thought you were a member of the church.'"[66]

For people in such a restrictive setting, gospel lyrics set to popular tunes proved especially welcome. Gospel songs tended to be simple songs that could be sung easily with only a moderate amount of musical training. As a result, they appealed to the reform spirit of the age, offering the distinct possibility that the musical habits of a generation would be altered for the better. Although some conservative Protestants found the obvious secular influences distasteful and unnecessary, the overwhelming majority of those being influenced by the new evangelicalism accepted the music enthusiastically.[67] By the late nineteenth century, the theological implications of evangelicalism also had melded nicely with this attitude of acceptance. One recent historian noted that singing evangelicals often took the perspective that, like their own souls, such songs had been "rescued from popular profanation to nobler ends and that thousands of converted souls who formerly sang these tunes to the 'devil's songs' were now singing them to the songs of Zion."[68]

Years before the "conversion" of sacred songs, the tunes that were later associated with Sunday morning Protestant worship had often known another life altogether. Reminiscent of the early camp meeting days, popular chorus tunes were sometimes added to well-established hymns. One such case involved a melody that originated as a minstrel song in the early 1850s under the title "Take Me Home." The song was subsequently converted in 1864 into a Confederate patriotic tune by John Hill Hewitt, the celebrated "bard of the Confederacy." During the decade following the war, gospel writer Ralph Hudson composed a few new lyrics for the melody and attached them to Isaac Watts's famous verses from the English hymn "Alas! And Did My Savior Bleed?" The result was "At the Cross," a new gospel song created from mostly old lyrics and a melody that had flourished on both sides of the Mason-Dixon line.[69]

Fear of moral decline stood at the heart of some evangelicals' concern over the secular nature of the new songs. In the late nineteenth century, many rural southerners moved north in search of opportunities in the growing urban and suburban industrial centers. At the same time, evangelicals made a concerted effort to convert the cities' inhabitants through urban revivalism. Optimism over revival success was more than tempered, however, by concern for the expanding nightlife and seeming hedonism of urban living. The city's glitz and the accompanying allure of amusements simply offended evangelicals' sense of Christian morality and their concern for family stability.[70]

By the early years of the twentieth century, several important religious developments helped establish the particular boundaries of the evangelical front that would support the world of gospel music in the decades to come. One such development was the emergence of premillennialism as a theological framework. Most nineteenth-century evangelicals had seen the future of God's kingdom through a millennial lens. Given America's enviable position as a place of opportunity and the overwhelming confidence bred throughout the reform-oriented years of the early nineteenth century, most evangelicals had adopted the older Puritan view of postmillennialism. Under the postmillennial scheme, Christians anticipated that Christ's Second Coming would occur after the millennial reign, which was alluded to in Revelation 20. The theological presupposition led to a fairly optimistic social program, with Christians seeing their work in society as fitting hand in glove with the divine plan of God. Most deemed the positive signs of reform in their midst as proof positive that things were indeed improving and advancing toward a period of relative peace in which overt sin, at any rate, was repressed. Missionary zeal and revival success both contributed to this overweening confidence, as did a national obsession with individualism and manifest destiny.[71] Even given the catastrophic results of the Civil War, most

The Roots of a Musical Genre

American evangelicals clung to their belief that, within just a few generations, they would be the bearers of God's final plan.

By the late decades of the century, however, a dramatic shift took place in the way many evangelicals viewed their future. Unconvinced by the tenor of events occurring in their midst and attached to a biblical literalism that opted for an alternate interpretation as more accurate for the eschatology of the Book of Revelation, these Christians adopted a premillennial view of Christ's return. From this new perspective, believers anticipated that the Second Coming would occur prior to the dawn of a millennial reign. The shift was significant in part because it presupposed a more pessimistic worldview and one in which the values of modern society might be more easily questioned and criticized.[72] As more and more evangelicals moved toward the premillennial camp, the songs they sang reflected the siege mentality of a people out of step with contemporary values. Increasingly, the distinction was a badge that evangelicals wore proudly.

Also emerging in the late years of the nineteenth century were a host of new denominations advocating more radical doctrines and a strict ethical code of conduct. Emerging first in the 1880s as groups no longer comfortable with what they considered the social accommodation of the mainline denominations, a band of believers formed independent Holiness organizations and continued a rapid program of evangelism particularly among working-class and rural Americans. By the turn of the century, these believers were beginning to secure their place on the landscape, though few in the mainstream denominations dreamed that they could become a viable alternative for most evangelical Christians. In the first decade of the twentieth century, however, a Holiness-inspired revival sparked a movement that, over the course of the next hundred years, would have remarkable repercussions among American Protestants and indeed within Christianity worldwide.

Pentecostalism emerged through sporadic revivals that occurred in the Midwest from 1901 through 1905. The theological legacy of an itinerant evangelist named Charles Fox Parham, the movement achieved its security through a three-year revival launched in Los Angeles in 1906 by one of Parham's students, William J. Seymour. Parham was a white former Methodist from Kansas, Seymour, a black former Baptist from Louisiana. Both men had been profoundly influenced by the Holiness movement and both shared an intense desire to seek the fulfillment of the Holy Spirit in what they believed to be history's final days. Though the two men broke ties during the dynamic period of Pentecostal growth beginning in 1906, they represented the interracial character of the earliest days of the movement. Such integrated worship attracted attention during a period when Jim Crow laws and racial segregation were rapidly becoming the standard both inside and outside the South.

From Seymour's base at the Azusa Street Mission in Los Angeles, the Pentecostal movement would grow ultimately to influence astounding numbers worldwide. In addition, the movement's emphasis on the moving of the Spirit and an acceptance of emotional worship would influence Protestants despite the stereotype that Pentecostals were simply unlettered and unsophisticated zealots. Along with those influences came a new audience for gospel music, an audience much less encumbered by the traditions of the past and much more attuned to incorporating secular musical influences into their brand of religious experience. Though Pentecostals would remain small in number until the middle decades of the twentieth century, their influence in gospel music, both black and white, loomed large.[73]

The Roots of a Musical Genre

Springdale, Arkansas, August 2, 1996

I sit and watch as seven hundred people gather for an afternoon sing billed as "an old-time singing convention." There are a handful of recognizable performers in the audience, most notably James Blackwood, an icon in the southern gospel music industry; Glenn Sessions and Cecil Pollock, former members of the Rangers Quartet; Robert S. Arnold, who sang in the late 1920s with the Carr Quartet and still publishes an annual shape-note convention songbook; Les Beasley, lead singer for the Florida Boys for the past four decades; and Bob Brumley, son of the legendary songwriter Albert Brumley and host of the annual Albert E. Brumley Memorial Sing. These men arrive without fanfare to spend a few hours singing the old tunes with the audience. Unlike the concerts I've attended on the previous two evenings, this event promises to include the fans. Many know what to expect; a few come just because it is free of charge.

It does not take long to figure out how this gathering will be different from a regular concert. Paperback songbooks are passed out, and the "concert" begins with several rousing congregational numbers. Then several of the older singers are called on to sing a few tunes. Although this is a performance, fans are encouraged to join in and the atmosphere is extremely relaxed. Then the highlight: the announcer calls up to the front all singers, special guests and audience members, who have been trained in the "do-re-mis." Only forty or so clamor to the front to take their positions near the piano, eyes intently focused on their open songbooks. How these singers are different from the others now becomes clear. They are singing tunes with an eye out for the peculiar shape of the notes and with total disregard for the lines and spaces of traditional musical notation. In the old days, this kind of performance was the staple, the "meat and potatoes" of convention singing.

Now, it is also clear how very different the gospel music industry is in 1996. Today there is an obvious distinction between singer and fan. One comes to sing, the other to listen. Even this attempt to re-create an old convention singing falls short of the mark. At a genuine singing convention, the audience participated in shape-note singing. Fans became performers and, in practicing the new songs together, helped teach each other — sopranos, altos, tenors, basses . . . everyone grouped together by part to sing the latest compositions precisely because the ability to master new songs demonstrated a singer's skill. There are still convention singings, back in the rural havens of the South, tucked away in ever more remote locations . . . but this is not one of them. If it were, the rest of us in the audience would know what the folks on stage know. Here, the crowd listens intently as the chosen few sing a hymn "the old way." Ignoring the lyrics in one verse, they substitute the shapes, singing only do, re, mi, fa, so, la, and ti whenever the symbols dictate. The crowd is curious and they applaud, but then the old-timers return to their seats, and the regular program continues. Even so, the point has been made. This small group of singers reminds us that the roots of the gospel music industry are embedded in a handful of curious shapes.

2
SHAPE NOTES & A MUSICAL TRADITION

Few things captured the spirit of a rural southern community a hundred years ago more than the singing school. In some ways, it demonstrated the remoteness that helped shape the unique history of the South and southerners, while, in other ways, it demonstrated the degree to which the region and its people were integrally tied to the nation and its history. Shape notes were not born in the South, but they were adopted by the region and preserved there as in no other region of the country. As such, they were a significant import, an import that southerners actively encouraged and, in time, came to claim as one of their own most cherished devices.

More precisely, shape notes became the peculiar musical vision and property of rural southerners. It was in their region that, for well over a century, "square-toes" defended their system from the abuse heaped on them by tradition-minded "round heads." It was also there that proponents of the old four-shape system, dubbed "Moveable-Doists," argued with their progressive-minded seven-shape brethren, the "Fixed-Doists," in language that outsiders could have only puzzled over.[1] And, as a result, it was there in the South, in the midst of a unique campaign for another lost cause, that the southern gospel music industry was born. Even after use of the shape-note system had been reduced to a declining number of singing seminars and *Sacred Harp* reunions, the industry would live on as a testament to the influence that the little shapes once held.[2]

Singing schools dated to the early eighteenth century, when an interest in reforming church music led to their establishment throughout New England. Shape-note schools dated at least to the early nineteenth century, when music teachers like Daniel Steele of Albany, New York, began teaching the old four-note system to aspiring students.[3] In the South, the singing schools of the shape-note variety grew in force while their northern counterparts waned with the introduction of traditional music instruction in the expanding public school system. Given the rural-to-urban shift under way in the late nineteenth century as well as the recent sectional split, it is not surprising that shape notes would survive, and even flourish, in the South while slipping into obscurity in northern states. Public education also lagged in the South, while traditional evangelicalism found fertile soil for sinking its theological roots. All these factors help explain how the shape-note system became, by the early years of the twentieth century, one of the region's most unique possessions.[4]

Part of the mystique of shape notes was that they provided a talented rural youngster with one of the truly unique opportunities that might come along over a lifetime. Singings were prestigious social events that could mark a person as a citizen of note. An individual with a talent for singing and the ability to teach music might ultimately find an occupation outside the difficult and unpredictable world of southern agriculture. It would not be the first or the last time that enterprising young southerners seized an opportunity to exit the perilous economics of cotton.[5]

Oftentimes the urge to escape the farm and move into the greener pastures of musical education came with an enthusiasm that pushed a bit too fast and too hard. In one of the early issues of James Vaughan's *Musical Visitor*, an aspiring young teacher wrote music educator B. C. Unseld with a question that revealed his naïveté: "I found two pieces of music, both in the B-flat, one is written in simple four-pulse measure, the other in compound two-pulse measure. The one that is written in four-pulse measure begins with Mi on the added line below, and the one in compound two-pulse measure begins with Sol on space above first line. Now both are written in the same key of B-flat. Which piece is to be sung the highest is what I want to know? My aim is to go to teaching at once."[6] Though Unseld noted the possibility of "a misprint in the copy" with respect to the key of one of the music pieces, he spared few words in admonishing the reader of his need for a more in-depth education before he would be able to go into business as a singing-school teacher:

The Roots of a Musical Genre

You are certainly mistaken in the key of one of the pieces, or there is a misprint in the copy. Mi in the key of B-flat is not represented by the added line below. The measure sign has nothing whatever to do with the key to the piece. You say your aim is to go to teaching at once. Brother, let me advise you not to do so until you know more about the simplest things in music. Attend a few sessions taught by a a [*sic*] competent teacher followed by a session or two at the normal and then you will be able to do your pupils some good. To attempt to teach with your present knowledge—or rather, lack of knowledge— you will do your pupils more harm than good.[7]

Singing schools became far more than occasions for ironing out one's grasp of musical theory, however. From the beginning, they doubled as social events. Young men and women understood that, in addition to whatever passion they shared for learning music and improving their vocal ability, these short-term sessions provided much-needed relief from daily chores as well as an opportunity to enjoy the company of the opposite sex. As early as 1782, one New England singing school student admitted that his chief objective in life at the moment involved "the Hopes of going to singing-meeting tonight & indulging myself a little in some of the carnal Delights of the Flesh, such as kissing, squeezing &c. &c."[8] For generations, rural students would enjoy a mix of pleasures associated with the singing schools, only part of which involved a considerable improvement in their musical ability.

Singing schools represented a primary example of free enterprise even as they demonstrated the isolation of rural America and its inhabitants' desire to improve and enjoy the progress of modern America. Teachers crisscrossed the rural paths of the South, setting up local ten-day schools and working their class meetings around the everyday needs of those willing to pay the few dollars required.[9] Classes, often held at night, included a rigorous program introducing students to the rudiments of shape-note music and vocalization techniques. Students were routinely drilled until the shape-note system was memorized both for sight-reading of musical selections and for recognition of pitch and harmony. The conclusion of a school "term" became a community event with graduating students often putting on a public concert to display their newfound talents.[10]

Attending the singing school of a well-known shape-note teacher was a mark of distinction in many areas of the South. In time, certain teachers became revered, and students clamored to attach themselves to their reputation. One Alabama resident born in 1910 remembered of T. B. Mosley, an associate of A. J. Showalter's Dalton, Georgia, publishing business, that "you was a nobody at a singing if you didn't go to his singing school. You'd have a hard time getting a place to sing." [11] As a result of this kind of reputation, experienced singing-school teachers commanded a much larger fee for their services and also gained demand for conducting more involved sessions, called "normals," to advance the training of particularly talented singers and establish the credentials for a new generation of singing-school teachers. [12]

Southern singing conventions dated to the 1840s and were initially associated with geographical areas such as river valleys. Some conventions became devoted to a particular songbook and, as in the case of those using the *Sacred Harp*, might well forbid singing from any other source. [13] Others remained more generally within the shape-note camp. Particularly as the seven-note books coalesced in the latter decades of the nineteenth century, singing conventions looked more and more to emerging shape-note publishing companies for leadership in the selection of singing material.

The success of singing schools in rural southern communities allowed for the organization of local, regional, and ultimately national singing conventions. Usually annual or biannual affairs, singing conventions purported to bring together the best singers of a given area for a time of fun, fellowship, and mutual training. New gospel songs, often called "convention songs," introduced by paperback songbook publishers, were the highlight of a convention. One-half to three-quarters of a typical convention book of a hundred songs would feature new songs, with the remaining entries consisting of older standards or more recent favorites. Since shape-note singing highlighted a singer's ability to pick up an unfamiliar piece of music and sight-read it perfectly, convention participants took particular pride in being able to tackle the new songs. [14] Probably in response to this aspect of convention life, many gospel songwriters by the 1930s were styling their songs with elaborate harmony parts. Featuring echoes and an alternating melody, the songs often resembled giant puzzles that, once the timing and harmony were perfected, came across to both singer and listener as a finely tuned production.

In rural southern communities, singing conventions provided one of the few social outlets available to residents. Organized with annual meetings, a working constitution, and a regularly elected slate of officers, singing conventions were uniquely suited for tying together the combination of interests that dominated the southern social scene—joyous music, religious energy, and democratic policy.[15]

By the early twentieth century, singing conventions flourished in almost every southern state and boasted organizations on the county, district, and state levels. Conventions were routinely one of the larger local gatherings, rivaled only by the annual agricultural fair and perhaps a well-attended camp meeting.[16] Newspapers took occasion to print news from the conventions on a regular basis, noting the minutes of the annual meetings as well as the schedule of activities and featured singers.[17] Many music publishers recognized the conventions as the bread and butter of their annual distribution efforts and utilized the meetings for advertisement and sales.[18] In 1936, the most prominent of the shape-note publishers who used the seven-note system joined forces to form and cosponsor the National Singing Convention. The constitution of the national convention was rewritten in 1949 to allow for the inclusion of voting representatives from the various state organizations as well, but the convention remained, nonetheless, tied to the fortunes of the paperback songbook companies.[19]

Not all southerners supported the growing fascination with the singing conventions and convention songs. William Denham, a Southern Theological Seminary student, took upon himself the chore of investigating the new "gospel song movement" and published his results in a Th.D. dissertation in 1916. Acknowledging that the positive effects of the movement might outweigh the negative, Denham was nonetheless concerned that "the ultimate spiritual effect" had been of "very doubtful value." Chief of his worries was that the weak theology contained in many of the songs contributed to "a superficial and emotional type of Christian character," which, in the end, was "more of harm than of good to American Christianity."[20]

Despite his objections, Denham admitted that some of the gospel songs, notably the recent offerings of Fanny Crosby, were of considerable value and were thus destined to become hymns of the church. His chief objection, however, was that much of the gospel song movement had become commercialized, with publishers producing mostly new songs packaged cheaply in paperback books and distributed widely for the greatest profit.[21] Denham offered a rather practical suggestion—that denominational leaders in his own Southern Baptist Convention, in addition to implementing other safeguards, regularly revise the denominational hymnbook. A revised hymnal could include standard hymns along with the most worthy gospel songs. That combination, along with an effort to price the books in a range affordable to most churches, would go a long way toward controlling the spread of gospel songs among Southern Baptists. Denham minced no words when he concluded: "We are passing through a critical time in our religious history, when there is an increasing tendency to ignore the deeper needs of our religious selves, and to cater to the superficial and emotional. Wise and systematic control of the singing of our people would go far toward remedying this condition, and it is with the prayer that such control may result that I bring to a close this discussion of 'The Gospel Song Movement.'"[22]

Even more caustic in his appraisal was Dr. H. M. Poteat, professor of Latin at Wake Forest College, located just north of Raleigh, North Carolina. Blasting "the cheap hymn," Poteat argued that such music drew heavily on secular music—principally on the likes of "blues, jazz, waltzes, [and] ragtime." Songs of such "slushy sentimentality" had become so popular "outside the church, that the same sort of thing, with a poor, thin veneer of religion, is demanded in the church." Publishers of such "sacred rags" were pandering to the public taste for profit with little or no concern for the larger spiritual message of their product.[23]

Like Denham, Poteat was chiefly concerned with the commercial aspects of the songbook business. His description of the singing convention was colorful if condescending: "In some sections of the South 'singing conventions' are quite popular. The people come together from all parts of the surrounding country, bring the babies and abundant baskets of dinner, and spend the day (or, sometimes, several days) whooping and squalling and bellowing songs out of sundry cheap books. Various 'singing teachers' are on hand, each extolling the glittering merits of the book for which he is agent, and vieing [sic] with his fellows in oily piety and those acrobatic and vulgar antics that are deemed necessary to the successful leadership of choir and congregational singing."[24]

Poteat's analysis of the value of the new gospel songs contained an obvious disdain for the culture of the common man. One of the chief faults of the gospel songs, according to Poteat, was the incessant habit of emphasizing the chorus, a portion of the song made easy to sing and remember. The Wake Forest professor noted that songs like "Love Lifted Me," "Brighten the Corner," and "There Is Power in the Blood" were composed in such a fashion that there remained "a paucity of ideas and expressions." With that dearth of inspiration was a musical challenge that

The Roots of a Musical Genre

detracted rather than aided the worship experience. Poteat found objectionable the very challenge that singing convention adherents loved—the "gymnastic contortions for the basso, death-defying gyrations for the tenor, peripatetic circumambulations for the alto," and all this "while the soprano bravely pegs away at the tune." Poteat admitted that the songs provided "*pep*" but opined that "the *pep* thus engendered is a poor, specious counterfeit of that deep religious enthusiasm aroused by the hearty singing of a real hymn." [25]

Despite Poteat's ardent criticism, a growing number of rural southerners were becoming enamored with the lively strains of the new gospel music. Aiding this growth were the number of Holiness and Pentecostal churches that sprang up in the early decades of the new century. Holiness and Pentecostal adherents were not about to be swayed by the lofty rhetoric of a college professor like Dr. Poteat. In addition, their theological leanings reinforced a desire for the very "*pep*" that Poteat warned against. Since the middle years of the nineteenth century, Holiness advocates had yearned for a more intense religious experience and had often recognized the value of music in at least setting the mood for the reception of such an experience. Even more ardent in this respect were the Pentecostals, many of whom identified spirited singing with their open worship of the Holy Spirit and the reception of spiritual signs. In the inaugural issue of *The Apostolic Faith* from Los Angeles in September 1906, supporters of the Pentecostal revival had even allowed that God was bestowing the "gift of singing" as well as "playing instruments" upon those with no prior training. Such claims were consistent with a movement in which believers were convinced of the miraculous outpouring of God's Spirit in the exciting last days of human history.[26]

Holiness and Pentecostal worshipers assumed a pragmatism that fit well with the innovative and popular sound of the new gospel songs. Early Pentecostals, as one student of the movement has noted, valued music as "a language beyond aesthetic, let alone theological, judgment" and, more than anything else, viewed the art form as a way to attract potential believers.[27] As a result, they worried less than their contemporaries about the dangers of accommodating their religious music to modern tastes.[28]

As a general rule, Pentecostals harbored few biases against religious music and, more often than not, frowned on traditional music rather than the contemporary songs that appealed to believers' emotions. Throughout the early decades of the twentieth century, many Pentecostal churches were stretched to afford the pianos and organs that became standard in most of the mainstream churches in their midst, so they were more likely to allow inexpensive instruments, especially guitars, that members could bring from home.[29]

Even so, a few Pentecostal writers feared that their fellow believers were going too far in their acceptance of modern gospel music. Especially by the early 1930s, when a second generation of Pentecostal leaders were concerned with institutional building and acceptance into the evangelical mainstream, critics began to favor the traditional hymns over the simple choruses. Robert Brown, an Assemblies of God minister from one of the landmark Pentecostal churches in New York City, ably expressed the new position in an article published for his church members in early 1937:

> We have noticed in many Pentecostal meetings that sacred songs are now put to ragtime music, and that people work themselves into a frenzy playing and singing in the effort to please their listeners. . . . Singing and playing Gospel songs and music is a part of the worship of a holy God, just as much as is preaching or praying. We should therefore enter into His Courts, whether it is to sing or play, with holy reverence and with Godly fear. . . .
>
> Jazzy music and singing is merely a *substitute*, and instead of appealing to deep spirituality it caters to the natural man, and bespeaks two things. First, that the person who thus entertains has largely lost the deep touch of God they once possessed. Second, that their audience, who applauds, have [*sic*] drifted in the same direction.[30]

Despite this kind of concern, Pentecostals provided a ready market for the new gospel songs of the early twentieth century. Not surprisingly, they would also contribute more than their share of writers and performers as well.

The shape-note music that Holiness-Pentecostals and assorted Baptists in the South came to share grew out of a combination of love for music and the successful business ventures of southern entrepreneurs. By far the most successful music company in the South during the late nineteenth century was the Ruebush-Kieffer Company, which emerged from the Funk family of Virginia's Shenandoah Valley.

Joseph Funk, born March 9, 1777, created a literal music dynasty in the western regions of the state of Virginia. His *Harmonia Sacra* endured multiple editions and inspired one of the most loyal followings in the

The Roots of a Musical Genre

South. Funk's earliest inroad into music publishing had been to publish a German collection, *Die Allgemein Nutzliche Choral-Music*, in 1816 to serve the sizable German immigrant population in western Pennsylvania as well as the numbers filtering down into the Shenandoah Valley. His first English edition appeared sixteen years later.[31]

Funk's love of music translated over to his entire family. Though he was sometimes criticized for it within his Mennonite tradition, he taught his sons to play various instruments, including the violin and the flute. Indeed, he would establish a long-standing tradition of talented gospel music families, most notably the Speer, LeFevre, Blackwood, Carter, and Lewis families.[32]

From the 1830s up to the Civil War, Joseph Funk and several of his sons conducted shape-note singing schools throughout rural central and western Virginia. As they traveled, they sold the Funk songbooks, of course, expanding the family business as they spread the democratic principles of shape notes. The work, though arduous, was no doubt exhilarating and often lucrative. In a November 1845 letter, Joseph Funk reported that he and his son Timothy had found Spotsylvania County, Virginia, ripe for the new musical theory. Netting a profit of $200 from a total of eight separate singing schools, he remarked to his family that "teaching music, to a competent teacher is, in this place, pretty good business."[33]

Funk was also instrumental in setting other gospel music precedents. In July 1859, he launched a periodical titled *The Southern Musical Advocate and Singer's Friend*. Published by his own printing company, the monthly journal was an unabashed promoter of Funk's work. Specifically, it proclaimed the need for Funk's musical and religious revolution, arguing that "hundreds of Christian congregations assemble weekly, oftentimes without having one member capable of conducting this part of Divine worship to acceptance. The service of SONG is often presented to Heaven as a sacrifice, 'Maimed, and blind, and halt.'"[34] One of the first such publications in the South, *Southern Musical Advocate* presaged twentieth-century gospel music publications that would help identify a host of southern publishing houses.[35]

Funk was adamant that music as an act of worship was to be a participatory activity and not a spectator sport. Noting the "prominent error" that had arisen in making religious music in church services "a mere instrument of sensuous gratification," the old Virginian spoke eloquently in favor of increased, as well as improved, congregational singing:

And hence, in some of our churches, a *select few* perform the singing services, in a sort of theatrical style, whilst most of the true worshippers take no part, and the only effect upon the congregation is, the fancy is amused, whilst the heart remains unmoved, and the emotions unawakened.

For these reasons, we shall not advocate SPECIAL CHOIRS *of the select few*, but choirs composed of *the whole congregation*, who may desire, and have the capacity to take part in the service. Singing will never have its legitimate influence in the Church, in strengthening and encouraging the Christian, in his devotions, and in awakening the sinner from his death-like slumber, until the congregation can unite their voices in singing, not only psalms and hymns of praise and devotion, but in pealing forth the grand and solemn anthem. This anticipated result is not a mere chimera of the fancy; we look forward with confidence, to the day, when Christians generally will be awakened to the importance of musical cultivation and training, and when *all* Christians may unite in praising God with melodious voices.[36]

In addition, Funk's publication stood solidly behind the new trend toward using seven, rather than four, shape notes. Although he chose his own unique shapes for the three additional symbols, his switch to seven character notes meant that the musical patriarch and his descendants would adapt their empire after the tradition established by Jesse Aikin. The editor recognized that the conflict to follow would come not from advocates of the older four-note system so much as from those as of yet unconvinced about the advantages of shape notes in general. Announcing that "our music will be printed on the figurate or *'patent note'* system of notation," Funk explained that, whereas "instructions are not necessarily less thorough under this system than under any other, . . . the singer can learn to read music with much more readiness and certainty, by this system, than by the 'round notes.'" At any rate, Funk promised that "upon this subject, however, we do not desire to be controvertial [*sic*]" and maintained that "our columns shall be open for disscussion [*sic*] upon this subject." His position proved to be one that his heirs would find difficult to maintain.[37] Through the work of Funk's grandson, Aldine Kieffer, and Kieffer's partner and brother-in-law, Ephraim Ruebush, the shape-note system would be promoted and encouraged throughout the South in a saga that at times would resemble another "musical war."[38]

Born August 1, 1840, in Saline County, Missouri, Aldine Silliman Kief-

The Roots of a Musical Genre

fer inherited his grandfather's love of music and, more than any other of Joseph Funk's heirs, possessed the desire to promote and continue to build the family's musical empire. Kieffer's attachment to his grandfather grew initially as a result of the tragedy of his own father's death. In June 1847, John Kieffer, a singing-school teacher who had married Funk's daughter, Mary, ten years earlier, died prematurely, forcing his widow and her three children to pack up and move back in with her father in Mountain Valley, Virginia (later renamed Singer's Glen). As a result, the young boy, having already attained an appreciation for music from his father, entered the world of the musical Funk family. For the rest of his life, he would immerse himself in and then take control of this world. By the age of nine, Kieffer was learning to set type in his grandfather's printing shop, in between his other chores and schoolwork. By ten, he was attending weekend singing schools taught by his grandfather and uncles and, by sixteen, had begun teaching his own singing school classes.[39]

Of importance to the future of shape-note publishing was Kieffer's friendship with Ephraim Ruebush, a young man seven years his senior who moved to Mountain Valley in 1853 to secure a job as a bookbinder's apprentice in Funk's publishing house. Funk himself took an interest in the young Ruebush and taught him music on the side. Within a few years, Ruebush and the precocious young Kieffer became both friends and committed warriors in the cause of shape-note music theory. By the end of the decade, the two young men formed a partnership with several of their fellow students and, like Funk before them, set out on horseback to teach area singing schools. Though the enterprise proved slow in the early going, by the time the Civil War began in April 1861, Kieffer and Ruebush had built a promising beginning as a teaching team attached to Joseph Funk's music house.[40]

The outbreak of the war was traumatic for the two young music teachers. The previous month, Ruebush had married Virginia Kieffer, Aldine's older sister. What might have been a happy time proved tense for more reasons than the separation of family and young friends. Ruebush, originally from Augusta County, Virginia, opposed the secession of his native state and soon enlisted in the Union army, in which he apparently served for the duration of the war. Kieffer, on the other hand, joined the Tenth Virginia Volunteer Infantry and became a member of the Confederacy's Army of Northern Virginia.[41]

Undaunted by the national schism that threatened both his life and his family ties, Kieffer found occasion to pursue his musical interest during wartime. During their winter encampment late in 1861, he and a fellow Confederate taught a two-and-a-half-month singing school to almost five hundred of their compatriots in a log church building they constructed near Fairfax Station, Virginia.[42] The following winter he participated in a band "concert" along the Rappahannock River, where encamped Union and Confederate troops displayed their talents for their foes across the frozen expanse of river.[43] Kieffer's military service came to an abrupt halt when he was captured at the Battle of Spotsylvania Court House in May 1864 and imprisoned in Fort Delaware, where he was allowed a few music books to study during his confinement.[44] He was released in April 1865 shortly after Lee's surrender at Appomattox.[45] Kieffer returned to Singer's Glen and, picking up the pieces of his life, resumed both his music business and the delayed partnership with his brother-in-law, now a discharged captain from the Union army. The elder Funk had passed away late in 1862, but he left behind, even in the midst of the desolation of the war, two ambitious supporters of shape notes who would ably carry on his passion.[46]

Taking a cue from their musical mentor and his *Southern Musical Advocate*, Kieffer, along with his brother, L. Rollin Kieffer, and two uncles, Solomon and Timothy Funk, formed the Patent Note Publishing Company and launched *The Musical Million and Singer's Advocate* in 1870. The family had attempted a reprisal of *Southern Musical Advocate*, which folded three years earlier as a result of the war, but that enterprise had ended in failure by 1869. Now Kieffer determined to embark on an even more ambitious publication. He chose the name *Musical Million* in the hopes that the new vehicle would reach a million people with its musical message—which decidedly praised the virtues of shape notes. The publication also became the central medium for advertising the Funk family's printing company. It began modestly with the three hundred or so former subscribers of the *Southern Musical Advocate* receiving an initial six-month subscription as recompense for the discontinued *Advocate*.[47]

Two years later, in January 1872, the family business was reorganized to reflect the reunion of Kieffer and his old partner and brother-in-law. Ephraim Ruebush assumed control of business matters, while Kieffer continued as editor of the journal and as the major artistic force behind the music company. Ruebush, Kieffer and Company (also known simply as the Ruebush-Kieffer Company) would have a far-reaching impact on the shape-note music publishing business, particularly in the

The Roots of a Musical Genre

South, throughout the remainder of the nineteenth century. Over the next two generations, *Musical Million* would stand as the staunchest advocate of shape notes that the nation had ever known and, by the turn of the century, served 10,000 subscribers across the nation.[48]

In conjunction with the founding of *Musical Million* in 1870, Aldine Kieffer apparently was having some kind of crisis — becoming much more fanatical on the issue of shape notes than his grandfather or other shape-note enthusiasts had ever been up to that point. A little over a decade later, he was essentially predicting that the use of shape notes would soon eclipse that of round notes nationwide. He argued that the evolution toward the exclusive use of shape notes represented a kind of scientific determinism:

> It affords us but a melancholy pleasure to know that most of the musical journals of twenty, fifteen and ten years ago, who maligned the cause we advocated, have dropped like snowflakes into the stream of time, and have been borne into the great ocean of eternity. But times change. Monkish customs and superstitions of five centuries ago, however beautiful, no longer possess the power to charm the devotee. The beliefs and the creeds of a century past have fled like the stars of the morning. Evolution and change of order are found in all things, and he who thinks musical notation is to be an exception to this law might as well step out and from under, unless he is an Atlas, a Sampson [*sic*] or a Hurcules [*sic*], to hold up, tear down, or clean out this universe by his power and might.[49]

During this period, Kieffer helped facilitate one of the most important developments within the shape-note publishing world. From the outset of the *Musical Million,* he believed that to be successful in his quest to make shape notes the norm two important goals would have to be achieved. First, shape-note publishers would have to agree upon one uniform set of characters and reduce for the consumer the degree of competition within the southern shape-note industry. Following Aikin's invention of three additional notes in 1846, no fewer than six competing systems had emerged. Since all used the same four shapes associated with the older four-note system, Kieffer theorized that it would be a relatively minor — though important — achievement for publishers to decide on the single most functional of the available alternatives. Despite his apparent open-mindedness, Kieffer strongly favored the seven-note system created by his grandfather, in no small part because his publishing company was already using it with some success. Nevertheless, events conspired to convince him ultimately to bow to the acceptance of the older, competing system of Jesse Aikin.[50]

Aikin visited Singer's Glen late in the spring of 1876 to meet with Kieffer about the problem of multiple systems of character notes. In relatively short order, the elder publisher convinced Kieffer to abandon Funk's system for the one that he himself had devised back in 1846. Kieffer perhaps was forced to recognize that the older gentleman's seven-note system predated by several years the system that his grandfather had adopted. In addition, Aikin proved to be a forceful arbiter, threatening at one point to seek a restraining order against the Ruebush-Kieffer Company. Aldine Kieffer would later assume the high road, claiming that the decision to adjust his shapes was a result of his concern for the greater need of solidarity in the shape-note reform movement.[51] Nevertheless, Aikin's influence no doubt weighed heavily in Kieffer's agreement to shift to the older system. Beginning in October 1876, Ruebush-Kieffer publications used Aikin's system, which became recognized as the standard.[52]

The second order of business in the campaign to popularize shape notes was to barrage the country with singing-school teachers who would win converts from the masses of rural folk who, in Kieffer's mind, would always form the backbone of the nation. Kieffer's attachment to rural life stemmed from several sources. His own boyhood in the Shenandoah Valley had endeared him to rural folk and rural ways. In addition, his involvement in the Civil War had in some ways instilled in him romantic notions about the quality of freedom and independence that could only come when people were tied to the rural landscape. Finally, by nature, Kieffer was a romantic given to long bouts of depression. Indeed, he told a coworker once that "the blues of five hundred years rested on him." His friends believed that, as in the case of his grandfather, who suffered from a similar disorder, this moodiness gave the young publisher an artistic insight demonstrated by his love of English poets and his uncanny ability to wield the pen in dramatic, flowery fashion.[53] As did Thomas Jefferson a century earlier, Kieffer looked with a bit of naïveté on sacred rural soil and saved his harshest attacks for the scourge of urban life. By the mid-1880s, he gave readers of the *Musical Million* a taste of Jeffersonianlike rhetoric in regard to urban spaces and their impact on the sacredness of the human family and home.

The Roots of a Musical Genre

At no time in the history of our common country has impure and sensational literature secured such a wide circulation as at present. No one fact can be more deplored by our people than this. The impure literature of the age is filling our jails, penitentiaries, and asylums with criminals and lunatics. It is turning our homes into hells, our society into communistic mobs, and our churches into atheistic, deistic, infidelic and universal societies. . . . Throw this viper of society into the fire, as did St. Paul the serpents that wound themselves about him on the island Mileta. Secure for your homes chaste publications, no matter under what denominational auspices such publications may be conducted. . . . Let every professor of Virtue, Knowledge, Temperance, Brotherly Love and Human Sympathy see to it that journals advocating moral and mental purity visit their homes, and that the trashy, obscene and devilish publications emenating [*sic*] from our great cess-pools of vice, the large cities, are tabooed.[54]

Kieffer's ability to flood the backcountry with shape-note teachers peddling both the message of "musical democracy" and a backpack full of publications from Singer's Glen was conditioned on finding enough devoted disciples. At the center of this effort was the opening in August 1874 of the Virginia Normal Music School, considered by some to be the first such institution in the South.[55] Unlike the typical singing school, this Ruebush-Kieffer-backed institution promised students a faculty who specialized in various aspects of musical instruction and who were also sympathetic to the concept of notation reform via shape notes. Setting the standard for the annual Virginia Normal, Kieffer hired Benjamin C. Unseld, a former teacher at the New England Conservatory of Music in Boston and an associate of Theodore F. Seward, editor of the *New York Musical Gazette.* Unseld served as the school's first principal and remained on the faculty through most of the late nineteenth century. Ironically, Unseld personally favored round notes and succeeded in convincing Kieffer to allow both notation systems to be taught at the Virginia Normal. Kieffer seems to have accepted the idea as consistent with his vision, since music teachers trained in the normal would be expected to know traditional music theory in addition to having the skill to teach the masses to read shape notes.[56]

Most southerners continued to learn shape notes from the ranks of traveling singing school "professors," and now the Virginia Normal provided the shape-note enthusiasts with their own institution for educat-

ing the future teachers expected to carry the tradition into the twentieth century. Though the "school" was essentially an annual conference
without a permanent campus, it nonetheless lent a sense of stability to
the shape-note cause. Meeting for the first six years in facilities rented
in New Market, Virginia, the school survived primarily through advertising in the *Musical Million*. The important influence of the Ruebush-
Kieffer organization was also evident in the reorganization of the normal
in 1880 and the simultaneous move from New Market to Dayton, Virginia. The school's move to Dayton followed the transfer of the Ruebush-
Kieffer headquarters to the same town two years earlier. It also placed
the school in the same location as the Shenandoah Seminary, another
Funk family educational enterprise, which had opened its doors to the
public in October 1878. The seminary's campus now provided the Virginia Normal with a new home. Classes at the institution, renamed the
Shenandoah Normal Music School, began meeting in seminary facilities in the summer of 1880. A total of 101 students were enrolled for a
four-week course of instruction. The association of the normal with the
Dayton campus continued into the early twentieth century.[57]

Students of the Shenandoah Normal, popularly referred to as the
Ruebush-Kieffer Normal, took with them advanced music training and
the inspiration of Aldine Kieffer's plan for saturating the countryside
with shape-note instruction. Soon, the concept of a four-week normal
to train particularly gifted students in music theory and the principles
of effective music teaching was adopted in various locations across the
South. Experienced singing-school teachers simply advertised for students interested in taking a more advanced course of study and, if enough
students responded, a normal would be set up.

Generally, students gauged the worth of a normal by the reputation of
an individual teacher. If a student had received instruction by a teacher
who was widely known and respected, his career as a singing-school
teacher could begin with the mere advertisement of having studied under
such a master. One Ruebush-Kieffer student, Ephraim T. Hildebrand,
gained this kind of respect and ultimately taught advanced normals as
well as the regular singing schools offered to the rural public. By the
late years of the century, Hildebrand's contact with an ambitious young
Tennessee student named James David Vaughan inaugurated the next
chapter in the history of the southern gospel music industry. Ultimately,
Kieffer's dream of reaching a million people with the shape-note message

The Roots of a Musical Genre

would come true several times over in the labor of shape-note enthusiasts influenced by Vaughan and others like him.[58]

The work of Ruebush, Kieffer and Company had a dramatic impact on the musical history of the American South. Other publishing houses were spawned in the wake of the successful business emanating from Dayton, Virginia. One of the more important disciples molded by the company was Anthony Johnson Showalter, another Funk family relative. Showalter's great-grandmother was a sister of Joseph Funk, and his ancestors settled in the countryside only a few miles outside Singer's Glen. His father, John A. Showalter, became a talented young associate of the Funk enterprise and, along with Joseph Funk and the Funk sons, Timothy and Solomon, prospered as one of the most successful singing-school teachers in the valley. When the Virginia Normal opened its third session at New Market in the summer of 1876 under the direction of B. C. Unseld and P. J. Merges, eighteen-year-old Anthony was in attendance, and, from the beginning, he made an impression and became a valuable part of the family business.[59]

Like Kieffer before him, A. J. Showalter was something of a child prodigy. Born May 1, 1858, he began his musical training in the singing schools and private classes taught by his father. By the age of fourteen, he was conducting singing schools on his own and, within four years of first attending the Virginia Normal, was hired to help teach the annual sessions there. He also jumped headlong into the publishing business, producing his first book of songs in 1880 and following it with several books on music theory, one of which he widely touted as "the first work of its kind by a southern author."[60]

By the early 1880s, Showalter revived memories of a young Aldine Kieffer by establishing himself as one of the most ambitious young teachers associated with the Ruebush-Kieffer music enterprises. As a businessman, he was relentless, building his reputation throughout the states of Mississippi, Alabama, Texas, South Carolina, Georgia, Arkansas, North Carolina, and Missouri. After marrying in 1881, he took the opportunity to establish a branch office for Ruebush-Kieffer in Dalton, Georgia, and moved his family there in 1884. Not long afterward, however, Showalter broke with the Ruebush-Kieffer Company and formed his own music business. Young music dynamos leaving the nest to establish rival organizations would become a perennial theme in American gospel music.[61]

Showalter began publishing titles under his own name in 1884 with the release of *Good Tidings*. Nevertheless, he proceeded slowly and did not formally incorporate the A. J. Showalter Company until 1890. Rather, he seems to have used his growing popularity as a music teacher and his connections with other aspiring gospel publishers to test the free-market system. Under the influence of his talent and ferocious drive, his business grew rapidly, with the publishing house employing close to a hundred workers by the turn of the century.[62] He also formed *Our Musical Visitor*, a music journal that was renamed *The Music Teacher* after only a handful of issues were published.[63]

Showalter's publication was clearly modeled on the format of the successful *Musical Million* and was designed specifically to promote his new publishing business. Largely due to its promotion, the A. J. Showalter Company became in a brief period of time "the second most important publishing house in the South for the spread of this shape-note tradition."[64] By the early twentieth century, there were branch offices of the Showalter Company in Dallas, Texarkana, and Chattanooga, each run by one of a number of promising graduates from the Showalter music program.[65]

By the late 1880s, Showalter was commanding "$50 and Expenses" for a five-day singing school and "$90 and Expenses" for the more typical ten-day affair. At the same time, his former students and many other southern singing-school teachers were content with the market rate of $50 and expenses for a ten-day school alone.[66] In addition, he became involved in local Dalton enterprises, becoming, among other things, a stockholder and the director of a local lumber company, director of a regional insurance company, and owner of a 20,000-tree peach orchard. He was also a prominent member of the First Presbyterian Church in Dalton, serving as elder until his divorce and remarriage in 1912, which apparently caused some disruption within the community. Showalter spent most of his remaining years in Denver, Colorado, because of his second wife's deteriorating health. He also lived for part of each year in Chattanooga, Tennessee, where he rented a room in the Park Hotel.[67]

By 1904, Showalter had sold close to two million copies of a total of sixty different songbook titles. In addition, he was a noted writer, composing more than a thousand songs. Office workers recalled that he would generally arrive in the morning "before breakfast and compose a song or two; after writing them, he would try them on the office piano."[68]

The Roots of a Musical Genre

By far, his most enduring contribution was "Leaning on the Everlasting Arms," a song he wrote in consultation with Elisha Hoffman.[69]

Not surprising, Showalter also started his own music normal, advertising the opening of the Southern Normal Institute in 1885. Like its counterpart in the Shenandoah Valley, the Southern Normal ran for four weeks and was held in a number of different locations in various states. With the establishment of the institute, later renamed the Southern Normal Conservatory of Music, Showalter had successfully duplicated in Dalton, Georgia, all of the influential enterprises that the Ruebush-Kieffer Company had made so well known in the rural South.[70]

One of the Showalter graduates was a young Lebanon, Alabama, musician named Jesse Randall Baxter Jr. Baxter would learn the ropes from Showalter and, when the time was ripe, would also find occasion to stake his own territory in the highly competitive world of gospel music publication.[71] The innovative publisher from Dalton, Georgia, also influenced Thomas Benjamin Mosley, an Albertville, Alabama, native. Mosley worked closely with Showalter during the early twentieth century and took over as editor of *The Music Teacher* upon the founder's death in 1924. His familiarity with the talented singers of the Sand Mountain area in northeastern Alabama helped promote what one recent writer has labeled "a regional stronghold in perpetuating southern gospel music."[72]

Showalter's influence, as well as that of his successors, was a credit to the musical vision and philosophy of Aldine Kieffer. *Musical Million* continued to advertise singing schools taught by a host of associates who allied with the Ruebush-Kieffer establishment. The journal also provided major exposure for the more than one hundred different songbooks printed in shape notes that the company marketed throughout the rural South. Lowell Mason and other music educators may have failed to see the advantage of shape notes for public education, but Kieffer made an impressive case through the sheer volume of his sales. The Ruebush-Kieffer Company's 1878 move to Dayton, Virginia, had been made in large part to facilitate the shipping and receiving of orders. Many of the songbooks sold extremely well. The 1877 *Temple Star* sold a phenomenal 500,000 copies alone by the early years of the century.[73]

In addition, Kieffer succeeded in convincing a host of music teachers throughout the South to follow in his footsteps and to traverse the rural landscape teaching local singing schools. By the turn of the century, regular visits by singing-school teachers were a staple in rural southern communities, with such teachers earning the honorary title "professor" and a commensurate level of respect perhaps only slightly below that afforded a Confederate colonel. Kieffer himself was revered as only a handful of his contemporary southerners would be. When George Jackson penned his study of southern shape notes in 1933, he expressed surprise at the number of babies he discovered named after the venerable promoter from Singer's Glen.[74]

Nevertheless, Aldine Kieffer's dream of a total revolution in musical training via shape notes proved elusive. However strong the system was in rural regions of the South, it never tapped into the growing urban marketplace, where industry and commerce were dramatically shaping the nation's future during the latter part of the nineteenth century. Ignored, and thus, in the words of one historian, "the victim of the killing indifference of the musical leaders in the urban centers," shape notes faced an uncertain future at the turn of the century.[75] They would surely not supplant traditional musical notation, as Kieffer and others had hoped, but neither would they disappear quite yet.[76]

Shape-note singing school conducted in Crisp County, Georgia, by John M. Spivey, 1913. Courtesy Southern Gospel Music Hall of Fame and Museum, Sevierville, Tenn.

James David Vaughan, ca. 1930. Courtesy Southern Gospel Music Hall of Fame and Museum, Sevierville, Tenn.

Vaughan School of Music, Lawrenceburg, Tennessee, 1913. B. C. Unseld is seated second from the left; James Vaughan is seated third from the left. Courtesy Southern Gospel Music Hall of Fame and Museum, Sevierville, Tenn.

Vaughan School of Music, Lawrenceburg, Tennessee, 1920. Note the increased enrollment in the school. Courtesy Southern Gospel Music Hall of Fame and Museum, Sevierville, Tenn.

WOAN, Lawrenceburg, Tennessee, mid-1920s. Courtesy Southern Gospel Music Hall of Fame and Museum, Sevierville, Tenn.

WOAN Orchestra, mid-1920s. Otis McCoy is on the far left holding the banjo. Vaughan's son-in-law, William Walbert, is in the back row, third from the left. To his left is music editor and songwriter Adger M. Pace. Courtesy Southern Gospel Music Hall of Fame and Museum, Sevierville, Tenn.

*Virgil Oliver Stamps,
ca. 1935. Courtesy
Southern Gospel
Music Hall of Fame
and Museum,
Sevierville, Tenn.*

*Stamps-Baxter
Music School, Dallas,
Texas, 1935. Courtesy
Southern Gospel
Music Hall of Fame
and Museum,
Sevierville, Tenn.*

II
THE BIRTH OF AN INDUSTRY

Springdale, Arkansas, August 3, 1996

He's ninety-one . . . and he still sings tenor. This is my first glimpse of Robert S. Arnold. He sings a few songs at the nightly Albert E. Brumley Memorial Sing held in an old rodeo arena and then is also one of the featured performers at the singing convention held in a small auditorium located on the complex grounds. The tenor part is amazingly smooth for a nonagenarian and the crowd amply expresses its approval. I not only listen in amazement to the voice so well preserved but also watch in awe at the way the aged gentleman handles himself and the way he enjoys the stage, the way he prizes the music.

Gospel performer and a songwriter most noted for the classic "No Tears in Heaven," Robert S. Arnold is also a music publisher whose business dealings go back six decades. Founder of the National Music Company in 1937, he has weathered the fortunes of singing conventions and shape-note publishing for longer than most members of his audience have lived. And his constitution reflects the heartiness of a sure trouper, a survivor of the taxing schedule required of singers to succeed in the gospel music business. When I approach him for the interview, I am cautious: "What would be a good time for you, Mr. Arnold? I don't want to overload your schedule." But his reply is a classic tribute to a gospel singer's unconventional schedule: "Oh, tonight after the concert will be fine. Just come by and ring my room when we all get back to the hotel."

Like many gospel concerts, this one ends after midnight. By the time I get to Bob Arnold's room for the interview, it is 1:00 A.M. "Are you sure you want to do this now, Mr. Arnold? We could reschedule for tomorrow." "Oh, no. Come on in. Let's talk." By the time I leave, it is almost 2:00 A.M. As I head back to my room, I note with a chuckle that these gospel singers are killing me—even if they are more than twice my age.

3
JAMES DAVID VAUGHAN, PIONEER

Had James David Vaughan not happened upon the gospel music scene in the late nineteenth century, the expansion of the gospel music industry in the South might well have peaked with the contributions of Aldine Kieffer and Ephraim Ruebush. Already much had been accomplished. The campaign for shape notes was successful in the rural South, if nowhere else. And the gospel music publishing business was putting out more and more product each year, particularly through the auspices of the Ruebush-Kieffer disciple A. J. Showalter. In addition, gospel singing was popularized by the great revivalists of the era, most notably Sam Jones in the South and Billy Sunday in the North.[1]

Sam Jones, whose career spanned the late decades of the nineteenth century, became, next to Dwight L. Moody, the nation's best-known evangelist. A self-styled spokesman of the South, Jones enjoyed remarkable success in northern cities by the end of the century and, for many, represented the dawn of a new era of cooperation and harmony between the regions. Billy Sunday, a converted baseball player, reached the peak of his career in the first two decades of the twentieth century and, much more than Jones, suffered from the division of fundamentalists and modernists within Protestant ranks. Both evangelists, and many others of lesser notoriety, successfully emulated Moody's emphasis on music.[2]

Jones employed two music specialists, E. O. Excell, a robust music dynamo from Chicago, and Professor Marcellus J. Maxwell, a quieter, but nonetheless effective, singer and songwriter from Oxford, Georgia. The celebrated "Ex and Max" formed a team that made the southern evangelist's campaigns memorable for more than just Jones's colorful preaching and proclamation to "quit your meanness."[3] C. J. Miller, a singing-school teacher who traveled the rural landscape of Alabama beginning in the 1880s, recalled hearing Sam Jones remark in a sermon that "while I preach ten persons into the kingdom—E. O. Excell sings 100 there."[4]

Sunday's music man, Homer Rodeheaver, became an even more widely recognized national figure. A multitalented singer, songwriter, and businessman, Rodeheaver continued to popularize the congregational singing that Ira Sankey had pioneered a generation earlier. "Rody" grew to be a crucial part of the Sunday campaigns, able to fascinate children with magic tricks just as he could "twitch the smallest finger of his left hand and ignite a huge choir."[5] Rodeheaver established his own music publishing firm in the early twentieth century and, with songwriter Charles H. Gabriel, was responsible for the appearance of *The Gospel Choir*, a monthly journal promoting the establishment of church choirs. He also invested in the new phonograph recording business and reportedly sold a million copies of his own recording of "The Old Rugged Cross."[6] Though never espousing the southern emphasis on shape notes, he would be well known in many southern gospel circles in part because "Brighten the Corner Where You Are," a catchy song written by his associate Gabriel in 1913 and popularized through the Sunday-Rodeheaver campaigns, ultimately became a quartet standard.[7]

But, if gospel music in the South had remained simply the province of gospel evangelists and audience-participatory singing conventions, the southern gospel music industry might never have been born. Something unique was needed to merge shape notes, popular religious singing, and convention-style songbooks into a thriving industry. That something was the development of professional quartets.

James David Vaughan, born December 14, 1864, grew up in the obscure rural environs of Giles County in the southern part of middle Tennessee. Despite the recent war, he enjoyed certain advantages. In part because of the efforts of its native son and the nation's seventeenth president Andrew Johnson, Tennessee had weathered the destruction of the war fairly well. As the only state to avoid formal reconstruction and the first to achieve readmittance to the Union, its economy progressed surely, if slowly, in the decades following Appomattox.[8] Vaughan's father, George Washington Vaughan, a native North Carolinian and Civil War veteran, prospered enough in the decades immediately after the war to send his son to a local private school. In time, the gifted student excelled academically and embarked on a career as a schoolteacher. He taught local schools in southern Tennessee beginning in the late 1880s and seemed intent, for a time, to make his name as a southern educator.[9]

But young Vaughan also developed an early aptitude for music. Members of his mother's family, the Shores, were avid devotees of William Walker's four-note-based *Southern Harmony*, and it is likely that the young boy absorbed much of that influence. In the late 1870s, when Vaughan was just a teenager, a traveling singing-school teacher, James Berry, conducted a series of ten-day shape-note schools in the Giles County area. Berry's musical influence came from the powerful Ruebush-Kieffer Company of Dayton, Virginia. Vaughan attended two of these sessions, absorbed the ideology of shape notes, and fantasized about becoming a music teacher himself. Within a few years, he moved decisively to make his dreams into reality. At the tender age of eighteen, he taught his first singing school to a handful of local residents, including his three younger brothers, at the local church where his family and friends worshiped.[10]

To advertise the school's success and publicize his own plans for future sessions, Vaughan organized a family quartet, which locals came to call the Vaughan Boys Quartet. Taking the lead part himself, he coached his fifteen-year-old brother, John, to sing bass, his twelve-year-old brother, Will, to sing tenor, and his baby brother, Charles—only seven at the time—to sing alto. Four decades later, Charles Vaughan remembered that his older sibling "took us three brothers with him to fill singing dates that he made and he seldom failed to make a school after this quartet had gone to a place and took part in the day's singing."[11] While essentially a local phenomenon, the quartet was nonetheless important in shaping the older Vaughan's early grasp of how performance harmony could be used to publicize the gospel music business.[12]

Shortly after his marriage to Jennie Freemon, a local girl, in May 1890, James Vaughan packed up his belongings and moved to Cisco, Texas. The move was an abrupt one, but it is likely that family members already in the Cisco area influenced his decision to join them. Vaughan's uncle, Richard B. Vaughan, probably enticed his nephew to pursue a teaching career in rural central Texas, where he served as a Methodist minister. Within a year, most of the family, including James Vaughan's parents and his brothers John and Charles, also made the move to Cisco.[13]

The young couple no doubt reveled in the opportunity to begin their

The Birth of an Industry

life together in a new setting and with a promising career in education. By May 1891, they celebrated the birth of their first child, a daughter, whom the couple named Grace. The talented James Vaughan quickly made an impression in the new town. In addition to his work as a public school teacher, he continued to offer friends and neighbors the opportunity to learn music via his shape-note singing schools. More importantly for the future of his publishing career, he stumbled upon the opportunity to pursue his own thirst for musical knowledge. At some point around 1892, he came into contact with Ephraim Timothy Hildebrand, a young graduate of Shenandoah Seminary and a protégé of the Ruebush-Kieffer Company.[14]

Hildebrand and a partner operated the Hildebrand-Burnett Music Company of Roanoke, Virginia, and as part of the company's music promotion taught advanced normal schools in addition to conventional ten-day singing schools. These traveling normals were designed with students like Vaughan in mind. Talented singers who had shown an ability for picking up musical knowledge but who did not have the time and means to attend a music school like the one in Dayton, Virginia, could nonetheless pursue their musical interests. Vaughan arranged local support for a Hildebrand-directed normal and attended the three-week session himself sometime during 1893. Charles Vaughan later remembered that the school had a profound influence on his older brother and that "he became more deeply interested in music."[15]

Significantly, Hildebrand also inspired Vaughan to try his hand at composing music, and the two young men both published songs in the 1896 Ruebush-Kieffer collection titled *Crowning Day, No. 2*.[16] Soon the team collaborated on several songs and worked together to publish two songbooks, *Onward and Upward* and *Onward and Upward No. 1*, printed by Hildebrand's company in Roanoke.[17] In 1894, Hildebrand had become principal of the Ruebush-Kieffer school in Dayton, Virginia, a position he held for five years. Though Vaughan never actually attended the Virginia school, his connection with Hildebrand was key to—at least indirectly—his own association with the famous Shenandoah Valley shape-note operation. The influence had already been manifestly implied when, in March 1893, Vaughan had named his second child, a son, Glenn Kieffer Vaughan.[18]

The visit of E. T. Hildebrand to Cisco, Texas, clearly set James Vaughan on a new path. It rekindled his earlier love for music and made him more determined than ever to pursue this important avocation. It also pushed him closer to the world of shape-note publishing. But all was not happy for the Vaughans in Cisco. The joy at the birth of two children was tempered by the loss of two older family members. Both George Washington Vaughan and his son John died of tuberculosis during the family's brief residence there. Ultimately, however, another unanticipated tragedy forever turned the young schoolteacher's fortunes away from the Texas frontier and back toward the valleys of middle Tennessee. Six weeks after the birth of his son, Kieffer, a deadly cyclone destroyed most of what made up Cisco, Texas, and killed twenty-nine of its residents. Included in the destruction was the Vaughan home, which reportedly literally fell down around family members huddled inside. Miraculously, all the Vaughans survived, but, once the storm subsided, they decided to abandon their experiment with the central Texas plains. Devastated and with little of their dreams surviving, the family packed up what few belongings they could still claim and headed back to the familiar environs of Giles County and southern Tennessee.[19]

Back home, near old friends, James Vaughan resumed his career as a public school teacher, ultimately rising to the position of principal of the school in Elkmont Springs, Tennessee. For the next decade, he continued his work in education and furthered his reputation as a singing-school teacher. In addition, he taught his children shape notes and, along with his brother Charles, his daughter, Grace, and a family acquaintance, Fay Springer Collins, sang occasionally at local Methodist churches.[20] Maintaining his friendship with Ephraim Hildebrand, he sponsored several more music normals and managed to have a few more gospel songs published. Gradually he gained more confidence in his ability to write and publish music. In 1900, he compiled enough of his own tunes and, securing the rights of others he came into contact with, published his first independent songbook. As with most of his later songbooks, the title was that of an original Vaughan composition and the first song to appear in the new collection. *Gospel Chimes* was just one of many shape-note hymnals floating around the rural South by 1900, but, as James Vaughan's first solo effort, it lit a spark that would produce a music publishing legacy that would last for the next sixty years.[21]

Spurred by his new opportunity, Vaughan left his position as principal following the 1901–2 school term and moved his family to Lawrenceburg, the county seat of neighboring Lawrence County. There he took a job as an office clerk for his brother-in-law, James C. Springer, who had acquired the position of county register of deeds. But, Vaughan calculated from the beginning that the clerking position was a temporary hindrance. Using the back room of the office as the unofficial storage space for his James D. Vaughan Music Company, he continued to market his publication, reprinting and revising another edition in 1903. In addition, he hawked the books relentlessly through his contacts in the shape-note music world and via his accelerated work as a singing-school teacher. Within a year of the release of the revised version of *Gospel Chimes*, Vaughan was forced to secure permanent offices for his publishing company. Over the next six years, he produced five additional titles, selling a total of 60,000 books annually.[22]

By 1910, Vaughan sensed that his gamble and hard work had paid off. He was in the process of purchasing additional downtown office space to house his expanding business, and he maintained a growing correspondence with contacts who might use his publications in singing schools or at annual singing conventions. Also, by that year, he had begun to publish at least one songbook per year—a practice that his company would continue well after his death in 1941. His newfound confidence triggered several important changes in his operation, and over the next few years, those changes would revolutionize the gospel music business in the South.[23]

Vaughan's most important business decision in 1910 was to sponsor, beginning in May, a traveling quartet to attend singing conventions and peddle his growing line of gospel songbooks. The idea had apparently originated a few years earlier but had met with only limited success. One member of the original quartet later recalled the significance of James Vaughan's decision:

About that time a Texas company tried quarteting a little but did not do much good. Then, in the spring of 1910, the first Vaughan quartet was started out in Lawrenceburg. It was several years before any other song book publisher tried a male quartet on the road. In fact, James D. Vaughan is the only song book publisher in the south to have kept several quartets the year round at good salaries. It was not for several years after the first Vaughan quartet commenced traveling that the quartet "fever" seemed to strike over the southland. But, when it did start, a great wave of quartet singing started over the country. Not many paid singers in the quartets but nearly every community had one or more quartets, although not many of them would have been considered very good singers.[24]

James David Vaughan

The original Vaughan Quartet, managed by Charles Vaughan, was understood from the beginning to be a crucial link between the publisher and the large number of churches and singing conventions across the rural South. By hiring singers and financing their travels, James Vaughan theorized that he could make his works more popular than those of the more established and well-known publishing houses like Ruebush-Kieffer in Dayton, Virginia, and A. J. Showalter in Dalton, Georgia. The initial quartet included Charles Vaughan, who sang bass, George W. Sebren, who carried the lead part, Ira T. Foust, who sang the alto line an octave low, and Joseph Allen, who sang tenor.[25]

The decision to sponsor a quartet came also from the desire of some of Vaughan's students to visit and sing together. Vaughan's younger brother, Charles, and local friend Joe Allen began discussing how they might combine "a short vacation and a little 'singing trip' at the same time." Hoping to form a trio, they contacted Ira Foust in Eaton, Tennessee, a small town on the western end of the state. The two had met Foust the previous year at the Lawrence County Singing Convention and now arranged for the young singer to conduct a local singing school. The engagement would pay his expenses and provide the necessary time for the new trio to practice and decide where they might be able to travel and sing. In the course of their preparation, two important events occurred. First, a local minister, Rev. B. J. Reagin of the Cumberland Presbyterian congregation, told the young men about the annual assembly of his denomination later that month and offered to arrange for the group's appearance. Apparently impressed with the size of the upcoming Presbyterian convention, James Vaughan agreed to sponsor his brother's group and their "vacation" if they would advertise his growing list of songbooks and sell as many as possible at the gathering. A second circumstance turned the ambitious trio into a quartet just four days before the scheduled appearance at the Cumberland Presbyterian Assembly in Dickson, Tennessee, almost a hundred miles due north of Lawrenceburg. George Sebren, another one of Vaughan's acquaintances from the tightly knit singing community, contacted the elder Vaughan seeking employment, noting, "[I]f you have anything for me, I will come over there." Convinced that Sebren's baritone lead would complement the group, Charles Vaughan—with his brother's approval—wired Sebren to come as soon as possible, guaranteeing him a month's pay of $50.00.[26]

The Vaughan Quartet's debut at the 1910 annual Cumberland Presbyterian Assembly in Dickson proved to be even more fortuitous than the

The Birth of an Industry

band of young adventurers or their sponsor-publisher James Vaughan could have imagined. Charles Vaughan recalled later that the large tent meeting was attended by close to 1,500 Presbyterians plus additional town residents interested in the spectacle. With no other music competition, the quartet easily wowed the crowd and ultimately stayed to sing "for every service of the assembly for the rest of the time." Aided by rainstorms, which kept the crowd of several thousand under the tent, the quartet managed to sell 5,000 of the Vaughan songbooks, in addition to a large number of promotional group photos, which the members had hastily acquired. By the time they reported back to Lawrenceburg after the conclusion of the five-day affair, James Vaughan clearly understood the dynamics of their success and resolved that they represented the advantage he needed over his competitors in the shape-note industry. The quartet continued to make appearances as employees of the Vaughan company, performing at church revivals as well as the more established singing conventions. By 1916, their popularity had grown such that James Vaughan purchased one of the new Ford automobiles to facilitate the group's excursions, which soon included a five-day trip to Illinois.[27]

The songbook publisher obviously profited from his willingness to gamble on quartet advertising. When Vaughan representatives arrived in south central Kentucky in 1912, the shape-note music craze "swept across the hills, hollows, and flatlands like a wild fire fanned by a strong wind." The quartets graphically demonstrated what knowledge of shape notes could mean in a rural community, and, as a result, singing-school teachers became "respected, appreciated, and admired beyond all measure." Their status, according to one historian, existed "just a notch below God in the eyes of local residents."[28] By the summer of 1917, Vaughan had established three additional branches of operation. In addition to Lawrenceburg, Vaughan publications were now marketed from regional bases in Greenville, South Carolina, Midlothian, Texas, and Fitzgerald, Georgia.[29] Within a few years, Vaughan employed additional quartets and, by the late 1920s, sponsored as many as sixteen quartets—many of which traveled under the generic name the Vaughan Quartet.[30]

In addition to the tremendous advertising that came via the quartets, Vaughan also strengthened his company by organizing a permanent school of music in January 1911. The Vaughan Normal School of Music, clearly modeled on the earlier Ruebush-Kieffer effort in Virginia, was nonetheless the first of its kind in Tennessee and quickly drew students

interested in advancing their knowledge of music beyond the level provided by the ten-day singing schools. Demonstrating how far Vaughan
had come in the decade since abandoning his career in public education,
Benjamin C. Unseld, the former principal of the Ruebush-Kieffer Normal, moved to Lawrenceburg in 1913 to became dean of the new school.
Securing the seventy-year-old music teacher gave Vaughan and his new
enterprise instant credibility.[31]

Benjamin Carl "Uncle Ben" Unseld held almost legendary status in
music circles of the rural South by the early years of the twentieth century. Born in Shepherdstown, Virginia (later West Virginia), on October 18, 1843, he developed a love for music early in life and demonstrated
both talent and an intense desire to improve his musical ability. As a
young man, he secured a position in a Pennsylvania railroad office only
to take advantage of a six-month leave-of-absence to pursue his musical avocation. The decision turned into a lifelong career. In 1866, he attended the Musical Institute of Providence, Rhode Island, and studied
with Dr. Eben Tourjee. Shortly thereafter, when Tourjee established the
New England Conservatory of Music in Boston, young Unseld went
along and served as the institution's first secretary. In the early 1870s,
he continued his training, working with notables such as Theodore F.
Seward and Dr. William Mason.[32] In addition, he taught music at Fisk
University in Nashville and helped develop the internationally known
Fisk Jubilee Singers, a black gospel ensemble that toured Europe as well
as America throughout the late nineteenth century.[33]

But it was Unseld's association with Aldine Kieffer and Ephraim Ruebush that linked him indelibly to the fortunes of shape-note publishing
and ultimately to southern gospel music. His decision in 1874 to become principal of the celebrated Virginia Normal, the first music school
in the South, placed him in direct contact with more than one generation of music teachers — an association that was cemented by his decision to join the Vaughan campaign and conduct music normals in 1911.
Unseld personally favored round notes and was instrumental in convincing both Kieffer and Vaughan to include round-note instruction in
their schools alongside shape-note instruction.[34] Nevertheless, he shared
the enthusiasm that the shape-noters elicited for the mass education of
rural southerners — and particularly churchmen — in the rudiments of
sight-reading. He also shared their passion for improved music quality
in church congregations across the land. Long after his death in 1923, he

was remembered in gospel music circles as the "musical father or grand-father of nearly all the successful normal teachers of the South."[35]

The normals that James Vaughan began organizing and advertising in the summer of 1911 were similar to those that he had attended and occasionally taught in previous years.[36] Vaughan recognized that if his books were to become more successful, the singing schools that began flooding the country as a result of Aldine Kieffer's influence forty years earlier would need to continue. What was also needed, Vaughan believed, was a constant stream of singing-school teachers trained via normals with the credentials and ability to conduct the rural schools. If future teachers were trained by Vaughan and his associates, they were much more likely to use Vaughan books in their schools as well as to recommend them at the larger singing conventions. Vaughan believed so firmly in his annual normal that, in later years, he paid the expenses and salaries of those teachers who would travel to New York for advanced musical training.[37]

Initially, the Vaughan Normal moved around—quite literally taking the education to promising students throughout the region. As the Vaughan company grew, however, and its reputation in the music industry spread, the normals found a permanent home in Lawrenceburg.[38]

Assisting in the spread of Vaughan's reputation was his music monthly, *The Musical Visitor*. Vaughan had begun publishing the *Visitor* in 1911 and in 1913 turned over the job of editing to B. C. Unseld.[39] Unlike Vaughan's songbooks, which were printed by the Armstrong Printing Company of Cincinnati and then shipped back to the Vaughan company for distribution, the music journal was published and printed in Lawrenceburg.[40] By 1915, the journal enjoyed 5,000 subscribers; by 1923, it claimed to have "the largest circulation of any Southern music journal."[41] In Vaughan's mind, the school and the journal clearly fit together as part of a package. The *Visitor* would advertise the recurring normals and would inform the public about the progress of singing-school teachers who improved their craft by attending the music sessions. Likewise, sessions of the Vaughan Normal would ensure that young men—and, to a lesser degree, young women—would advertise the importance of the journal and the publishing enterprise it represented. In turn, the normals also fueled Vaughan's growing interest in sponsoring quartets at singing conventions and having the singers sell songbooks there. Through it all, *The Musical Visitor* (renamed *Vaughan's Family Visitor* shortly after World

War I) served as a convenient advertisement for all of Vaughan's activities. When the journal was sold in the mid-1960s, Vaughan's daughter-in-law, Stella, served as editor. She recalled with pride the role the literary piece had played in promoting both the Vaughan enterprise and shape-note singing in the South. "As you know, she wrote in a pamphlet about her father-in law, "the *Vaughan Family Visitor* is for the people who enjoy the singing conventions and attend them and who buy our publications and in it we have published the lives of many of the Gospel Composers and also we try to publish a fairly complete Convention Slate so that the readers may know where the conventions are being held and are therefore able to attend. It has blessed the homes of thousands of subscribers."[42]

By 1915, the Vaughan company sponsored a four-week normal in Lawrenceburg each winter and the following year increased the term to six weeks. Attendance at the annual event varied but generally reached between fifty and a hundred students.[43] In addition, the firm contributed the teaching staff for several other normals held across the South during the summer months.[44] Students who could not attend an entire term at a normal took as many classes as possible, a practice Vaughan facilitated at the Lawrenceburg Normal by scheduling both day and night sessions for students. Vaughan recognized that his school, and indeed his entire industry, catered to the needs of rural people, and, not surprisingly, he extolled their virtues. Reprinting a selection from the *Musical Million* that opined, "There is no life that will compare with a country life" and "country people are the best people," he sought to reinforce the beliefs of rural churchmen, who feared the modernism they believed to be creeping in among their urban brothers and sisters. "To the country we look for our noblest boys and girls, sturdiest men and women. . . . Our best music students usually come from the rural districts, and this is encouraging to those who are forced to live a quiet, secluded life. Such a life is to be preferred above that of a rushing, zigzag city life—where the attractions are so many that the mind has no time for mature deliberation. In the city, it is go, go, go. Tonight, it's a club meeting, tomorrow night prayer meeting—next night a sociable and so on to the end of the chapter."[45]

In addition to the daily music instruction and practice sessions of the Lawrenceburg Normal, James Vaughan himself taught daily Bible classes. Like Kieffer before him, the young publisher saw his role as more than a producer of gospel songbooks and a promoter of popular singing.

Vaughan's personal devotion and commitment to American evangelical ideals was captured often in his work but never more poignantly than on the opening page of his 1910 songbook *Voices for Jesus*. Under a distinguished portrait of himself in a well-tailored three-piece suit, Vaughan inserted the words: "Yours in Christ and Song" above his name. He then included the following note: "May this book, through the influence of the Holy Spirit[,] bless mankind wherever it goes, and win many precious souls for Jesus, is my prayer. THE AUTHOR. 'Sing unto the Lord a new song.'—Bible"[46]

Such devotion carried over to the instructional normals. Singing the gospel ensured that the evangelical message of the Christian gospel would also flood the countryside, and Vaughan felt sure that his students needed to exhibit a firm faith as well as a solid musical foundation. Though men dominated the normal rolls, women were encouraged to participate and were sometimes granted free tuition to encourage their attendance.[47] Vaughan's educational mission and Christian devotion took precedence over all his work. His evangelical zeal and New South optimism convinced him that he could literally change the landscape. Years before his publishing empire began to flourish, he had shared this vision with Aldine Kieffer and the readers of *Musical Million:* "Young men of the sunny South, the land of flowers and song, where the magnolias wave in the gentle zephyrs, and all nature is rife with fragrance, do you aspire to true greatness? Would you, like the immortal Grady, win the love and admiration of a nation? Then build your manhood on Jesus Christ. He is the perfect model. If you build on the 'sinking sand,' when the storms of life assail you, you will fail; but if you build on the solid rock, you will be able to stand."[48] Vaughan remained committed to the evangelical nature of his work long after his financial success had been assured. By the 1920s, he renamed the annual normal "The Vaughan Conservatory of Music and Bible Institute" and lengthened the term to five months.[49]

Unlike formal college institutions, which offered advanced degrees for specialization in a given field, music normals operated under the assumption that pupils would return often and continue their training on a regular basis. In fact, the scheduling of three-week, four-week, and six-week sessions implied as much, offering singing-school teachers a variety of options to stay sharp in their craft. A 1915 Vaughan promotional advertised the normal as a school that "prepares men and women for teaching [and] composing, trains for conducting, quartet singing, writing, or anything in the gospel song work line."[50] Just as important, the normals created a music fraternity by linking singing-school teachers from across the South to a central agency. Vaughan's January 1915 session drew almost seventy students to the daytime classes and an additional fifty for the evening alternative. Students came from eleven different states, and Ben Unseld felt sure that the "hard times" of the previous year had hampered recruitment such that attendance was "hardly half of what it would have been had times been good."[51]

Students who left the Lawrenceburg Normal peddled their talents in rural singing schools but also distributed the shape-note convention books that Vaughan's presses produced at least annually. In addition, they sold subscriptions to the *Musical Visitor.* Their activities received regular press in the pages of the monthly journal. During January and February 1915, 479 new subscriptions of the *Visitor* were sold despite the fact that many of the "hustlers" (as they were called) had been involved as students or staff of the January normal. Praising their efforts, Vaughan noted triumphantly that "with such an array of hustlers, we can make the *Visitor* the most widely circulated music journal in the world."[52]

And, indeed, Vaughan's army of salesmen—singing-school students and quartet members alike—continued to pay dividends. The most recent Vaughan songbook, *Crown Carol,* released at the beginning of the year, had, by May 1915, sold over 100,000 copies. Reporting the success in the pages of the *Visitor* and announcing another press run of 20,000, Vaughan exhorted his troops in the summer of 1915, "Cheer up, brothers, there is plenty of business ahead of us. We wish you a liberal share of it."[53]

With the success of his journal and the music school continuing through the war years, Vaughan was ready to try even more innovations by the 1920s. In part as a result of his acquaintance with Fred C. Green, a local Lawrenceburg resident who had served in the Signal Corps during World War I, Vaughan invested in early radio. Applying and receiving a license from the U.S. Department of Commerce in November 1922, Vaughan began broadcasting on 150 watts in early 1923 under the call letters WOAN. The station was one of the first functioning stations in the state of Tennessee.[54] Soon, Vaughan built two 125-foot towers with a vertical antenna near his publishing headquarters in downtown Lawrenceburg, and, on January 1, 1925, the station was upgraded to 500 watts.[55] The station's broadcast originated at 833 kHz on the AM dial but moved frequently over the next eight years. For a brief period in 1925–26, the station shared the 1060 spot with WSM of Nashville, another recently established station that, in later years, would become known for its support of country music. By 1928, the dial setting was fixed permanently at 600.[56] WOAN's power, though small by radio standards just a few years later, was strong enough in the early 1920s to reach literally across America. Soon the Vaughan company had acquired fans from as far away as California and Canada. Readers of *Vaughan's Family Visitor* were encouraged to "hear the famous 'Vaughan Quartet' . . . them and more too!" by purchasing "a complete Aeriola Senior Radiophone Receiver."[57]

Licensed as a noncommercial broadcasting station, WOAN was restricted from selling ads to other businesses and, as a result, never proved financially viable. Nevertheless, programming for WOAN presented a host of opportunities for the many Vaughan enterprises. Vaughan envisioned radio in much the same way he viewed the Vaughan Normal and the increasing number of Vaughan Quartets touring the countryside. The broadcasts would feature Vaughan music and the Vaughan music center in a way that would increase the songbook sales throughout rural America.[58] In addition, the station could be used to give valuable experience to the students who attended the annual normal. Many Vaughan groups were first exposed to radio in the small studio located in downtown Lawrenceburg.[59]

Radio also introduced Vaughan's music to a host of new fans and, in that sense, paved the way for a generation of quartets to come. From the beginning, the station drew a fairly conservative musical audience. One listener from Bloomington, Indiana, wrote in 1926 to praise the station for offering the kind of music that his age group could appreciate. "The South is certainly furnishing the North with good music. About all we are able to get up here from our northern stations is 'jazz.' Young people like 'jazz' but we older people like to hear real music like that which your station puts on the air."[60] Southern listeners were no doubt equally impressed with the advantages that the new technology provided.

Even before founding the station, Vaughan had launched Vaughan Phonograph Records in 1921 and soon began advertising the recordings of the Vaughan Quartet in the pages of the *Visitor* and on the back of his songbooks.[61] Vaughan no doubt was aware of the impressive growth of the phonograph industry in the years after World War I. Making contact with a Wisconsin company that issued custom recordings, he arranged to send a quartet there under the direction of his son, Glenn Kieffer Vaughan, to make three ten-inch double releases. The initial recordings were the spirituals "Couldn't Hear Nobody Pray" and "Steal Away." In addition, the quartet recorded the more recent "Magnify Jesus," by W. W.

Combs; "Look for Me," by V. O. Stamps; and "Someday," by L. C. Taylor. A duet version of James Rowe and Howard E. Smith's "Waiting at the Gate" concluded the session.[62]

Although it is not entirely clear who made up the earliest of the Vaughan recording quartets, it seems likely that the members were J. E. Wheeler, M. D. McWhorter, Adlai Loudy, and Herman Walker. It is possible that Kieffer Vaughan may have also sung with the group since he was present and clearly took the lead vocal on the duet number. The Vaughan company's arrangement on these first three records was undoubtedly linked to its association with Homer Rodeheaver, who had recently become involved in promoting the Rainbow Records label from his Winona Lake, Indiana, home. Years later, Kieffer Vaughan's widow, Stella, placed both Kieffer and this quartet at Rodeheaver's home in August 1921, noting that "they were in Indiana to make records."[63] Though the personnel would change frequently, the quartet led by Kieffer Vaughan was successful enough in packaging and selling recordings—usually at $1.00 each—that by the early 1920s it was known in Lawrenceburg almost exclusively as the Vaughan Recording Quartet.[64]

Within months of this initial recording effort, the Starr Piano Company of Richmond, Indiana, contacted Vaughan with an offer to record the quartet at their Gennett Records studio. Wilson Taggart, a company representative, had happened upon one of the early Vaughan discs at a camp meeting and, out of curiosity, bought it and played it. He recalled later that the quality "was worse than our records!" Recognizing an economic opportunity, he decided to contact Vaughan and offer his services: "So I wrote and got him up here to start making records. We imprinted the envelopes for them on their label. We sold them quite a lot of records. They were as good financially as they could be."[65] Over the next decade, the Vaughan label issued more than sixty records. Most were gospel recordings by the Kieffer Vaughan–led quartet, but a few solos and instrumentals were also released. Occasionally, secular tunes, such as "Kentucky Babe" and "I'll Take You Home Again Kathleen," were also recorded.[66]

In addition, the Vaughan Recording Quartet, with Kieffer Vaughan singing lead, traveled to New York in 1924 to make a recording in the studios of the Edison Company. By now, the group included Hilman Barnard on first tenor, Walter B. Seale on baritone, and Roy L. Collins on bass.[67] Despite the advertisement that Vaughan Phonographs produced "the first and only Southern records to be placed on the market," Vaughan's records had a clear connection with the northern record industry.[68] Subscribers to the magazine were treated to occasional references to the new recording technology becoming available to them along with its advantages for lovers of gospel singing. S. C. Beall, a *Visitor* reader from Texas, wrote in to extol the virtues of the industrial 1920s and specifically the Vaughan company's decision to tap into the new technology: "People who do not read the *Visitor* and do not have the Vaughan records to play for them at night when tired and weary from our days of toil, have never learned just what the world has in store for them. It is a fine way to have a Vaughan quartet with you all the time. Since having tried a few of the Vaughan records we hardly realize that we have any others."[69] Don Hooper, also of Texas, reminded readers early in 1923 of yet another virtue of the phonograph machines: "The owners of talking machines are now enjoying the music of these famous Quartets in their own homes. Mr. Stamps says its cheaper, 'you do not have to feed them,' and I guess he is right."[70]

In many ways, James Vaughan was a big fish in a little pond. His commercial success ensured that he would become the most important citizen of Lawrence County, and he seems to have achieved that status at least by the 1920s. In 1919, he purchased the fledgling *Lawrence News* and, for the next twenty years, published the countywide weekly newspaper.[71] Not surprisingly, he became involved in town politics. He served on the local school board, was a member of the city council, and, beginning in 1923, served a four-year term in the mayor's office. He also was for a time president of one of the local banks. Friends remembered him as "an independent in politics, he voted for the man rather than for the party." That view may well have been reinforced by Vaughan's stance as "an ardent prohibitionist by precept as well as practice." In a predominantly Democratic region, he was no doubt reluctant to support a national platform that in the late 1920s called for a repeal of the Eighteenth Amendment.[72]

Vaughan also enjoyed friends and acquaintances in the larger circle of southern rural music. Uncle Dave Macon became a close friend who visited with Vaughan regularly to discuss his own love of gospel music.[73] In addition, Vaughan's willingness to share broadcasting time with a new Nashville radio station, WSM, when it opened in 1925 won him friends at the station's parent company, the influential National Life and Accident Company. As a result, WSM maintained a long-term appearance agreement with the Vaughan Quartet that stretched through 1939.[74]

Vaughan's position became even more significant as the Depression reached Lawrenceburg and the town declined in relative importance to the larger trade centers of Nashville, Memphis, and Birmingham. Partly because of the financial downturn, Vaughan lost WOAN in 1929, selling the station's equipment and frequency to WREC, Memphis, for $9,000. The station had been a financial drain anyhow, and, with the arrival of hard times, the experiment in another outlet for advertising the James D. Vaughan Music Company came to an end. During the 1930s, quartets associated with Vaughan would bring plenty of free publicity by securing radio programs on larger stations in bigger markets. Perhaps realizing that, Vaughan sold the WOAN license and equipment to Memphis investors, who ultimately succeeded in turning the station into a profitable commercial investment. In much the same way, Vaughan Phonographs also failed to achieve sustained success and gave way to larger and better-operated labels. In 1935, five years after his last new releases appeared, Vaughan discontinued Vaughan Phonographs. The Vaughan label had always been, like most of James Vaughan's enterprises, a way of extending the commercial appeal of the publishing company. With the onslaught of the Depression in the late 1920s, sinking additional funds into those additional advertising venues simply no longer made sense.[75]

Vaughan probably understood that with the popularity of the quartets additional profits would come from the recordings themselves. But the popularity of radio in the 1920s ironically undermined the early commercial success of recordings as consumers opted for the variety and convenience of live commercial radio. In addition, the recording industry of the 1920s and 1930s was controlled almost exclusively by northern production companies that contracted separately with southern distributors like Vaughan or that sent crews to centers like Bristol, Tennessee, and Atlanta, Georgia, to record the latest in country and gospel talent. Modest gains would be made in the industry during this period, especially in the quality of the recordings themselves, but neither large-scale profits nor a distinctly southern industry would materialize until after the Second World War.[76]

Not even the Depression, however, could interrupt Vaughan's string of successful paperback publications. At least one new book appeared in each of the Depression years, and Vaughan managed to market two such titles during the dark days of 1933. Just two years before the crash of 1929, his company reported cumulative sales in excess of 3.5 million, the overwhelming majority having come in the two decades following the Vaughan Quartet's founding in 1910. Vaughan continued to sell an average of approximately 200,000 songbooks per year, passing the 6 million mark by 1941.[77] If anything, the Depression made his inexpensive paperbacks more attractive to consumers. In 1931, the Vaughan presses produced *Vaughan's School Songs*, complete with lessons for music classes in Tennessee's public schools.[78]

James Vaughan's pioneering efforts in songbook publishing, radio, and the phonograph industry were significant in keeping alive a particular genre of gospel music. More important, his personal attachment to four-part male harmony backed by a simple piano accompaniment, and his willingness to invest in quartets as a suitable vehicle for advertising his publishing empire across the rural South, introduced the economic possibilities of gospel music harmony. In many ways, Lawrenceburg spawned the modern southern gospel music industry, although, ironically, Vaughan's innovations would make it possible for quartets — within just a couple of decades — to operate quite independently of songbook publishers and even singing conventions. Though neither WOAN nor Vaughan Phonographs lasted beyond the 1930s, they foreshadowed a significant shift in the power structure of the gospel music industry in the South.

Dallas, Texas, July 28, 1996

"Mary, would you mind playing a little piano for me? Anything will do. I'd just like to sing a few songs and to hear you play." That's how I end the interview, not sure if my subject is willing. She's in a retirement home now and it's been fifty years since the musician shortage caused by the World War II draft convinced her husband, Frank, to have her play as the full-time pianist for his famous Stamps Quartet. She was known as "Sally" then—a nickname that Frank gave her though she's not sure why.

But here on this hot July afternoon, she willingly obliges, if my wife, Connie, and I will help her from the wheelchair onto the piano stool of the baby grand located here in the visitor's lobby of the small retirement home just outside Dallas. Our kids are with us, and they join us as we gather around the piano. Others in the lobby watch with a detached bemusement as we all begin to sing. "Do you know this one?" Sally asks as she breaks into the V. O. Stamps and Luther Presley arrangement of "When the Saints Go Marching In." "Oh, yeah, that's a good one," my kids respond immediately. Then the classic Stamps-Baxter number composed by Cleavant Derricks, "Just a Little Talk with Jesus." A few more and then something I don't recognize . . . an elaborate, lilting number. "That was pretty. What was it?" "I don't know, Sally says. I just made it up."

We conclude with a couple of verses of "Amazing Grace." The singing is suspect, though we enjoy it and no one complains. But there's no mistake that the little lady behind the ivories has done this before. For a few moments, she plays them just as she did back in the early 1940s—complete with those classic southern gospel runs. And this day, there are no convention books. It's all by ear and memory as she remembers the tunes and I try to remember the words. I have a confession . . . both her ear and her memory are better than mine.

4
STAMPS-BAXTER: A TEXAS GOSPEL MUSIC EMPIRE

Virgil Oliver Stamps faced a difficult decision in the fall of 1923. All his life, he had dreamed of a career in gospel music and now he seemed perched on the edge of achieving that dream. As James Vaughan's chief agent in Texas, he oversaw the Lawrenceburg operation west of the Mississippi — contributing monthly to the pages of the *Vaughan's Family Visitor*, conducting a summer normal, and hustling the annual songbooks. In addition, he was a noted writer himself and had enjoyed some success as a dynamic music teacher. At one point he had left the Vaughan fold for what promised to be greener pastures, but he had returned to the Lawrenceburg fraternity that he knew so well and had risen higher than anyone else, save members of the Vaughan family. Clearly, he owed much to the visionary from Tennessee.

Nevertheless, Virgil Stamps knew, as he pondered his situation that fateful fall, that he could rise no further up the Vaughan ladder. James Vaughan's son, Kieffer, and he were essentially the same age and it would be Kieffer who would someday inherit the Lawrenceburg company. Grateful though he was for James Vaughan's mentorship, Stamps knew his burning ambition could never be sated working for someone else. Even as he conducted the Vaughan business from his Jacksonville, Texas, office, he contemplated the consequences of a break toward independence. Instinctively, he knew that his magnetic personality and network of gospel music friends across the Southwest would support him once he became an independent in competition with his old boss. Shortly after 1924 dawned, Stamps took the plunge, resigning as head of Vaughan's Western Department and opening Virgil O. Stamps Music Company.[1]

Predictably, Stamps's defection from the Vaughan ranks created hard feelings within the southern gospel publishing community. For a number of years, the Vaughan company's sales declined as did the attendance at its annual winter normal. Vaughan scrambled to hang on to part of the southwestern market, appointing Robert Jordan to take the post vacated by Stamps.[2] But Virgil Stamps was not easily replaced. He took with him his own network of admirers and a decade of work in the Texas-Arkansas corridor.

Stamps had been a robust, energetic young man of twenty-three when he first entered the Vaughan Normal School in the summer of 1915. Quickly, he proved himself one of Vaughan's top hustlers, the term affectionately given to those who, in the course of teaching singing schools and singing at various conventions, sold more Vaughan books than their peers. Together with his brother, Frank, a bass singer who led one of the most popular Vaughan quartets during the years immediately after World War I, he linked the name Stamps with the fortunes of the Vaughan company.

Still, Virgil Stamps faced long odds in 1924. By leaving Vaughan, he cut himself off from the most successful shape-note publisher in the South at precisely the time when the Lawrenceburg operation seemed poised for its greatest wave of success. Radio and early Vaughan recordings both seemed promising in 1924, and the *Visitor* had clearly provided an important vehicle for advertising both the new songbooks and the travels of the various quartets. Like Vaughan, Stamps had ambition, musical talent, and a supportive bass-singing brother with traveling in his blood. And, also like Vaughan, he had an undying passion for the message and sound of southern gospel music.

Virgil Stamps was born in Upshur County, near Gilmer, Texas, on September 18, 1892. His parents, William Oscar Stamps and Florence Rosser Stamps, were rural east Texans who frequented singing conventions and, like many of their neighbors, came to love the shape-note gospel hymns and the musical performances of local quartets. William Stamps operated a sawmill and a rural general store. In addition, he owned some interest in other local business ventures. Though not wealthy, he was more prosperous than many of his neighbors, and, as a sign of their respect, he was twice elected to represent his district in the Texas state legislature and also served for a while as U.S. Post-

The Birth of an Industry

master in Ore City, Texas.[3] In addition, he encouraged all six of his sons to develop musical skills and to follow the teachings of the local Methodist church. As a teenager, Virgil Stamps learned music first through a local singing school taught by Richard M. Morgan in 1907 and, just a few years later, began teaching his own singing schools and working on his own musical compositions.[4] In March 1909, at the age of sixteen, he married Addie Belle Culpepper, another Upshur County native, and, eleven months later, they celebrated the birth of a daughter. By 1911, the young couple secured some independence from parents and in-laws when William Stamps purchased a general store in nearby Ore City and offered the job of managing the business to his son. For the next three years, during which time he and Addie announced the birth of a son, Virgil Stamps ran the store and got involved in a variety of other business interests owned by his father.[5] In addition, he earned a little extra money teaching his singing schools. Despite his new obligations, Stamps continued investing in his own music education. He attended music normals whenever he could and, as a result, "acquired debts that . . . took him years and years to pay."[6]

In 1914, two momentous events in Stamps's young musical career would change him forever. First, he wrote and published his first song, "The Man Behind the Plow," which he marketed independently for ten cents per sheet, and, second, he decided to travel away from home to receive additional music training.[7] Though not a gospel song, "The Man Behind the Plow" prompted Stamps to pledge to make a career in gospel music "or starve to death." His newfound determination proved invaluable as he headed into the unpredictable business world of gospel music publishing. Years later, after becoming the most successful shape-note publisher in the nation, he modestly noted, "Well, we escaped starvation at least."[8]

Late in 1914, shortly after the publication of "The Man Behind the Plow," Stamps traveled to Lawrenceburg, Tennessee, to attend the Vaughan Music School. His first reports back from the school were glowing, and the *Musical Visitor* was happy to accommodate his words of praise. "I am having a great time," he wrote. "You all should be with me. Where am I? Why, in the Lawrenceburg Normal, of course. You don't know what you are missing. This is the greatest Normal ever. It is well worth coming from Texas to attend."[9] When he returned to Texas early in 1915, it was as a traveling representative of the Vaughan company.[10]

Stamps approached his new career with a driving ambition, and his quick success added to the significant competition that already existed within the small community of shape-note publishers in the South. A third child, another son, arrived in September 1915, and Stamps would have to push hard if he were to make a living by indulging his passion for music. At some point around 1916, however, he mysteriously disappeared from the pages of the *Musical Visitor*, though the precocious young man had clearly been a bright star as a music teacher and company hustler. The previous year, James Vaughan himself had noted in the magazine that "Virgil is a sure enough hustler. We are mighty glad to have him as a member of the Vaughan bunch."[11] Late in the year, the music publisher was still sold on the young man's potential, noting, "Virgil has the qualities that make him a winner." Vaughan also continued to run advertisements for "The Man Behind the Plow."[12]

In June 1917, as Americans followed news of the war in Europe and American troops' entry into the fray, an explanation finally came. Stamps had "made a mistake in running off after strangers."[13] He had served briefly as manager of the Atlanta, Georgia, branch of a rival songbook company, the Samuel W. Beazley Company of Chicago.[14] Now he was "back to the loving fold of the Vaughan fraternity" and "working in one of our popular quartets." Vaughan noted, with humor but no doubt with a degree of self-satisfaction as well, that "we forgave him, and took him back, and he says that he is with us to stay this time."[15] The time was a low one for Virgil Stamps for another reason: In the midst of his failed opportunity in Atlanta, he and Addie had lost their twenty-month-old son.[16] It was no doubt comforting when Vaughan extended a hand, invited him back to the company, and placed him in a popular Lawrenceburg-based Vaughan quartet with J. M. Allen, I. T. Foust, and Vaughan's son-in-law, W. B. Walbert.[17]

This time, Stamps would make the most of his Vaughan association, and, apparently seeking to make the most of the ambitious young man's talent, James Vaughan created more and more opportunities for him. In 1918, Vaughan dispatched Stamps and his family to the east Texas town of Timpson to establish a branch house for distribution and promotion of the Vaughan publications. The following year, Stamps relocated to Jacksonville, a slightly larger town sixty miles west, and there he operated the Vaughan interests for the next five years.[18]

In Jacksonville, Stamps built the most successful arm of the Vaughan organization. By 1922, he was issuing his own monthly report in the pages of *Vaughan's Family Visitor*, touting the virtues of Texas and of

The Birth of an Industry

shape-note singing in the western regions.[19] When Vaughan expanded into recordings and radio in the early 1920s, Stamps understood the magnitude of the effect technology would have on the future of gospel music. Extolling the technology behind the new Vaughan records, he urged readers to check out the new discs and reminded them that they could now enjoy the music of a Vaughan quartet without the burden and expense of having to feed the individual members.[20]

In all areas, Stamps's ambition paid off for the Vaughan company. Quartets identified with him in part because he was himself an accomplished bass singer who had spent time on the road with a quartet. Students no doubt admired his passion for music and his ability to utilize shape notes. Most of all, aspiring music publishers envied his salesmanship and the easy way in which he communicated with the rural people who bought and used the books. As the early 1920s progressed, Stamps received more and more praise in the pages of *Vaughan's Family Visitor.* "He has made the Vaughan schools in Texas a household word," one writer gushed, "and has placed many on the road to success. He is one of the best gospel songwriters in the South, a fine singer, possessing a deep basso profundo voice, is considered by those *who know* to be a teacher of rare ability and has an abundance of what it takes to make any business go—PUSH."[21]

It was obvious by late 1923 that Virgil Stamps, now known to his business associates as simply "V. O.," was getting restless. He clearly challenged others within the Vaughan organization to keep up with the pace of his western office. Among his other accomplishments, he managed a successful branch of the Vaughan Modern Normal School of Music held from mid-November to Christmas at his office in Jacksonville, drawing 119 students, a number rivaling the attendance enjoyed by Vaughan's annual school in Lawrenceburg.[22] Company publications noted with pride that "Mr. Stamps bears the distinction of having taught more normal music schools than any man of his age."[23] Largely because of that success, he was advertised as a featured teacher at the upcoming Vaughan Normal, scheduled to open in Lawrenceburg on New Year's Day 1924.[24] Ominously, as the new year approached, he warned others to "watch us in 1924. We have a loyal organization that is going to be felt and heard from in the west."[25] Stamps's rhetoric was no doubt meant as a friendly challenge intended to boost the morale of the James D. Vaughan Music Company's employees, but it was clear that his drive might soon lead him to move on to bigger and better things: "Some records will be broken in this territory in the next 12 months. WE have over 600 teachers lined up with us. WATCH OUR SMOKE you fellows in the east. We expect to build the largest school and business in the south in Texas. Boys, let's all get in line and do our best. Nothing short of our best is worthy of the Vaughan Fraternity."[26]

V. O. Stamps's decision to form his own company must have been a difficult one. He no doubt felt genuine affection and gratitude toward James Vaughan for giving him a chance in the music business. He must also have been unsure about what might happen without the financial backing of the tried and true Vaughan company. As late as the summer of 1923, however, Stamps's "Western Department" section in the *Family Visitor* gave no hint that he would form new competition as he blasted those who failed to remain loyal to the home office. His tone highlighted the highly competitive world of 1920s shape-note publishing: "Judas Iscariot betrayed the Savior of the world for a few pieces of silver. Men today are still betraying their friends for small amounts of money. Some men who owe all they are to some man or company of men are willing to 'Bite the hand that helped them,' if some one will offer them books two cents cheaper. The sin of ingratitude is one of the basest of sins, think well before you commit it. Be a booster—a booster, for those who have boosted you."[27]

There is evidence that Stamps's competitive nature created jealousy and ill will within the small community of shape-note music teachers. In August 1923, *Vaughan's Family Visitor* published a letter from Stamps in reply to a critical article published by Will M. Ramsey, a rival shape-note music publisher in Little Rock, Arkansas. Ramsey's *Musical Advocate* had accused Stamps of disrupting a singing convention by unfairly eliminating his competition. The controversy had initially broken when both men had attended "the great Plateau Singing Convention at Plainview, Texas," two months earlier.[28] According to Stamps, the article erroneously reported that he "engineered the proceedings of the convention and met its officers at Plainview FRIDAY night and directed the whole business." Apparently, Ramsey accused Stamps of securing an inside track on what songs would be featured at the singing convention and had thus established an unfair advantage for the Vaughan company's product. In denying the charge, Stamps added an uncharacteristically confrontational note to the monthly journal: "I will give Mr. Ramsey $100.00 in cash if he will prove that this writer saw any one connected with the convention at Plainview, FRIDAY night."[29] The incident again

The Birth of an Industry

confirms the contentious nature of shape-note publishing at the time and specifically illustrates that Virgil Stamps himself had become, by 1923, a major force to be reckoned with.

Whether by expressing such devotion to the Vaughan cause Virgil Stamps was masking his own plans for independence or simply fighting a subconscious urge to move out on his own is not clear. In any case, he decided that a proposed move was not something he could easily discuss with his mentor, even as he carefully planned for financial backing from several acquaintances in Texas. In 1924, he finally took the plunge, breaking with Vaughan to form the V. O. Stamps Music Company, headquartered in Jacksonville. Predictably, the break did create hard feelings that would last for the rest of Stamps's life. When Stamps's company published *Radio Song Album,* "a book of special songs by the South's favorite composers—their photographs, and a 'thumb-nail' sketch of their lives," in 1937, the Vaughans of Lawrenceburg were conspicuously absent. Noting in the index that the publication was "not designed to be a 'Who's Who'" of southern publishers, Stamps apologized to a few notables who had been omitted because their photos had arrived late. He also included the telling comment, "We are sorry that others refused to cooperate with us."[30]

Not surprisingly, the Vaughan company published a collection of biographical essays that same year. *Who's Who among Southern Singers and Composers,* by one of Vaughan's most devoted singers, Ottis J. Knippers, was even more ambitious than the Stamps collection. Whereas Stamps's *Radio Song Album* included 105 brief entries with photos, Knippers's collection contained 145 photos accompanied by more extensive biographical information. In addition, while the Stamps collection was woven between pages of classic Stamps-Baxter songs, the Lawrenceburg publication avoided any musical content. Though songwriters and singers associated with both publishing companies found their way into each of the books, V. O. Stamps was noticeably absent from the Knippers publication.[31] Years later, Ottis Knippers noted with regret that he had omitted V. O. Stamps from his collection, recalling that "that old feud was still going on then."[32]

Part of the reason James Vaughan felt so betrayed by Stamps's departure in 1924 was the discovery that his employee had been earning money on the side in an attempt to finance his new company. Otis McCoy, an employee of Vaughan's, remembered that a copy of a music book that was published by the A. J. Showalter Company and being marketed by

Stamps using Vaughan company envelopes was mistakenly returned to the Vaughan home office in Lawrenceburg. That accidental discovery tipped Vaughan off in advance of any public announcement by his junior employee, and it was probably this incident, more than anything else, that led to the intense rivalry that existed between them for the next fifteen years. Rumors subsequently circulated that Stamps had been holding out the best songs sent to the Vaughan Texas office, waiting to use them in his own books. When Stamps's first independent publication, *Harbor Bells*, appeared in 1924, Vaughan devotees believed their suspicions confirmed.[33] According to a later Stamps publication, that initial songbook was "an instant success, the sales not only far exceeding those of any similar book issued by a new concern, but also surpassing sales records made by many old-established publishing companies."[34]

Stamps's role in the collection of copyrights remains shrouded in mystery, but one thing is clear: he used his former connections to Vaughan to promote his songbook business. One of his earliest acquaintances through Vaughan was Jesse Randall Baxter Jr., a music teacher trained by and working for the A. J. Showalter Company in Dalton, Georgia. Just three years older than Stamps, Baxter was, like Stamps, a Methodist who had fallen under the spell of shape-note singing. Also like Stamps, Baxter had worked his way up and gained the confidence of his employer, ultimately securing control of Showalter's branch house in Texarkana, Texas. It was Baxter who arranged for Stamps's early books to be printed on the Showalter presses, and it was probably Baxter's connection that had led to Stamps's selling Showalter books on the side during 1924.[35]

Despite the success of *Harbor Bells*, by 1926 the V. O. Stamps Music Company was struggling to compete with the more established shape-note publishers.[36] In desperate need of financing and with his earlier business investors now developing cold feet, Stamps convinced Baxter to invest in the new company. The death of Showalter in the fall of 1924 and the success of Stamps's first book both played a role in Baxter's decision to purchase stock from the timid investors in the spring of 1926. The following year, the two men jointly bought out all of Stamps's remaining backers and incorporated the new arrangement under the name the Stamps-Baxter Music Company.[37]

Even after Baxter bought into the company in 1926, the convention books from Jacksonville, Texas, were still being printed by the Showalter printing firm from Dalton, Georgia. The practice was not unusual given

The Birth of an Industry

the expense of investing in separate machinery; James Vaughan continued to have his songbooks printed in Cincinnati until well into the 1930s.[38] By 1928, the Stamps-Baxter alliance seemed set; Virgil Stamps would operate the home office from his base in Jacksonville and J. R. Baxter would run a branch office in his familiar territory in Chattanooga. Clearly both men sought to undercut the singing convention business of the Vaughan and Showalter companies.

It may have been the intense competition that convinced V. O. Stamps to relocate the home office to Dallas in 1929. Dallas was a growing city, and the move would prove fortuitous for the future of the Stamps-Baxter company. Baxter continued to operate the branch office from Chattanooga, and soon the company opened yet another branch office in Pangburn, Arkansas, managed by gospel songwriter Luther G. Presley.[39] After several years, the company invested in printing machinery and, beginning in 1934, published and printed its own songbooks from a small Dallas office on Beckley Avenue. As the business grew, larger quarters were needed, and, by 1936, a permanent location on South Tyler in the prominent subdivision of Oak Cliff was secured.[40]

Over the next five years, Stamps-Baxter became the most prominent name in all of gospel music. Company songbooks outsold all their competitors, and prominent quartets rushed to associate themselves with both the Stamps-Baxter name and the new songs appearing in the paperbacks now being published several times each year.[41] Like Vaughan before them, Stamps and Baxter understood the significance of maintaining strong ties with popular gospel quartets. Making use of V. O.'s talented brother, Frank, a man known and loved throughout the gospel quartet circuit, the men sought to make the Stamps-Baxter name representative of the best in gospel quartet music. Frank Stamps had traveled for several years as manager of the Vaughan-Stamps Quartet, and, beginning in 1924, he formed the first Stamps Quartet, which stood as the sole representative of his older brother's enterprise.[42] Continuing to represent the thriving new Stamps-Baxter company after 1926, Frank's group—despite several personnel changes—grew in popularity. By 1927, the Frank Stamps Quartet was operating out of Chattanooga, Tennessee, and the group achieved notoriety throughout the South by means of concert appearances and 78 rpm recordings made with the Victor Company.[43] In addition, they, and lesser-known groups who contracted to use the Stamps-Baxter name, met the Vaughan competition head-on at state and regional singing conventions, hoping to achieve mass sales by popularizing the newest tunes in their convention books.[44] Virgil Stamps himself formed a version of the Stamps Quartet during the late 1920s and, taking the bass part himself, promoted the company around the Dallas area. To distinguish the group from the many now sporting the Stamps-Baxter name, he dubbed his group "The Old Original Quartet."[45]

As the 1930s wore on, in most every way, the Stamps-Baxter company's accomplishments exceeded those of the Vaughan company. *Stamps-Baxter News*, a four-page newsletter begun in 1927, was converted into a full-fledged monthly publication, *The Southern Music News*, by the summer of 1934. Stamps himself initially served as editor, but, as the business grew and the demands on his time increased, in 1939 the company hired a full-time editor, J. I. Ayres. Shortly thereafter, with business growing outside Texas and the South, the publication was renamed *Gospel Music News* to reflect its more national character.[46] The publishers' mission statement was displayed proudly under the masthead: "Dedicated to the Interest of Gospel Music, Practical Christianity and Better Homes." The first issue under the new name featured photos of Stamps and Baxter along with the following letter to readers:

The News has outgrown its name. When it was launched years ago its sphere was the South. Now it has subscribers in every state in the union and several foreign countries. Its sphere today is National and International. The News will continue to serve the South that gave it birth . . . the South we dearly love. Our prayer is, that it will grow in influence and usefulness, and that it will be a big factor in our fight to make all America "Gospel Music Conscious." We hope it will always be worthy of your confidence and support.

Your friends,

V. O. STAMPS

J. R. BAXTER, JR.[47]

At its height, the Stamps-Baxter publication enjoyed a circulation of close to 50,000, probably about double that of *Vaughan's Family Visitor* during the 1920s.[48]

The Stamps-Baxter firm's efforts mirrored those of the Vaughan company in other ways as well. Beginning in 1924, the V. O. Stamps School of Music began offering courses for both aspiring singers and music teachers. After Baxter's arrival in 1926, the schools were expanded. A six-week session held in Chattanooga beginning in November was generally followed by a similar session conducted from the home office in Dallas

The Birth of an Industry

shortly after the first of the year. In the late 1930s, session lengths were reduced to three weeks and the Dallas school—the larger of the two—was moved to June.[49]

The success of the Stamps-Baxter publications and the quartets that publicized the company drew to the Stamps-Baxter schools instructors from a wide talent pool across the evangelical South. By 1929, Stamps and Baxter lured William W. Combs, a celebrated voice teacher with years of experience in the Vaughan Normal, to join their staff as the backbone of the annual schools. For a brief period, Combs even held interest in the Stamps-Baxter company—an indication of the importance that both Stamps and Baxter placed on the annual educational events.[50] And the move paid dividends. By the dawn of World War II, more than 500 students were attending the sessions held in Dallas each summer.[51]

Also like Vaughan, Virgil Stamps and Jesse Baxter understood the growing importance of radio in spreading the gospel music business. By 1936, the team secured a relationship with radio station KRLD in Dallas that promoted the V. O. Stamps Quartet and the Stamps-Baxter publications daily.[52] With a catchy bass-lead, the fast-paced "Give the World a Smile Each Day" introduced a program of Stamps Quartet music that could be heard in homes across the Midwest. Even more important was an arrangement that V. O. made with XERL, a powerful 500,000-watt operation located just across the Mexican border from Del Rio, Texas. With no restrictions from American authorities, the station's broadcasts, in particular its nightly programming, reached much of North America. Stamps's agreement to provide fifteen-minute transcription discs for replay over the air several times late at night and early in the morning made the Stamps Quartet name, Stamps-Baxter products, and the sound of southern gospel–style quartets instantly accessible. In addition, as the Stamps-Baxter fraternity of quartets grew, the company allowed both its name and its signature song to headline radio programs across the South.[53]

Closely associated with the Stamps-Baxter School of Music was another radio promotion that would have far-reaching implications for the future of gospel quartet music. In 1938, Stamps promoted an "All-Night Singing" as a part of the conclusion of the school. Students formed a major part of the talent pool for the one-evening performance carried live over KRLD. In addition, a large audience gathered to witness the event. The first in what became an annual sing was broadcast from the state fairgrounds in Dallas. Stamps scheduled the second one, in 1939, to be broadcast from the Cotton Bowl, though inclement weather ultimately caused the concert to be moved to a local church. In 1940, participants performed before a crowd of 7,500 at the Dallas Sportatorium and the event was broadcast continuously for eight hours. This annual all-night sing continued to be associated with the school well into the 1950s.[54]

Part of the reason for Stamps-Baxter success was the willingness of each partner to allow the other the luxury of concentrating on his own strength. According to coworkers and associates, Stamps utilized his skill as a promoter at singing conventions, as a jovial friend of quartet men everywhere, and as a singer in the Dallas-based V. O. Stamps Quartet. Baxter, on the other hand, concentrated on the business of efficiently running and operating the publishing firm, though he also sang in a Chattanooga-based Baxter Quartet and conducted his own local radio program.[55] Associates later remembered Virgil Stamps as "a visionary," as someone who dreamed of new ways of propelling gospel music into the limelight. Baxter, on the other hand, was remembered as "a wonderful music man" with "keen business ability."[56]

While Stamps-Baxter and James D. Vaughan competed for the lion's share of shape-note songbook business in the 1930s, a number of other publishers built small firms in an attempt to carve out their own share of the market. When George Pullen Jackson published *White Spirituals in the Southern Uplands* in 1933, he noted twenty-nine different seven-character shape-note convention publication houses hailing from the southern United States. Among the more prominent were the Teachers' Music Publishing Company of Hudson, North Carolina; the Morris-Henson Company of Atlanta; the Athens Music Company of Athens, Alabama; the John Benson Publishing Company of Nashville; the Trio Music Company of Waco, Texas; the Central Music Company of Little Rock, Arkansas; and the Tennessee Music and Printing Company of Cleveland, Tennessee.[57] Specific areas of the South tended to be remarkably loyal to a particular shape-note company in large part because of the personal relationships built between the local inhabitants and singing-school teachers and company representatives. This loyalty led to a proliferation of songbooks, since individual churches and local singing associations expected new material on an annual or biannual basis.[58]

One struggling company proved to have a particularly important influence on the development of the southern gospel music industry. The Hartford Music Company was a marginal operation located in the small

The Birth of an Industry

mining town of Hartford, Arkansas, just thirty miles south of Fort Smith. Founded in 1918 by Eugene M. Bartlett, John A. McClung, and David Moore, the company achieved some recognition in the 1920s with Bartlett's "Victory in Jesus" and "Everybody Will Be Happy over There." McClung would also ultimately capture attention with his lovely composition "Just a Rose Will Do," written shortly before his death in 1942. But another partner, a young man who did not enter the picture until 1926, would force fans across the gospel music world to take notice of what was appearing from the little hamlet not far from the Oklahoma border. Albert E. Brumley would become the best-known southern gospel songwriter of all time.

Hartford's musical heritage began in 1904 when David Moore, a shape-note singing-school teacher, relocated there and opened the David Moore Music Store. A coal mining boom in the late 1880s had turned Hartford into a thriving little town of 4,000, thanks to "the railroad and a 7-foot vein of the highest grade smokeless coal."[59] Moore sold pianos, organs, and a variety of musical instruments along with songbooks and sheet music. His specialty was gospel music. Within a few years, he teamed up with Will M. Ramsey to form the Central Music Company, publishing shape-note convention books for several years until Ramsey relocated the company to Little Rock.[60] One of the employees of the Central Music Company was a local Hartford boy, an aspiring songwriter named Eugene Monroe Bartlett.[61]

After Ramsey moved to Little Rock, Bartlett convinced Moore and McClung to help him form another company, which Bartlett also agreed to manage. Bartlett followed the same route to success with the Hartford Music Company that James Vaughan had taken in Lawrenceburg.[62] In 1921, he opened the Hartford Musical Institute, a shape-note normal that offered sessions twice a year, in January and June. By the early 1930s, close to 400 students were annually attending the Hartford school; one of the special instructors at the school was Homer Rodeheaver, who attended the winter session in 1934.[63] Likewise, Bartlett published a monthly magazine, *The Herald of Song*, intended to promote shape-note music and to advertise several full-time quartets the company sponsored to promote Hartford products. One of those quartets was the W. T. "Deacon" Utley Quartet, which could be heard regularly on several midwestern radio stations. By 1930, Bartlett's company had branches in Nacogdoches, Texas, and Hartshorne, Oklahoma.[64]

In the end, however, Bartlett's greatest contribution to southern gospel came in his mentoring of a young singer and songwriter named Albert Edward Brumley. Brumley was born on October 29, 1905, in the Indian Territory near what would become Spiro, Oklahoma. His parents were sharecroppers, eking out an existence in the eastern Oklahoma soil. With a few good cotton harvests, William and Sarah Brumley ultimately saved enough to buy their own place near the Oklahoma-Arkansas line in LaFlore County, Oklahoma, in a community known as Rock Island. Young Albert Brumley's enthusiasm caught the attention of locals, and he excelled at music after attending a singing school early in 1922. He was recognized as a competent bass singer in his youth, but it was his fascination with music and his ability to compose lyrics drawn from his solid rural upbringing that ultimately endeared him to the gospel music community. Brumley later recalled that when the teacher drew the scale notation on the board and began explaining the basics of music theory to the class at that first singing school, it was a revelation: "When he . . . said that all the songs and melodies that had ever been written came from that little scale up there on that blackboard . . . and all that ever would be written could be found in that scale . . . that set me afire! That's when I decided that if other people could do it [write music], I could do it."[65]

Brumley spent the next few years working on the family farm, though he continued to write gospel music and achieved a reputation in the Rock Island community as "that hot shot bass singer."[66] In 1926, at age twenty, Brumley set out to try to turn his interest in music into a dream come true. On the advice of one of his singing-school teachers, he left the farm and traveled to Hartford, Arkansas, to meet the man in charge of the well-known music company there. Brumley had seen Bartlett only once before, at a singing convention held near Rock Island. Now he arrived on the famous songwriter's porch with only $2.50 in his pocket, not even enough to pay the $5.00 tuition for the upcoming Hartford Normal, much less his own room and board. After explaining his plight and eagerness to pursue a musical career, Brumley ended up not only enrolled in the upcoming school but also a guest in Bartlett's home. It was an act of kindness he never forgot and one that E. M. Bartlett could not have guessed would be returned to him in such an immediate way. Over the next ten years, Brumley worked off and on as an employee of the Hartford company, attending music classes and, in his spare time, writing songs. By 1929, he and several other students were representing the company as members of the Hartford Quartet. For six months, Brumley sang bass and occasionally played piano for the group consisting of

The Birth of an Industry

Marvin P. Dalton on first tenor, Burgess Bell on lead, and W. A. McNinch on the baritone part.[67] In addition to the gospel numbers promoting the Hartford songbooks, the quartet occasionally provided a comedy routine featuring E. M. Bartlett's own "Take an Old Cold Tater and Wait." The performances demonstrated the ability of gospel music quartets to provide varied entertainment to the members of the rural communities they visited.[68]

In 1931, Brumley married Goldie Edith Schell, a young woman he met at a singing school he was teaching in Powell, Missouri. With the marriage, he decided to settle down in Powell and concentrate on his love for songwriting, since his "heart was set on a writing career." His first published song, "I Can Hear Them Singing Over There," had appeared under Bartlett's label in 1927 but, in Brumley's words, was "not one of my better tunes."[69] Without the constant rush of quartet life, he entered into one of the most successful periods that any gospel songwriter has ever enjoyed. Goldie Brumley encouraged her young husband to push his songs, noting, "They're good, Albert. . . . Any publisher would be glad to publish them."[70] Beginning with "I'll Fly Away" (1932), the list of songs that became gospel and country music standards seems almost endless: "Jesus, Hold My Hand" (1933), "I'd Rather Be an Old-Time Christian" (1934), "I'll Meet You in the Morning" (1936), "There's A Little Pine Log Cabin" (1937), "Did You Ever Go Sailin'?" (1938), "Turn Your Radio On" (1938), "I've Found a Hiding Place" (1939), "He Set Me Free" (1939), "Rank Strangers to Me" (1942), "If We Never Meet Again" (1945), "I Just Steal Away and Pray" (1946), and "I'm Bound for that City" (1954).[71]

Brumley was easily the most recognizable songwriter to come out of the white gospel quartet music industry. "I'll Fly Away" has been recorded well in excess of 500 times by a remarkably diverse assortment of artists.[72] Brumley's talent lay in converting the rural flavor of evangelicalism into nostalgic, sentimental ballads and upbeat, happy rhythms that resonated with an American Christian audience adjusting to the technology and the fast pace of twentieth-century life. One admirer called Brumley the "Gershwin of the Rural Route."[73] Most remarkable about Brumley's talent was his ability to compose rousing gospel standards like "I'll Meet You in the Morning" alongside lilting sentimental favorites like "Did You Ever Go Sailin'?" This gifted Oklahoman was able to transcend and broaden the musical horizon of many artists within both the gospel and the country fields. His approach to songwriting was simple, and therein lay his success. After many years at the top of his craft, he commented that "basic simplicity has been the earmark of nearly all great songs . . . the reasoning is simple; they are easier to understand and easier to remember."[74]

In addition, Brumley recognized the value of songs, eventually reclaiming the copyrights to his early work that had been signed over to Hartford, Stamps-Baxter, and other music publishers. By 1943, he organized his own music company, ultimately owning the remains of the Hartford company that had given him his start a generation earlier.[75] All-told, by the time of his death on November 15, 1977, Brumley had produced close to 700 songs, the popularity of which was unprecedented in gospel music circles.

By the time of Brumley's success, companies like Stamps-Baxter and Hartford had already paved the way by popularizing the southern gospel style. In the future, the companies' strength would wane as individual songwriters and singers took more and more of the spotlight upon themselves. As the publishing companies declined, an industry characterized by participation and singing conventions came to a close. In its place, a business geared more toward entertainment emerged. The future of southern gospel belonged to the performers and their stage.

The Vaughan Radio Quartet, ca. 1927. Left to right: Hilman Barnard (tenor), Otis McCoy (lead), W. B. Walbert (baritone), and Adger M. Pace (bass). Courtesy Southern Gospel Music Hall of Fame and Museum, Sevierville, Tenn.

The Vaughan Recording Quartet, ca. 1925, Gennett Records Studio, Richmond, Indiana. Left to right: Hilman Barnard (tenor), Glenn Kieffer Vaughan (lead), Walter B. Seale (baritone), Roy Collins (bass), and Ted Shaw (piano). Courtesy Southern Gospel Music Hall of Fame and Museum, Sevierville, Tenn.

The Vaughan Quartet, ca. 1916. Manager and bass singer Charles Vaughan is third from the left. Courtesy Southern Gospel Music Hall of Fame and Museum, Sevierville, Tenn.

Hartford Quartet, late 1920s. Left to right: Marvin P. Dalton (tenor), Burgess Bell (lead), W. A. McNinch (baritone), and Albert E. Brumley (bass). Courtesy Southern Gospel Music Hall of Fame and Museum, Sevierville, Tenn.

The Vaughan Radio Quartet, 1933. Left to right: *Cecil C. Knippers (baritone), Ottis J. Knippers (lead), James D. Walbert (piano), W. B. Walbert (baritone), and Adger M. Pace (bass). Courtesy Southern Gospel Music Hall of Fame and Museum, Sevierville, Tenn.*

Vaughan Radio Quartet, January 1937. Left to right: *Dwight Brock (piano), Palmer Wheeler (tenor), Glenn Kieffer Vaughan (lead), John Cook (baritone), and Jim Waits (bass). Courtesy Southern Gospel Music Hall of Fame and Museum, Sevierville, Tenn.*

The V. O. Stamps Old Original Quartet, 1936. Left to right: Jim Gaither (baritone), Walter Rippetoe (tenor), V. O. Stamps (bass), Bob Bacon (lead), and Marion Snider (piano). Courtesy Southern Gospel Music Hall of Fame and Museum, Sevierville, Tenn.

The Frank Stamps Quartet, 1927. Left to right: Palmer Wheeler (tenor), Roy Wheeler (lead), Dwight Brock (piano), Odis Echols (baritone), and Frank Stamps (bass); Brock is holding a ukulele. Courtesy Southern Gospel Music Hall of Fame and Museum, Sevierville, Tenn.

CONCERT

Frank STAMPS *All-Star* QUARTET
FAMOUS
RADIO AND RECORD ARTISTS

AT _____

Night Of_____

Admission Only 15c and 25c

Your Friends of the Air Invite You to Hear Them In Person

Frank Stamps All-Star Quartet concert poster, 1937. Left to right: *Palmer Wheeler (tenor), Roy Wheeler (lead), Lawrence Ivy (piano), Odis Echols (baritone), and Frank Stamps (bass). Courtesy Southern Gospel Music Hall of Fame and Museum, Sevierville, Tenn.*

LeFevre Trio, ca. 1921. Left to right: *Alphus LeFevre (tenor and fiddle), Maude LeFevre (alto and guitar), and Urias LeFevre (lead and banjo). Courtesy Southern Gospel Music Hall of Fame and Museum, Sevierville, Tenn.*

Speer Family, mid-1930s. Left to right: *Rosa Nell Speer (alto and piano), Ben Speer (tenor and ukulele), Lena Speer (soprano and accordion), G. T. Speer (baritone/bass), Mary Tom Speer (soprano and mandolin), and Brock Speer (bass and guitar). Courtesy Southern Gospel Music Hall of Fame and Museum, Sevierville, Tenn.*

Blackwood Brothers,
ca. 1937. Left to right*:*
Roy Blackwood (tenor),
James Blackwood (lead),
R. W. Blackwood (baritone),
and Doyle Blackwood (bass).
Courtesy Southern Gospel
Music Hall of Fame and
Museum, Sevierville, Tenn.

Sand Mountain Quartet, 1937. Left to right*: Denver Chafin (tenor), Alton Jolley (lead),*
Erman Slater (baritone), and Corby Gardner (bass); Hixon Bell is seated with the guitar.
Courtesy Southern Gospel Music Hall of Fame and Museum, Sevierville, Tenn.

The John Daniel Quartet, late 1930s. Left to right: *John Daniel (tenor), Troy Daniel (lead), Wallace Fowler (baritone), Carl Rains (bass), and Albert Williams (piano). Courtesy Southern Gospel Music Hall of Fame and Museum, Sevierville, Tenn.*

The Sunshine Boys in *Columbia Pictures* Prairie Roundup, *1950.* Left to right: *Ace Richman, Fred Daniel, Smiley Burnette, Eddie Wallace, and J. D. Sumner. Courtesy Southern Gospel Music Hall of Fame and Museum, Sevierville, Tenn.*

Sunshine Boys advertisement, 1955. Courtesy Southern Gospel Music Hall of Fame and Museum, Sevierville, Tenn.

Swanee River Boys, 1941. From bottom left, clockwise: *George Hughes (tenor), Buford Abner (lead), Billy Carrier (baritone and guitar), and Merle Abner (bass). Courtesy Southern Gospel Music Hall of Fame and Museum, Sevierville, Tenn.*

III
THE EMERGENCE OF PROFESSIONAL QUARTETS

Bedford, Texas, July 29, 1996

I pull into the parking lot of the Black-Eyed Pea. It was his suggestion—
somewhere between my motel outside Irving and his farm south of Fort
Worth near Morgan, Texas. As I enter the restaurant, I look around.
Will we recognize each other? There he is. A completely unassuming
man, naturally shy and polite. "Hi, Mr. Carter, I'm Jim." "Nice to meet
you. Call me Roy. . . . Have you ever eaten here before? They have good
cornbread. Just about everything here is good to eat. Let's go ahead and
order and then you can tell me about this project of yours."

That begins my interview with Roy Carter, for many years the bass
singer and manager for the famous Chuck Wagon Gang. Roy's father,
brother, and two sisters had formed the group more than six decades
earlier and, over the years, no one had more success on radio and in
recordings. Their simple style thrilled hearts across America in part because it rarely changed. Dad Carter believed the music should be featured, not the singers, and the Chuck Wagon Gang followed that formula
to success. Roy and almost all his eight brothers and sisters sang with
the group at one time or another.

As my afternoon meal with Roy Carter stretches into its third hour,
long after the dessert and coffee, I have finally come to know this man . . .
at least a little. People loved the Chuck Wagon Gang because they came
to love the Carters . . . just regular friendly folks who poured their heart
and soul into a song. Roy explains that Dad Carter believed that the
group would fail if they ever thought of themselves as more than just
average singers. "People enjoy and like what they understand," Roy explains. "Dad told me one time, 'Son, there's ten thousand farmers out
there plowing on the plow and listening to a radio or a cassette tape that
believe sincerely that they can sing bass just as good as you can. It's because they understand it. It's simple.'" There's wisdom in what the father
told the son, and Roy knows it. Gospel music is about touching people
with a song.

Before I leave, Roy hands me a book on the history of the Chuck Wagon Gang. On the front inside cover, he pauses to write the following words: "To My Friend Jim, I hope this book will help you to know us a little better. Your friend, Roy and 'the Gang.'" Indeed it has, Roy, but not as much as that three-hour lunch. . . .

5
EARLY QUARTETS:
ON THE ROAD
THE FIRST TIME

The first generation of professional gospel music singers drew their strength from singing conventions and rural churches. They were the best at what they did, the most accomplished students from singing schools and publisher-organized normals. As they sang, they became something else—recognized celebrities of local radio, regional recordings, and rural concerts. In that transition from songbook salesman to professional quartet singer, the gospel music performer shifted from being an important part of the shape-note publishing world to becoming part of an industry in and of itself.

In the wake of James Vaughan's decision to underwrite the travels of his brother's quartet during the summer of 1910, other publishing firms began to provide expenses and salaries for talented singers who were willing to make the rounds of annual singing conventions and promote the latest company material. By 1918, the A. J. Showalter Company, the most successful shape-note publisher in the South at the turn of the century, had copied the formula at least in a limited fashion. Four of Showalter's associates, T. B. Mosley, J. D. Patton, H. M. Eagle, and B. B. Beall, formed The Big Quartet and traveled promoting their own *Big Quartet Book* along with Showalter's latest releases. All four men were well-known shape-note teachers who had worked at Showalter's Southern Normal Institute, and it is likely that their brief association as a quartet reflected their personal ambitions as music teachers as well as their affiliation with Showalter's company.[1]

The fact remained that quartet music, and especially the very talented voices producing it, attracted the crowds at singing conventions. In addition to the other crowd attraction, the new songs themselves, quartets offered the shape-note companies the best advertisement for their product. Furthermore, they introduced potential students of company-sponsored normals to some of the most talented singers the business had to offer and, in doing so, helped establish gospel music as an entity apart from other forms of music developing in the early years of the twentieth century. The distinction was important, since, from the beginning of musical recordings and radio, sacred songs proved commercially viable in the secular marketplace. Adding to popular recordings by well-known northern soloists like Homer Rodeheaver, southern religious singers found success via the new technology as well. For example, in August 1922, Andrew Jenkins and the Jenkins Family began a popular program on Atlanta's WSB radio. Jenkins, a partially blind evangelist and newsstand operator, had been loosely associated with the gospel music industry as a songwriter for the Morris-Henson Publishing Company of Atlanta. His marriage in 1919 to an Atlanta widow with three musically inclined children prompted him to combine his own love of music with theirs. The result was a religious variety program that featured not only gospel singing but also instrumental numbers and Jenkins's preaching.[2]

The city of Atlanta also witnessed some of the earliest gospel recordings. Frank Smith, a barber from nearby Braselton, Georgia, literally stumbled onto success after forming a local quartet to sing at area singing conventions and churches. Like many amateur groups, Smith's quartet appeared on WSB in early 1926 as part of Sunday afternoon gospel programming. The quartet captured the attention of a talent scout for Columbia Records and was subsequently invited, in April 1926, to record in a temporary studio in the Kimball House Hotel in downtown Atlanta. The success of the recordings was immediate and prompted other major recording labels like Okeh and Brunswick to promote similar products.[3] Under the name Smith's Sacred Singers, the group recorded sixty-six songs for Columbia Records from 1926 to 1930, in the words of one authority, "more than any other single gospel group in that time recorded for any company."[4] Despite his success, Smith showed little inclination to market his group beyond the occasional recording sessions and refused offers by publishing companies to take his group on the road and promote songbooks. Significantly, Smith preferred older gospel songs, recordings of which in the short run proved successful in terms of record sales but which limited Smith's value to the growing gospel music market.[5]

From the beginning, gospel music publishing companies kept their focus on new material with only some allowances for old convention standards and crowd favorites. From their perspective, the success of the new songs was crucial. As country and other forms of popular music made their presence known during the 1920s, religious songs, too, played a part in the repertoires of well-known singers. But, as with Smith's Sacred Singers, those religious hymns and gospel songs were invariably older songs already established as favorites within the fabric of Protestant worship in America. Singing a well-known gospel favorite could help even a secular singer establish rapport with an audience and reinforced the tremendous impact that evangelical Protestantism had on American culture throughout the nineteenth century. But, within the world of shape-note publishing, new material had to be introduced and accepted in order for songbooks to continue to find their way into homes and churches.

As a rule of thumb, the inexpensive convention books introduced the new material, and some of it, after having been tested and tried by time, would find its way into hardback hymnals. A few songs might become revered enough to be performed by popular secular singers. Nevertheless, the decision to accept them into a repertoire did not make one a gospel singer. Rather, it reflected the success of the song itself. Indeed, if a popular secular artist chose to record and sing a gospel number, it meant that that song had attained a status approaching cultural nostalgia. That gospel songs became so popular was not surprising given the important role of evangelical religion in the life of the population. Still, as a defining element of the gospel music industry, the distinction between new and old material remained crucial. More than anything else, it helped establish gospel music as an entity apart from both secular music and the religious music of the Protestant church service.[6]

Within the world of southern shape notes, not everyone accepted the arrival of quartets as a good thing. From the beginning of the shape-note system in the early nineteenth century, singing had been a community event with publishers, through their songbooks and music journals, eventually jumping on the bandwagon to promote better singing by more people. One objective had always been the improvement of Sunday singing in church services, since participants in the annual county or state singing conventions were expected to bring back both knowledge and new materials for the local church choir and congregation. Though quartets did not initially prevent this give and take, their presence and popularity by the mid-1920s did begin to obscure what had always been the primary mission of the singing societies. Now, suddenly, the emphasis of the conventions seemed to focus on just a handful of individuals who held the bulk of vocal talent.[7] In 1925, one convention attendee complained that "quartettes seem to be the rage" and, though "they do good singing, . . . they seem to want to do most all of it." He continued, arguing that "the singings we have now are nothing more than a contest between these 'Special singers,' local or imported. Even where they use the same book the same fight is on to see who can make the biggest hit. Class and church singing has gone down to where it is a thing of the past. The 'special' singers are always too busy, going about making dates to show off or giving concerts, to attend church and help do the singing there. Now what I want is some way to get the people singing so we can have singing when we are in need of it, and the kind we need."[8]

Another concern was that quartets added an unseemly degree of humor and silliness to conventions. Accustomed to entertaining rural audiences with concerts that included secular numbers as well as to making their annual pitches at singing conventions, quartet members were beginning to display an air of showmanship that some churchmen considered inconsistent with the bounds of gospel singing. The result was "religious or sacred songs sung in the same light, indifferent, meaningless spirit."[9] The conflict was the beginning of an uncomfortable relationship between professional quartets and the singing conventions up through the Second World War.

VAUGHAN QUARTETS

The first Vaughan Quartet, composed of Joseph Allen, George Sebren, Ira Foust, and Charles Vaughan, hit the road in May 1910 as much for the adventure and enjoyment of travel as with a concern for expanding the business of the James D. Vaughan Music Publishing Company. All four of those young men envisioned a future in music as singing-school teachers or songbook publishers; the entertainment value of a specific quartet of voices simply did not register with them. For them and many others like them, their choice of livelihood was a matter of available options. Life as a singing-school teacher or a music publisher simply promised more than life on the farm or a job at the mill. Quite a few early singers

Professional Quartets

came from humble roots, where most anything seemed better than the constant battle of survival as a southern sharecropper or mill worker.[10]

Life on the road attracted young men for a variety of reasons, not the least of which was the camaraderie of their fellow singers. Almost two decades after he began his singing career, Joe Allen recalled a road trip during which he and three other country boys suddenly found themselves in urban environs: "We stopped in a very fine restaurant in a city for our breakfast, all being presented with the bill of fare to select from, all reading everything we could understand, waiting for some one to call out what he wanted so the others could call for the same thing. Finally Charlie called for ham and eggs (which a person usually does after he finds he don't know what the other stuff is). The waiter called back to the cook and says 'Countryman in town and his three brothers with him,' which meant to the cook to prepare four orders ham and eggs."[11]

When the young singers were not approaching with a sense of humor their first contact with the outside world, they were taking occasion to play modest tricks on each other. Allen remembered that such was the case on the very first trip the Vaughan Quartet made out of the state of Tennessee:

> We were billed to sing in a little north Georgia town. Foust, a very timid bashful fellow and then his first time ever out of the state, at that time wore a brown derby hat that fit very closely to his head (might have been the same brown derby that played some part in the last presidential election). As we passed a bunch of boys on our way to the school building just outside the little town, Foust heard one of 'em say "I wish we had some eggs tonight." That didn't sound good to Foust. So, after the concert was over he and I were walking back to the hotel—he being much lower in stature than I, and walking in a low place I just reached down and thumped that brown derby; he hollered "eggs," and said "Come on Allen—"When I got to the hotel he was there; he said "Allen, only one hit me on the head and my derby is so much the same color I don't think it will ever show."[12]

As Charlie Vaughan and his trio of friends ventured out in the summer of 1910, they quickly sparked success for the young Vaughan company. Songbook sales improved, and reports from the singing conventions seemed to reinforce the notion that the group's presence gave the company an advantage over its competition. With sales nearing 90,000 books by the end of the 1912 season, James Vaughan clearly understood that his new advertising gimmick promised to become a staple of the industry. Nevertheless, "quarteting" remained a seasonal phenomenon, with travel to singing conventions occupying members' time during the mild southern months from spring into early fall. During the winter, quartet members generally taught in the Vaughan school and brushed up on their own musical skills. Since quartets traveled to conventions as company representatives, there was little need for individuals to establish an identity apart from the Vaughan name, and changing personnel became a routine procedure during the early years.[13]

In the fall of 1912, James Vaughan reorganized his original quartet, adding several of his employees and essentially forming two new groups. Foust and Allen came off the road, and Charles Vaughan sang bass surrounded by three new quartet men: P. B. Burress, L. H. Harber, and Fred Austin.[14] Meanwhile, George Sebren's lead vocal was complemented by the voices of Horace M. Ferrell, Oliver Todd, and John Todd. One of the reasons for the shift was a desire to show off a new technique practiced in the annual Vaughan Music School. Austin and Ferrell both took the new "first tenor" part, singing the female alto line in traditionally written hymns. The high-pitched voices established what would become for male gospel quartets an enduring trademark—a flashy high harmony part balanced by the gruff low bass.[15]

Over the next few years, different combinations of Vaughan quartets traveled to singing conventions and churches across the South. Charles Vaughan was the only constant, managing quartets into the early 1920s, when he took over the responsibility of editing *Vaughan's Family Visitor*.[16] In time, James Vaughan's son, Kieffer, and his son-in-law, William B. Walbert, served similar roles as managers of long-term Vaughan quartets. Depending on the distance from Lawrenceburg, the earliest groups traveled by horse-drawn carriage or, more often, by train. By 1916, a few of the groups were traveling in automobiles, which frequently had large placards attached announcing their arrival and advertising their schedule.[17] As company representatives, they carried along large supplies of the latest convention book and sample copies of the *Musical Visitor*. In addition, they advertised upcoming sessions of the Vaughan Normal and urged audiences to support a local shape-note singing school using one of their own as a teacher. Wherever they went, they promoted the Vaughan name and popularized the quartet style of gospel singing.[18]

One of the more unique groups to emerge in the first decade of professional quartet singing was the Vaughan Saxophone Quartet. Composed initially of Joe Allen, Adger Pace, Ira Foust, and William Walbert, the group first traveled and performed instrumental numbers in 1917. All were accomplished singers as well as musicians, making the brass instrumentals an addition to what singing convention audiences expected from a Vaughan quartet. Reporting on the group's progress from the field in the spring of 1917, Allen jokingly noted that the members were thrilled with their new accompaniment and that "sometimes some people really seem to enjoy our playing."[19]

Though quartet travel slowed down somewhat during the First World War, members of the Vaughan association were back on the road in full force by the early 1920s.[20] With the establishment of radio station WOAN in late 1922, the great variety of Vaughan musical talent could reach a wider audience and then could be taken, via the quartets, into local communities. Since the establishment of the Vaughan Normal in 1911, an incredibly diverse assortment of gospel music styles had been encouraged by the company. Now, radio offered the means to share that diversity with the world. In addition to four-part harmony quartets, nightly concerts from Lawrenceburg featured brass ensembles, piano solos, live orchestras, and an occasional novelty act such as someone "playing the handsaw." Performances always depended on who happened to be present at the Lawrenceburg headquarters, with guests and students encouraged to perform on a regular basis.[21]

Radio also created the identity of one of the more enduring of Vaughan's many quartets in the 1920s. In 1923, William B. Walbert, Hilman Barnard, Otis McCoy, and Adger M. Pace formed a quartet that was eventually dubbed the Vaughan Radio Quartet.[22] Barnard sang tenor and McCoy took the lead while Walbert sang baritone and Pace sang the bass part. Focusing initially on evangelistic work, the quartet stayed especially busy and traveled extensively across the entire nation. When the depths of the Depression forced many groups off the road, the Vaughan Radio Quartet continued as "the only quartet traveling solid time for James D. Vaughan."[23] The group's popularity was such that they remained together with only a few changes in personnel until the early 1930s,[24] after which Walbert continued the quartet for a few more years with a cast that included his talented son James on the piano, Pace, and two brothers, Cecil and Ottis Knippers.[25] By the late 1930s, Walbert was on the road again with a group known as the Vaughan Office Quartet.[26]

Another group, led by Glenn Kieffer Vaughan, was known locally as the Vaughan Recording Quartet because of its popularity on early Vaughan releases dating to 1921.[27] A proficient vocalist, the young Vaughan sang lead surrounded by an equally talented cast that included Hilman Barnard singing tenor, Walter B. Seale, baritone, and Roy L. Collins, bass.[28] By 1927, Claude Sharp had replaced Barnard on tenor and F. Pierce Heatwole had succeeded Collins on the bass part. This group, with Kieffer Vaughan as manager, then became a regular touring quartet.[29] In addition, Pierce Heatwole's brother, Luther, began traveling with the group as a full-time piano accompanist.[30] The Vaughan Recording Quartet traveled extensively in the late 1920s, even making an appearance at the famed Angelus Temple of Sister Aimee Semple McPherson in Los Angeles, California. In addition to recordings on the Vaughan custom label, the group made an appearance on WSM's Grand Ole Opry in Nashville in 1927 and recorded several songs in 1928 for the Victor Company.[31] The group disbanded at the beginning of 1930, though Kieffer Vaughan organized yet another quartet in the mid-1930s. For several years, this new quartet appeared daily on WSM, with Vaughan singing lead, Palmer Wheeler singing tenor, John Cook carrying the baritone part, and James ("Big Jim") Waits growling out the bass notes. Vaughan's nephew, James D. Walbert, and veteran quartet man Dwight Brock alternately held the position as group pianist.[32] By 1937, this group had resurrected the old name Vaughan Radio Quartet, which W. B. Walbert had abandoned a few years earlier.[33]

An unusual but extremely popular Vaughan arrangement was the duet of Arthur B. Sebren and Cullie G. Wilson. Featuring Wilson's remarkable lead vocals, the twosome dubbed itself "the Vaughan Happy Two" and, beginning in 1925, traveled across the country presenting a program "of sacred and secular songs, monologues, impersonations, handsaws played with violin bow and three tunes played at one time by one person on piano."[34] For six years, the pair appeared in the monthly reports published in *Vaughan's Family Visitor*, almost invariably topping the list with the number of new subscriptions and songbooks they sold. They drew a loyal following from among the convention crowds in the late 1920s. One enthusiastic listener wrote in to the Vaughan paper noting that "the Vaughan 'Happy Two' has it on any thing musically in the south today and if that 'Funny Two' or 'Lonesome Two' or Stamps' quar-

Professional Quartets

tet or any other twos or fours want to but [*sic*] up against them they will lick them more ways than a country man could pick a banjo."[35] In addition, the Happy Two made recordings on both the Vaughan and Victor labels and created somewhat of a sensation with the Sebren composition "Rocking on the Waves."[36]

During the 1920s, an increasing number of quartets came to align themselves with Vaughan's enterprise. Some came simply as associates interested in gaining credibility by using the company name, but as many as fifteen separate groups at one time were employed to travel on salary as Vaughan representatives.[37] Prominent groups affiliated with Vaughan by the mid-1930s included the Vaughan Office Quartet, the Speer Family, the Vaughan-Daniel Quartet, the Oliver Jennings Family, Vaughan's Sand Mountain Quartet (with Erman Slater), the Vaughan Melody Girls, the Vaughan Victory Four (with Fred C. Maples and Aycel Soward), and the LeFevre Trio.[38]

Vaughan groups clearly understood that they represented the company first and gave little attention to their own viability as quartets. Few as late as the 1930s envisioned that a gospel quartet might successfully travel apart from the umbrella of a music publishing company. There was also security in what a particular company came to represent, and some singers had become convinced by the late 1920s that a reputable music company served to keep gospel music within the bounds of good taste. With the arrival of jazz and other innovative music forms, quartets occasionally offended the propriety of some church folks when they included secular music in their repertoire. Vaughan quartets had been mixing an occasional secular number into their performances for years, and Charles Vaughan later recalled that his early quartets had "learned to let [audiences] help pay some of the quartet's expenses by giving them a chance to contribute" to "a concert program of clean, secular songs." Now, however, he lamented that "others have gotten so far away from it, and real gospel singing" that "we wonder if it was the best thing."[39] During the same period, a member of a Texas-based Vaughan quartet led by M. D. McWhorter explained that gospel concerts by company quartets were something audiences could depend on when it came to questions of content and presentation: "Good, clean concerts are the ones that count. Our singings have been pulled down some on account of some low grade concerting over our country with some low grade jokes. We quatets [*sic*] are doing our best to bring these concerts to the people in the Vaughan way."[40]

As the Dallas-based Stamps-Baxter company gained prominence in the shape-note publishing world in the early 1930s, so did the quartets associated with the firm. Both V. O. and Frank Stamps had experience with Vaughan groups in the years immediately following World War I. When the brothers set out on their own in 1924, Frank Stamps took his name, his reputation as a bass singer, and several singers from former Vaughan groups to form the first traveling quartet to represent the new company and its songbooks. The group was comprised of Stamps, J. E. Hamilton, Lee Myers, and Johnny E. Wheeler.[41] Personnel changed frequently over the next few years as both Virgil and Frank Stamps traveled to singing conventions to push the new company and its first convention book, *Harbor Bells*. During the mid-1920s, V. O. worked the home office in Jacksonville, Texas, in addition to traveling sporadically with a quartet that included Jeff Duncan and identical twins Bill and Zeke Kitts.[42] He even experimented with a handful of custom label recordings with his quartet during this period in Waco, Texas. Significant as these early efforts were, neither of the Stamps quartets achieved much recognition, and, despite early encouragement from the success of *Harbor Bells*, Stamps's investors were anxious to pull out of the deal by 1926. However, conditions improved when Stamps's old friend and competitor J. R. Baxter Jr. bought into the company as the only other shareholder. The former Showalter employee opened up a company office in Chattanooga, Tennessee, and immediately brought needed contacts and a good head for business.[43]

Shortly after the Baxter merger in March 1926, Frank Stamps moved east to join his brother's new partner and began operating his quartet out of the Chattanooga branch office. Not long after his arrival, his quartet, composed of himself, Lee Myers, Odis Echols, and Austin Williams, recorded a few custom releases for the Dixie Phonograph Company.[44] These recordings had no discernible impact, but fortunes turned soon as a result of a Frank Stamps combination that would become one of the most famous of the Stamps-Baxter-related quartets. Johnny E. Wheeler, a veteran of Frank Stamps's earlier quartet, had introduced his brothers, Palmer and Roy, to the business when they toured together briefly as the Wheeler Brothers Trio. Operating out of Durant, Oklahoma, the trio caught Frank Stamps's attention around 1926 when they performed a program of popular music in a series of concerts in Kentucky that were sponsored by local Lions Clubs. Soon, all three of the Wheeler brothers were singing with the quartet: Johnny on lead, Palmer on tenor, and Roy on baritone.[45] Odis Echols had replaced Johnny Wheeler by 1927 and assumed the baritone part, with Roy Wheeler switching to the lead. One other important change in 1927 brought the addition of a "fifth man," the pianist Dwight Brock. Most traveling quartets had consisted of only the four singers; one member played piano and sang, or, just as often, the quartet simply sang without accompaniment. Echols recalled years later that he had heard Brock playing piano at a drugstore in Haleyville, Alabama, and was so impressed that he convinced Frank Stamps to hire him as a permanent—and additional—member of the group.[46] Brock quickly revolutionized the piano accompaniment with his trademark improvisation between verses of a song, a short piano solo that became known as a "turnaround." The turnaround became second nature to gospel piano players of the next generation. Brock's rhythmic style placed the instrumentation of gospel music in the forefront and did much to encourage other groups to improve their own accompaniment.[47]

By the late 1920s, black gospel quartets were beginning to score success with 78 rpm recordings in northern markets. This increased interest in gospel music and the growing popularity of quartet groups on radio probably was responsible for the introduction of major labels into the southern market. In the fall of 1927, Okeh Records approached several members of Frank Stamps's Chattanooga-based group about the possibility of a recording session. Before he could make a decision on the offer, Frank Stamps received a letter from a representative of the Victor Company that noted, "I understand you've got a colored quartet that's making a hit in the South" and offered an audition for a recording session. Obviously excited, Frank Stamps replied, "They're not colored but I'll put 'em up against any quartet in competition."[48]

Ralph Peer of the Victor Company set up an audition, and, on October 20, 1927, the "all-star" combination of Frank Stamps, Odis Echols, Roy Wheeler, Palmer Wheeler, and Dwight Brock met at the Grady Hotel in Atlanta to record the first two of twenty-five records that Frank Stamps's quartets would record for Victor over the next five years.[49] Their initial recording, at the request of Peer, included two gospel music standards, "Bringing in the Sheaves" and "Rescue the Perishing." After these selections, Frank Stamps suggested that the group record a number that had become popular with their audiences. Their rendition of "Give the World a Smile," a song written just two years earlier by Otis Deaton and M. L. Yandell, became one of the first major gospel hits. Before long, all the major Stamps-affiliated groups were using the song in their programs and it became famous as a lead-in to all Stamps-Baxter quartet radio programs.[50] By the mid-1930s, Frank Stamps had dubbed his quartet the Frank Stamps All-Star Quartet as a way of distinguishing it from the many Stamps and Stamps-Baxter groups covering the landscape, including the one that Virgil Stamps promoted in regular broadcasts on Dallas's KRLD and on recordings for Columbia.[51]

Groups associated with the Stamps-Baxter company dominated quartet gospel music in the white communities of the South by the end of the 1930s. Most of them secured daily programming on radio stations to advertise their concerts and promote company products. As the quartets, who ordinarily sang out of the most recent Stamps-Baxter convention book, gained notoriety, so did the company name and musical product. Virgil Stamps's Old Original Quartet, with Stamps singing bass, Walter Rippetoe singing tenor, Robert E. Bacon singing lead, J. E. Gaither singing baritone, and Marion Snider playing piano, was extremely popular on Dallas's KRLD in a program that originated in 1936.[52] The Frank Stamps All-Stars, comprised of Stamps, Roy Wheeler, Lawrence Ivey, Wilkin "Big Chief" Bacon, and Eiland Davis, were regulars on WHO in Des Moines, Iowa. Other groups associated with Stamps-Baxter could be heard on stations across the country: for example, W. T. "Deacon" Utley's Smile-A-While Quartet was headquartered at WMAZ in Macon, Georgia; the Daniel Stamps-Baxter Quartet appeared daily on WSM in Nashville; the Deep South Quartet appeared on WAPL in Birmingham; the Blackwood Brothers Quartet was with KWKH in Shreveport, Louisiana; and Herschel Foshee and the Stamps-Baxter Melody Boys appeared on KARK in Little Rock.[53]

By the time of Virgil Stamps's death in 1940, the Stamps-Baxter company was sponsoring more than forty quartets across the country. The company provided a handful of groups, like the Frank Stamps All-Stars and the Blackwood Brothers Quartet, with salaries, travel expenses, and a vehicle. More common was an indirect sponsorship, whereby groups were approved to use the company name in exchange for singing and handling Stamps-Baxter material exclusively. These groups profited from the name and drew income from a percentage of their sales.[54] Most of the quartets with radio programs were male, but a sizable number of family groups included one or more female members. In addition, as with the Vaughan company, quite a few all-female groups represented Stamps-Baxter at regional singing conventions. By the late 1930s, female groups associated with the company included the Beulah Girls Quartet of Georgia; the Bashful Trio from Jonesboro, Arkansas; the Thompson Sisters Trio of Monroe, Georgia; the Mayes Sisters Quartet of Attoyac, Texas; and the Pennington Quartet of Geary, Oklahoma.[55]

Although groups handled their own appearance schedules and juggled those concerts around the demands of their individual radio commitments, they were intensely loyal to the Stamps-Baxter family of quartets. Most of them arranged to be present at V. O. Stamps's big all-night concerts in Dallas, which originated in 1938 after a fan remarked, "Mr. Stamps, I could listen to you sing all night."[56] The connection between the company and the quartet, however, remained a loose one based on mutual friendship as well as the company's value as a promoter of quartets. After V. O. Stamps's death, many of the more prominent groups left Stamps-Baxter when Frank Stamps formed his own competing company in 1945. This new Stamps Quartet Music Company created confusion within the shape-note publishing world because it duplicated the Stamps name. Many fans of southern gospel simply never grasped the distinction between the Stamps Quartet and the Stamps-Baxter companies. The confusion was compounded by the fact that Frank Stamps's new company was headquartered in a facility literally around the corner in the Oak Cliff subdivision of Dallas. Frank immediately duplicated the services of Stamps-Baxter, publishing several new songbooks each year, contracting with traveling quartets, sponsoring an annual music school, and producing a monthly journal, the *Stamps Quartet News.* Among the groups lured from the Stamps-Baxter organization, now run by J. R. and Clarice Baxter and V. O.'s widow, Trueman, were the Old Original Quartet on Dallas's KRLD (with Frank Stamps singing bass), Frank's old Stamps All-Stars, the Blackwood Brothers, the Deep South Quartet, and Harley Lester's Stamps Quartet. Frank Stamps also ambitiously recruited new talent, adding groups like the Blue Ridge Quartet from WBBB in Burlington, North Carolina; the Dixie Four from WIBC in Indianapolis; and the Weatherford Quartet from KGER in Long Beach, California.[57]

HARTFORD AND OTHER COMPANY QUARTETS

By the late 1920s, the Hartford Music Company of Hartford, Arkansas, also began to profit from traveling quartets. Songwriter Albert Brumley traveled extensively in 1929 as a bass singer in a group that included Marvin Dalton on first tenor, W. A. McNinch on baritone, and Burgess

Bell singing lead and playing piano. Members of the group earned $50 a month—not bad for young men on the eve of a national depression.[58] Like other publishing companies, Hartford used music students to make the rounds of annual singing conventions to sell its products. Ordinarily, those groups changed personnel annually. One version of the Hartford Quartet jump-started a long successful gospel career for W. T. "Deacon" Utley. By the late 1930s, Utley was appearing daily on radio in Macon, Georgia, as head of the Smile-A-While Quartet.[59]

Other, smaller companies formed quartets to tap into the songbook business, though few were able to compete beyond a local market. Robert S. Arnold, a singing-school teacher in the early 1920s, sang with a variety of such quartets at singing conventions and local churches. After a stint with the Carr Quartet, named after Arnold's teacher J. H. Carr, the young singer joined the Central Quartet, which represented Will Ramsey's shape-note company in Little Rock, Arkansas. By 1927, he had returned to work on his Texas farm but had joined with several friends to form one of the most unusual gospel groups of the era. Arnold combined his tenor voice with lead singer Bill Bynum, baritone Cecil MacDonald, and a bass singer named Bernie Horner in a compilation known as the Over-all Quartet. Dressed in white shirts, black bow ties, and neatly pressed blue overalls, compliments of a sponsor, the J. C. Penny Company, the four young men performed off and on in Texas and Arkansas for the next seven years. Their unusual appearance demonstrated the possibility of marketing shape-note quartet music using homespun rural imagery. It also symbolized the way in which a blending of secular and sacred themes permeated the everyday lives of most southerners.[60]

FAMILY QUARTETS: THE SPEERS AND LEFEVRES

Along with talented singing-school instructors, a handful of family groups moved onto the gospel music scene during the prosperous years of the early 1920s. Already popular in local churches, at singing conventions and sometimes in convention-sponsored talent contests, these groups offered additional exposure for music publishers. In addition, an attachment to a well-known name like Vaughan or Stamps lent credibility to the group itself. Although a few groups represented a publishing company on salary, most simply entered into an arrangement whereby, in exchange for use of the company name, they agreed to sell songbooks and earn a commission for those sales. Furthermore, they agreed not to promote a competing company while under contract. If they were particularly successful, a company might also hire them to appear at the annual normal schools as instructors and pay a percentage of their expenses to allow for more extensive travel. Family groups brought a new dimension to the gospel music business. In addition to offering the unique sound of close family harmony, the groups tended to be more stable than the typical music publishing groups, which reorganized each year with new members in an effort to keep the annual singing convention audience interested. Family groups also had a natural appeal, particularly if they included children, whom audiences could follow over the years and adopt as almost a part of their own families.

Such was the case with the Speer family, a group that aligned with the Vaughan company in the late 1920s. George Thomas "Dad" Speer and his wife, Lena, formed a singing partnership with his sister and brother-in-law, Pearl and Logan Claborn, in order to promote Tom Speer's singing schools near his farm in Double Springs, Alabama. Tom Speer sang bass, and Lena sang the soprano lead. Pearl Claborn carried the alto part and Logan, tenor. The Speer Quartet traveled to area singing conventions and became one of the more popular of the many family groups that frequented the annual events in exchange for usually no more than a freewill offering.[61]

Eventually, Speer came to believe "that his music was supporting his farm." On one memorable day in the summer of 1923, while plowing a field behind his two mules, Kate and Beck, the young singing-school teacher reached an epiphany of sorts. When he struck a root and broke a part of his plow, he sat down under a tree and contemplated his dilemma. Dreading the four-mile walk to the nearest store and doubting that the plow part in question would even be in stock, he decided then and there to change professions. Looking heavenward, he promised God, "If you'll help me sell this farm and if you'll help me make a living for my family in the gospel music business, I'll never walk behind a plow again."[62] It was a promise that the talented singer would find easy to keep. Within a year, he sold the farm and purchased a house in town, from which both he and the Speer Quartet entered the music business full time.[63]

Freed from the confines of the farm, Tom Speer expanded his musical circles as much as possible, taking the group to more singing conventions and arranging concerts with an admittance fee. In the concert appearances, the group performed secular tunes as well as the gospel songs they had perfected at singing conventions. Sometimes, the quartet would be joined by Lena Speer's father, C. A. Brock, head of the Athens

Music Company in Athens, Alabama. Brock would take the bass part and Tom Speer would switch to lead, while Lena accompanied the group on piano.[64]

Since they were only moderately successful, both the Speers and the Claborns found it difficult to make a living even with their expansion into rural concerts. As a result, late in 1925, Logan Claborn returned to his job as a carpenter, and he and Pearl joined the Speers only occasionally at local singing conventions. Tom and Lena Speer pressed on, continuing the singing schools and enlisting their young children to fill the vacant parts of the quartet. Their oldest, Brock (named after his maternal grandfather), born in December 1920, was not quite five when he began to sing with his parents. Rosa Nell, born in September 1922, was only three. Although their parents sang most of the programs as a duet, Brock joined in on the alto part and little Rosa Nell would take the lead on several special numbers that Tom Speer drilled into the children's heads in regular practice sessions. Both remembered their father as a strict taskmaster when it came to music and admitted that they literally "learned to sing with Daddy's razor strap across his lap." By 1930, the Speers were a regular four-part harmony group again with the two oldest kids traveling with their parents, except when school attendance made it impossible.[65]

In early 1930, the family moved north to Lawrenceburg, Tennessee. Lena Speer had relatives in Lawrenceburg, and, with the Depression promising tough financial times, Tom and Lena sought to affiliate themselves with the powerful Vaughan publishing company. Soon the Speers were receiving notice and endorsements in *Vaughan's Family Visitor*, and they undoubtedly used Vaughan songbooks and sold them on commission. As a result, they forged an alliance with Vaughan that would grow stronger over the next ten years. In addition, the family, which had increased by two with the birth of Mary Tom in June 1925 and Ben in June 1930, traveled to singing conventions and concerts whenever they could.[66]

The Speers' big break came in 1934 when James Vaughan offered Tom Speer a full-time position with the company as a music instructor and songbook representative. Late in that year, Vaughan's paper even featured a prominent photo of the entire family, noting that "the Speer family is a real singing aggregation, the father and mother both coming from singing families, and their children have been well trained."[67] Over the next seven years, the Speers faithfully represented Vaughan, work-

Professional Quartets

ing in the summer and winter normals as well as traveling and singing to promote Vaughan music materials. In addition, Tom Speer continued his songwriting and sold several of his songs as sheet music printed on the Vaughan presses. By the mid-1930s, *Vaughan's Family Visitor* was noting that the family "makes about as big a hit as anybody and they get calls from many places, so many that they cannot be filled."[68]

Recognizing the attraction of his talented family, Tom Speer taught each of his children to play an instrument. Brock mastered the guitar and Rosa Nell the piano, while, despite her objections, Mary Tom managed some proficiency on the mandolin. Five-year-old Ben instinctively took to the ukulele and, with Lena Speer taking up the accordion, the family formed a small band. All four of the children sang as well. Mary Tom usually took the lead part, while Rosa Nell sang alto, Ben, tenor, and Brock, bass. On some numbers, all six family members would sing because Tom Speer had worked out a program with a variety of harmony parts and instrumentation. The arrangement was a huge success, and, by 1938, the Speers and the Vaughan quartets led by Kieffer Vaughan and William Walbert were considered the three major groups representing the company.[69]

After James Vaughan's death in early 1941, the Speers ended their affiliation with the Lawrenceburg company and moved to Montgomery, Alabama, where they secured a job with radio WSFA performing live daily morning and afternoon programs. They continued their singing convention and concert schedule but now as representatives of the Stamps-Baxter company. Association with the station gave the Speers greater name recognition as well as free advertisement for their singing engagements, and, as World War II erupted, they seemed poised for the greatest success of their career. Within a few months of Pearl Harbor, Brock Speer joined the Air Force and served for the duration of the war. In the years before he left for the war, the elder son had assumed the permanent role as the group's bass singer, and his absence forced further creativity on "Dad" Speer's part. The result was seventeen-year-old Mary Tom taking over the bass part, singing it an octave higher than normally written. With this kind of adaptation, the Speers remained at the forefront of the developing gospel quartet industry.[70]

Another family that successfully cracked the profession during the 1920s was the LeFevres, a group that first emerged in 1921 as a trio of children singing country tunes. Originally from Smithville, Tennessee, Urias, Alphus, and Maude LeFevre made up the first version of more than five decades of LeFevre groups. Eleven-year-old Urias sang lead and picked the banjo, nine-year-old Alphus sang tenor and played the fiddle, and thirteen-year-old Maude took the alto part and strummed the guitar. Initially, the group sang only country but, after a religious experience, began singing gospel songs in mostly Pentecostal-style churches across the South. Both brothers played guitar, and Alphus excelled on banjo, violin, and almost every other stringed instrument. By 1927, their instrumental ability landed them some work on Nashville's WSM.[71]

In the mid-1920s, Maude married and left the group but Urias and Alphus persevered. Another sister, Peggy, filled in for a time, but she soon married and gave up performing as well. Much of their concert work had become affiliated with the Church of God, and both boys decided to attend the denomination's Bible Training School in Cleveland, Tennessee. While students there in 1930, they formed one of several groups that took the school's name and traveled to sing for evangelistic services. The earliest version of the Bible Training School Quartet included Urias on lead, Alphus on tenor, James McCoy singing baritone, and Johnny Yates singing bass.[72]

Out of school by late 1934, the quartet—now with B. C. Robinson singing the bass part—affiliated briefly with the Vaughan company, where Alphus LeFevre's instrumental ability soon landed him a job with the Vaughan winter normal.[73] About the same time, another change substantially altered the future of the group. In September 1934, Urias married Eva Mac Whittington, the seventeen-year-old daughter of Rev. H. L. Whittington, a Church of God pastor. The two had met more than eight years earlier when the LeFevre Trio had sung at her father's church in Chattanooga. Though only eight years old at the time, Eva Mae attracted Urias's musical interest as well as his heart. This young musical prodigy, who was able to play piano and organ by ear at the age of six, made quite an impression on the older LeFevre brother. Reportedly, Urias remarked to Alphus LeFevre, "I met my wife tonight."[74] Years later he would joke that "the main reason I married her was because she was such a good pianist!"[75]

By January 1935, the LeFevre boys had dropped their quartet and once again formed a trio, this time with Eva Mae singing alto and accompanying the group on piano. Because of Urias's lead guitar and Alphus's assortment of instruments, some gospel groups eventually referred to them as "the Salvation Army."[76] But the act immediately caught the attention of rural audiences in the mid-1930s, with one music publication

Professional Quartets

noting that the trio "in some ways have a way of getting hold of the public different from other members of the Vaughan fraternity."[77] After traveling briefly as representatives of Vaughan in 1935,[78] the LeFevre Trio concentrated its efforts on singing in widespread evangelistic meetings, despite the birth of several children to Urias and Eva Mae during the early years of their marriage. With the heavy demands of their schedule, the couple considered the road their home and used their parents' addresses as their only permanent residences. The Singing LeFevres found a niche performing in Holiness and Pentecostal churches, oftentimes appearing alongside Rev. Whittington, who now served as pastor of Atlanta's Hemphill Church of God but frequently held revivals for Church of God congregations across the nation.[79] Through Whittington's contacts, the LeFevres secured a regular Sunday morning radio program on Atlanta's WGST, and, before long, their talent and energy raised eyebrows. The NuGrape and Orange Crush Soft Drink Company, for example, eventually sponsored the group and paid for transcription discs to be played on several stations throughout the South. As a result, in some areas, the group began to be billed as the Suncrest Trio, though they remained known as the LeFevres in their home base of Atlanta. By the time America went to war late in 1941, the group was enjoying regular airplay on a daily radio program and was popular enough to stay busy in concerts within a day's driving distance of Atlanta.[80]

GROWING COMMERCIALIZATION
AND AN ECONOMIC DOWNTURN

Recordings and radio marked the future of the music business, and by the late 1920s, the achievements of groups like the Frank Stamps All-Star Quartet demonstrated that gospel music could succeed as a viable form of American entertainment. Gospel and country music seemed to be following a similar path of success. Both aspiring country and gospel artists tapped into the growing technology that was making musical entertainment affordable for most American families.[81] Yet, shape-note songbook publishers and rural churches offered quartets a market that was far more identifiable and stable. The negative side, one that gospel musicians would struggle to deal with for decades, was that this music was, like religion in general, tied to the volunteer fortunes of American Christianity, and many church members would resist overt entertainment by gospel singing groups as well as any attempt at "paid concerts." For too many years, linked as they were with singing conventions and religious services, gospel singers would have to be content with freewill offerings from church folk. A handful would find a more stable source of income in radio, an extension of the secular market that, more than anything else, drove the success of country music and other forms of entertainment.[82] A few others would work to include comedy in their act, hoping to draw a larger audience by expanding their entertainment focus.[83]

With the coming of the Great Depression by the early 1930s, gospel music lost the euphoric spirit of expansion that had dictated the 1920s. The market for convention books and quartet singing had been a rural market. Hard times affected everyone. By the end of 1932, an election year shaped by the economic downturn, quartets that had tasted success just a few years earlier were finding it tough to stay on the road.[84] Schedules were cut back, and only the most successful quartets, backed by both publishing company support and radio programs, were able to continue their travel. A few worried that the economic disaster had forever changed the fortunes of quartet music. Reflecting on the progression of quartets since he first went on the road back in 1910, Charles Vaughan noted that radio and a proliferation of local groups at singing conventions had effectively diluted the market for the professional quartet singer. In addition, the Depression had "made it so that no quartet can do much toward making a living no matter how good they are." The most extensive work lay in "evangelistic meetings," but, even there, "the depression has caused many churches who would like to have them for a meeting to have to refrain from doing so." As a result, he feared that the heyday of the gospel quartet had come to an end:

> A male quartet in the country is not looked upon as it was years ago. Then it was an unfailing attraction that people would pay money to hear sing, because it was rare. Now while people like to hear a good male quartet they can hear one over the radio for nothing and they do not go any great distance out of their way to hear one any where [sic]. . . .
>
> We do not want to be misunderstood in this article, and do not mean that quartets have played out, for there are some good local quartets in lots of sections of the country, which are doing a good work. What we meant was that traveling quartets can no longer make enough to pay salaries and expenses.[85]

Nevertheless, the shock of the Depression was probably diminished by a couple of factors. Rural areas had already endured economic hardship

as a result of a chaotic farm market during the early years of the twentieth century, so it is likely that the economic crash of 1929 was not nearly
the initial blow to the southern agricultural world that it was to business
interests elsewhere. Still, if times were hard off the farm, they would become harder still on the farm, and there was little comfort in this kind of
preparation for economic disaster. On the other hand, convention singing and convention songbooks offered relatively cheap entertainment, a
fact that ensured that the gospel music business would survive the rough
years of the early 1930s.[86] James Vaughan was able to continue publishing songbooks each year and managed to sneak a second release in for
1933. Beginning in 1935, he began a five-year run that produced three
books annually. Likewise, the Stamps-Baxter company enjoyed tremendous success during the thirties, building a name that would become
almost synonymous with shape-note publishing in the South. After producing an annual book since Baxter's arrival in 1926, the company managed at least two releases a year beginning in 1932 and four beginning
in 1939.[87] One new company even got its start during the dark days of
the Depression. Headed by former Vaughan employee Otis L. McCoy,
the Tennessee Music and Printing Company emerged in 1931 with the
advantageous backing of the Cleveland-based Church of God. Founded
and operated as a division of the denomination's Church of God Publishing House, the new company would not only survive the Depression
but would ultimately play a crucial role in perpetuating the tradition of
shape-note music.[88]

FROM THE CARTERS TO THE CHUCK WAGON GANG

One family group whose fortunes hinged almost entirely on the commercialization of gospel music rapidly taking place during the 1930s was
the Chuck Wagon Gang. Known originally as the Carter Quartet, the
group forged its style from late-night gospel singings in migrant camps
during the darkest days of the Depression.[89] David Parker Carter was
born in 1889 in Milltown, Kentucky, but his family soon relocated to
north central Texas. As a teenager, he attended a singing school in Clay
County, Texas, where he met Carrie Brooks, another recent émigré. The
two married in 1909 and, after a brief stint farming the Texas countryside, moved to Noel, Missouri, where Dave Carter secured a steady position working for a railroad line. The young couple remained a part of
the rural singing-school tradition, keeping abreast of the new material
from the shape-note companies and singing for their own enjoyment in

a quartet with Dave Carter's sister Nan and her husband, Lee Brooks (also Carrie Carter's brother). By 1926, Carter had transferred to Oklahoma, where he continued to work for the railroad and to do farm work on the side.[90]

A railroad accident near El Reno, Oklahoma, in 1927 began a series of misfortunes that landed the Carters in dire economic straits. Dave Carter was injured when he lost his balance after the engineer unexpectedly applied the emergency brake. His injuries forced him from his job, and a long legal battle to claim medical expenses proved unsuccessful. As a result, the Carters were ill prepared for the economic downturn that hit the nation over the next two years. Aggravating the situation was the fact that the couple now had eight children to feed. The oldest, Ernest, was born in 1910, a little over a year after the couple married. Another son, Clellon, came in 1913. Two daughters followed, Rosa Lola in 1915 and Effie in 1917. A third son, Eddie, arrived in 1919, followed by two more daughters, Anna in 1922 and Ruth Ellen in 1924. A final son, Roy, was born in 1926, the year before the accident.[91]

The late 1920s and early 1930s were trying times for Dave and Carrie Parker. They moved back to Texas and, like many others, survived on whatever work they could find for themselves and the children as well as government handouts and occasional secret hunting trips for illegal antelope and prairie chicken. A final daughter, Bettye, arrived to the couple early in 1930. By the mid-1930s, the family was barely scratching out an existence in a migrant circuit that led almost all of the Carters into the cotton fields of Texas during the fall and Dave Carter and his oldest sons into the wheat fields of Kansas during the spring. Despite the tough conditions, the family held on to a handful of prized instruments they had collected over the years. Along with nearby relatives, family members learned to play several stringed instruments, as well as the harmonica and an old pump organ. Late at night, both at their Texas home and in the migrant camps, they would sing songs, mostly gospel but also folk and western tunes, with the accompaniment of Ernest's guitar. Roy Carter recalled years later that family members "would see the glow of a cigarette under the nearby cottonwood trees and know that neighbors were gathered to hear the music."[92]

When his eighteen-year-old daughter Effie grew ill with pneumonia in 1935 and there was no money for medicine, a desperate Dave Carter took the advice of other migrant workers to try his fortunes with the radio. Leaving the rest of the family at a nearby migrant camp, he,

Ernest, and Rosa walked into the small, 250-watt radio station KFYO in Lubbock and auditioned for a job to sing on a daily fifteen-minute program. Miraculously, the Carters received the job and immediately improved their financial fortunes with a regular income of $12.50 per week.[93] Dave Carter secured a week's advance on the program and, after receiving medical help for Effie, included her as a member of the quartet. Rosa's strong soprano lead and Effie's clear alto voice merged with Ernest Carter's bass and Dave Carter's tenor on a variety of songs, including shape-note-style gospel hymns, western ballads, and traditional folk songs. Over the next year, the group, accompanied by Ernest Carter on guitar, proved remarkably popular with the local rural audience.[94]

Recognizing opportunity, Dave Carter drove the family to Fort Worth in 1936, and auditioned at a string of smaller radio stations in the area. Discouraged after a host of refusals, the group considered a return to Lubbock, where a raise to $15.00 per week and a couple of local sponsors had at least allowed the family to escape the harsh cotton fields. However, Dave Carter convinced his children to try one more audition, this time with Fort Worth's large 50,000-watt WBAP. The station manager immediately recognized the Carters' unique style and hired the group for a morning spot sponsored by Morton Salt. From the beginning of their association with WBAP, the Carters drew heavily on western imagery. They sang western tunes on a morning program called "The Roundup." In addition to Ernest's guitar, the group was now backed by Dave Carter on the mandolin. Oftentimes, they included in their daily repertoire a sacred number accompanied only by the guitar.

Shortly after the Carters' appearance on "The Roundup," a Fort Worth milling company, Bewley Flour Mills, decided to expand its own advertisement campaign with the station. A local singing group called the Chuck Wagon Gang performed the company-sponsored morning program and, like the Carters, employed the traditional western theme. In addition, the all-male group made afternoon trips to local towns and sang while a cook made biscuits from Bewley's Best Flour to pass out to the crowd. The company wanted this group to travel across the state and needed another group to continue the regular morning radio program as the resident "Chuck Wagon Gang." At a salary of $15 per week per member of the quartet, the Carters jumped at the opportunity to carry the daily Bewley Mills show and agreed to the name change. After a couple of seasons, the traveling group disbanded and the Carters remained the sole Chuck Wagon Gang.[95] For the next fifteen years, the quartet appeared daily on the Fort Worth radio program and became one of the most recognizable groups in gospel music, despite the fact that it made few personal appearances. Although the group's new name conjured up western imagery, their style remained rooted in the tradition of shape-note convention singing.[96]

It was also in Fort Worth that the personal identity of the group members changed forever. At the insistence of Cy Leland, the group's new agent, Ernest became "Jim" and Dave Carter became simply "Dad." Likewise, Rosa Lola took the shortened name "Rose" while Effie became known as "Anna."[97] No one could have predicted how enduring the name changes would become. WBAP's 50,000-watt signal was among the strongest in the South, and, given the intense competition among southern flour companies, Bewley Mills pushed the name and identities of their new singers through occasional guest appearances at the opening of new food stores in the Dallas–Fort Worth area. Over the next few years, other major affiliates that participated in the Texas Quality Radio Network provided the group with widespread coverage across the Southwest. The Carters as the Chuck Wagon Gang became one of the most popular groups on southern radio stations during the years before America's involvement in the Second World War. Unlike most other groups, they accomplished this feat without an association with one of the major music publishing companies.

As their popularity grew, the Carters also fine-tuned their repertoire. Although they began with only one gospel song per program, they quickly learned through fan mail that listeners preferred the gospel songs. They added more sacred material and, by 1940, eliminated all their western ballads and folk tunes to concentrate on a program of all gospel music.[98] Still feeling the effects of the Depression, rural listeners came to identify with the Chuck Wagon Gang's simple style and especially the "comforting songs . . . with their visions of a caring Saviour and a Heavenly reward."[99] Dave Carter remained convinced that the secret to his family's success was that fans embraced simple music and a sound that, with some practice, they could emulate.[100]

The group got even more exposure when a scout for Columbia Records heard them and contracted with Dad Carter for a series of 78 rpm recordings beginning in November 1936. The family's earliest sessions in San Antonio in late 1936 and in Dallas in the summer of 1937 included a considerable number of secular songs, but, by the April 1940 session in Saginaw, their repertoire had turned exclusively gospel. Recordings

Professional Quartets

relayed the group's simple style literally around the world. The arrangement with Columbia would be a successful financial pact for both partners that would last almost four decades.[101]

THE BLACKWOOD BROTHERS

At about the same time that Dad Carter forever altered his family's future by auditioning for a Lubbock radio program, another family group began to seek its own fortunes in the rural farm counties of northern Mississippi. William Emmett Blackwood, the son of a shape-note singing-school teacher, his wife, Carrie, and their three sons and a daughter began their singing career in church. Early on, the family attended a local Baptist congregation, but, by the mid-1920s, they were deeply immersed in the local Pentecostal community, joining the Cleveland-based Church of God and singing at local services. The church's influence was critical, James Blackwood later recalled: "It was into this Spirit-filled, miracle-working family that I was born."[102] The oldest son, Roy, began preaching in the early 1920s and studied for the ministry in the Church of God. Doyle, born in 1911 and a little more than a decade younger than Roy, was captivated early on by the family's love of music and became a fan of the smooth harmony of the country duo the Delmore Brothers and of the legendary Jimmie Rodgers. He learned to play guitar and mandolin and even practiced voice projection from the top of tree stumps near the family home in rural Choctaw County.[103]

In the early 1930s, Doyle and his younger brother James, born in 1919, attended a shape-note singing school conducted by Vardaman Ray, a well-known teacher who represented the Hartford Music Company, at the nearby Clear Springs Baptist Church. The cost for the ten-day course was $3 per student, and the boys later recalled fondly how their financially struggling parents had actually sold several chickens to provide the money for the tuition. Both boys made good on the investment. After the school ended, Ray invited the two young men to join him and another singer as part of a quartet singing in a few local concerts. Given Ray's credentials, the Blackwood boys jumped at the invitation. With Ray singing the lead; James, tenor; Doyle, baritone; and Gene Catledge from nearby Ackerman, bass; the quartet performed for most of a year as the Choctaw County Jubilee Singers. The experience was the earliest proving ground for two of the members of what would become the Blackwood Brothers Quartet.[104]

At the same time that Doyle and James ventured out locally with the Choctaw County Singers, Roy Blackwood sang in the Church of God congregations he pastored in various locations across the South. Almost always, he sang in a quartet that included his son R. W. In 1934, Roy moved his family back to Choctaw County and, with that move, the Blackwood Brothers Quartet was formed, with thirty-four-year-old Roy singing lead; fifteen-year-old James, baritone; and thirteen-year-old R. W., alto. Twenty-three-year-old Doyle sang bass and played guitar.[105] For a little more than a year, the Blackwoods sang locally for churches and at area singing conventions. They crisscrossed the rough, rural roads of Mississippi in Roy's 1929 Chevrolet, dreaming of somehow carving out a musical career that would take them off the farm. The dreams settled most firmly in the hearts of the two youngest Blackwoods, who, only two years apart in age, grew to be more like brothers than uncle and nephew. As the younger boys' voices matured, part assignments changed. James assumed the lead part, while R. W. sang baritone; Roy then switched to tenor, and Doyle continued to sing bass and accompany the group on guitar.[106]

The Blackwood Brothers Quartet disbanded late in 1935 when Roy returned to full-time ministry and accepted a pastorate in Texas. Nevertheless, over the next few years, the Blackwood boys continued to make good use of their singing talents. Roy and R. W. resumed singing in a local church group, and Doyle taught singing schools and sang briefly with the Homeland Harmony Quartet in Birmingham, Alabama. James, "afire with ambition to make my mark in the Gospel Singing field," remained on the farm but maintained his focus by performing "with every group I could find, trying to stay in the singing business."[107]

The Blackwoods reunited in 1937 when Roy and his family returned to Choctaw County and Doyle gave up his stint with the Homeland Harmony. The boys worked on the family farm and supplemented their income by taking jobs with a local timber company, all the while reformulating their plans for a singing career. When a small 250-watt radio station opened in Kosciusko, Mississippi, the boys drove the forty miles from the farm to audition for a live radio program. WHEF was just a one-man operation with no formal procedure for auditions, but the owner gave the boys fifteen minutes of live air time just to see how they sounded. Before their time expired, phone calls streamed in from listeners who wanted to request specific songs. Consequently, the fifteen-minute audition stretched into an hour-and-fifteen-minute pro-

Professional Quartets

gram, during which the station received fifty-nine calls. The overwhelming response led to an offer for a regular thirty-minute program of live music on Sunday mornings. The boys enthusiastically accepted, agreeing to sing for free provided they had the opportunity to advertise their local concert bookings.[108]

The success in Kosciusko soon gave the Blackwoods confidence to seek greener pastures. Early in 1938, they headed south for 5,000-watt WJDX in Jackson, Mississippi, but were initially unable to secure a daily program. Still, the new setting forced the boys to push their singing schedule. They attended singing conventions for freewill offerings and organized schoolhouse sings, where they charged ten cents for adults and a nickel for children. At a meeting of the Mississippi State Singing Convention, the Blackwoods made the acquaintance of Frank Stamps. Impressed with the boys' talent, the well-known bass singer called his brother V. O., who agreed to pay the group a commission for selling Stamps-Baxter songbooks. Even more good news arrived when Tommy Gentry, a local country artist with a morning show on WJDX, invited them to sing regularly on his program. Fan mail from Gentry's show convinced the station to offer the brothers their own daily spot, which ran from 9:15 to 9:30 A.M. The radio engagement, though again unpaid, continued to give the group valuable exposure as well as an opportunity to hone their skills.[109]

Singing initially both country and gospel tunes, the group soon returned to their gospel-only repertoire. James Blackwood later recalled that they convinced the station that they should sing only gospel by taking a straw vote among the listeners of the daily program. "The response was tremendous. The vote was overwhelming," he remembered. "We went to an all-Gospel program. We never sang 'pop' music again."[110]

By early 1939, the Blackwoods had secured a position with KWKH in Shreveport, Louisiana, singing on both a morning and a noon daily program. The Shreveport station was in the process of upgrading from 10,000 to 50,000 watts, and the increased exposure soon launched the Blackwoods into the thick of the southern gospel music scene. V. O. Stamps increased his commitment to the group, furnishing them an automobile and a sweeter deal as book representatives. In addition to a 1939 Mercury, the group now enjoyed a guaranteed salary of $18.50 per member each week. If songbook sales exceeded an agreed-upon minimum, members would receive even more. Stamps also influenced the group's style, convincing them to abandon Doyle Blackwood's guitar accompaniment and add Joe Roper, a Stamps-Baxter contact, as the group's first pianist.[111]

Ultimately, the Stamps-Baxter influence moved the group to a distant location. In an attempt to get his brother more involved in company work near the home office, V. O. suggested that the Blackwoods replace Frank Stamps's quartet as representatives in Iowa by taking a position with the 50,000-watt station KMA in Shenandoah. Frank Stamps's quartet would thus leave a spot on WHO, Des Moines, to assume the radio slot at KWKH in Shreveport. Though the move meant leaving their family behind in Mississippi, the Blackwoods agreed. They saw the move as an opportunity to spread their music in another region of the country and as a favor to V. O. Stamps, who had helped make much of their recent success possible. Years later, James Blackwood remarked that "V. O. was like a daddy to us and, of course, if he'd said to go to China, we'd have gone to China, I guess."[112]

In August 1940, the Blackwoods opened their daily program on KMA. Over the next couple of years, they carved a niche in the Iowa countryside, using the radio program to promote concerts within several hours' driving distance of Shenandoah and even securing occasional sponsors for their show. With Hilton Griswold now serving as group pianist, they became one of the most popular quartets linked to the Stamps-Baxter company. One promotional campaign that took place not long after the group arrived in the region produced 10,000 pieces of fan mail from over twenty-seven U.S. states and three Canadian provinces. An advertising agent associated with KMA reasoned that such a response meant that the group's daily airings, now expanded to three separate broadcasts, drew close to a million listeners. Consequently, the Stamps-Baxter company raised the group's guaranteed salary to $40 a week per member.[113]

Radio's potential to spread the popularity of gospel music was underscored during the Blackwoods' first winter in Shenandoah. Returning late one night from a performance in northeast Missouri, the group underestimated the strength of a driving snowstorm and ran out of gas. Doyle Blackwood, who routinely served as the group's radio emcee, walked to a nearby farmhouse and tried to rouse the sleeping family for help. Years later, the Blackwood brothers delighted in recounting what happened next: "Hellooo [sic] there!" the young announcer called several times. "We're motorists stuck on the highway . . . and we're out of gas! Would you please let me in to use your phone?" Momentarily, a light came on in an upstairs bedroom and a man stuck his head out to yell, "Just a minute, Doyle. I'll be right down." The husband and wife had recognized the familiar voice from the program that played daily on the radio in their home. Such was the power of radio in the era immediately preceding the Second World War.[114]

THE HOMELAND HARMONY AND JOHN DANIEL QUARTETS

A number of other groups that would play an important role in southern gospel also emerged during the Depression years of the 1930s. In Cleveland, Tennessee, one of the Bible Training School quartets sponsored by former Vaughan employee Otis McCoy eventually began performing as the Homeland Harmony Quartet. Though the group's role was minor until its reorganization after World War II, McCoy's contacts and influence at the Church of God school was significant for several singers who would play major roles during the next two decades. In addition to the LeFevre brothers, bass singer Aycel Soward, baritone Fred C. Maples, tenor Connor B. Hall, and songwriter Vep Ellis all fell under McCoy's tutelage.[115]

The John Daniel Quartet was another group coming into its own by the mid-1930s. Formed near Sand Mountain, Alabama, a hotbed of shape-note music since A. J. Showalter left his mark in the late nineteenth century, the quartet emerged first in the early 1920s along with the Speers and LeFevres. John Tyra Daniel, born in 1903 near Boaz, Alabama, and his younger brother, Troy Elbert, born in 1906, sprang from a musical family. They both did their first singing on the front porch with their parents, brothers, and sisters. As they grew up, the pair could never free themselves from the attraction of the music and, by their late teens, had formed the Daniel Family Quartet—an arrangement that included their sisters Mary and Ora as well as their brother Luther. By the mid-1930s, John and Troy Daniel were still in the quartet business, now as representatives of the A. J. Showalter Company. Combining his tenor voice with Troy's lead, John arranged for Carl Rains to sing bass and E. C. Littlejohn to sing baritone. Littlejohn's wife, Daisy Bell, played piano for the group. By 1937, the quartet had secured a better business deal with a rival company, agreeing to "push the Vaughan publications exclusively."[116]

Over the next few years, the Daniel Quartet traveled the singing convention circuit as well as arranged their own concert engagements. The group traveled to thirty-eight different states during the period and toured in Canada. By 1940, with a revamped quartet that included Wally Fowler singing baritone and "Big Jim" Waits singing bass, the quartet left Vaughan and spent the next two years representing the Stamps-Baxter company. The Stamps-Baxter connection placed the group—now billed exclusively as the John Daniel Quartet—in an enviable position: the company provided them a regular salary and covered their travel expenses. However, the agreement prohibited the Daniel brothers from competing for radio time with other groups that represented Stamps-Baxter. Consequently, they left Stamps-Baxter in 1942 and secured a position headlining a live morning program on WSM in Nashville. The arrangement with WSM also opened up dates for them on the Saturday night Grand Ole Opry, and the quartet soon became one of the best known acts in gospel music.[117]

THE CYCLING RANGERS AND THE SWANEE RIVER BOYS

Perhaps the most unique combination to grace the company of gospel music quartets in the days preceding America's entry into the Second World War was the Rangers. Originally known as the Texas Rangers Quartet because they got their start around the time of the Texas centennial celebration in 1936, the group moved quickly to make a name for itself. Comprised of guitarist and lead singer Vernon Hyles, his bass-singing brother Arnold, baritone Walter Leverett, and tenor George Hughes, the quartet displayed a tight harmony blend and considerable skills at self-promotion. Performing at the Texas Centennial Exposition held in Dallas, they captured the attention of Governor James Allred, who christened the four "honorary Texas Rangers and 'Ambassadors of Good Will' for the state of Texas."[118]

Even before the Texas centennial, the group had hatched a plan to build the name of the quartet by traveling to New York and appearing on the radio network program "The Major Bowes Amateur Hour." By advertising their plan at the centennial, the boys secured several major sponsors by agreeing to ride bicycles from Texas to New York and to perform in concerts en route. Montgomery Ward provided bicycles, and the Justin Boot Company furnished each of the men with a new pair of cowboy boots. Topping off their attire were complimentary white Stetsons, which the boys wore along with light-colored pants, dark shirts, and light-colored ties.[119]

Benefiting from newspaper coverage, in which they had been dubbed the "Cycling Rangers," complete with photos of the four heading down the highway, the group had no trouble getting offers for concerts along the way. With headlines touting Arnold Hyles as "America's lowest basso," the quartet gave gospel performances in Texas, Arkansas, Tennessee, and Kentucky on its way north.[120] The bicycling stunt was an ingenious promotion, and the four men clearly saw it as such. Two decades later, Vernon Hyles's wife recalled the adventure:

> The laughs we have had from their experiences on those bicycles would make a book. Of course what Mr. John Q. Public didn't know was that a car and driver followed rather closely behind them and it wasn't unusual at all to see all four boys inside the car with their bicycles on the bumpers. Nor was it unusual to see one of them on each side of the car "hitching" a ride up a long hill. I'll assure you that there were numerous bruises "where they hurt the most," and that one of the boys (don't let him know I told you, but his name is VERNON) has never had any desire to own a bicycle since. He will assure you that "riding a bicycle" is NOT one of his major accomplishments.[121]

By the time the group reached Louisville, Kentucky, late in 1936, they had sold the bikes and were traveling exclusively by car. Though they had a booking in Cincinnati and still hoped for an audition to appear on the Major Bowes program, their schedule abruptly changed when Louisville's WHAS radio offered them a spot on the 5:00 to 7:00 A.M. daily farm report. The job paid well, $32.50 per man per month, and provided the group free advertising for all its concerts. Within weeks, the Texas Rangers had more dates than they could fill. Ironically, the quartet also benefited from the widespread coverage of a disastrous flood that brought a national radio hookup to WHAS in January 1937. Their reputation grew, and, by the late 1930s, they—still with their western persona—were one of the best-known gospel quartets in the entire nation.[122]

One key personnel change came to the Rangers in the summer of 1938 when Denver Crumpler replaced George Hughes on the first tenor part. Crumpler's Irish tenor complemented the group perfectly, and the four men soon began billing themselves simply as the Rangers Quartet. They also looked to expand their appeal in more traditional gospel quartet markets. Believing they could benefit from the economic boom occurring in the Carolinas with the growth of the cotton industry, they made a move to Charlotte, North Carolina's WBT in January 1939. There they performed several evenings each week on a program sponsored by B. C. Headache Powders on the CBS Dixie Network as well as on a local morning broadcast twice a week. Soon the Rangers were again swamped with requests for personal appearances and, with their popularity growing, even made a handful of 78 rpm recordings for Decca Records in New York. The affiliation with the 50,000-watt WBT lasted for five years, during which time the Rangers abandoned their guitar accompaniment for the more traditional piano. Marion Snider, a veteran pianist of V. O. Stamps's Old Original Quartet as well as the Blackwood Brothers, joined the group in 1941. Like the Chuck Wagon Gang before them, the Rangers were unique in that they forged a successful career via radio with no connection to the music publishing companies. Unlike the Gang, the Rangers also relied on their personal concert schedule to supplement their income. Along with the MacDonald Brothers Quartet of Missouri and the Johnson Family Singers of North Carolina, they foreshadowed changes soon to come to the gospel quartet industry.[123]

Like earlier gospel groups that came to rely on their personal concert schedule for part of their regular income, the Rangers sang secular tunes to augment their mostly gospel repertoire. The Swanee River Boys, a quartet that emerged in Chattanooga, Tennessee, in 1939, focused on a similar mixed program.[124] With experience in the Vaughan Four Quartet, a group that sang regularly on Knoxville's WNOX in the late 1930s, Buford and Merle Abner decided to try to form their own traveling quartet. They convinced fellow group member Billy Carrier to join them and, along with former Ranger George Hughes, arranged for a regular spot on Chattanooga's WDOD. Buford Abner's lead vocal was balanced by brother Merle's bass, Carrier's baritone, and Hughes's tenor. By early 1941, the Swanee River Boys had moved to Atlanta to become a part of the successful WSB Barn Dance program, on which, with Carrier's guitar accompaniment, they performed until late the following year, when the war forced the Abner brothers into military service. Though the group favored gospel, they remained more tied to secular music than most early gospel groups and, for that reason, lingered on the perimeter of the developing gospel quartet industry.[125]

While newcomers to the industry like the Rangers and the Swanee River Boys were establishing themselves as major forces in the industry, the two most powerful men in shape-note songbook publishing and quartet promotion passed away, marking a watershed in southern gospel. On August 19, 1940, Virgil Stamps died from an apparent heart attack suffered while recuperating from a recent stroke. Though Stamps was in poor health for several weeks prior to his death, the sudden loss was a shock to devotees of shape-note convention music. A crowd of several thousand flocked to Dallas for the funeral, and tributes poured in from across the nation. Less shocking, given his advanced age, but no less a loss to the community, was the demise of James Vaughan on February 9, 1941, also from a heart attack. According to local news reports, almost 7,000 people crowded outside Lawrenceburg's Nazarene Church to pay their respects. Untold thousands of others mourned both these men through the pages of the *Gospel Music News* and *Vaughan's Family Visitor*, and gospel quartet members paid their respects on radio and in concerts.[126]

By the end of 1941, America would be at war and the focus of attention would turn to defeating Nazi Germany in Europe and the Japanese empire in the Pacific. Quartets would struggle to survive. Those who did faced the inevitable loss of personnel to the armed services as well as the uncertainties of travel during a time of gas and rubber rationing. Many quartets broke up, at least temporarily. By the time they reunited a new era of southern gospel music had begun.

The Oak Ridge Quartet

The Oak Ridge Quartet, 1945. Left to right: Curly Kinsey (bass), Johnny New (tenor), Wally Fowler (lead), and Deacon Freeman (baritone). Courtesy Southern Gospel Music Hall of Fame and Museum, Sevierville, Tenn.

Promoter Wally Fowler (center) reviews the mail from the successful All-Nite Sings at the Ryman Auditorium, ca. 1949. Courtesy Southern Gospel Music Hall of Fame and Museum, Sevierville, Tenn.

The master showman Hovie Lister, ca. 1955. Courtesy Southern Gospel Music Hall of Fame and Museum, Sevierville, Tenn.

The Statesmen in concert, mid-1950s. Left to right: *Jake Hess (lead), Denver Crumpler (tenor), Hovie Lister (piano/vocals), and James "Big Chief" Wetherington (bass). Not pictured is Doy Ott (baritone/piano). Courtesy Southern Gospel Music Hall of Fame and Museum, Sevierville, Tenn.*

The Blackwood Brothers with the McGuire Sisters, June 1954. Left to right: Jackie Marshall (piano), James Blackwood (lead), R. W. Blackwood (baritone), Bill Shaw (tenor), Bill Lyles (bass), Christine McGuire, Phyllis McGuire, and Dorothy McGuire. Courtesy Southern Gospel Music Hall of Fame and Museum, Sevierville, Tenn.

The Blackwoods in their new bus, 1955. Courtesy Southern Gospel Music Hall of Fame and Museum, Sevierville, Tenn.

The Blackwood Brothers on stage, ca. 1956. Left to right: Bill Shaw (tenor), James Blackwood (lead), Cecil Blackwood (baritone), J. D. Sumner (bass), and Jackie Marshall (piano). Courtesy Southern Gospel Music Hall of Fame and Museum, Sevierville, Tenn.

The Rangers Quartet, ca. 1949. Left to right: *Arnold Hyles (bass), David Reece (piano), Denver Crumpler (tenor), Erman Slater (baritone), and Vernon Hyles (lead). Courtesy Southern Gospel Music Hall of Fame and Museum, Sevierville, Tenn.*

The Melody Masters, Tampa, Florida, 1946. Left to right: *Wally Varner (piano), Alvin Tootle (tenor), Lee Kitchens (lead), Mosie Lister (baritone), and Jim Wetherington (bass). Courtesy Southern Gospel Music Hall of Fame and Museum, Sevierville, Tenn.*

The Homeland Harmony Quartet, 1945. Left to right: *Connor Hall (tenor), Otis McCoy (lead), Hovie Lister (piano), James McCoy (baritone), and Big Jim Waits (bass). Courtesy Southern Gospel Music Hall of Fame and Museum, Sevierville, Tenn.*

Palmetto State Quartet at WFBC, Greenville, South Carolina, late 1940s. Left to right: Jamie Dill (piano), Clarence Owens (tenor), Malone Thompson (lead), Woodrow Pittman (baritone), and Paul Burroughs (bass). Courtesy Southern Gospel Music Hall of Fame and Museum, Sevierville, Tenn.

The Harmoneers, mid-1940s. Left to right: Fred C. Maples (lead), Charles Key (piano), Bob Crews (baritone), Bobby Strickland (tenor), and Seals "Low Note" Hilton. Courtesy Southern Gospel Music Hall of Fame and Museum, Sevierville, Tenn.

*Blue Ridge Quartet, early
1960s.* Left to right: *Elmo
Fagg (lead), Kenny Gates
(piano), Ed Sprouse (tenor),
George Younce (bass), and
Bill Crow (baritone). Courtesy
Southern Gospel Music Hall of
Fame and Museum, Sevierville,
Tenn.*

*The Chuck Wagon Gang,
mid-1950s.* Left to right,
ascending: *Eddie Carter
(tenor), Rose Carter Karnes
(soprano), Anna Carter Gordon
(alto), and Roy Carter (bass);*
bottom right: *Howard Gordon
(guitar);* inset: *Dave "Dad"
Carter. Courtesy Southern
Gospel Music Hall of Fame
and Museum, Sevierville,
Tenn.*

In 1957, southern gospel promoters dubbed former Louisiana governor Jimmie Davis (right) "Mr. Gospel Singer"; "Miss Gospel Singer" went to Ruth Green (left), and "Gospel Disc Jockey" went to Rick Maze (center). Courtesy Southern Gospel Music Hall of Fame and Museum, Sevierville, Tenn.

Imperial Sugar Quartet advertisement, ca. 1950. Left to right, standing: Floyd Gray (bass), Jake Baumgardner (baritone), Homer Tankersley Jr. (lead), and Charles Speed (tenor); seated: Marion Snider (piano). Courtesy Southern Gospel Music Hall of Fame and Museum, Sevierville, Tenn.

The Crusaders, 1953. Left to right: *Dickie Matthews (piano), Bobby Strickland (tenor), Buddy Parker (lead), Bervin Kendrick (baritone), and Herschel Wooten (bass). Courtesy Southern Gospel Music Hall of Fame and Museum, Sevierville, Tenn.*

The Jordanaires, 1951. Left to right: *Bill Matthews (tenor), Monty Matthews (baritone), Culley Holt (bass), Gordon Stoker (piano), and Bob Hubbard (lead). Courtesy Southern Gospel Music Hall of Fame and Museum, Sevierville, Tenn.*

The Goodman Family on stage, late 1940s. Left to right: *Sam, Eloise, Stella, Gussie Mae, Ruth, Rusty (with guitar), and Howard (at piano). Accordion player is unidentified. Courtesy* Singing News *magazine, Boone, N.C.*

The Rebels Quartet, early 1950s. Left to right: *Horace Parrish (tenor), Lee Kitchens (lead), John Mathews (baritone), and Jim Waits (bass). Courtesy Southern Gospel Music Hall of Fame and Museum, Sevierville, Tenn.*

Stamps Melody Boys, 1949. Left to right: *Clarence Heidelberg (baritone), Doug Jones (bass), Richard Smith (lead), Jack Pittman (tenor), and Reece Crockett (piano). Courtesy Southern Gospel Music Hall of Fame and Museum, Sevierville, Tenn.*

The Lester Family, Lester's Music Store, St. Louis, Missouri, mid-1950s. Left to right, standing: *Harvey "Dad" Lester, Opal "Mom" Lester, Alene Lester, and Herschel Lester;* left to right, seated: *Brian Lester and Donna Lester. Courtesy Southern Gospel Music Hall of Fame and Museum, Sevierville, Tenn.*

The Lewis Family of Lincolnton, Georgia, 1956, shortly after the Lewis Family Show *debuted on Augusta, Georgia's WJBF-TV.* Clockwise, from bottom left: *Little Roy (with banjo), Talmadge (with fiddle), Polly, Miggie, Janis, Pop (with bass), and Wallace (with guitar). Courtesy Southern Gospel Music Hall of Fame and Museum, Sevierville, Tenn.*

The Plainsmen, late 1950s. Left to right: *Thurman Bunch (tenor), Jack Mainord (lead), Larry Denham (piano), Howard Wellborn (baritone), and Rusty Goodman (bass). Courtesy Southern Gospel Music Hall of Fame and Museum, Sevierville, Tenn.*

The Golden Gate Quartet, 1951. Clockwise from bottom left: *Alton Bradley (baritone), Orville Brooks (lead), Clyde Riddick (tenor), and Orlandus Wilson (bass). Courtesy Southern Gospel Music Hall of Fame and Museum, Sevierville, Tenn.*

Springdale, Arkansas, August 2, 1996

"Mr. Blackwood, maybe we could continue our interview later this afternoon. I hate to ask you, but could you give me a lift back to the hotel?" That begins a memorable experience with one of the legends of gospel music. James Blackwood has been singing since he, his older brothers Roy and Doyle, and a nephew, R. W., formed the Blackwood Brothers Quartet in 1934. "I'll be happy to give you a ride, if you don't mind helping me set up my table for tonight's concert," he begins. "No problem, I've got plenty of time," I reply. Now, after an afternoon at the singing convention sponsored by the Brumley Sing, we prepare to head back several miles across town to the hotel.

But we go first to the rodeo grounds where the evening concert will take place. Then, from the back of James Blackwood's trunk, we unload boxes of cassettes, CDs, videotapes, and photographs, carefully setting up the table that will, in just a few hours, host fans and admirers coming by for a chat and to purchase the latest James Blackwood release. The old quartet is gone, and now there is just James . . . and me . . . unloading and setting up a table in much the same way he has been doing since 1934, first with convention songbooks from the Stamps-Baxter company and later with RCA records and other products proudly displaying the famous Blackwood name. Nine Grammys, seven Dove Awards, and four *Singing News* Fan Awards later, he can't resist the urge to set up another table and pitch another product. It's an old habit, but it's an honest habit, and one that, at age seventy-seven, he performs with the urgency of a young man concerned with his first musical release. The table set just so, the products dusted and available . . . as we leave, I glance up in admiration. Life on the road must be in his veins.

6
THE BOOM YEARS: GOSPEL MUSIC PROMOTERS & THE ALL-NIGHT SINGS

The early months of 1946 brought fresh opportunity for American citizens. The rationing of the war years had ended, the boys came home from overseas, and, across the nation, Americans were once again ready to return to the activities of peacetime. More important, the war had spurred new technology and placed the nation in a position to reap unprecedented prosperity over the next generation.

Southern gospel quartets and promoters recognized their own opportunity for success during the years immediately after the war. Significantly, music publishers came to play a declining role in that success. Part of the reason for this decline was the gradual disappearance of the rural singing conventions. Gospel music had thrived, in large part, because it provided inexpensive entertainment for rural audiences. That entertainment was participatory first and performed for spectators second. More and more during the late 1940s, gospel quartets were singing to large audiences via radio, in concerts, and on 78 rpm recordings. As they prospered, the power and prestige of the shape-note music companies that had dominated the gospel music scene since the early years of the century diminished. As a result, the number of publishing companies that specialized in annual shape-note convention books also declined and their product—whose sales were once described as ranking "second only to the Bible in this area"—reached fewer and fewer southerners.[1] By the late 1960s, much of what remained of the industry had coalesced into the holdings of the Tennessee Music and Printing Company.[2]

Tennessee Music and Printing, an auxiliary of the Church of God of Cleveland, Tennessee, was established in 1931 with former Vaughan employee Otis Leon McCoy at the helm. It enjoyed the stability of a denomination that grew steadily during the Depression years and even more dramatically after the war.[3] In 1948, Tennessee Music and Printing acquired the holdings of the old A. J. Showalter Company from the L. A. Lee Printing Company, which had owned the remains of the Dalton, Georgia, firm since 1941. During the late 1960s, it expanded even further by purchasing the inventory that had previously belonged to Vaughan Music. The growing independence of gospel music quartets corresponded with the growth of Tennessee Music and Printing, since the church press had no interest in sponsoring traveling groups.[4]

Music companies' decline was also due in part to internal politics and conflicts. Five years after the death of V. O. Stamps, for example, when responsibility for day-to-day operations and the lion's share of control of the Stamps-Baxter company remained with J. R. Baxter, Frank Stamps bolted from the company and formed the rival Stamps Quartet Music Company. He also started a rival school, which he scheduled directly opposite the annual Stamps-Baxter school. The rift damaged the credibility of both companies in the eyes of some gospel music fans as both J. R. Baxter and Frank Stamps struggled to capitalize on V. O. Stamps's legacy.[5]

With music companies like Vaughan and Stamps-Baxter on the wane, individual quartets' independence grew as they assumed more and more control over the development of the industry and the songs that were produced. Increasing numbers of artists began writing and recording their own material; some also began to contract separately with songwriters. The result was a new direction for gospel music. A number of groups had proven they could earn a living apart from the publishing houses. For example, the Chuck Wagon Gang's alliance with radio in Fort Worth, coupled with their Columbia recordings, not only made them independent but also afforded them a remarkable amount of personal and financial success. In addition, the Rangers had proven that hard work and ingenuity could put a quartet into the marketplace via radio and incessant concert appearances. But, in the days after the Second World War, virtually all groups would achieve an independence that only a handful had dared in earlier decades.[6]

World War II also precipitated changes in the way the nation addressed the issue of race. Segregated combat units became a thing of the past after President Harry Truman's integration of the armed forces in 1948.[7] The dramatic shift marked the beginning of a series of events that would spark the civil rights movement and bring remarkable change to the American social landscape. Ironically, the same set of events inaugurated a greater degree of segregation in the world of gospel music—at least in the short run. Southern fears and agitation over the *Brown* decision of May 1954 reduced the already small number of black gospel groups performing before predominantly white audiences. A decade that began with frequent appearances of the Golden Gate Quartet, one of the most famous black groups in the nation, on concert venues headlined by major white gospel quartets thus ended with the almost total segregation of gospel music. It would not be until the revolutionary changes of the 1960s had taken place that audiences of both black and white gospel would once again cross the color line.[8]

The war also occasioned technological advances that would hasten the self-sufficiency of the gospel music quartets. The interstate highway system championed by the Eisenhower administration in the mid-1950s grew in part from wartime concerns (and particularly those of the Cold War) about transportation of national resources and military mobilization. With the growth of the nation's automobile, tourist, and freight transportation industries in the decade after the war, interstates became a part of the life of most Americans. As they did, they opened the way for more convenient and far-flung travel by gospel and other musical entertainers. In addition, the end of wartime gas rationing meant that quartets could resume their heavy travel schedules. By 1956, the first musical group was touring by custom bus.[9]

Advances in radio at the end of the war introduced just the beginning of a series of technological avenues for promoting and sustaining a successful group. Within just a few years, better sound equipment, more widely available and affordable recording studios, and the arrival of local and syndicated television programming would all take gospel quartets to larger and larger audiences.

Entertainment had always been part of a quartet's appeal along with a love for the music born in the devotion of American evangelicalism. Nevertheless, some conservative Christians had a hard time reconciling the music's entertainment value with the seriousness of religious devotion. In the late 1930s, the Vaughan company had urged several of its quartets to concentrate on evangelical meetings and went to great lengths to explain to their supporters that, while some groups included "other numbers to their programs with a little comedy," all Vaughan-supported singers "use nothing that is not clean and wholesome along with the entertaining features."[10] Shortly before the outbreak of the war, some members of the Vaughan fraternity were disapproving of even that. Hilman Barnard, a fifteen-year veteran of the Vaughan Radio Quartet who left the group in 1932 to become a full-time evangelist, wrote to *Vaughan's Family Visitor* in 1940 to say that secular and sacred music should no longer be mixed. "Hymns and gospel songs are being made 'common' because every 'Tom, Dick and Harry' are using them on their radio program, be it 'Grand Ol [*sic*] Opry,' 'barn dance' jamboree or what have you. We just cannot do it and glorify God."[11]

Despite concerns about mixing evangelical music with entertainment, gospel music grew increasingly commercialized in the years immediately after the war. While only a handful of groups—most notably the Chuck Wagon Gang and the most famous Vaughan or Stamps groups—had been able to make recordings prior to 1941, almost all professional groups produced 78 rpm discs in the ten years after the war. By 1949, *Billboard Magazine* listed four hundred record companies, some of which specialized in gospel music. Labels such as Bibletone and White Church offered many quartets their first opportunity to carry a product of their own, independent of a powerful music publisher.[12] In addition, gospel artists and producers joined professional organizations like SESAC, one of the three major licensing organizations in the recording industry.[13]

With the growth of the professional gospel music industry, convention singing declined. Already hampered by the growth of urban and suburban neighborhoods as well as the increase in entertainment options that came with rural electrification and the introduction of television, conventions sought to survive by bending the rules to allow the most popular quartets more performance time. Naturally, quartets relished the opportunity to expand their influence.[14] Though their roots lay in singing schools, where church choirs and better congregational hymn singing had been stressed, quartet members now found themselves in the entertainment business. For them, shape notes remained only as tools in the recruitment of new talent to ensure that all members of a quartet could rapidly learn new material.[15]

New technology played an important part in artists' transition from singing conventions to concert-oriented performances. Already radio had converted groups like the LeFevres, the Chuck Wagon Gang, the Blackwoods, and the Rangers into household names. Once introduced

Professional Quartets

by that powerful medium, quartets stood a good chance of drawing instant publicity and a large crowd when staging area concerts. Familiar with a group's sound, audiences came to listen to gospel music, not to participate in the harmony. By the mid-1930s, groups were using "loudspeakers" to project sound and, as a result, could sing to outdoor audiences numbering in the thousands.[16] The singing schools and shape-note normals that survived became launching pads for talented singers interested in making a living by singing gospel music. By the mid-1950s, almost a thousand gospel quartets dotted the landscape, although most were required to supplement their singing income by working regular jobs. All dreamed, however, of making it big in gospel music.[17]

In fact, successfully carving a career in gospel music became a greater possibility than ever before. Crucial was the musician's ability to identify with an audience and to understand what fans of the music liked best. Gauging fan interest moved gospel singers closer and closer to the boundaries of other forms of popular music, since expanding the market often meant following some new appeal. In this regard, quartets relied on their intimate understanding of American evangelicalism and their recognition that musical taste reflected sociocultural status. In the South, such status was also reflective of denominational affiliation. A courtroom exchange in a 1957 civil case involving publishing rights of gospel music reflected publishers' awareness of the religious market for their quartet songs:

A: Well . . . some people would call it a gospel song that maybe has a bouncy rhythm effect to it that naturally you wouldn't sing it in your first Churches, nor any of your Churches, maybe, yet it would be a religious lyric, with Biblical words, and all of that.
Q: Isn't it true that that type of gospel music is mainly sung over the radio and for popular mass consumption rather than religious purposes?
A: Not exactly. You have different planes of religion, some will buy a rhythm tune, some won't. And in the work that I do, I have visited with a lot of denominations and I find that sometimes maybe your Church of God or some of those people will like the bouncy, rhythmical type of song whereas my First Baptists down here won't.[18]

Integrally tied to the growing demand for the "bouncy, rhythmical" gospel quartet numbers was the phenomenal success of Pentecostalism. Born in the millenarian fever that swept the nation during the early years of the twentieth century, the movement appealed to both white and black working-class Christians. Initially interracial, Pentecostalism had evolved by the 1930s into a string of largely segregated denominations. Pentecostals' vibrant worship style stressed the immediate presence of the Holy Spirit and the miraculous "signs and wonders" of the last days before the Second Coming. It also reflected the strong degree of immediacy in their religious devotion and taste. Interested in evangelism above all else, they accepted popular music styles as long as the lyrics were consistent with their theological assumptions. They disassociated themselves from the formality of traditional worship and argued that reaching the lost with the message of salvation meant using creative and innovative tactics. As a result, Pentecostals were most receptive to the music of the masses and saw little difficulty in combining the sounds of popular music with gospel lyrics.[19] For that reason, a sizable number of Pentecostals comprised the ranks of gospel quartets in the years after James Vaughan's decision to finance his brother's group in 1910.

Among the early groups emanating from Pentecostal circles and utilizing those connections to their advantage were the LeFevres and the Blackwoods. James Blackwood remembered years after his career began that some denominational churches were biased against the "Stamps-Baxter" style of music, believing that "the message wasn't deep enough." Although "some of the criticism was justified," he noted, "much of it wasn't."[20] He recalled fondly that "the Pentecostals were the first denomination to use our type of Gospel music. They were more given to singing songs with a beat. They weren't afraid to clap their hands and pat their feet."[21]

A number of individuals in the publishing company quartets also came from Pentecostal churches. Otis McCoy, the Vaughan Radio Quartet member who helped form the Tennessee Music and Printing Company in 1931, and John Daniel Sumner, a young bass singer who got his start with the Sunny South Quartet in central Florida in 1945 were two examples. R. E. Winsett, a shape-note publisher from Dayton, Tennessee, had strong ties to the Assemblies of God.[22] A number of songwriters also added a strong Pentecostal flavor to their music, particularly Herbert Buffum, Vep Ellis, and Ira Stanphill.[23] Dottie Rambo, a young talent who emerged in the 1950s from a United Pentecostal tradition would become, by the mid-1960s, perhaps the best-known female songwriter in recent gospel music history.[24]

Similarly, many early quartets sprang from the Holiness denomina-

Professional Quartets

tions that held a parallel, though theologically distinct, position in favor of jubilant worship. The Church of God of Anderson, Indiana, and the Church of the Nazarene both contributed key individuals to the early gospel music scene. James Vaughan and his family were worshiping at the Church of the Nazarene by the mid-1920s and were instrumental in leading the Speer Family into the denomination as well. Bill Gaither, a young struggling songwriter and schoolteacher in the mid-1950s, emerged from the Indiana-based Church of God to become one of the century's most prominent gospel songwriters.[25] In both Holiness and Pentecostal circles, a rigorous pattern of devotion reigned while unnecessary frills and certain forms of entertainment, including motion pictures, dancing, and secular youth music, were frowned upon. As a result, gospel music emerged as a powerful outlet for young people in these denominations, providing what one researcher has dubbed "worldly pleasures within a sanctified form."[26]

Early in the century, Pentecostals cast their lot in favor of joyous singing, a logical response to their acceptance of emotional displays during worship. The result was a greater inclusion of musical instruments than in other Protestant circles. Music thus became more varied in Pentecostal services, and adherents who worshiped there came to appreciate the diversity of styles that were indicative of the gospel music industry by the end of World War II. In a 1954 article in which he provided an extensive exposition on the Greek words for "sing," Assemblies of God writer J. J. Mueller opined that the Scriptures overwhelmingly supported singing as an activity both inside and outside the church. He was also adamant in his belief that a diverse assortment of instruments were acceptable in the arena of gospel music: "After years of worshiping God in music, and now after a thorough study of the New Testament on the subject, I am convinced that the Lord does not frown upon our use of instruments to worship Him, but that He actually is pleased for us to glorify Him by their use."[27]

By the 1950s, however, some Pentecostal denominations were questioning their heritage of allowing popular Christian music in churches with little censure. Predictably it was the larger denominations that had begun to achieve a higher socioeconomic stature during the years after 1945 that first made this self-conscious analysis. In 1955, the official organ of the Assemblies of God reprinted an article titled "Shallow-Pan Christianity," spelling out the dangers inherent in the music popularized by traveling quartets:

A tropical hurricane of a different but equally devastating character is moving northward. *The Prarie Overcomer* calls it a "musical monster." It says: "Capacity crowds come to be entertained and, occasionally converted during an 'All-nite Sing,' colloquially called 'gospel boogie' or 'jumping for Jesus.' Admission charges in one city, where 6,500 attended, were $1.25 to $1.60, children half price. We warn God's people not to be swept into supporting the gospel show business . . . May God make us as serious as the days in which we live. Fun, froth, and religious frolic are indicative of shallow-pan Christianity."[28]

Nevertheless, most rank-and-file Pentecostals continued to express an openness for popular gospel music, restricting their opposition to gospel singers who did not lead upright Christian lives or to music that was too closely associated with the sound of jazz or rock 'n' roll, the new teen music. In a 1963 address, Reverend James Hamill of the First Assembly of God in Memphis—the home church of the Blackwood Brothers and the minister's own son, Jim, lead singer with the Blue Ridge Quartet—blasted "the disgusting examples of ungodly persons singing hymns and religious songs on radio, television and elsewhere across this country, which must be nauseating to a holy God."[29] "I get a little tired of people who have appreciation for only one type of religious music," Hamill said in support of the gospel quartet style but then went on to note that "I do not believe there is any place in the church for rock and roll, or jazz, in the name of religion."[30]

As the power of the gospel music publishers declined, a handful of innovative concert promoters became more and more important in dictating the success of quartets. In the late 1940s, Wilmer B. Nowlin, a Methodist schooled in the popularity of the V. O. Stamps's all-night radio broadcasts ten years earlier, and Wallace ("Wally") Fowler, a quartet singer and country music songwriter, became the chief forces in organizing a string of concerts across the South. Initially mixing country and gospel acts, both men capitalized on quartets' association with local radio stations. They also hedged their bets by booking several quartets together in one concert appearance, thus ensuring a large enough crowd and getting both the public and the quartets used to the idea of late-night engagements.[31]

Nowlin jumped into the gospel music promotion business when, in June 1948, as president of the DeLeon, Texas, Community Club, he helped organize the annual DeLeon Peach and Melon Festival. Spending

$750 of his own money to attract country superstar Eddy Arnold, Nowlin was then forced to promote the concert in an effort to get the club's investment back. Given their popularity in Texas, he hired the Frank Stamps All-Star Quartet to open the Arnold show and the Stamps-Ozark Quartet to close it. When the festival drew over 12,000 people, the event turned Nowlin into a regular concert promoter.[32] He continued to book gospel quartets alongside established country stars. Quartets were popular locally throughout the South because of their regular radio programs, and having them on a concert schedule ensured a certain amount of free publicity for Nowlin's upcoming events. This interaction of gospel and country artists throughout the 1950s opened up new opportunities for some gospel singers. By the latter years of the decade, groups like the Blackwoods and the Jordanaires of Nashville, Tennessee, were providing backup vocals for popular country and rockabilly stars like Hank Snow, Red Foley, and Elvis Presley.[33]

A committed Christian, Nowlin soon became enamored with the gospel quartets. In 1950, he organized his first "Battle of Songs," an event that featured the top gospel quartets in a late-night format in head-to-head competition. Fans were urged to attend and cheer on their favorite quartet. Over the next four decades, Nowlin successfully advertised concerts from his home base in Fort Worth. In 1962, he began promoting gospel music exclusively.[34]

Wally Fowler's move into gospel music promotions also took place in 1948. Already an established singer in quartet circles and rapidly making his name in the country music arena as well, Fowler borrowed a concept that V. O. Stamps had introduced a decade earlier and began promoting a series of all-gospel performances, touting them as "All-Night Sings." Holding one of the first talent-packed affairs on Friday, November 5, 1948, in Nashville's Ryman Auditorium, the young promoter convinced local affiliate WSM to broadcast two hours of the spectacle live. Despite cold, rainy weather, Fowler packed the house and, with enthusiastic listeners calling in, was able to get an extension of an additional hour on the radio. After that concert, he brought the All-Night Sing and the most popular gospel groups to most major southern cities through the 1950s.[35] To critics who charged that mixing gospel and popular music styles bordered on blasphemy, Fowler replied, "We're doing what the Lord wants us to do. . . . If we sing hymns to practically every beat except the tango and the mambo, it's because it doesn't matter how you honor the Lord, just so you honor Him." In 1955, *Colliers* referred to Fowler's concerts as "the largest and most successful of a dozen religious musical road shows that attract an estimated 2,000,000 paying fans a year" and estimated that they drew "up to 15,000 a week in some 200 towns and cities in 38 states each season."[36]

As had been the case between rival publishing companies, influential promoters began to compete. Over the next two decades, Nowlin and Fowler expanded their bases of operations across the South, though Nowlin dominated Texas, Arkansas, and Missouri and Fowler controlled areas east of the Mississippi. A few other promoters, notably Loy McCormick in Georgia, J. G. Whitfield in Florida, Lloyd Orrell in the Midwest and northern states, and Polly Grimes in California, also carved out successful careers in the gospel music business.[37] As quartets became dependent on the promoters for successful concert appearances, major groups were also likely to feud with an individual promoter over arrangements promised or not promised in advance. The most popular groups, especially the Blackwoods and Statesmen in the 1950s, however, were able to command larger advances and dictate appearance time.[38]

Capitalizing on the growing professionalism of the industry, a gospel music fan and former journalist for the *Atlanta Constitution*, E. O. Batson Jr., of Sylacauga, Alabama, founded the *Gospel Singing World* in November 1954. Joined initially by Jack House of Birmingham, Alabama, and endorsed by Wally Fowler, Batson secured complete ownership of the magazine within just a few months. Unlike the publications of the shape-note music companies, Batson's journal focused almost exclusively on the concerts and activities of the most popular gospel music quartets and songwriters. With tidbits about singers' personal lives and quality photographs, the monthly included a handful of product ads and a regular schedule of major concert dates throughout the South. Though occasional mention of singing conventions, including the quartet activity at those gatherings, was also included, the focus of the journal revealed the direction that the more popular groups were headed.[39] Operating successfully for four years, *Gospel Singing World* achieved a level of quality that would not be reached consistently by another organ of the industry for another three decades.[40]

THE TRANSITION FROM THE WAR YEARS
TO THE BOOM YEARS

Most of the gospel music groups that had prospered prior to World War II moved rapidly down the path of professionalism once the war was

Professional Quartets

over. Family groups like the Chuck Wagon Gang and the Speer Family had been able to survive the war with other family members often stepping in to fill the spaces of sons called into military service.[41] Others, like the Blackwoods, struggled with frequent personnel changes in order to keep active and to maintain name recognition. James Blackwood later remembered introducing an entirely new audience to the southern-style quartets after he and members of the group relocated to California to work in aircraft plants. Though R. W. Blackwood was drafted into the army in 1944 and served in the Pacific during the last year of the war, substitutes enabled the group to perform weekend concerts.[42] Eva Mae LeFevre even sang for a time with the Homeland Harmony Quartet when both Urias and Alphus LeFevre were serving in the army. By doing so, she kept that prominent music family name before the public eye and helped prepare for the group's return in 1945.[43]

The war's end also saw a brief revival of company-sponsored quartets. Frank Stamps's new Stamps Quartet Music Company promoted the fortunes of several prominent groups, especially Frank's own All-Star Quartet. The company also briefly organized a female quartet known as the Stampettes, a group managed and accompanied by Frank's wife, Sally.[44] After the war ended, longtime Stamps-Baxter and Stamps Quartet associate Harley Lester hired Glen Weldon Payne, a veteran of the Stamps-Baxter school and a former employee of the company, to sing. Payne, destined to become one of the premier lead singers in southern gospel history, would sing for several Stamps Quartet Music Company groups through the mid-1950s.[45]

The quartets who early on established themselves apart from music publishing companies paved the way for more and more independent gospel groups. The Chuck Wagon Gang moved from their position as exclusively a radio quartet to a very successful association with gospel music concert promoters beginning in 1951. Largely due to the strength of exposure from a Knoxville, Tennessee, radio evangelist and gospel music aficionado Rev. J. Bazzel Mull, their name became a household word in the Southeast. As early as 1939, Mull had begun broadcasting his sermons and playing gospel music on local radio in Gastonia, North Carolina. In time, he established links with a series of southern radio stations. Mull and his wife, Anna, established the "Mull Singing Convention of the Air," a program of gospel music favorites that was regularly featured on several large southern stations by the mid-1950s.[46] Mull's promotion of the Chuck Wagon Gang, together with the group's resumption of recording sessions with Columbia in 1948, led the group to legendary status.[47]

Other groups moved in similar directions at the war's end. The Speers relocated to Nashville from Montgomery, Alabama, to take an early morning radio program with WSIX, a move that enabled Brock Speer to attend classes at Trevecca Nazarene College. Within a few years, the group also began making their first 78 rpm recordings on the Columbia and Bullet labels.[48] The LeFevres regrouped after the war and continued their concerts and radio promotions from Atlanta. By the late 1940s, they were also making 78s on the Bibletone label.[49]

Success led the Swanee River Boys a bit further away from gospel music in the decade after the war. Broadening their repertoire to include folk songs and popular ballads, they established themselves as radio favorites, performing again on Atlanta's WSB and then on Charlotte's WBT. From 1948 through 1954, the Swanee River Boys worked in Cincinnati, performing on the NBC radio network and appearing on one of the earliest television programs, *The Swanee River Boys Time.* Their success with popular music—by one account, requests at concerts "ran almost two-to-one in favor of the secular material"—set them apart from the gospel circles that were rapidly moving toward professionalism in the late 1950s.[50]

The Rangers Quartet entered the 1950s as one of the most successful gospel quartets of all time. Their affiliation with WBT in Charlotte ended in 1945, and the group enjoyed momentary stints at radio stations in Wheeling, West Virginia; Richmond, Virginia; and Atlanta, Georgia, over the next two years before rejoining the Charlotte station briefly in 1947. From there, the quartet moved west to Topeka, Kansas, then back to Raleigh, North Carolina, before finally settling in Shreveport, Louisiana, by the early 1950s. A car accident in January 1951 killed baritone singer Erman Slater and seriously injured veteran bass Arnold Hyles. Forced to curtail their travel, the quartet still sang regularly on the Liberty Broadcasting System in a series of radio programs that took them to every state in the union.[51] In addition, the group continued to make records, many on their own Ranger label in a promotion known as the "record of the month." In 1955, they made yet another move, this time to the West Coast, where they starred in a weekly television program produced in Hollywood. Despite their achievements, personnel changes became more frequent and travel became more difficult for the aging Hyles brothers. In 1956, the group disbanded. Rights to the quartet name were sold to pianist David Reece, who, by the 1960s, had reformed the group as a trio, which had begun another successful stint at Charlotte's WBT.[52]

THE STATESMEN

In addition to the older groups, a series of newly formed groups dotted the southern landscape during the years immediately following the conclusion of World War II. Of all the established groups, none would become more successful or influential than the Statesmen Quartet from Atlanta. Formed in 1948, the group was the brainchild of Hovie Lister, a twenty-one-year-old pianist and gospel music zealot from Greenville, South Carolina. Born into a textile mill family on September 17, 1926, Lister began learning piano at the age of six and, by his teenage years, was playing at his local Baptist church and for the Lister Brothers Quartet, a group comprised of his father and uncles.[53] In addition, he achieved some local acclaim when he was selected to play at a series of revivals conducted by the celebrated evangelist Mordecai Ham. During the Ham crusades, he accompanied the legendary songwriter and soloist Austin C. Miles, whose compositions included standard gospel favorites "In the Garden" and "Dwelling in Beulah Land."[54]

During the war years, Lister attended the Stamps-Baxter School of Music and subsequently played piano with some of gospel music's most influential groups, including the Rangers, the LeFevres, and the Homeland Harmony Quartet. By 1947, he had settled in Atlanta and secured a job playing gospel recordings on radio station WEAS in nearby Decatur. Most stations still used live broadcasts of local groups, and Lister's short tenure as a deejay foreshadowed the key role that recordings would play in the promotion of all forms of popular music in the immediate future.[55]

Even before settling in at the radio station, Lister had dreamed of forming his own quartet. Years later, he admitted, "That had been the dream all the time I was with the other groups. . . . I wanted to do something different . . . I had a sound in mind."[56] Always brash and filled with confidence from his early success in gospel music, Lister used his friendship with Barry Howell, the son of *Atlanta Constitution* owner Major Howell, to land a spot on Atlanta's brand-new WCON. Owned by the Atlanta daily, the station had sufficient funding and was willing to hire steady talent. Lister convinced Howell that he could put together a quartet composed of the best voices in the business and secured the coveted 6 A.M. and noon time slots for the new group. In addition to providing valuable advertising for area concerts, the station agreed to pay Lister's new group $50 a week per member. This influential backing gave Lister the clout to raid other quartets and entice some of gospel music's best voices to join his group.[57]

When the new station opened in August 1948, Lister left WEAS and took charge of the promised time slots on WCON by playing gospel recordings. In the meantime, he hastily scoured the gospel music quartet world seeking the mix that would produce his new sound. The initial lineup included baritone singer Mosie Lister, who had experience with both the Sunny South and the Melody Masters, and tenor Bobby Strickland, a veteran of the Sand Mountain Quartet and the Harmoneers. Bervin Kendrick was selected to sing lead and Gordon Hill, to sing bass. This group went on the air in October 1948 to fill WCON's daily lineup with live gospel music. Choosing the name from a small newsletter published by Georgia governor Herman Talmadge, Lister called his group the Statesmen. Before finalizing the name, he actually approached Talmadge with the idea and received the governor's blessing. In time, the Georgia politician became a Statesmen fan, proclaiming the members "Ambassadors of Good Will for the State of Georgia."[58]

From the beginning, however, the lineup was understood to be temporary. Mosie Lister was not interested in venturing outside Atlanta on the concert circuit and, within a few weeks, was replaced by W. Jake Hess, a young lead singer with experience in the John Daniel Quartet and several smaller groups. To make room for Hess, Kendrick assumed the role of the group's baritone. Other quartet members, however, were also unsure to what degree they were willing to commit to the endeavor.[59]

Hovie Lister continued to seek a particular blend of voices and sound that would set his quartet apart. Through a series of personnel changes from late 1948 to mid-1949, Lister toyed with the mix and ultimately assembled a collection of voices that he believed held the potential for greatness. When the quartet began touring extensively in the summer of 1949, it was comprised of Jake Hess on lead, Bobby Strickland on tenor, Bervin Kendrick on baritone, and James "Big Chief" Wetherington on bass. Within the next two years, Strickland was replaced by Claris G. "Cat" Freeman and Kendrick by Doy Ott. Hovie Lister served as master of ceremonies, played piano, and occasionally joined the group as a fifth voice. Like Hess, Wetherington was a veteran of several quartets, most recently the Melody Masters of station KFAB in Lincoln, Nebraska. Ott had played piano for the Rangers and had also demonstrated his ability

Professional Quartets

on vocals, occasionally providing backup with his smooth baritone voice. His versatility allowed Lister the freedom on occasion to take to the stage himself during concert performances.[60] Freeman was also a veteran singer with experience in several quartets. From the rich shape-note tradition in the Sand Mountain region of northern Alabama, he had contributed his efforts in recent years to the Melody Masters and the Blackwood Brothers.[61]

Over the next few years, Hovie Lister's Statesmen advanced faster than any other group in gospel music. Their affiliation with WCON gave them considerable clout, and Lister's relentless search for perfection pushed the quartet rapidly down the path of greatness. In addition, few individuals in gospel music circles had the drive and stage presence of Hovie Lister. He understood intuitively the way to move an audience, selecting numbers that allowed his quartet to glide through a program with a delightful mix of slow, reverent classics and rousing, foot-tapping convention numbers.[62] He also became quite proficient at adapting black spirituals and arranged a number of them for his quartet. Probably his most famous adaptation was "Get Away Jordon," a song introduced and taught to the Statesmen in the early 1950s by the Gospel Harmonettes, a black female gospel trio from Birmingham, Alabama.[63]

One final personnel change, however, would come before the Statesmen would move into their own as one of the premier groups of the gospel music world of the 1950s. In 1953, Freeman left the quartet and Lister convinced Denver Crumpler, the venerable tenor singer from the Rangers Quartet, to join his group. Long a fan of Crumpler, Lister understood that his Irish tenor voice would perfectly complement the other members of the group. For the next four years, the Statesmen achieved recognition as the finest of white gospel quartets.[64]

Part of the reason for the Statesmen's success was their close affiliation and friendship with the Blackwood Brothers. By 1952, the Blackwoods were the only group that rivaled and outdrew Lister's quartet. Instead of competing head-to-head, however, the two quartets actually joined forces to form a partnership that would last for the next fifteen years. The combined effort proved appealing to fans of gospel quartet music, and the two groups used their slightly contrasting styles to their advantage. Often concert promoters pitted fans of the groups against each other in order to see which of the two could draw the most applause.[65] The financial return on the arrangement was also impressive. Averaging $250 per group before the partnership, the Blackwood-Statesmen team was able to command up to $1,500 per appearance by the end of the decade.[66]

<h2>SUCCESS AND TRAGEDY</h2>

Over the next few years, both the Statesmen and the Blackwoods enjoyed unprecedented success in the world of gospel quartet music. Beginning in late 1945, the Blackwoods had begun releasing 78s on their own label from Shenandoah, Iowa, and issued several numbers on the White Church label. Their concert success, however, and their successful promotion on radio after their move to Memphis in 1950 led to a national contract. Beginning in 1951, the Blackwoods offered regular releases through their recording deal with RCA Victor.[67] The Statesmen followed a similar path, issuing a handful of 78s on Capitol from 1949 through 1953 as well as on their own custom label. Two years after the business deal that linked the two quartets in 1952, the Statesmen signed their own exclusive deal with RCA.[68]

Radio continued to provide an important source of income and advertisement for the two groups. In 1950, the Blackwoods left station KMA in Shenandoah to appear daily on WMPS in Memphis. As a music center in its own right, the city provided plenty of opportunity as well as a central location for touring nationally over the next two decades. By the mid-1950s, the Blackwoods were also appearing on local television station WMCT, sponsored by Dixie Lily Flour—the staple product of the Memphis-based Buhler Mills.[69] With the merger of the *Atlanta Constitution* and the *Atlanta Journal* and the subsequent sale of WCON in early 1950, the Statesmen moved to WSB, the more powerful 50,000-watt station controlled by the city's major newspaper. By mid-decade, via a regular program called *Singing Time in Dixie*, they were recording transcription discs that allowed the quartet to be heard in more than thirty-five separate markets.[70] The quartet also picked up an impressive sponsor, the National Biscuit Company. With the support of Nabisco, the Statesmen launched a weekly syndicated television program that ran from 1953 to 1957. The program originated in some thirty-five markets but ultimately was carried on more than a hundred southern television stations. With innovative staging for introducing new gospel tunes, the program was filmed at the Belon King Film Company in Atlanta.[71]

In 1954, both the Blackwoods and the Statesmen received national exposure when, just two months apart, they won first place on the

Professional Quartets

weekly CBS national television program *Arthur Godfrey's Talent Scouts.* The Blackwoods turned the trick first on Monday, June 14 when they sang "Have You Talked with the Man Upstairs?" earning the right to appear alongside the McGuire Sisters the following week on Godfrey's morning television show in New York. Partly as a result of the show's promotion, the song became one of RCA's top-selling singles over the next few weeks. The Statesmen matched the feat, winning on *Godfrey's Talent Scouts* in August 1954 with a lively Stuart Hamblen number titled "This Ole House."[72]

In the midst of such rousing success, tragedy struck the new gospel quartet team. Before an appearance at the annual Peach Festival in Clanton, Alabama, on June 30, 1954, Blackwood members R. W. Blackwood and Bill Lyles were killed while making a test landing of the group's newly purchased twin-engine Beechcraft. The Blackwoods had pioneered air travel by gospel quartets just a few months previously and were one of only two gospel groups (the LeFevres being the other) to experiment with airplanes as a regular mode of transportation. Crushed by the loss of his nephew and friend, James Blackwood contemplated giving up on his gospel career. However, encouraged by his friends and companions in the Statesmen Quartet as well as fans, he rebuilt the quartet within the next six weeks, hiring R. W. Blackwood's brother, Cecil, to sing baritone and John Daniel "J. D." Sumner of the Sunshine Boys to sing bass.[73]

Sumner's addition as a full partner in the quartet, though forged in tragedy, would prove momentous. His career had begun a decade earlier when he began singing for the Tampa-based Sunny South Quartet. Briefly organizing and managing the Dixie Lily Harmoneers, a Tampa group sponsored by the local Dixie Lily Milling Company, Sumner had quickly achieved distinction in the industry for his deep, bass voice.[74] With Bill Shaw's high tenor and his low bass, the new version of the Blackwood group quickly re-established the quartet as a continuing force in gospel music. On Monday, September 17, 1956, James Blackwood's tenacity was rewarded when the group took home for the second time the top honor on Arthur Godfrey's television program.[75]

The Blackwood-Statesmen enterprise also led to the origins of what would become, in time, the largest annual gathering of fans and quartets in the industry. The National Quartet Convention, the brainchild of Sumner, featured all the major groups in a three-day concert held in October 1957 in Memphis's Ellis Auditorium. At a cost of $15,000 for production, the event was risky, but, after breaking even the first year, the convention proved to be a financially promising event. By the mid-1960s, the NQC had been stretched into a week-long affair that drew more than 20,000 people.[76]

J. D. Sumner also proved influential in another innovation that changed the course of gospel music and ultimately the entire entertainment business. Early in 1955, after the Blackwoods had returned to touring by car following the fatal plane crash of the previous year, he convinced his partner James Blackwood to invest in a bus for the group's travel. Sumner purchased a 1938 Aerocoach from Trailways and customized it, installing five reclining chairs in which quartet members could both relax and sleep. In time, cots and other more elaborate accommodations were installed in the bus. As singing groups became popular, more and more adapted to the new mode of travel, as did singers and traveling performers in other areas of the entertainment world. Significantly, bus travel solved the emerging problem of inventory that resulted from the increased availability of 78s and, beginning in 1952, the 33⅓ rpm discs. Better sound systems added to the freight that quartets hauled from concert to concert. Coupled with the federal interstate highway program inaugurated in the late 1950s, the bus significantly improved a quartet's ability to travel and tour successfully.[77]

THE OAK RIDGE BOYS

While no group in gospel music gained the success and national attention of the Blackwoods and Statesmen in the 1950s, other groups prospered and built their own identities among a growing core of fans in the southern gospel music market. Influenced by the creative genius of promoter and songwriter Wally Fowler, the Oak Ridge Quartet grew out of a country music group formed during World War II.[78] In 1943, in Oak Ridge, Tennessee, the U.S. Defense Department was building a facility related to the government's effort to develop nuclear weapons. Fowler's group, known as Wally Fowler and the Georgia Clodhoppers, sang frequently for construction workers at their campsite just outside of Knoxville. Anchored by Fowler's lead vocal, the group featured Johnny New on tenor, Lon "Deacon" Freeman on baritone, and Curley Kinsey on bass. Talented singers and musicians, the boys occasionally performed as a gospel quartet—though they concentrated on spirituals more than the gospel songs coming out of the rural singing conventions. Shortly after the atomic bomb was dropped on Hiroshima in August 1945, Fowler—

Professional Quartets

always one to capitalize on available publicity—renamed the group the Oak Ridge Quartet.[79]

Fowler's new gospel quartet created a sensation in the gospel music world as a result of his successful promotion of the all-night sings at the Ryman beginning in November 1948. By the spring of 1949, Fowler had arranged for a sing at the Ryman on the first Friday night of each month and, for several years, that event reigned as perhaps the most popular one in gospel music. It also publicized the all-night sing as the vehicle by which gospel music would gain popularity over the next two decades. Nevertheless, Fowler had difficulty keeping his quartet together. When the first Ryman broadcast aired on WSM, Curley Kinsey had already left the group, replaced on the bass part by Curley Blaylock. By this point, the Oak Ridge Quartet as the gospel component of the musical entourage was clearly taking over. In 1949, the Georgia Clodhoppers simply ceased to exist. The addition of talented electric guitar accompanist Neal Matthews Jr. and piano player Boyce Hawkins put the group in a unique position. Given Fowler's many promotional duties, the group could hit the road without him by having Matthews take the lead vocal part. Personality clashes, however, led to the dissolution of the group. By the end of 1949, all the members had left Fowler and formed their own group, the Stone Mountain Quartet, an experiment that proved to be short-lived.

Never one to worry about personnel changes, Fowler simply moved on. He hired another group, the Calvary Quartet, from Statesville, North Carolina, to fill the last group's shoes and to carry on the Oak Ridge name. This talented, young, more traditional gospel quartet included Joe Allred on tenor, Bob Weber on bass, and Pat Patterson on baritone. Fowler resumed his customary lead part but hired Billy Joe Campbell, the fourth member of the original Calvary Quartet, to accompany the new group on guitar and, during Fowler's absence, sing baritone while Patterson switched to the lead part.[80]

This revamped version of the Oak Ridge Quartet, sometimes referred to by Fowler and their fans as the Oak Ridge Boys, continued to draw heavily from country music. Like the Chuck Wagon Gang before them, their preferred backup came from the guitar. They used only Campbell's guitar accompaniment for their performances on WSM radio in early 1950. Even after adding piano player Bobby Whitfield in May 1950, guitars remained an important part of their concert presence. On one swing through Tennessee in 1951, Fowler hired a young guitar player named Glen Allred to replace Campbell, who had recently left the group. Influenced heavily by country guitarist Merle Travis, the sixteen-year-old Allred played lead guitar and sang on the occasions when Fowler's schedule forced him to miss concerts. Years later, Allred remembered that Fowler routinely joined the group only on weekends and that, during the week, he would—like Campbell before him—pick up the baritone part while Patterson sang lead.[81]

During the 1950s, the Oaks continued to endure frequent personnel changes. When the quartet let young Glen Allred go in late 1952, Bob Prather assumed the baritone part. Johnny New returned as the group's tenor but was then replaced by Joe Allred, the man he had himself replaced less than a year earlier. During the first months of 1953, Patterson's spot was taken by lead singer Calvin Newton; shortly thereafter, Joe Allred left again, this time replaced by veteran quartet tenor Cat Freeman. Frequent turnover was an obstacle in the path of many gospel quartets, but for a group as young as the Oaks such constant change threatened extinction.

Given his heavy involvement in promotions, Fowler eventually tired of managing and, in 1952, agreed to sell the group to Bob Weber. In exchange for the interest on a $10,000 loan, Weber took ownership of the group, and the Oak Ridge Quartet set out to make its own future.[82] Within a few years, however, the group had folded. Even so, by the end of 1956, Fowler had suddenly re-emerged as a key player in the fortunes of the Oak Ridge Quartet. Hiring a talented young singer named E. Smith "Smitty" Gatlin to serve as manager, Fowler essentially reclaimed the group name. In January 1957, another set of faces hit the road as the reorganized Oak Ridge Quartet. At that point, the group was comprised of Gatlin on lead, Ronnie Page on baritone, Hobart Evans on tenor, and Bill Smith on bass. Powell Hassell joined the group on piano as the quartet moved toward more traditional accompaniment under Gatlin's direction.[83]

In 1958, Fowler once again "sold" the Oak Ridge Quartet, this time to Smitty Gatlin and the other members in exchange for forgiveness on a debt of several thousand dollars owed to the group for recent concert appearances. By the early 1960s, the quartet, still under Gatlin's direction and having endured several lean years, finally began to prosper—primarily under the name Oak Ridge Boys. The 1960 combination became one of the best known, with Gatlin singing lead, Willie Wynn singing tenor, Ronnie Page singing baritone, and Herman Harper singing bass. Tommy Fairchild accompanied the group on piano.[84]

With the Oaks' success and increased popularity as "Boys" rather than "Quartet," Fowler emerged again at the heart of a controversy over ownership of the group's name. Hoping to capitalize on his previous association, he organized a new quartet and billed the members as the "Oak Ridge Quartet." When efforts to force Fowler to stop using the name failed, Gatlin and the Oaks filed suit on October 5, 1964. The following year, the case was ultimately settled in the group's favor and Fowler relinquished any right to use the name or any variation in the future.[85] Shortly after the case was cleared up, Gatlin took a position as a minister of music in Dallas, Texas, turning his share of the group over to the other singers, Harper, Wynn, and Bill Golden. The trio hired a new partner, Duane Allen, lead singer for the Prophets Quartet, and the Oaks continued to headline gospel concerts for another decade. Despite incessant controversy throughout the group's history, the Oak Ridge Boys survived and in the late 1960s were one of the premier groups in gospel music.[86]

HOMELAND HARMONY

Formed in the 1930s as part of the Church of God Bible Training School ministry, the Homeland Harmony Quartet underwent a major reorganization after the war. By 1942, the group consisted of Tennessee Music and Printing chief Otis McCoy on lead, James McCoy on baritone, B. C. Robinson on bass, and young Connor Brandon Hall on the tenor part. Within the next few years, Hall, a devoted singer with strong ties to the Church of God, acquired use of the name, moved the group to Atlanta, and put together a collection of voices that ranked as one of the top quartets of the next decade. Over the years, Hall sang tenor but made other frequent personnel changes. Through most of the 1950s, James McCoy continued to sing baritone for the group while a list of talented singers, including Paul Stringfellow, Wayne Groce, Jim Cole, and Bob Shaw, anchored the lead part. Likewise, an impressive string of bass singers served Hall's quartet, including Jim Waits, Aycel Soward, George Younce, and Rex Nelon. Hall and the Homeland Harmony also alternated piano players frequently. Among those playing for the group from 1942 to 1958 were Hovie Lister, Lee Roy Abernathy, Reece "Rocket" Crockett, Wally Varner, Jack Clark, and Livy "Lightnin'" Freeman.[87] The group sang regularly on Atlanta's WAGA radio, with each member earning as much as $75 apiece for a week's work of three live programs daily.[88] By the mid-1950s, the group also ventured into the regional television market with more than fifty stations carrying the Atlanta-based show.[89]

SUNSHINE BOYS

Organized around 1939 as a country-and-western group performing on WMAZ in Macon, Georgia, the Sunshine Boys became one of the best-known gospel groups in the 1940s and 1950s through a unique combination of talent and good fortune. Original personnel included John O. "Tennessee" Smith, singing tenor and playing mandolin, fiddle, and lead guitar; his brother A. L. "Smitty" Smith, singing lead and playing rhythm guitar; Milton "Ace" Richman, singing bass and playing bass fiddle; and Pat Patterson, singing baritone and playing the accordion. In 1941, this quartet of talented musicians moved from Macon to Atlanta, where they performed regularly on WAGA. Patterson was drafted in early 1942 and replaced by a young Atlanta piano player and singer named Eddie Wallace. With the addition of Wallace, the group expanded its repertoire to include gospel numbers accompanied by keyboard. Over the next three years, they worked alternately on Atlanta radio stations WAGA and WSB and became a part of the popular *WSB Barn Dance* aired each Saturday night.[90]

The versatility of the group proved valuable as the Sunshine Boys struggled to advance their career during the war years. At WAGA, they actually appeared on the air as two separate groups—providing back-to-back programs without the audience suspecting their identity. At 12:30 A.M. daily, the quartet sang a fifteen-minute set as the Light Crust Doughboys, sponsored by the local Light Crust Flour concern. The set featured western swing numbers accompanied by the two Smith brothers and Richman on strings. Taking only a thirty-second break to adjust the set, the four men then launched into the 12:45 program as the Sunshine Boys, with Wallace on keyboard and the entire repertoire consisting of standard gospel quartet songs. Wallace later recalled that the charade continued for three years "and nobody around Atlanta ever knew it was the same group."[91]

In local concert appearances, the quartet billed itself as the Sunshine Boys and concentrated on a program that, while more diverse than those of other gospel quartets, drew its strength from the four-part-harmony gospel tunes. Off the concert tour, however, the Sunshine Boys were anything but traditional. Late in 1945, the quartet traveled to California, where they auditioned and received a contract with PRC-Eagle-Lion to appear in a series of western films starring Eddie Dean and Lash Larue. Over the next seven years, they appeared in as many as two dozen films, including a series of Durango Kid westerns produced by Columbia Studios, in which they played roles opposite film stars Charles Starrett and Smiley Burnette. Singing occasional western tunes and spirituals, the Sunshine Boys forced a new awareness of the talent in the gospel quartet industry and forged valuable links that allowed them on occasion to cross over and sing popular secular material.[92]

Eventually the Sunshine Boys' playing in different fields led to a major personnel change. The Smith brothers, wanting to further their careers in the more mainstream country market, left the group in mid-1949 to form their own duo, the Smith Brothers. Richman and Wallace, content to continue playing gospel music with occasional forays into secular music, hired tenor singer Fred Daniel and an impressive young bass named J. D. Sumner to fill the vacant spots. To build a following for the revamped quartet, the four men took a job at WWVA radio in Wheeling, West Virginia, where they performed twice a day on their own program in addition to appearing as part of the famed Saturday night *WWVA Jamboree* on weekends. This foursome continued to make occasional trips to Hollywood for film appearances and recorded 78s for Bullet, Decca, and several other labels. In 1951, they backed up country star Red Foley on the recording of Thomas Dorsey's "Peace in the Valley." The song was quickly catapulted into one of the best-known and best-selling gospel songs of all time. After Sumner's decision to leave the group and join the Blackwood Brothers in the summer of 1954, the group replaced him with Johnny Atkinson and, two years later, with veteran bass singer Burl Strevel.[93]

BLUE RIDGE QUARTET

One of the popular combinations to emerge in the postwar period was the Blue Ridge Quartet. In 1946, Elmo Fagg, a baritone singer with the Lone Star Quartet, a group featured on Raleigh's WPTF, joined a recently organized group sent by the new Stamps Quartet Music Company to do radio work in Burlington, North Carolina. As the group's manager and lead singer two years later, he moved to Spartanburg, South Carolina, where he reorganized the quartet to appear regularly on WSPA radio. From that location, the Blue Ridge Quartet became well known across the South, performing alongside other major gospel groups for the next three decades. By the mid-1950s, the group—now independent of the Stamps Quartet organization—featured Fagg's lead vocals along-side tenor singer Ed Sprouse, bass singer Burl Strevel, and a baritone accompanist named Kenny Gates. As did other quartets, the Blue Ridge endured frequent personnel changes yet remained one of the premier quartets in the southern market through the mid-1960s.[94]

IMPERIAL SUGAR QUARTET

Another quartet that took advantage of the increased interest in radio advertising was the Imperial Sugar Quartet. Organized by Marion Snider, the former pianist for the V. O. Stamps Old Original Quartet, the Blackwood Brothers, and the Rangers, the group launched a successful career in 1946, shortly after Snider's release from the navy. Original personnel were George Moffett on the lead part, Charles Speed on tenor, Dudley Hughes on baritone, and Floyd Gray on bass. Snider personally recruited the group and had them rehearse until a half dozen songs could be performed flawlessly. He then called an old friend who worked as program director for WFAA radio in Dallas.

Unbeknownst to Snider, his audition for the radio spot caught the ear of representatives from the Tracy-Locke Advertising Agency, which was in charge of a program for advertising the Imperial Sugar Company. In a stroke of good fortune, the chance encounter catapulted the quartet into a final audition, after which they were chosen to perform live on WFAA radio three times a week in a program broadcast across a growing network of stations linked as the Texas Quality Network. Since the quartet had not yet chosen a name, they became the Imperial Sugar Quartet. For the next nine years, with Snider on piano and serving as manager, the group traveled across the Southwest, expanding their reputation on the concert circuit as well as through 78 rpm recordings. Like other successful groups of the period, they mixed occasional secular songs into their radio repertoire. They also had the good fortune of relatively few personnel changes. By 1949, Homer Tankersley had replaced Moffett on the lead part, and, a few years later, Jake Baumgardner replaced Hughes on baritone.[95]

PALMETTO STATE QUARTET

The Palmetto State Quartet also emerged in 1946. Operating out of Greenville, South Carolina, the quartet, by the late 1950s, was comprised of Jack Bagwell on lead, Jack Pittman singing baritone, Claude Hunter singing tenor, and Ken Turner singing bass. Jamie Dill provided piano accompaniment. Officially a part-time group, Palmetto State demonstrated how a regional quartet dedicated to regular weekend performances could build a loyal following. The quartet ultimately played an influential role in southern singing circles—developing a unique harmonic style that would persist for the remainder of the century.[96]

THE PROLIFERATION OF MALE QUARTETS

An amazing number of gospel quartets sprang up in the South during the 1950s. Some lasted only a few years; others endured to occupy a prominent place on the state and local level if not in national circles. Veteran bass singer Jimmy Jones organized and managed the short-lived Deep South Quartet in Atlanta from 1954 to 1957.[97] More enduring were the Stamps-Baxter Melody Boys from Little Rock, Arkansas. Successful on local KARK radio even before the outbreak of World War II, the quartet members—led by seasoned pianist Joseph "Smilin' Joe" Roper—built a name for themselves in the Midwest. As the 1940s drew to a close, the Melody Boys ended their formal affiliation with the Stamps-Baxter Music Company and became popularly known as Joe Roper and the Melody Boys Quartet. With continued radio exposure and a successful stint on early Little Rock television, the group laid a foundation that would keep them before the public for the remainder of the century. After Roper's departure in 1960, the group—now simply the Melody Boys Quartet—retained strong fan appeal in part through the efforts of longtime bass singer Gerald Williams.[98]

Equally enduring were the Harmoneers, organized around 1943 by Fred C. Maples in Knoxville, Tennessee. During the decade after the war, the group rose to prominence with a lineup that first featured Maples on baritone, Bobby Strickland on tenor, Erman Slater on lead, and Aycel Soward on bass. A later famous configuration of the quartet included Maples on baritone, "Happy" Edwards on tenor, Bob Crews on lead, and Seals "Low Note" Hilton on bass. Charles Key played piano for the Harmoneers throughout their tenure in gospel music and occasionally joined members on vocal numbers. The Harmoneers recorded for RCA Victor and sang on radio station WNOX, and later on WROL, on a program sponsored by Scalf's Indian River Medicine. Traveling widely across the South, the group remained one of the most popular performing quartets throughout the 1950s.[99]

Elsewhere, former Harmoneers and Statesmen tenor Bobby Strickland formed the Crusaders and operated the new quartet out of Birmingham, Alabama, from 1950 to 1953. Unfortunately, the talented Strickland perished in an automobile accident in September 1953 while en route to a sing in Chattanooga, Tennessee. Unable to overcome the tragedy, the rest of the group disbanded shortly thereafter, although several of the members—Buddy Parker, Herschel Wooten, and Bill Hefner—reunited as components of the Harvesters Quartet, singing at WBT radio in Charlotte, North Carolina.[100] Also popular in the Charlotte area was Arthur Smith and the Crossroads Quartet. Smith, a proficient songwriter and musician, formed a group in the late 1950s comprised of his brothers Ralph and Sonny, along with Tommy Faile and Lois Atkins. Radio and television appearances kept the group before the public for more than two decades.[101]

During the heyday of the 1950s, gospel singers hoped and prayed for some sequence of events that would help set them and their associates apart from the growing number of quartets. In this highly competitive atmosphere, the chance for success hinged on many factors beyond the creation of a harmonic blend. Connections with promoters, a lucky break with a powerful radio station, friendship with other successful groups— these circumstances oftentimes provided the crucial elements behind success. Personalities also played a key role in the creation and dissolution of quartets. Members would leave a group and form another, hoping for the elusive success that always seemed right around the corner.

The Sunny South Quartet, initially formed in Tampa, Florida, in 1941 by Horace Floyd, Mosie Lister, Lee Kitchens, Clyde Cain, and R. D. Ginnett, lasted only a few years, but the individual members spawned two other significant groups.[102] After disbanding during the war years, Floyd, Lister, and Kitchens reorganized the group in early 1946. Young James S. Wetherington replaced Cain on the bass part, and Quentin Hicks replaced Ginnett as pianist. In late 1946, Wetherington, Kitchens, and Lister left the group to form the Melody Masters. After a year of barely surviving, the new group ended up on the staff of KFAB in Lincoln, Nebraska—now comprised of Wetherington, along with Cat Freeman, Jake Hess, Alvin Toodle, and Wally Varner. Although the Melody Masters lasted only another year or so, the former members persevered. Wetherington, Hess, and Freeman played primary roles in the success of the Statesmen Quartet, and Varner served in the late 1950s and early 1960s as pianist for the Blackwood Brothers.[103]

Another spin-off of the Sunny South was the Rebels Quartet, whose roots illustrate the volatile nature of competitive quartet life. In late 1946,

Horace Floyd was faced with rebuilding the Sunny South Quartet by hiring three new singers. He chose Stacy Selph to sing lead, Joe Thomas to sing baritone, and young J. D. Sumner to sing bass. Nevertheless, personnel changes continued as all the men in the group struggled to make a living. Within a couple of years, Floyd left the Tampa area and reorganized his group in Orlando. Sumner took a remnant of the old quartet and organized the Dixie Lily Harmoneers, assuming the former quartet's affiliation with Tampa's WFLA. Joined by Thomas on lead, he hired tenor Horace Parrish and baritone John Mathews to round out the group.[104] After Sumner left to join the Sunshine Boys early in 1949, Lee Kitchens, the former Sunny South and Melody Masters member, joined Mathews, Parrish, bass singer Jim Waits, and pianist Jimmy Taylor to form the Rebels Quartet. When Kitchens and Waits left in the mid-1950s, two men whose futures would also be influential in the quartet business replaced them. Jim Hamill's lead vocals anchored the group for most of the late 1950s, alongside the smooth bass voice of London Parris. Headquartered in Tampa, Florida, the Rebels remained a top group throughout the 1960s, traveling mainly in the Deep South states, where, as their name suggested, they were best known.[105]

FLORIDA BOYS

Among the male quartets making a name in the 1950s, none would be more influential than the Florida Boys. Originally known as the Gospel Melody Quartet, the group was the brainchild of Jesse Gillis "J. G." Whitfield of Pensacola, Florida. After leaving the Army Air Corps shortly after the conclusion of World War II, Whitfield, who had grown up attending Florida singing conventions and singing with a local quartet known as the Happy Hitters, organized the Gospel Melody "just because we liked to sing."[106] The group made the rounds of nearby convention singings and concerts but continued to struggle until Whitfield's success in the local grocery business gave him the resources to bankroll the group and advertise more heavily. Eventually, Whitfield would own "a chain of food stores, three drug stores, a department store, a trading stamp company, a mail order merchandise house and a promotion company."[107] Along the way, he became a primary figure in the expansion of gospel music in the South.[108]

Whitfield's earliest Gospel Melody Quartet was comprised of Roy Howard, a close friend and fellow former Happy Hitter, singing lead; Guy Dodd singing tenor; and Edward Singletary singing baritone. In addition to managing the group, Whitfield sang bass. A young man named "Tiny" Merrell played piano for the group. In late 1951, after singing at a local Pensacola radio station, Howard suffered a heart attack and died. Though shaken, Whitfield persevered, reorganizing the quartet with young men experienced in the gospel quartet industry. In 1952, he hired Glen Allred, the former guitar player for Wally Fowler's Oak Ridge Quartet. In addition to providing guitar accompaniment to the Gospel Melody, Allred contributed his smooth baritone voice on vocals. The following year, Whitfield hired Les Beasley, formerly with the McManus Trio from Texas, to sing lead. By 1954, Buddy Mears was singing tenor and Emory Parker had taken over as group pianist. It was this group that also began promoting itself by another name. The inspiration behind the name Florida Boys was promoter Wally Fowler, who had begun to use the quartet in some of his concerts. Fowler, who opposed the name Gospel Melody because he felt it was not distinctive enough, began billing the quartet as "the boys from Florida, who have sand in their shoes and a song in their heart," tying them to their Pensacola base."[109] Whitfield ultimately accepted the name and abruptly informed the rest of the group at a morning rehearsal in 1954: "Fellows, this morning we're the Florida Boys."[110]

The Florida Boys profited from Fowler's support as well as Whitfield's willingness to begin local promotions on his own. As his business interests became lucrative, the energetic bass singer willingly contributed more of his capital to ensure his group's success. The quartet also benefited from unfailing stability. After hiring Derrell Stewart to replace Livy Freeman at the piano in 1955, the nucleus of the quartet was set. Beasley, Allred, and Stewart were destined to remain Florida Boys for more than four decades. Ironically, Whitfield would not remain a part of that core, although his relationship with the Florida Boys as an active promoter and friend endured. Having been widowed tragically in the early 1950s, he decided to come off the road in 1958, shortly after his second marriage. With this additional commitment, he found it difficult to balance his expanding business interests and continue full-time quartet travel. Beasley took over as manager, and, as the new decade dawned, the group continued as one of the top traveling quartets in the South.[111]

KINGSMEN

Another up-and-coming group of the mid-1950s was the Kingsmen Quartet of Asheville, North Carolina. Formed by three McKinney

Professional Quartets

brothers—Lewis on lead, Raymond on baritone, and Reece on bass—the original Kingsmen also included tenor singer Charles Colyer and pianist Charles Matthews. By the early 1960s, the group was under the control of Eldridge Fox, a talented pianist, singer, promoter, and songwriter. Through Fox's leadership and the group's irrepressible stage presence and showmanship, the men gradually emerged from the shadows of part-time service to become one of the industry's leading quartets. With veteran lead singer Jim Hamill joining the group in 1971, Fox was able to build a group that, by the late 1970s, featured Johnny Parrack on tenor, Hamill on lead, Fox on baritone, and Ray Dean Reese on bass.[112]

COURIERS

Members of the Couriers, one of the most unique groups to emerge in the 1950s, began their singing careers on the campus of the Assemblies of God Central Bible Institute in Springfield, Missouri. After a 1955 concert by the Blackwood Brothers held at the local Shrine Mosque, as many as eight student groups began singing on campus and in area churches. One of those groups formed by young men studying for the ministry took the name Couriers to signify their role as messengers of the gospel message.[113]

Within a couple of years, the Couriers Quartet had solidified its personnel with Neil Enloe singing lead; Duane Nicholson, tenor; Don Baldwin, baritone; and Dave Kyllonen, bass. Fellow student Eddie Reece served as group accompanist. Finding some success with weekend travel, the youngsters persevered, even recording a tape at the school, mailing it off to have inexpensive records pressed, and then hand-making their own album jackets. In 1958, the five decided to leave Central Bible Institute to test their fortunes in the world of professional gospel quartet music.[114]

Lacking the stage presence of the better-known quartets and virtually unknown in the strong southern market, the Couriers opted for a unique location. Neil Enloe recalled that group members discussed their predicament. "We were so bad and we knew it . . . so we said, 'Let's settle somewhere where the people haven't heard much and they don't know the difference.'"[115] Choosing western Pennsylvania as an area where they would face no major competition, the boys capitalized on a network of Assemblies of God contacts that they had cultivated during their college years. They settled in Harrisburg in 1958 and, after a successful audition, secured an unpaid position singing weekly on radio station WCMB. The Sunday morning program provided the group with prime exposure to local churches and, before long, they found themselves busy in a market where few had heard the gospel quartet style. Over the next twelve years, the Couriers continued the weekly program on WCMB and eventually recorded the programs for play on ten other stations in the Northeast.[116]

The Couriers' success sprang from more than the lack of immediate competition in the gospel music marketplace. Harrisburg, Pennsylvania, was a strategic location in that the group did not have to travel great distances to hold concerts in the major population centers of the Northeast and Midwest. In addition, the group's Bible college background and strong devotion to church ministry provided an edge over other quartets that, by the 1950s, had become more and more dependent on community- rather than church-based concerts. With the number of conservative evangelical churches growing at an unprecedented pace during the decades following the Second World War, the Couriers quite naturally were ready to respond with a presentation that mixed gospel preaching and testimony alongside traditional quartet music. The approach proved especially effective in northern churches unfamiliar with the nuances of gospel quartet concerts in the South.[117] Their insecurities aside, the group's members were talented performers who in time established their own unique style within the gospel quartet world. Though never extremely popular or well known in the South, by the early 1960s, the Couriers were themselves sponsoring and promoting concerts in Pennsylvania and surrounding states that brought "outsiders" from the larger southern market into a whole new arena for gospel quartet music. Likewise, they became one of the first southern gospel groups to travel extensively in Canada, where they found a remarkably warm reception.[118]

By the early 1960s, success loomed large for a number of male southern gospel quartets. For most groups, the work was hard and the hours long. Still, the financial clout and professional quality of the Blackwoods and Statesmen proved that, with enough talent and perseverance, a gospel group might break through the ranks to enjoy genuine acceptance and celebrity. At the same time, however, a cadre of innovative southern singers and songwriters sought success through a slightly different avenue. Frequently drawing on the mixed-voice tradition of the Speers, LeFevres, and Carters, these gospel singers hoped to prove that there was more than one way to fulfill the dream.

The Segos, early 1960s. Left to right: James Sego (lead), unidentified member (piano), Naomi Sego (alto), Lamar Sego (bass), and W. R. Sego (baritone). Courtesy Southern Gospel Music Hall of Fame and Museum, Sevierville, Tenn.

The Sons of Song, late 1950s. Left to right: Don Butler (baritone), Calvin Newton (tenor), and Bob Robinson (lead). Courtesy Southern Gospel Music Hall of Fame and Museum, Sevierville, Tenn.

Wendy Bagwell and the Sunliters, ca. 1960. Left to right: *Jerri Morrison (alto), Wendy Bagwell (baritone), and Jan Buckner (soprano). Courtesy Southern Gospel Music Hall of Fame and Museum, Sevierville, Tenn.*

The Weatherfords on the cover of The Answer, *a publication of Rex Humbard Ministries and the Cathedral of Tomorrow, in Akron, Ohio, ca. 1960. Left to right: Glen Payne (lead), Henry Slaughter (piano), Lily Fern Weatherford (alto), Earl Weatherford (baritone), and Armond Morales (bass). Courtesy of* Singing News *magazine, Boone, N.C.*

The Couriers, Harrisburg, Pennsylvania, early 1960s. Clockwise from bottom left: *Neil Enloe (lead), Duane Nicholson (tenor), Dave Kyllonen (bass), and Don Baldwin (baritone). Courtesy Southern Gospel Music Hall of Fame and Museum, Sevierville, Tenn.*

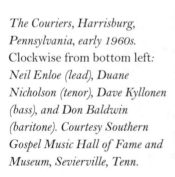

The Dixie Echoes, Pensacola, Florida, ca. 1970. Left to right: *Dale Shelnut (lead), Ken Turner (bass), Randy Shelnut (guitar), Joe Whitfield (baritone), Larry Ford (tenor), and Sue Whitfield (piano). Courtesy Southern Gospel Music Hall of Fame and Museum, Sevierville, Tenn.*

The Florida Boys on the set of The Gospel Song Shop, *ca. 1962.* Left to right: *Coy Cook (tenor), Glen Allred (baritone), Billy Todd (bass), Derrell Stewart (piano), J. G. Whitfield (promoter), and Les Beasley (lead). Courtesy Southern Gospel Music Hall of Fame and Museum, Sevierville, Tenn.*

The regular cast of The Gospel Singing Caravan, *ca. 1963. Pictured are members of the LeFevres, the Blue Ridge Quartet, the Prophets, and the Johnson Sisters. Courtesy Southern Gospel Music Hall of Fame and Museum, Sevierville, Tenn.*

The regular cast of The Gospel Singing Jubilee, *ca. 1967. Pictured are members of the Florida Boys, the Dixie Echoes, the Happy Goodmans, and the Blackwood Singers. Courtesy Southern Gospel Music Hall of Fame and Museum, Sevierville, Tenn.*

The LeFevres and their new bus, 1963. Left to right: *Paul Hughs (bus driver), Alphus LeFevre (tenor), Jimmy Jones (baritone), Urias LeFevre (lead), Eva Mae LeFevre (piano/vocals), Pierce LeFevre (guitar/trumpet/vocals), and Rex Nelon (bass). Courtesy Southern Gospel Music Hall of Fame and Museum, Sevierville, Tenn.*

The Klaudt Indian Family on the set of Bob Poole's Gospel Favorites, *Greenville, South Carolina, mid-1960s.* Left to right: *Bob Poole, Vernon Klaudt (bass), Melvin Klaudt (tenor), Betty Klaudt (piano), Ken Klaudt (lead), Lillian "Mom" Klaudt (alto), and Raymond Klaudt (baritone). Courtesy Southern Gospel Music Hall of Fame and Museum, Sevierville, Tenn.*

The Kingsmen and their band, mid-1970s. At microphones, left to right: *Johnny Parrack (tenor), Jim Hamill (lead), Eldridge Fox (baritone), and Ray Dean Reese (bass). Courtesy of* Singing News *magazine, Boone, N.C.*

The Imperials, 1973.
Left to right: *Terry Blackwood (lead), Armond Morales (bass), Joe Moscheo (piano), Sherman Andrus (baritone), and Jim Murray (tenor). Courtesy of* Singing News *magazine, Boone, N.C.*

The Inspirations, ca. 1970. Left to right: *Archie Watkins (tenor), Ronnie Hutchins (lead), Eddie Dietz (baritone), Marlin Shubert (bass), and Martin Cook (piano). Courtesy of* Singing News *magazine, Boone, N.C.*

The Hinsons, early 1980s. Left to right: *Yvonne Hinson Johnson, Ronny Hinson, Kenny Hinson, and Eric Hinson. Courtesy of* Singing News *magazine, Boone, N.C.*

*Jerry Goff, "Mr. Gospel Trumpet,"
ca. 1980. Courtesy Southern Gospel
Music Hall of Fame and Museum,
Sevierville, Tenn.*

*Jerry Goff and the Thrasher Brothers
from the* America Sings *television
program, pictured at Meramec Caverns,
late 1960s.* Left to right: *Jerry Goff,
Jim Thrasher (lead), Ellis "Moose"
Hill (bass), Buddy Thrasher (baritone),
Joe Thrasher (tenor), and Randy
McDaniel (piano). Courtesy Southern
Gospel Music Hall of Fame and
Museum, Sevierville, Tenn.*

Bill Gaither Trio, ca. 1970. Left to right: *Danny Gaither (baritone/tenor), Gloria Gaither (alto), and Bill Gaither (lead). Courtesy of* Singing News *magazine, Boone, N.C.*

The Downings, mid-1970s. Left to right, standing: *Fred Satterfield, Ann Downing, Joy Dyson, Paul Downing, Dony McGuire, and Mack Peters. Courtesy of* Singing News *magazine, Boone, N.C.*

The Dixie Melody Boys, early 1970s. Left to right, standing: *Delmar Tillman (baritone), Jerry Dunbar (bass guitar), Ed O'Neal (bass), and John Jarman (lead).* Left to right, kneeling: *Everett Harper (piano) and Charles Forehand (tenor). Courtesy of* Singing News *magazine, Boone, N.C.*

Teddy Huffam and the Gems, early 1980s. Left to right, standing: *Therlow Foy, Morgan Stevenson, Connie Oliver, and Timothy Echols;* left to right, seated: *Robert Smith, Teddy Huffam, and Phillip Thomas. Courtesy of* Singing News *magazine, Boone, N.C.*

*J. D. Sumner and the Stamps,
1972.* Left to right,
standing: *Donnie Sumner
(baritone) and J. D. Sumner
(bass);* left to right, seated:
*Ed Enoch (lead), Richard
Sterben (bass), and Bill Baize
(tenor).* Courtesy of Singing
News *magazine, Boone, N.C.*

The Speer Family, late 1960s.
Left to right: *Susan Speer,
Sue Chenault, Bob Johnson,
Jeanne Johnson, Ben Speer,
Harold Lane, and Brock
Speer.* Courtesy of Singing
News *magazine, Boone, N.C.*

The Rambos in concert, ca. 1970. At microphones, left to right: *Buck Rambo (baritone), Reba Rambo (soprano), and* Dottie *Rambo (alto). Courtesy of* Singing News *magazine, Boone, N.C.*

The Rex Nelon Singers, 1977. Left to right: *Greg Cothran, Janet Paschal (soprano), Rodney Swain (lead), Kelly Nelon (alto), Rex Nelon (bass), Lamar Newton (piano), and Robbie Willis (drums). Courtesy of* Singing News *magazine, Boone, N.C.*

*Nashville, Tennessee, September 28, 1992, and
Durham, North Carolina, August 12, 1996*

"When I hear your music, I hear elements of white gospel and elements of black gospel. Is that by design?" I ask Charles Johnson. He pauses and then replies, "If you hear that, then you have a good ear because that's exactly what I try to do. I consciously mix the two." Thus begins my first meeting with the most successful black artist in southern gospel. But Charles, who entered the southern gospel field only eight years ago, in 1984, is not new to gospel music. For more than two decades, he sang with the Nightingales, a prominent black gospel quartet. Now he sings southern gospel and believes that there is room for expanding the market, for reaching both white and black Americans with all that is good about gospel music. "I was led to do it," he tells me with obvious conviction in his voice. For too long, he says, the music has reflected the segregation of Sunday mornings. Now he hopes to encourage others to celebrate the music that speaks to the religious needs of everyone, regardless of skin color.

It's a few years later, I am spending a day with Charles—at his home in Durham and in the home of his friend Joseph Wallace, a fifty-year veteran of the Nightingales—still singing and still good friends with his old buddy Charles. As we reminisce, I ask both men about the dual roots of American gospel music. Charles becomes serious, and Joe gets excited because he feels the sermon coming on. "This thing's been called black gospel," Charles begins. "They call it white gospel. Gospel don't have no color to it. . . . This is programmed from man. . . . Man formats his radio station to play white gospel or man formats his station to play what they call black gospel. . . . And a black person will turn over on the black station and listen to gospel . . . and a white person will turn over here because a white person is singing. And I want to know, 'Did God die for everybody?' Jesus Christ came back and won on the cross and He died for the sins of the world. And when Jesus comes back, He's coming back after the ones that accept Him regardless of what color they are. Now how am I going to put a tag on the gospel of God—God's Gospel? It don't have a color."

You're right, Charles. It's about the music and it's about the message. It always has been.

7
THE GOLDEN AGE CHALLENGE: UNCONVENTIONAL GROUPS AND SONGWRITERS

As the Blackwood Brothers and the Statesmen carried southern gospel to new heights of popularity in the 1950s, innovative sounds and arrangements erupted throughout much of the gospel quartet world. For every group that sought success through imitation, another seemed to emerge dedicated to winning acceptance by defining a new niche in the gospel music marketplace. Spurred on by songwriters willing to experiment with new instrumentation and popular music styling, these performers helped expand the boundaries of southern gospel and collectively drew a host of new fans into its arena.

The decade and a half after the conclusion of World War II witnessed the emergence of more mixed ensembles onto the gospel music circuit. In the prewar era, only a handful of professional groups included both male and female singers, though, through perseverance, those groups had achieved success. The LeFevres, the Speers, and the Chuck Wagon Gang had all survived despite a strong penchant within the industry for traditional four-part-harmony male quartet singing. Now, other groups began to make a similar statement within the gospel music world. In the same way that the war had opened the industrial marketplace to women through the absence of male employees drafted into service, it had opened gospel quartet singing to more female musicians and singers. Even the Blackwood Brothers experimented with a short-term husband-and-wife replacement team that included LaVera Humphries on the piano.[1]

One of the earliest mixed groups to find success after the war was the Weatherford Quartet, originally of Southern California. Earl Weatherford, a diehard for the traditional four-part-harmony male quartet sound, married Lily Fern Goble, the daughter of a Church of the Nazarene minister, in 1945. For several years after their marriage, Weatherford's wife filled in on the tenor part whenever his part-time group was short-handed. By the end of 1948, with the group sponsored by the Stamps Quartet Music Company, Lily Fern's beautiful alto voice had convinced her husband that she should remain a regular member.[2]

In 1949, the Weatherfords became a full-time quartet and moved to Fort Wayne, Indiana, where they worked on the staff of WOWO singing on a daily gospel program. In the mid-1950s, they relocated to Akron, Ohio, where the personnel became staff members at the Reverend Rex Humbard's Cathedral of Tomorrow. During one period of the Akron years, the quartet, consisting of Lily Fern Weatherford on alto, Glen Payne on lead, Earl Weatherford on baritone, and Armond Morales on bass, became one of the smoothest-sounding gospel quartets of all time. Accompanied on piano by Henry Slaughter, the group sang in a style different from many other quartets of the era and enjoyed the exposure of Humbard's weekly radio and television programs. Worshipful and always concentrating on blend, the group built a name that made them particularly popular in church concerts. When the Weatherfords left Akron in 1963 to return to regular touring, they became one of the groups that would pave the way for the future of southern gospel as a vehicle for evangelistic ministry.[3]

SEGOS

Another male quartet that marked its rise to success with the inclusion of a talented woman was the Segos. The first Sego family quartet was established in Macon, Georgia, in 1946 when brothers James, W. R., and Lamar Sego joined with bass singer Charlie Norris Jr. to sing locally on a part-time basis. Norris's mother played piano for the original group. Over the next few years, a number of bass singers and pianists joined the three Segos as they sought to carve out a place in the small local market. The Sego Brothers' country styling landed them frequent appearances on Macon's WMAZ-TV on the *Uncle Ned and His Hayloft Jamboree* program. Its exposure across middle Georgia put the group in contact with gospel music promoters, and, by the early 1950s, the Segos appeared at a handful of recognized concert venues across the South.[4]

After a brief period of inactivity in the mid-1950s, the group re-appeared in 1958—this time with the three brothers singing alongside James's talented wife, Naomi. Though James Sego initially doubted the wisdom of including a female singer in the group, Naomi's strong voice gave the quartet a quality it had lacked in earlier years, and soon the group was traveling simply as the Sego Brothers and Naomi. Largely on the strength of the song "Sorry, I Never Knew You," released in 1962, the group suddenly jumped to the top of the gospel music industry, with requests for personal appearances and record sales thought impossible just a few years earlier. A somber ballad, the song became a jukebox stan-dard at truck stops across the South. Sales of the 45 of the song, as well as album sales made it one of the first legitimate hits by a gospel music group. After this song's success, the Segos moved into full-time status.[5]

LESTERS

The Singing Lester Family had also found success by the 1950s. Origi-nating as a family trio in the early 1930s, the group revolved around the music ministry of Harvey and Opal Lester and their young son Her-schel. From their base in St. Louis, the Lesters ran a thriving music busi-ness, including a downtown music shop that offered shape-note singing schools to students during the week. By the late 1940s, the family trio had expanded to a quartet that included Herschel's wife, Mary Alene. Family members played a variety of musical instruments and, as Her-schel and Alene Lester's children grew up, each became a part of the singing family. With profitable ventures into St. Louis radio and tele-vision in the late 1950s, the family charted a course for southern gospel in the Midwest—launching their own annual homecoming event inside the scenic Meramec Caverns near Stanton, Missouri, in 1968.[6]

HAPPY GOODMANS

From northern Alabama came the Goodman Family, a collection of brothers and sisters that emerged from poverty on the rural outskirts of Birmingham to become a major force in the gospel music industry by the 1960s. By the late 1940s, the group included Howard Goodman, who managed the group and served as pianist, and his younger brothers, Sam, Charles ("Rusty"), and Bobby, and his sisters, Ruth, Eloise, Stella, and Gussie Mae. When Howard Goodman married Vestal Freeman, the sister of veteran tenor singer Cat Freeman, in late 1949, he added yet another talented singer to the family. Still, the Goodmans remained in relative obscurity in the larger gospel music world until the mid-1960s, when a new combination, consisting of Howard, Vestal, Rusty, and Sam singing, and various other family members on instruments, caught the attention of southern gospel fans. Largely through the promotion of television, the group—at this point known as the Happy Goodmans— reached new heights of success with a string of hits and record sales that placed them at the pinnacle of the industry. Over the next two decades, appearances on syndicated gospel music programs and on Jim and Tammy Faye Bakker's PTL network would make the Goodmans some of the most recognized faces in the world of gospel music.[7]

LEWIS FAMILY

Another innovative group emerging in gospel music during the 1950s comprised a talented assortment of family members from Lincolnton, Georgia. The creation of James Roy "Pop" Lewis, an avid bluegrass musician, the Lewis Family carved out their own unique place in southern gospel—maintaining ties to the genre despite the fact that their music often seemed to fit more in bluegrass festivals than in rural southern gospel concerts. Strictly a local phenomenon until the early 1950s, the Lewis Family, under the tutelage of their father, began singing at Fowler concerts in 1951 and on local television and radio about the same time —drawing increased interest in their versatility and presentation. The Lewises ultimately featured a trio of female voices, ably provided by daughters Polly, Miggie, and Janice Lewis. The sisters were joined on vocals and accompanied on an assortment of stringed instruments by the elder Lewis and his four sons, Esley, Wallace, Talmadge, and "Little Roy." Little Roy, the precocious youngest sibling, developed an irrepressible stage presence, injecting infectious humor and energy into the family's presentation. He also became especially adept on the five-string banjo. By the mid-1960s, few fans of gospel singing had not heard of the "First Family of Bluegrass Gospel Music" that hailed from north Georgia.[8]

KLAUDTS

The Klaudt Indian Family, probably the most unique mixed group to emerge in the 1950s, added an element of diversity to the southern gospel music world. Gospel quartet music among American Indians dated to at least the mid-1930s, when the Vaughan company had sponsored the

Professional Quartets

Vaughan All-Indian Quartet, a family of Chickasaw tribesmen in Oklahoma City. Hamp J. Porter and his sons wore traditional native dress during their performances and even convinced Vaughan to publish "What a Friend We Have in Jesus" in the Chickasaw dialect.[9]

The son of a German cattle rancher and the daughter of an Arickara tribesman, the Klaudts incorporated a rich flavor into their gospel presentation. Reverend Reinhold Klaudt and Lillian Little Soldier, a direct descendent of one of George Custer's scouts at the Battle of the Little Big Horn, met on the Fort Berthold Reservation in North Dakota. Devout members of the Church of God, they married in 1929 and, preaching and singing together, they pioneered new churches across the Dakotas, Wyoming, and Montana. As their five children, Vernon, Ramona, Melvin, Raymond, and Kenneth, grew up, they were each added to the singing group and taught to play a variety of musical instruments. Together with their mother, the Klaudt children provided the group with accordion, guitar, piano, organ, saxophone, trumpet, trombone, banjo, and bass guitar accompaniment.

Determined that their children would be educated at the Church of God's Bible Training School in Cleveland, Tennessee, the Klaudts expanded their evangelistic efforts into the South in the early 1950s. Within a few years, the family settled in the Atlanta area and, led by Reinhold Klaudt's solid business sense, tapped into the thriving southern gospel concert market. Sometimes appearing in full Indian regalia, the family drew attention within an industry replete with traditional southern quartets and trios. Capitalizing on an American fascination with the West, similar to the way the Rangers had in the mid-1930s, the Klaudts had become one of the most attractive draws on Wally Fowler's all-night sings by the late 1950s.[10]

JIMMIE DAVIS AND THE PLAINSMEN

The gospel music industry profited during the 1950s from a genuine celebrity in its midst. Jimmie Houston Davis was born in 1899 to a sharecropper family on a cotton farm in the backwoods of Jackson parish in northern Louisiana. While attending classes at Louisiana College in Pineville, he sang with a college quartet that specialized in gospel songs and spirituals. Sometimes he sang literally on the street to make money to stay in school. After earning a master's degree from Louisiana State University in 1927, he began teaching history at the Shreveport-based Dodd College for Women, where he began to get some notice as a local singer. By 1928, Davis had achieved local fame mostly as a country music performer on KWKH in Shreveport, where he sang on a regular Friday night program. He also experimented with songwriting and in 1935 hit it big with "Nobody's Darling but Mine," a country ballad later recorded by Gene Autry, Bing Crosby, and a host of other artists. His success as a songwriter continued, and he achieved songwriting immortality after he and a friend, Charlie Mitchell, cowrote "You Are My Sunshine" in 1940.

On the strength of his singing and good looks, Davis received roles in Columbia Pictures Westerns during the early 1940s, playing opposite well-known actors like Charles Starrett and Tex Ritter. His growing reputation helped him land several positions in local Louisiana politics and, in 1944, he rode that reputation into the Governor's Mansion. Leaving office in 1948, Davis returned to singing and spent considerable time with the gospel groups that he loved so well. For a brief period in the late 1950s, he traveled with the regionally popular Plainsmen Quartet, appearing on a number of concert billings with the best-known gospel groups of the day.[11] This increased visibility helped Davis secure another term as the Louisiana governor in the early 1960s, but, for many of his fans, he was always best associated with the music, and particularly the gospel songs that he helped produce. Among his most notable gospel recordings were "Suppertime" and "Mansion over the Hilltop," two songs composed by contemporary writer Ira Stanphill. Davis's own compositions, particularly "Someone to Care" and "Sheltered in the Arms of God" (which he cowrote with Dottie Rambo) also cemented his place in the gospel music industry.[12]

QUARTETS ... MINUS ONE

Particularly innovative in the late 1950s was a collection of talented trio combinations. The LeFevre Trio had long held an appeal, though, during the fifties, they most often retreated to a quartet sound backed by one of several impressive bass singers—first Jim Waits, then Jimmy Jones, and finally Rex Nelon. A few other trios also made some inroads, most notably the Rangers Trio, formed after the retirement of members Vernon and Arnold Hyles from the Rangers Quartet in 1956. The Hyles brothers sold the rights to the quartet name to their pianist, David Reece, and he, along with Clark Thompson and Roy McNeil, entered the 1960s as the Rangers Trio.

One of the most celebrated trios of the 1950s was the Sons of Song, a combination formed in 1957 when several veterans of southern gospel

Professional Quartets

quartets convinced Wally Fowler to give them an impromptu opportunity at one of his all-night sings in Birmingham, Alabama. With Bob Robinson singing lead and playing piano, Calvin Newton adding a high tenor harmony, and Don Butler contributing a polished baritone, the group became popular in part because it was different. In many ways, the Sons of Song foreshadowed a shift in gospel music toward more diversity, where musicians would incorporate newer sounds and more innovative styling. Though the group was in a traffic accident in late 1958, which severely injured Robinson and Butler, the trio persevered for several more years.[13] David Young replaced Robinson as lead singer and pianist. Newton, who was not badly injured, continued with the group, as did Butler, who for a time after the accident appeared on stage on crutches.[14]

Similarly, the Johnson Sisters of Birmingham, Alabama, offered gospel music fans a different sound beginning in the mid-1950s. With older sister, Mary, at the piano, Margaret, Judy, and Anna Johnson forged a smooth trio harmony that earned them billing as the "Sweethearts of the All-Nite Sings." Modeling themselves after the McGuire Sisters, the siblings linked up with Wally Fowler around 1954 and made regular appearances on local radio and television as well as at major weekend concerts into the late 1960s.[15]

WENDY BAGWELL AND THE SUNLITERS

Another trio that became popular in the late 1950s made several unique contributions to the southern gospel music industry. Organized in Smyrna, Georgia, the versatile Sunliters combined the male baritone of Wendell Lee ("Wendy") Bagwell with the soprano of Jan Buckner and the alto of Jerri Morrison. By 1960, these three engaging singers gained national attention by virtue of a ballad titled "Pearl Buttons." Composed by Bagwell, the song's success landed them a date at New York's Carnegie Hall in 1963, making them the first southern gospel group to be so honored. More remarkable, the group suffered no personnel changes, other than an occasional change in instrumental accompanists, over a career that spanned four decades. Bagwell and Buckner enhanced the group's sound by playing a variety of instruments, but it was Bagwell's comedic genius that ultimately set the group apart from its competition. With impeccable timing, Bagwell knew how to mix down-home, rural humor with sentimental gospel lyrics and, by the early 1970s, literally no one else in the business could offer a similar repertoire. The Sunliters' recording of "Here Come the Rattlesnakes" in 1970 was released as a 45 single and, its sales, along with those of the album and the 8-track tape, exceeded one million dollars—an almost unprecedented feat for an artist in the gospel music field.[16]

CHANGES IN THE INDUSTRY

More than anything else, an annual convention of the quartets came to facilitate the growing professionalization of the industry—even as it dramatized the highly competitive environment that groups had endured since the heyday of the rural singing conventions. The brainchild of J. D. Sumner, the first National Quartet Convention (NQC) was sponsored by the Blackwood Brothers Quartet in October 1957. Held in Ellis Auditorium in the Blackwoods' hometown of Memphis, the three-day event involved almost all of the major quartets within the white segment of the gospel music industry. An unqualified success in its early years, by the mid-1960s the convention assumed the character of a power broker within the small industry. Major promoters and artists now had a place to meet, and, oftentimes, annual schedules for quartet appearances would be determined through the meetings that took place there.[17]

The NQC evolved into both a showcase for major gospel groups looking for an edge on the competition and a proving ground for new talent. Beginning with the first convention, an annual talent contest was held, with the winner receiving the valuable opportunity to appear in concert alongside major groups during the upcoming year. In 1964, a young local church group from Madison, North Carolina, known as the Hopper Brothers and Connie took first prize. Years later, its members would acknowledge that the NQC success had launched them toward a full-time career in gospel music.[18]

Also important in changing the face of gospel music was the introduction of new material made necessary by both the alienation of the music publishing companies and increased demand from concert audiences. Because of fierce competition, music publishers had generally required quartets to sing only those songs published by the company. The restriction ensured that, while quartets were free to use the firm's copyrighted material for their own advancement, no group would be plugging a competitor's music. As quartets became more independent and bucked the trend, publishers oftentimes retaliated by cutting off the supply of new gospel songs—a power that was a result of the fact that songwriters had traditionally contracted directly with the music companies. In the 1950s, this ploy backfired. Quartets turned increasingly to new sources for material, and innovative songwriters began pitching their material directly to popular groups, thus effectively bypassing the music publishers. The result was an innovative period of gospel music composition in which creative writers, most notably Lee Roy Abernathy and Mosie Lister, wrote almost exclusively for major quartets. The two men, who were gospel singers themselves, represented a generation of gospel musicians who became almost entirely independent of the publishing companies that had birthed the industry a half century before.[19]

A by-product of the estrangement between publishers and quartets was the introduction of black spirituals into the repertoires of some white gospel groups. In the preceding fifty years, gospel music in black communities of the South had developed along a similar path as that in white communities. Shape-note singing had become popular among some southern blacks, although economic factors and higher illiteracy rates inordinately hampered the availability and practicality of convention books among their friends and neighbors. The result was a continuation of the nineteenth-century call-and-response tradition.[20]

Nevertheless, as did white southern gospel music, gospel music of the black community proceeded down commercial channels.[21] Particularly successful by the 1930s were the jubilee ensembles and quartets operating out of most urban centers, north and south. Whereas radio dominated in the white market, recordings were actually a stronger link between black gospel artists and their fans. In an age when many southern blacks lacked access to rural electrification and when radio stations catered to the predominantly white market, inexpensive phonographs provided a unique opportunity for budding professional singers to share their talents. The resulting demand for "race records" often highlighted the unique styling of black gospel quartets.[22]

At least one prominent black songwriter wrote extensively for the Stamps-Baxter Music Company in the decade before World War II. Cleavant Derricks, a Baptist minister who hailed from Chattanooga and spent time in Knoxville, Tennessee; Beloit, Wisconsin; and Washington, D.C., became best known for quartet standards like "Just a Little Talk with Jesus," "We'll Soon Be Done with Troubles and Trials," and "When God Dips His Love in My Heart."[23] With an unmistakable influence from the shape-note convention arrangements and a style that often featured the bass part on the chorus, Derricks's songs found their way into southern shape-note hymnbooks, though few in the South would probably have guessed the author's racial origins.[24]

As the relationship between white quartets and shape-note publishing companies weakened, the tie between black and white gospel strengthened. Many of the songs and arrangements popularized in the 1940s and 1950s by black gospel quartets remained free from any restrictive copyrights. White quartets, admiring the vocal ability of their counterparts in the segregated South and in need of new gospel material, simply picked up on the arrangements by listening to records, radio programs, and concert performances.[25]

BLACK INFLUENCES AND CROSS-POLLINATION

The passive interaction of white and black quartets in the 1950s was actually quite extensive. Most white singers grew up familiar with the material and singing style of groups like the Dixie Hummingbirds, the Five Blind Boys, the Fairfield Four, the Nightingales, the Harmonizing Four, and the Golden Gate Quartet. As a result, it was relatively easy for white gospel quartets to adapt some of the material into their groups' repertoires. By 1953, the Blackwoods had recorded several spirituals, including "Swing down Chariot," "Rolling, Riding, Rocking," and "Rock-A-My Soul" and included them in their regular concert schedule.[26] In a few cases, such as Hovie Lister and the Statesmen's adaptation of the Gospel Harmonettes' "Get Away Jordon" and the Blackwoods' use of the Golden Gate Quartet's "Swing down Chariot," there was actual cooperation between white and black groups. More common, however, was a conscious borrowing of songs and styles heard on radio and recordings. Both white and black quartets appreciated the value of new material and innovative styling and took steps to expand their repertoires.[27]

The Golden Gate Quartet placed an indelible stamp upon the white industry. Formed in the early 1930s in Norfolk, Virginia, the group initially included A. C. "Eddie" Griffin on tenor, Henry Owens on lead, Willie "Bill" Johnson on baritone, and Robert "Peg" Ford on bass. Like their white counterparts, members of the Golden Gate began their professional careers through an association with radio. By 1935, they had worked briefly at WIS in Columbia, South Carolina, and were broadcasting live over WBT in Charlotte, North Carolina. Extremely talented and versatile, the group included in their music imitations of distinctive sounds such as train whistles, automobile engines, and boat motors.

Professional Quartets

They became best known, however, for their performance of spirituals, punctuated with staccato rhythms and syncopated beats. With Willie Langford replacing Griffin on tenor and Orlandus Wilson replacing Jones on bass, the group began recording for Bluebird and for Victor Records as early as 1937. Their success led to a move the following year to New York, where they produced a weekly radio program for CBS and began appearing on the local nightclub circuit, performing both gospel and secular tunes. They soon earned an appearance at Carnegie Hall and performed at President Franklin Roosevelt's 1941 Inauguration Gala.[28]

The Golden Gate Quartet traveled extensively across the nation in the 1940s. The group, with their smooth, often a cappella, style, attracted larger white audiences than did most other black quartets. As a result, promoters sometimes paired the Gates with prominent white quartets such as the Blackwoods and the Statesmen. James Blackwood later recalled fondly his own association with the Golden Gate even as he remembered the awkwardness of stopping at a roadside café for hamburgers and having members of the black group refused service.[29] Gospel audiences simply accepted the momentary abridgement of segregation when it came to the Gates' performance of gospel quartet numbers. With personnel that included veterans Wilson and Clyde Riddick (who had joined the group in 1940) and Orville Brooks and Alton Bradley, the quartet appeared in concert alongside white quartets throughout the early 1950s.[30] Predictably, the southern furor over the *Brown v. Board of Education* decision in May 1954 curtailed the appearances of the quartet in venues catering to white audiences.[31] Not until the early 1970s would another black gospel group find such appeal among white audiences.[32]

POPULAR MUSIC AND GOSPEL BOOGIE

Quartets' break with music publishers produced an unprecedented emphasis on songwriting within the community of gospel singers. For decades, the copyrights to works written by gospel music's most promising composers had filtered into the hands of music publishers like Stamps-Baxter. Arrangements sometimes included small sums of cash, but, more commonly, publishers traded a stack of convention books (which writers could then sell) for the rights to a new gospel song. In the 1930s, young writers such as Albert Brumley sold their compositions both for monetary gain and because of a lack of any other way to get the work into the hands of the quartets. Brumley soon grasped the long-term value of his work and succeeded in securing rights to most of it by buying into

the publishing business himself.[33] By the late 1940s, the concert orientation of the white gospel quartets and the success of commercial recordings made the value of gospel songwriting apparent to talented writers.
In addition, the estrangement of the quartets and the publishers gave
some writers greater incentive to write specifically for quartets and the
emerging recording market.

Foremost among the innovators in gospel songwriting was Lee Roy
Abernathy, a young pianist from Canton, Georgia, who inaugurated
an unparalleled career in gospel music networking and self-promotion.
Born August 13, 1913, in Bartow County, Georgia, near the little textile community of Atco, Abernathy inherited an interest in music from
both of his parents. His father, a sharecropper and textile worker, taught
singing schools and wrote gospel songs. His mother played piano and
avidly supported her husband's music — on one occasion bundling up her
young son a mere three weeks after his birth and carting him off to a
nearby singing school. As a result, young Abernathy was exposed early
to a world of both hard work and energetic gospel music. The family
moved a lot during the 1920s, trying their lot in no less than eight different mill villages and farming communities across northwest Georgia.
With the onset of the Depression, Abernathy's father hedged his bets by
settling on textile work in the small town of Canton, some thirty-five
miles due north of downtown Atlanta.[34]

By five years of age, Abernathy was singing regularly in his father's
quartet. The Atco Quartet was strictly a weekend group, but the experience proved valuable for the youngster. By the time he turned fourteen,
he had learned to play the piano — an instrument that would define him
for much of the rest of his life. Taking naturally to his musical heritage,
Abernathy formed his own group in the early 1930s. The Modern Mountaineers were a country band of sorts, featuring Paul Darnell on violin,
Bunk Dooley on guitar and mandolin, a young man remembered only
as Wilkie on guitar, violin, and French harp, and Abernathy on piano.
The Mountaineers played at local square dances and experimented with
"more modern stuff on the (style of) the Sons of the Pioneers."[35] The
country band played occasionally on Atlanta's WSB radio and recorded
a series of 78s in Chicago during the mid-1930s.[36]

Despite his penchant for popular country tunes, Abernathy was most
enamored with the style of the gospel quartets. As his musical appe-
tite grew, he studied under most of the legends of the shape-note gospel
world, including James Vaughan, A. J. Showalter, Adger Pace, and J. M.

Professional Quartets

Henson. He also studied music at Atlanta's Conservatory of Music. According to his testimony, he walked a distance of almost fifty miles every week for a thirty-minute session there and earned the five-dollar-per-lesson fee by giving music lessons of his own to local folks for twenty-five cents each.[37]

Abernathy's accomplishments were considerable. He wrote campaign songs for Franklin Roosevelt's 1936 re-election effort as well as for that of the popular Georgia governor Eugene Talmadge. In 1943, he began selling his own gospel compositions via sheet music despite ridicule from within an industry that was accustomed to selling collections of songs in the annual convention books. Abernathy later boasted that he actually sold more single-sheet copies at fifty cents each than many convention publishers sold of their larger compilations at the lower price of thirty-five.[38] The innovative Georgian even tried his own hand at politics with a run for governor in 1958. Though he finished a distant third, his campaign was a lively one punctuated by his own composition "Lee Roy's the Boy."[39]

All the while, Abernathy kept actively involved in gospel quartets. After his family moved to Canton around 1932, he renamed his father's group the Abernathy Quartet and played in local concerts. During the war, he organized the Four Tones and toured the country singing gospel and popular songs for the USO. When the Tones disbanded because of two members' active draft status, Abernathy joined the Swanee River Boys in a wartime arrangement that included Billy Carrier, George Hughes, and a young bass singer named Bill Lyles. By the end of the war, he was in Richmond playing piano for the Rangers on radio station WRVA.[40]

After the war, Abernathy entered another innovative enterprise, offering mail-order piano lessons. Again the butt of jokes, he was able to persevere and sell his product.[41] Always one to seek new avenues for doing business, the young songwriter also never missed an opportunity to capitalize on a public event. After Atlanta's tragic Winecoff Hotel fire on December 7, 1946, in which 119 people died, he wrote a controversial song detailing the event. "The Burning of the Winecoff" received a National Fire Protection award for 1946. It also demonstrated Abernathy's amazing versatility.[42]

Similarly, Abernathy created controversy in the world of gospel recordings. In 1947, he joined the Homeland Harmony Quartet as group pianist and, early the following year, convinced the members to record his new song "Everybody's Gonna Have a Wonderful Time up There." Borrowing from the celebrated "boogie beat" of the Chicago jazz musicians, Abernathy and the quartet found a receptive audience for the upbeat, unique gospel number. Recorded on White Church Records, the song (popularly known as "Gospel Boogie") sold in the neighborhood of 200,000 copies—well ahead of most other gospel songs from the era.[43] It also sparked an uproar. Connor Hall remembered singing at churches and singing conventions where religious leaders specifically requested that the group eliminate the number from the evening repertoire. Writers to the *Atlanta Journal* condemned the song for its immorality. Abernathy responded by pointing out that the song yielded a great opportunity for evangelizing: "When I wrote 'Gospel Boogie' I was inspired to write it. I felt it was one means of reaching the distant places where no ministers go . . . no singers sing, in juke jives, etc. In this way I was doing something the Lord said [to] do: 'Preach the gospel everywhere.' No other song in the world has ever reached the people in the secluded places like 'The Gospel Boogie.'"[44]

Abernathy understood that compositions like "Wonderful Time Up There" drew new fans to gospel music and lifted groups to a level of popularity and an income potential never dreamed of in the old world of shape-note music publishers. After fans began asking for "that boogie song," he added "Gospel Boogie" in parentheses next to the song's title on the White Church record for subsequent printings. Within months of the original recording in early 1948, black gospel artists and country artists issued versions of the song. A decade later, Pat Boone's version reached number ten on the *Billboard* charts and the song was established as a gospel music standard.[45]

Abernathy, and gospel musicians like him, understood clearly that their personal success hinged on their ability to enter the professional world of entertainment. While singing gospel required that they have respect for Christian beliefs and traditions, it did not mean that their music had to remain participatory or dependent on the freewill offerings of local church members. Abernathy angered some but emboldened others when he published his philosophy and a collection of his songs in a disjointed, rambling commentary titled "*It*" in 1948.[46] Intended as "a handbook for the new professional quartets," the book gave specific advice about copyrights, publishing, promotional ideas, and songwriting techniques.[47] The unusual collection by one of gospel music's most unique personalities symbolized the dawning of a new day for the gospel quartet industry.[48]

Predictably, the new trend in adapting gospel to popular styles served as a last straw for the association between many gospel quartets and the singing conventions that had nourished them a generation earlier. By 1950, *Vaughan's Family Visitor* had disassociated itself from many of the popular quartets, asking its readers, "Why should people who love the Lord and clean Christian society have to listen to the music of the 'juke box' to find a medium of expression toward God?" Allowing that there were "thousands of sincere Christian singers scattered over our land who will not stoop to participating in such programs," one of the journal's regularly featured editorialists pointedly noted that "Christianity has a place for all talented singers if they are first partakers of the fruits. If they are not, then they should come repenting and forever turn from their lives of wickedness."[49] In a statement indicative of the time period, the staunch defender of the singing conventions went on to compare the threat of the all-night sings with that of international communism.[50]

CRAFTING THE SOUTHERN GOSPEL MESSAGE AND SOUND: THOMAS MOSIE LISTER

In addition to Lee Roy Abernathy, several other songwriters in the 1950s pointed the gospel music industry away from its traditional ties to music publishing companies and singing conventions. Ira Stanphill, an Assemblies of God minister, penned several standards during the decade, the best known of which were "Mansion over the Hilltop," "I Know Who Holds Tomorrow," "Suppertime," and "Room at the Cross."[51] Another Assemblies minister, Vesphew B. "Vep" Ellis, was equally proficient. "The Love of God," "Let Me Touch Him," and "Do You Know My Jesus?" were some of his most popular contributions.[52] Stuart Hamblen, a Los Angeles radio celebrity who was converted in a 1949 Billy Graham crusade, drew even more national acclaim with songs such as "It Is No Secret What God Can Do," "First Day in Heaven," "This Ole House," and "Known Only to Him."[53] Also influential was Stuart K. Hine's "How Great Thou Art," an arrangement modeled on a Swedish gospel song from the 1880s. Popularized by George Beverly Shea during the Graham crusades of the 1950s, the tune became a gospel quartet standard as well as a familiar favorite of secular artists.[54]

By far the most influential gospel songwriter of the 1950s from the standpoint of the developing gospel quartets, however, was a young music store operator and piano tuner named Thomas Mosie Lister. Perhaps more than any other songwriter of the era, Lister enjoyed the overwhelming respect of his peers as a craftsman of innovative tunes with strong evangelical lyrics. A talented singer who served brief stints with the Sunny South Quartet, the Melody Masters, and the Statesmen, he developed short-term throat trouble from complications due to a bout with pneumonia and decided in the late 1940s that he did not want to continue the life of a traveling quartet man. Nevertheless, Mosie Lister continued to keep his finger on the pulse of the four-part-harmony quartet style, producing a string of gospel favorites, many of which he pitched initially to his old friends in the Statesmen Quartet. By 1955, *Gospel Singing World* was claiming that "it would be hard to find a known quartet not singing one of Mosie's compositions among their best loved numbers."[55]

Lister, who was born September 8, 1921, in Cochran, Georgia, was an incredibly diverse composer. From the reflective "How Long Has It Been?" (1956) to the rollicking, upbeat "Happy Rhythm" (1953)—in which, like Abernathy, he incorporated aspects of the "boogie" beat—his work complemented the growing professionalism of the gospel music industry. Writing songs specifically for quartets, Lister developed a solid sense for how well a song would be received commercially and combined that knowledge with his own standard of what a gospel song should possess lyrically. Foreshadowing the work of future writers in the gospel field, he wrote songs with specific groups in mind, even though sometimes his work was altered by the interpretation of a particular singer or musician. Lister remembered that he intended the song "I'm Feeling Fine" (1952) to be a slow ballad. However, after he pitched the song to the LeFevre Trio, Eva Mae LeFevre's rapid tempo transformed the song into a rousing harmony number.[56]

Lister also wrote with particular voices in mind. His old friend Jake Hess became the focus of several songs immortalized by the Statesmen, including the distinctive "Then I Met the Master" (1956). In 1960, Lister's "His Hand in Mine" (1953) was chosen as the title cut for the young Elvis Presley's acclaimed gospel album, signaling to many the commercial possibilities of gospel music within the broader market.[57] Other Lister standards included "Goodbye, World, Goodbye" (1955), "He Knows Just What I Need" (1955), "I've Been Changed" (1959), "'Til the Storm Passes By" (1958), "Where No One Stands Alone" (1955), "The King and I" (1954), and "While Ages Roll" (1970).[58]

Professional Quartets

As the 1960s dawned, major recording companies were issuing the top groups' albums, packed concerts were drawing from a growing number of devoted fans, and television was threatening to replace radio as the medium for reaching an even wider audience. Gospel groups also were experimenting with new sounds and, for the first time in their history, found themselves completely independent of publishing companies that might handicap their access to the labors of talented gospel songwriters. A greater degree of professionalism was emerging, and few participants in the developing industry doubted that an even brighter horizon was ahead.

IV
THE WORLD
OF SOUTHERN
GOSPEL

Live Oak, Florida, June 15, 1996

The setting is beautiful—a bowl-shaped, earthen arena with a rustic, wooden stage in the middle of the north Florida forest . . . within a quarter mile of the historic Suwanee River and under a canopy of live oaks covered with Spanish moss. Unlike many outdoor concerts, the sound is good—the oaks providing a kind of acoustical shelter. Outlining the outer rim of the concert area, venders sell hamburgers, ice cream, and boiled peanuts. The night is warm but not unbearably hot. The recent dry spell has solved the aggravation of combating mosquitoes and a casually dressed crowd of 2,500 sits in anticipation of an evening-long gospel concert.

Soon the harmonious sound of the quartets fills the air and the crowd turns its attention to the stage. This is nothing out of the ordinary for a gospel concert—the high tenors, the low basses, the precise endings, the constant piano runs . . . but, after intermission, the concert takes a unique turn. Three of the groups on the evening program are former members of the *Gospel Singing Jubilee,* a syndicated television program that dominated the Sunday morning ratings throughout the South and ran in all national markets for almost two decades beginning in 1964. When the stage lights return, the Dixie Echoes, the Inspirations, and the show's host group, the Florida Boys, walk to the front and strike a familiar pose. Taking his position, Derrell Stewart, the red-socked Florida Boys' pianist suddenly hits the refrain and familiar words fill the night air:

> Praise the Lord I've been invited to a meeting in the air.
> Jubilee, Jubilee.
> And the saints of all the ages in their glory will be there.
> Jubilee, Jubilee.
>
> Jubilee, Jubilee.
> You're invited to this happy jubilee.
> Jubilee, Jubilee.
> You're invited to this happy jubilee.

(from "The Happy Jubilee," Raymond Browning, lyricist;
Adger M. Pace, composer)

The crowd is enraptured, as I am. The nostalgia is strong, the lyrics taking us back to a seemingly more peaceful time, or less complicated, at any rate. For me, it was every Sunday morning . . . the sound I heard as Mama dressed me for Sunday school and church, on through the days when I dressed myself and went, not because she told me to, but because I wanted to. As I look around and see the glowing faces listening to the re-created television show, I'm suddenly aware that we have this in common. Having never met before, hailing from different parts of the region, we nonetheless grew up on and thrilled at the same sound. So when Les Beasley, the lead singer and longtime manager of the Florida Boys, begins announcing the numbers just as he did for so many years on the air, we listen and smile, for he is an old friend. For we southerners, we Americans of the television age . . . it is Sunday morning all over again.

8
QUARTETS &
THE NATIONAL
EXPANSION OF
GOSPEL MUSIC

The 1960s and 1970s were turbulent for many Americans. Debate over the nation's policy in Vietnam and the tragedy of Watergate led to a growing skepticism of politicians and politics in general. At the same time, early gains in civil rights for black Americans appeared muted by unrest and increased violence in the streets of the nation's largest cities. The war marshaled the country's youth to activism, and many older Americans developed a negative view of the music and appearance of high-school- and college-aged young people. Music clearly reflected the rapid changes taking place in American life and therefore became both balm and bane in a generational tug-of-war.

The period from 1960 to 1980 also brought tremendous changes to the world of gospel music. Never immune to what was happening in the larger culture, quartets and their fans struggled with the repercussions of international politics and endured the domestic unrest with much the same anxiety that other Americans felt. Through it all, they witnessed a remarkable evolution in the music industry they cherished. By the end of this period, many of the traditional outdoor sings had been replaced by concerts held in newer, more modern venues.[1] Likewise, the slicked-back hair and coat-and-ties that quartets generally sported gave way to the trendy, open-collar polyester leisure attire. More important, the gospel quartet sound also changed. The piano-dominated sound that had endured since the 1920s was now augmented by an assortment of new instrumentation. Styling and presentation also changed, and a different kind of gospel music—initially dubbed contemporary gospel—began to reflect the heavy influence of America's pop culture.

Though black gospel and white gospel endured as separate genres within the gospel music tradition, advances in civil rights brought changes there as well. Contemporary gospel emerged as a fine mixture of much that had made gospel music popular over the past half century in black and white communities across the nation. The sound was exciting and promised to draw a larger audience to gospel music and its message. At the same time, it threatened to redefine the method and scope of worship in Christian America. Ultimately, that same threat worked to redefine the religious mission of the traditional gospel quartets.

TELEVISION

The impact of television on America during the 1950s and 1960s was phenomenal. Just over four million Americans owned sets in 1950; by 1960, the number had jumped more than tenfold, to fifty million.[2] Like radio a generation earlier, the new medium came to alter not only what Americans did with their spare time but also their perspective of the world. Gospel music had adapted well to the force of radio during the 1920s and 1930s, coming to prosper in ways undreamed of when James Vaughan's first quartet traveled to Dickson, Tennessee, in 1910. Radio had provided a means of income, but, even more important, it had been the avenue for promotion.[3]

Gospel quartets eagerly embraced the new medium of television, intuitively understanding that it, too, would give them a promotional edge. Predictably, singers who had considerable experience with radio viewed television as its visual parallel. In the earliest days of television in Atlanta in 1948, Lee Roy Abernathy, then with the Homeland Harmony Quartet, composed a song reflecting the enormous interest in what the future might hold:

> Ev'rybody's talking 'bout what is coming next, What's the subject of the day, what's the golden text? There's one thing we know, it's true, God has willed it so, It's that wonderful invention for your radio.
> Television, what a wonderful invention, If it wasn't God's intention it would not be so;
> Television, life will be just one vacation, Meeting friends from ev'ry nation on our radio;

The World of Southern Gospel

We can sing the songs, new and old, anywhere we go, All the
 wondrous things we shall behold on our radio;
With television where we all can get together, Matters not what
 kind of weather, on our radio.[4]

Relative to radio, by the early 1950s, television reached only a handful
of homes. Still, its potential for providing gospel singers exposure and
bringing them future prosperity pushed some quartets into studios to
tackle the new marvel. Old habits had to be broken since quartets, accustomed to rising early and hitting the notes on radio with little regard for
personal appearance, were now required to contemplate the visual capacity of television. Even shape notes had seemed ready-made for radio
since singers well versed in the system could take requests over the air
and sing a brand-new song "cold" provided they had the music handy
in any number of convention hymnals. But television was different. It
demanded much preparation and calculation. Even regular stage appearances offered little in the way of practice. Antics on stage, dependent as
they were on the feel of the audience and the developing mood of the concert experience, would not work with the new medium. Quartets who
jumped into the television age now had to take into consideration stage
sets, makeup, precise planning, and time management.[5]

Another consideration was the national market that drove network
television. Most gospel quartets' forays into the new medium took place
in local markets where, as was the case with radio, local managers knew
the tastes of their audiences and scheduled area programming accordingly. In time, television would help transform the local and regional
markets into a national one.

Opportunities with television once again demonstrated the commercialization of gospel quartet music and its consequent growing incompatibility with the traditional, more conservative values of southern
church members. Gospel performers recognized that, given this en-
trenched conservatism and the religious nature of their product, they
faced an obstacle that secular performers did not. In a 1950 editorial,
Lee Roy Abernathy expressed his frustration with Christians who de-
cried innovative change and feared the onslaught of twentieth-century
technology. "THE HORSE AND BUGGIE days have come . . . and gone," he
wrote. "The automobile is here perhaps to stay. The airplane is here to
stay . . . rocket planes and other things. AMONG OTHER THINGS that are
here to stay we find the Devil and his termites gnawing away at every-

thing chosen to better the gospel field and God's work. People have even written their radio preachers and asked them if they could look at TELEVISION. I hope the Devil never gets hold enough on me to warp my conscience into his opinions."[6]

By the early 1950s, gospel quartets were eagerly seeking whatever exposure the new wonder of television could bring. The Sunshine Boys appeared briefly on Atlanta's WSB-TV shortly after the station went on the air in the fall of 1948, though their performances included an assortment of secular numbers as well as their trademark gospel.[7] The John Daniel Quartet appeared on some of the earliest broadcasts of Doc Tommy Scott's *Smokey Mountain Jamboree*. Similarly, the Stamps Quartet in Dallas experimented with a yearlong local program beginning in 1951.[8] As country music television programming spread through the South, and particularly the barn dance formula, a number of quartets made appearances in part because traditional gospel songs endured as a staple on such shows.[9]

By the late 1950s, popular quartets appeared more frequently on live local television shows and, with the advancing technology, taped them for rebroadcast on other stations. The Blackwoods' radio sponsor, Dixie Lily Flour, began promoting a fifteen-minute weekly television broadcast on Memphis station WMCT each Sunday. From Augusta, Georgia, the bluegrass gospel group the Lewis Family produced a weekly program every Sunday on WJBF. Drawing on his vast contacts in the gospel quartet community, Wally Fowler conducted a successful weekly program from Birmingham, Alabama's WBRC. Known as *Gospel Sing*, the program featured the Johnson Sisters and the Calvaleers Quartet on a recurring basis as well as special guests. Lee Roy Abernathy produced a similar show from Atlanta in the mid-1950s featuring his own Lee Roy Abernathy Quartet and then the delightful humor and sound of the Happy Two, a duet made up of himself and veteran quartet man Shorty Bradford.

By 1958, the Rebels hosted *Wake Up, Florida* on WFLA in Tampa in addition to several other live programs in north Florida. Even more remarkable were the Herculean efforts of the Speer Family. In addition to concert appearances, the Speers, under the sponsorship of Martha White Flour, appeared each weekday morning on Nashville's WLAC and then traveled several hours out of town for weekly live programs on Chattanooga's WRGP, Knoxville's WATE, and Jackson's WDXI. In Charlotte, North Carolina, both the Harvesters and Arthur Smith and the Crossroads Quartet brought gospel music twice a week to local audiences over WBTV and, in Spartanburg, South Carolina, Elmo Fagg and the Blue Ridge Quartet appeared each Tuesday on WSPA.

Atlanta proved to be a hotbed of gospel quartet television. On Monday evenings, the Statesmen appeared on WSB-TV followed on Saturdays by Connor Hall and the Homeland Harmony Quartet. Beginning in 1955, Atlanta viewers also enjoyed an hour-long program called *Gospel Jubilee*, hosted by "Happy Jack" Kilgore, on Saturday afternoons. Greenville, South Carolina, provided the home for *Bob Poole's Gospel Favorites* on WFBC. Within a few years, Poole was successfully syndicating the program in more than two dozen markets.[10] Dallas, Texas, a home for gospel quartet singing since the late 1920s, welcomed *Songs of Inspiration*, a Sunday afternoon program initially sponsored and hosted by local quartet enthusiast and singer Dudley Hughes and, beginning in 1959, by prominent gospel music pianist Marion Snider.[11]

Most important to the nationwide promotion of gospel music was the production of *Hovie Lister and the Statesmen Quartet*, a fifteen-minute program of gospel quartet music sponsored by the National Biscuit Company. The taped programs were a spin-off of the group's weekly live program on Atlanta's WSB-TV on Monday evenings, and they represented some of the most innovative and professionally produced gospel music television of the decade. Far ahead of its time, the program featured elaborate costuming and stage props, with numbers sometimes foreshadowing the concept videos that would emerge more than two decades later. In addition, the quartet sang Nabisco's catchy jingle.

Successfully syndicated from 1953 through 1957, the program showcased one of the best gospel quartets of all time singing a variety of traditional hymns, spirituals, and the newer gospel songs. With a lineup of Jake Hess, Denver Crumpler, Doy Ott, James Wetherington, and Hovie Lister, the Statesmen proved master entertainers and demonstrated as much as anything else the absolute professionalism in gospel quartet music. The energetic Statesmen manager and pianist Hovie Lister clearly understood the power of television. Like Abernathy, he was an innovator who had little patience for anyone in the Christian community who feared technological change and improvements. Lister's youth and easygoing stage presence meshed well with the peculiar demands of television, and his quartet's versatility showcased gospel quartet music as it existed in the postwar era.[12]

By the early 1960s, a number of gospel quartets were sufficiently experienced with television to participate more extensively. Late in 1961, the LeFevres launched the *Gospel Singing Caravan,* an innovative program that highlighted their own popular combination of singers and musicians along with several other top groups. With the Blue Ridge Quartet as partners, the LeFevres also featured the Johnson Sisters and the Prophets in a mingled assortment of talent that demonstrated the kind of variety now available in gospel music circles. The packaging of the groups was important since, taken together, they promised to appeal to fans of several different styles of gospel music. The four groups on the *Caravan* also began appearing in concerts together, thus increasing the popularity of the show. Promotional literature played up their diverse styles, hyping the LeFevres as "America's Most Versatile Singers and Musicians," the Blue Ridge as "The Sweetest Singing This Side of Heaven," the Johnson Sisters as "The Sweethearts of Gospel Music," and the Prophets as "The Most Unique Sound in Gospel Music."[13] Sponsored by Martha White Flour, the show was pioneered by the efforts of A. O. Stinson, an executive with Martha Flour who also initiated several syndicated country music programs, including the *Ernest Tubb Show, Flatt and Scruggs,* and *Jim and Jesse.*[14] Stinson left Martha White in the early 1960s and worked for several years with Programming, Inc., the Atlanta-based company organized by the LeFevres and Blue Ridge to produce the *Caravan* programs. Especially popular in southern markets, the *Gospel Singing Caravan* continued to be aired into the mid-1960s and ultimately appeared on more than forty stations.[15]

By far, the crown jewel of gospel music television proved to be the *Gospel Singing Jubilee,* produced by Showbiz, Inc. beginning in 1964. Hosted by the Florida Boys, the program was a combined effort of talented gospel singers, promoters, and savvy television executives. Owned by Noble Dury and Associates of Nashville, Showbiz, Inc., hoped to reproduce the success of country music television programs, which by the early 1960s were popular across the South. Due to the Florida Boys' impressive appearances on *The Gospel Song Shop,* a black and white gospel music program introduced in 1961 on several southern stations, the group received the invitation to headline the new color-formatted *Jubilee. Song Shop* had been a production of the Florida Boys' founder, J. G. Whitfield, the successful Pensacola grocer and one of the 1960s' most prominent gospel quartet promoters. Now with Whitfield shooting commercials and helping secure talent, the Florida Boys' manager Les Beasley coproduced the

The World of Southern Gospel

new show along with Jane Dowden, a representative of Noble Dury. Featuring a catchy theme song and a constantly revolving array of talent, the program soon became a major syndicated success. At its height in the late 1960s and early 1970s, *Jubilee* appeared in over ninety markets across the continental United States.[16]

As did the LeFevres, from the beginning, the Florida Boys consciously included a variety of gospel music talent in their show. The original lineup in 1964 featured the Pennsylvania-based Couriers along with the Happy Goodman Family and Whitfield's own Dixie Echoes. Together with the Florida Boys, the cast formed an exciting mix of gospel music styles. The program also added a touch of creativity, using sketches of angels and other church symbols as lead-ins to commercials. Most importantly, the show made syndication easy by offering local stations ready-made sponsorships. In return for the hour-long broadcast, television stations were given a fifteen-minute segment during which they could run local ads. The rest of the commercial time came as a package deal, with Chattanooga Medicine Company and Stanback Headache Powders providing both the revenue and the national clout needed to ensure an attractive production.[17]

The *Jubilee*, perhaps more than any other single factor in the 1960s and early 1970s, kept gospel quartets singing before the public—mostly in the southern market but increasingly in other regions of the country as well.[18] Produced for more than a decade, the program was responsible for introducing much of the new talent to the industry over that time period.[19] Significantly, it also demonstrated that concert promoters, the power brokers within the industry since the late 1940s, could be bypassed. The future of gospel music lay in successful media exposure and specifically in whether or not that media exposure could tap into the evangelical base of the gospel music message.[20]

The national success of the *Jubilee* dwarfed the efforts of other gospel quartets in television, but, on a local and regional level, other broadcasts also fared well. The *Lewis Family Television Show*, from Augusta, Georgia, was ultimately syndicated on as many as twenty-five stations across the South and became an enduring symbol of gospel music's strength on local Sunday broadcasts. The program ran continuously from 1954 to 1992 and, along with the *Jubilee*, was on Elvis Presley's regular viewing schedule.[21] Internal turmoil caused the *Caravan* to cease production in the mid-1960s at the height of the *Jubilee*'s popularity, but the show remained popular in reruns well into the 1970s. The LeFevres followed the production with the *LeFevre Family Show,* ultimately telecast in color in more than forty markets.[22]

Other programs also prospered. In the mid-1960s, the Blackwoods and Statesmen coproduced *Singing Time in Dixie,* an hour-long broadcast ultimately carried in over fifty markets across the South. In 1966, the two groups discontinued *Singing Time* in favor of the half-hour-long *Glory Road,* produced in the new color format for another couple of seasons.[23] Also enjoying a limited amount of syndicated success in local markets in the 1960s were *Gospel Roundup,* a show featuring the Chuck Wagon Gang and Rangers Trio, and *TV Gospel Concert,* starring the Prophets and Wendy Bagwell and the Sunliters.[24] With the help of former Martha White Flour executive A. O. Stinson, the Wills Family of Arlington, Texas, produced the *Wills Family Inspirational Time,* a program telecast across the Southwest during the late 1960s. Similarly, the Klaudt Indian Family, operating out of Atlanta, created the *Klaudt Indian Family Show* while the youth-oriented Oak Ridge Boys started the appropriately titled *It's Happening.* In Pennsylvania, the Couriers had also expanded successfully into television by the early 1970s—producing *Couriers,* a weekly production from Lancaster, Pennsylvania's WGAL that ultimately reached thirty-seven counties in the central and western parts of the state. Like their concerts, the Couriers' TV show introduced the predominantly southern style of white gospel quartet singing to a much larger, urban marketplace.[25]

Even more ambitious was Jerry Goff's *America Sings.* A talented singer and musician, Goff was experienced in television marketing—for two years he headed up Programming, Inc., the LeFevre–Blue Ridge agency that produced the *Caravan* show and, subsequently, the thirty-minute *LeFevre Family Show.* In 1967, he produced his own gospel variety program—this time anchored by him and the Thrasher Brothers, a relatively unknown group until the weekly show highlighted their ability as gospel singers and musicians. Goff financed *America Sings* through an investment in Akne-med, a new skin care product owned partially by the Thrashers and marketed through an advertising agency jointly owned by Goff, Jim Thrasher, and E. L. Wade. Ultimately appearing in ninety-one markets, the show ran successfully as a half-hour program for several years.

Perhaps more than anyone else, Goff represented the growing power of television in the gospel music field. Though *America Sings* ceased production in 1971, in large part because of the Food and Drug Administration's new restrictions on medical claims made on behalf of Akne-med, the exposure guaranteed Goff a place on the center stage of the gospel music industry. Forming his own gospel group, Jerry and the Singing Goffs, he combined singing with his evangelical preaching and varied musical skills to become a staple within the industry.[26]

Despite the growing array of television programs, the one foray by quartets into the motion picture industry proved disappointing. Perhaps inspired by the successful ventures of the Sunshine Boys in Hollywood almost two decades earlier, an enthusiastic fan of gospel quartets in 1966 funded the full-color production of *Sing a Song for Heaven's Sake*. Little thought went into the construction of a cohesive plot, however, and as a result, the film emerged as little more than a collection of some of gospel music's finest quartets singing on stage in a small, rural church. The production faithfully represented the growing variety of talent in gospel music, with performances by the Statesmen, the Blackwood Brothers, the Klaudt Indian Family, the Chuck Wagon Gang, the Lewis Family, the Oak Ridge Boys, the Blue Ridge Quartet, the Rangers Trio, J. D. Sumner and the Stamps, the Imperials, and the Swanee River Boys. However, promoters failed to find a suitable market in public theaters. Some individuals in the gospel music industry were frankly embarrassed by the portrayal and took occasion to say so, and no one more plainly than Pierce LeFevre. After the film premiered at the 1966 National Quartet Convention, LeFevre argued that those interested in promoting gospel music should "start a fund so that we may purchase the movie from its present owners. Then we can burn the movie and all copies so that no one else will ever get to see it. This is the best thing we could do for gospel music."[27]

A GROWING INDUSTRIAL APPARATUS

Despite the disappointing results of the movie, successful television exposure greatly increased the commercial success of gospel music groups in the 1960s. In 1959 the Blackwood-Statesmen team had expanded their interests to include Skylite Records, a Memphis-based company whose focus would be on gospel music alone. By the end of the year, the company boasted recordings by the Harmoneers, the Prophets, the Golden Keys Quartet, and the Singing Speer Family as well as rereleased material from earlier RCA recordings of the Blackwoods and Statesmen.[28] Similarly, the LeFevre-owned Sing label emerged in 1960 to promote a variety of gospel music enterprises from recording to music publishing. In 1963, the LeFevres opened a new studio in Atlanta, touting the operation as "the finest in gospel music." By the end of the following year, they had produced the albums of the Sego Brothers and Naomi, Wendy Bagwell and the Sunliters, and the Goss Brothers Trio, in addition to releases by the four groups that made up the *Gospel Singing Caravan* team.[29] The development of Skylite and Sing represented the growing control the powerful Blackwood-Statesmen and LeFevre–Blue Ridge teams had in the industry.

As significant as these companies were, they both revolved around major gospel groups. Eventually they began to encounter competition from other quartets who craved the opportunity to move out from under the shadow of the dominant labels. As television revealed the growing economic potential behind gospel music, new forces entered the industry and their presence ultimately proved attractive to these fledgling groups. By 1962, the John Benson Publishing Company of Nashville had established Heartwarming Records, with an emphasis on quality recordings for gospel music quartets. By the end of the decade, Heartwarming was a resounding success while Skylite had changed ownership and the LeFevre–Blue Ridge team had disbanded and lost its influence within the industry.[30]

Probably the greatest change in gospel quartet recording came with the introduction of Canaan Records in 1963. A division of Word, Inc., a large Christian publishing firm headquartered in Waco, Texas, Canaan soon secured recording arrangements with many of the major gospel groups. Significantly, their first major artist was the Florida Boys Quartet, the successful hosts of *Gospel Song Shop* and *Gospel Singing Jubilee.* Managed by Marvin Norcross, a highly respected businessman whose personal tastes and convictions had acquainted him well with the world of Christian music, Canaan set the standard by offering quality recordings that featured a growing assortment of gospel music talent.[31] Soon, Canaan was joined by other exclusively Christian labels, most notably Impact, a new division of the Benson company created in 1968, and Calvary Records, formed in Fresno, California, by Nelson Parkerson in 1971.[32]

Professionalism emerged in other quarters as well. The Don Light Agency, formed in Nashville in the fall of 1965, became an enduring partner for many groups in coordinating schedules and creating valuable links with smaller concert promoters. Light, a former disc jockey and employee of *Billboard* magazine, clearly understood the increased time and business savvy required of a quartet to function effectively in the world of gospel music. In a 1966 interview, he recalled: "Most of the groups were managed and booked by a member of the group. I felt it was virtually impossible to sing and be a performer, spend 30 to 100 hours a week on a bus going from one appearance to another and de-vote the amount of time on the phone required to do justice to the task of booking and keeping up on [the] latest happenings in the music busi-ness. It was common practice for gospel groups and promoters to operate without contracts which frequently resulted in misunderstandings and cancellations. I felt then, and still do, the gospel music business should be run as a business."[33] Famous bass singer J. D. Sumner, who had left the Blackwoods in 1965 to form J. D. Sumner and the Stamps, founded Sumar Talent in 1968 for much the same purpose and discovered a sig-nificant demand for the service. At about the same time, Oak Ridge bass singer Herman Harper retired from concert touring and joined the Don Light Agency, focusing the rest of his career entirely on promoting and booking gospel music talent. Ultimately splitting from Light in 1986 to form Harper and Associates, the engaging Harper and his company's success proved to be yet another cog in the wheel of gospel quartet professionalism.[34]

In the midst of this expanding infrastructure, the gospel quartet in-dustry established the Gospel Music Association. Formed in 1964 and initially envisioned as an umbrella organization to form a Hall of Fame similar to that operated by the Country Music Foundation in Nashville, the organization soon took on the challenge of promoting and coordinat-ing the rapidly spreading industry. In 1969, the organization hosted its first annual awards banquet—inaugurating the Dove, "the Gospel Music Association's answer to the Emmy, the Oscar and the Grammy," in the words of the *Singing News* editorial staff.[35] Ambitious plans were laid for the establishment of a Hall of Fame complex to house both plaques and appropriate museum artifacts. With a growing diversity of musi-cal styles, however, the organization ultimately faced the difficult task of coordinating the recognition of many different types of approaches to Christian music.[36]

The founding of an enduring mouthpiece for the industry also con-tributed to the professionalism of gospel quartet singing. J. G. Whitfield, by the late 1960s the most powerful promoter of the southern-based groups, borrowed the concept of an industrywide publication from the GMA. In January 1969, the organization launched what ultimately became a seven-year run of the promotional newspaper *Good News*. When Whitfield received his copy in the mail, he recognized immediately that a mass-produced publication could serve the same purpose as the bulk mailings he was already sending to advertise all-night sings in southern cities. Determined to cash in on the idea, he began producing his own monthly newspaper in May 1969.[37]

From the beginning of the *Singing News*, Whitfield was creative. The initial issue was mailed free of charge to everyone who had ordered songbooks related to the *Gospel Singing Jubilee* television program—a total of 100,000 copies. In addition to listing upcoming concert appearances, each issue of the *News* featured specific artists, complete with photos and behind-the-scenes industry information. As the concept unfolded, Whitfield pledged "more extensive news coverage of major concerts and singing events . . . with particular emphasis on improved photographic coverage."[38] Although the cost for a subscription was modest at $3.00 per year, little effort went into luring regular subscribers. Rather, Whitfield hoped to offset the cost of the publication by increasing concert attendance through advertisement. In time, he enlisted the cooperation of promoters Lloyd Orrell and W. B. Nowlin, agreeing to mail copies to each person on their concert mailing lists in return for a guaranteed amount of monthly advertising. The strategy prevented the magazine from building a hardcore subscription base, but it succeeded in placing the name of the publication in most gospel quartet circles in a relatively brief period of time. By the mid-1970s, as many as 300,000 *Singing News* issues were being mailed each month, though as few as 10 percent were routed to subscribers.[39]

Significantly, the magazine pushed the industry in the direction of popular music by emphasizing the success of particular songs. In January 1970, the "Gospel Hit Parade" became the industry's first monthly charting guide. Based on the formula used by *Billboard*, the *Singing News* chart relied upon "more than 200 gospel singing disc jockeys across the United States, in addition to reports of music and record sales from publishers, distributors and stores in the U.S."[40] Individual quartets had traditionally held more importance than specific songs, a fact that made it difficult for new groups to compete with the popularity of established artists. Nevertheless, as the 1970s came to a close, song charts and hit

The World of Southern Gospel

singles were becoming more important in defining the power structure of the industry.[41]

Another indication that gospel music was fast approaching professionalism was a bona fide scandal over the GMA's Dove Awards in the fall of 1971. The incident involved one of gospel music's premier groups, the Blackwood Brothers, who had captured nine out of fourteen awards. They were accused of having conducted "an extensive campaign to enlist new members, going to extreme means to encourage these members to vote for particular award nominees in the Dove balloting."[42] Their "more aggressive" recruitment of new members had resulted in approximately one-third of the total voting membership of the association.[43] Some individuals in the industry even accused the group of tainting the process by distributing "marked ballots, gifts and free memberships." Though no specific bylaw of the organization had been broken, the tactic created an industrywide concern over "voting irregularities and unethical ballot influence and solicitation."[44]

The GMA Board voted to nullify the entire process, thereby invalidating all the awards that had been presented at an October 9, 1971, banquet held in Nashville, and formed a committee to adjust the voting process with "safeguards against future irregularities in Dove Awards balloting."[45] James Blackwood, patriarch of the accused group and himself a member of the GMA Board, issued a statement in support of the organization's decision: "I take full responsibility for what I consider unethical solicitation of votes by members of our organization and personally guarantee there will be no repetition. I further pledge our complete support for the Gospel Music Association and subscribe to the statement of the ideals and concepts of this organization as set forth in the statement by the board. I strongly urge all other participants in the Dove Awards to subscribe and adhere to the code of ethics to be set forth by the Gospel Music Association."[46]

Ironically, the Dove Awards scandal demonstrated that the fledgling gospel music industry had emerged as a full part of the entertainment world. The Doves and the publicity that winning one generated were critical parts of a group's success. The awards made certain groups more attractive to concert audiences and provided valuable publicity for product sales.

In spite of the embattled organization's setbacks, it successfully established a Hall of Fame in 1971 — inducting "Dad" Speer in the deceased category and the legendary bass singer Jim "Pappy" Waits in the living category. Over the next decade, a sizable number of artists, songwriters, and industry promoters from all quarters of the gospel music industry would be so honored.[47]

THE BIRTH OF CONTEMPORARY GOSPEL

Increased organization and the success of television did more than give gospel quartets a new means for their commercial survival. More than radio, television encouraged groups to establish an image and forced them to identify a particular segment of the audience as their bread and butter. With the growing commercial appeal of the baby boom generation, many groups actively sought to engage teenagers and young adults. The *Jubilee* broadcast introduced several exciting new groups whose image and musical ability drew Christian youth. By the early 1970s, gospel music fans accustomed to tuning into the program on Sunday mornings had been introduced to a variety of groups like the Rambos, the Hinsons, the Downings, and the Inspirations. Likewise, a much larger variety of gospel talent was being showcased in stage concerts, reflecting the rapid changes occurring in the American music industry as a whole.[48]

The greatest change, often seen as a threat by many artists and fans steeped in the gospel quartet tradition, was the growing popularity of secular influences on the sound and style of gospel recordings and performances. Christened contemporary gospel by supporters, this new style of music emerged in the late 1960s in response to several trends taking place within American society. The expansion of television, and particularly syndicated gospel music programming, dramatically influenced the exposure of the musical style to families across the nation. At the same time, conservative evangelical churches—and particularly those with Pentecostal leanings—were building on successful revival campaigns of the previous decade. Groups like the Full Gospel Business Men's Fellowship International, founded by Demos Shakarian in 1951, demonstrated the degree to which this type of expressive worship was drawing from more middle-class American neighborhoods, where an increased financial base resulted in larger, more impressive church facilities and programs. Rather than surrender to the turbulent times of political and social unrest in the 1960s, these evangelical Christians actually marshaled stronger support—in part because their premillennial theology both promised hard times and explained why they would come. As a result, these churches looked particularly prophetic and relevant in a land where old values and assumptions were constantly questioned.[49]

The World of Southern Gospel

In addition, the youth culture of the 1960s proved far more influential than most conservative Christian parents wished. Young people raised in the church were increasingly pulled to the popular music of their generation, and their tastes proved difficult to change even when they sought to remain in the overall arena of American Christianity. Christian youth advocates sought to capitalize on the energy of popular music, particularly the campfire songs promoted early in the decade as a part of a nationwide folk revival on college campuses. Such tunes were used widely at youth retreats and evangelical revivals. Quite naturally, young people most often identified with Christian lyrics presented in music they liked and that was socially fashionable.[50]

In part, contemporary gospel emerged as a result of the success of these conservative evangelical churches and their influence on individual composers and performers. By the early 1970s, a number of popular entertainers and personalities had begun to profess publicly their faith in Christianity. Concerned with the impact of drugs and violence in the culture and oftentimes challenged by their own personal failings, national figures like Johnny Cash, Pat Boone, Debbie Reynolds, Noel Paul Stookey, Lulu Roman, Eldridge Cleaver, Tom Landry, and Roger Staubach emerged to make public professions, sometimes at major Billy Graham campaigns. They also published books and made appearances on national television talk shows.[51] As a result, Christianity became "hip" to a certain element of America's youth.

Many popular singers had themselves been strongly influenced by American Christianity and some specifically by the music of the gospel quartets. In the late 1950s, Elvis Presley was particularly open about the influence that the music of the gospel quartets—both white and black—had on his own musical orientation. As a young teenager, he and his family often attended church at Memphis's First Assembly of God, the home church of the popular Blackwood Brothers Quartet. An ardent fan of both the Statesmen and the Blackwood Brothers, Presley frequented the Blackwoods' performances at their live daily program on WMPS radio and took every occasion to become friends with and learn tips from the singers. He also attended the gospel concerts held in the city's Ellis Auditorium, sometimes receiving free entrance from singers such as James Blackwood and J. D. Sumner, who took to the boy and appreciated his eagerness to hear the music.[52] He even practiced with and auditioned for a position in a local part-time group, the Songfellows, shortly before his recordings at Sun Records positioned him for a successful career in the secular field.[53] Presley's meteoric rise to prominence in American popular culture in the late 1950s validated to a degree the world of quartet music, and his employment of the Jordanaires as backup vocalists generated hope among gospel singers that their fortunes were indeed on the upswing.[54]

Yet the impact of American evangelicalism on the larger culture by the 1970s was far from a one-way street. The image of Christianity—and thus the message and sound of gospel music—waxed quite different from that which had predominated in earlier decades, and the result, quite frankly, caught the gospel music establishment and much of evangelical Christianity completely off-guard. The new revival, born in the early years of the baby boom after World War II, included a youth focus entirely consistent with the marketing trends and cultural changes going on in the rest of American society. By the mid-1960s, youth-oriented gospel music written by major Christian composers like Ralph Carmichael and Kurt Kaiser began capturing a sizable audience among evangelical teenagers. Carmichael's "He's Everything to Me" (1964) and Kaiser's "Pass It On" (1969) were two of the most popular Christian youth songs of the era, and they demonstrated the degree to which music could be a powerful evangelistic tool for engaging young people in religious dialogue and faith. The trend was aided as well by the commercial success of popular music styles in the religious-oriented musicals of the period, particularly *Good News, Tell It Like It Is, Jesus Christ Superstar, Godspell,* and *Joseph and the Amazing Technicolor Dreamcoat.*[55] Though frowned upon and often misunderstood by parents and conservative church pastors, the revival of Christian themes in America's youth music ultimately proved to be a genuine and lasting phenomenon. Few areas of evangelical life felt the consequences more than gospel music.

As a distinctive genre, contemporary gospel music emanated from the Jesus movement begun in California coffeehouses in the late 1960s. Through the influence of a diverse assortment of youth-oriented evangelicals, popular music styles combined with Christian lyrics to form what many called "Jesus Rock." In some ways, the trend was not new. Since the 1920s, gospel music artists and composers had demonstrated—often with some resistance—the degree to which popular music styles might be combined with Christian lyrics to generate a new sound that challenged previous notions of the line between secular and sacred tunes. Perhaps more so than at any other time, however, conservative Christians in the 1960s were unprepared for such a mixing of popular and reli-

The World of Southern Gospel

gious cultures. Confused and fearful of the rapid sociocultural changes taking place, as demonstrated by continuing civil rights unrest, growing openness on sexual matters, Supreme Court decisions removing Bible-reading and sanctioned prayers in public schools, rising crime rates and drug use, and a bewildering American struggle in Vietnam, they tended to view popular culture as decidedly non-Christian and antagonistic to Christian values.

Many quartet members clearly cast their lot with the growing conservatism of Middle America. In the summer of 1964, a year after the Supreme Court's controversial *Abington School District v. Schempp* decision eliminating Bible reading in public schools, the Blue Ridge Quartet's bass singer George Younce included in his monthly column in *Sing* magazine a poem that had also aired recently on the group's *Gospel Singing Caravan* television show:

> I'd like to see the Bible placed where the Bible used to be,
> Upon the top of teacher's desk for every child to see;
> I'd like to hear the teacher say, as my teacher used to do:
> "Before we work or play, dear ones, I want to read to you."
> I'd like to see the teacher stand before the class again
> And lift with reverent care the Book that makes God's purpose plain,
> And ere the youngsters went to work I'd like to hear her voice
> Repeat those words of truth and faith that makes one's soul rejoice.
> . . . Yes, I'd like to see the Bible placed where the Bible used to be;
> I'd like to hear it read aloud in the schoolrooms of the free.
> I want my children taught to know God's matchless gift of love.
> The Book of books is wisdom's gate, the knowledge from above.[56]

Shortly thereafter, in the October 1964 issue of *Sing*, Pierce LeFevre included a strong endorsement of Republican nominee Barry Goldwater. Expressing specifically his fear of "creeping socialism," the young LeFevre noted that "since I left college, it has stopped creeping and started running."[57]

Perhaps the most outspoken critic was James Blackwood, by now an icon in gospel music circles. The venerable leader of the Blackwood organization complained of an "atheistic, communistic scheme to undermine the foundations of American life" and laid much of the blame on "the modernist, liberalist trend in the churches today."[58] Before he was through, Blackwood took on the theology of an Episcopal bishop who had reportedly questioned the divinity of Christ. In language stronger than that usually associated with quartet publications, he took a stand solidly on the side of America's fundamentalist Christians: "This is more of the damnable doctrine of the modernists and liberals. I am glad that the educated idiots who are preaching that Christ was not The Son of God got here too late to inform me because He lives within my heart."[59] Within a few years, Blackwood and the quartet that bore his name would make headlines in the inaugural issue of the *Singing News* for their "God and Country" petition decrying "the prohibiting of prayer and Bible reading in our schools." In just two months in the spring of 1969, the group collected more than 50,000 signatures. By the end of the summer, the petition held 193,000 names and the Blackwoods had helped to galvanize the opinion of the gospel music community.[60]

Despite the fears, Christianity proved remarkably resilient in the turbulent America of the 1960s. Within four years of provoking debate by asking, "Is God Dead?" on its April 8, 1966, cover, *Time* magazine was forced to ask on another cover, "Is God Coming Back to Life?" Concluding that "an aloof and alien technological society has already shocked man into a rediscovery of his own humanity, with all its hopes and miseries," the weekly recorder of American trends also acknowledged that "in every faith and in every believer, there is once again a burgeoning awareness of God—or at least a sense that every man is a priest to his fellow man."[61]

In the midst of the youth revolution, an unlikely evangelical revival emerged—asserting old ideals and concepts in a refreshingly new way. Predictably, the faith expressed by growing numbers of America's youth found its way into the larger culture. Popularized by a growing acceptance of gospel content in songs on the popular music charts, most notably the Edwin Hawkins Singers' "Oh, Happy Day" in 1969, Judy Collins's "Amazing Grace" in 1970, and Ocean's "Put Your Hand in the Hand" in 1971, young artists committed to Christian ideals began offering an entirely new type of gospel music. Led by Larry Norman's 1969 Capitol release *Upon This Rock*, the first commercial album composed entirely of the new gospel style, a new generation brought fundamental change to the world of gospel music. Within a decade, contemporary gospel grew to encompass a large share of the gospel music recording industry, with artists such as Steve Green, Andrae Crouch and the Disciples, the Second

Chapter of Acts, Randy Stonehill, Evie Tournquist, Randy Matthews, and Dallas Holm becoming staples within younger evangelical circles.[62]

One early proponent of the contemporary groundswell was Mylon LeFevre, the youngest son of gospel music pioneers Urias and Eva Mae LeFevre. In 1970, the younger LeFevre—already recognized in the gospel quartet world as a talented songwriter and singer—broke ranks with his family's singing tradition and released on Cotillion Records his own Jesus Rock album, *Mylon*. Within a few years, the young artist's interest in rock music as well as his unconventional hairstyle and lifestyle led to his complete break with his family's singing business. Upon his resignation from the group, he expressed a desire to "reach young people with what I believe in—that Jesus gave His life for my sins—but I'm not gonna shove religion at them."[63] LeFevre's interest in contemporary gospel, however, waned as, much to the chagrin of his family, he pursued secular music for a time. When his struggle with drugs was made public, many individuals in the more traditional gospel music camp felt that their concerns about the direction of contemporary gospel had been validated.[64]

Early contemporary artists suffered from a perception among most conservative evangelicals that rock 'n' roll was inherently evil and that the rhythm of the music itself was a "tool of the devil." Former pop musician-turned-evangelist Bob Larson minced no words in this regard in *Hippies, Hindus, and Rock & Roll*, the 1969 sequel to his widely circulated paperback titled *Rock and Roll: The Devil's Diversion:*

Initially, a tolerant society was fascinated by the hippies. Fashion trends, art motifs and advertisements exploited them. In one sense, the hippies were having a love affair with the society they professed to disdain. But soon the idealism of the novelty wore off and pragmatism took over. Racketeers muscled in on the marijuana trade. Love turned to hate, and even some hippies themselves were shocked to discover that their tribal society had not produced Utopia but rape and murder and disease. . . . Had the end of the hippie movement finally come? Hardly. After a brief transitional period during which its image was modified, "love" has been replaced by loneliness, fear and sporadic brutality. Militancy has seeped into their attitudes, as talk of "flower power" has been replaced by armed violence. . . . Aligned squarely with the policies of Moscow and Peking, the hippies' and the yippies' movements roll on. Satan's shock troopers have done their job well, but they could not have accomplished it without the savage, pounding beat of rock and roll.[65]

Facing this type of opposition, young Christian musicians bent on sharing their faith through the vehicle of rock music were often forced to look outside the organized church for support.

Influential in combating the negative image of the combined secular and gospel styles was Explo '72, an evangelical festival held in Dallas by the World Student Congress on Evangelism and supported by Bill Bright's Campus Crusade. Bright's organization, as well as this phenomenal gathering of young people, lent a degree of respectability to the infant genre of Jesus Rock, as did the appearances of Billy Graham and other major evangelical leaders. Filling the 80,000-seat Cotton Bowl at night and drawing a crowd twice that size for a downtown outdoor concert, many of the developing artists in contemporary gospel performed their new style of music before a sea of supportive young Christians. The huge turnout foreshadowed a series of annual Jesus Festivals that would take place across the nation during the 1970s and illustrated the degree to which the new contemporary sound had appropriated its way into Christian youth culture.[66]

Also sympathetic to the contemporary gospel movement was the Calvary Chapel in Costa Mesa, California. Serving as an early performance center for contemporary artists and giving sanction to their efforts, the large evangelical church formed Maranatha! Music in 1971. Maranatha!, which provided an assortment of publishing and recording services designed for evangelizing, became the first commercial outlet for many budding artists, including Love Song, one of the first gospel rock groups to achieve national exposure in secular music stores. The support of Calvary Chapel, as well as the name of the music company, illustrated the premillennial fervor behind the early years of Jesus Rock.[67]

Although hesitant at first, traditional gospel music companies by the early 1970s had begun recording contemporary material, and album sales, particularly among young people, ultimately guaranteed the genre a lasting place within the gospel music industry. In 1971, Word, Inc., established Myrrh Records as a purely contemporary arm of its growing gospel music business. Headed by Billy Ray Hearn, Myrrh actively sought new contemporary artists and encouraged their development. Likewise, Benson's Impact label purchased Larry Norman's earlier *Upon this Rock* project from Capitol Records and rereleased it with a new

The World of Southern Gospel

mix by Norman himself. By 1976, the Benson company had formed the Greentree label as a separate division focused entirely on contemporary artists. A handful of new companies, most notably Sparrow Records, which was established in 1976 by Hearn after his exit from Word, also joined the growing market, distributing an increasing number of products with each passing year.[68]

Though still controversial, contemporary gospel music endured in large part because of the active youth ministry promoted by many of its artists. During the 1970s, new publications, notably Frank Edmondson's *Rock in Jesus*, Lou Hancherick's *Harmony*, and John Styll's *Contemporary Christian Music*, focused exclusively on the genre, and a handful of radio stations scattered across the country began giving airplay to syndicated contemporary programs like Scott Ross's *The Scott Ross Show* and Paul Baker's *A Joyful Noise*.[69] A diverse assortment of groups, ranging from the Christian rock band Petra to Keith Green's Last Days Ministries, who provided a mission-oriented combination of preaching and singing, emerged, leading to an altered definition of gospel music itself. Commercial success within the growing youth market led some labels, particularly those owned by the Benson company, to focus almost exclusively on the new styles. Annual gospel music awards became categorized, with as many as eleven different genres identified.[70] By the late 1970s, performers and purveyors of contemporary gospel music—now termed contemporary Christian music—had found a permanent, if unsettled, place within the Gospel Music Association.

CONTEMPORARY INFLUENCES
WITHIN TRADITIONAL GOSPEL

Even in more traditional gospel circles there was a new look and feel to the music. Groups like the Speer Family successfully made the adjustment to include more instrumentation and innovative styling. Both "Dad" and "Mom" Speer died in the mid-1960s, in many ways symbolizing that the link between the singing-school teachers of the early 1920s and the performance-oriented industry of the baby boom generation had been severed. The elder Speers had indeed been pioneers in the industry, and they had also taught their children well. In the late 1960s and early 1970s, led by the solid management of Brock Speer and the creative musical genius of his younger brother Ben, the Speers moved in new directions. Joined by Brock's wife, Faye, and a succession of talented young singers, among them Sherrill Nielsen, Ann Sanders,

Sue Chenault, Harold Lane, and Bob and Jeanne Johnson, the brothers kept the group at the top of the charts and at the forefront of musical change.[71]

Other groups also stretched the boundaries of the gospel quartet world. Buck and Dottie Rambo first drew attention in the early 1960s when, with Judy Russell, they formed a trio known as the Gospel Echoes. Largely on the strength of Dottie Rambo's songwriting ability, the Echoes secured one of the coveted spots on the National Quartet Convention stage in 1964. Within a few years, Buck and Dottie became widely known as simply the Rambos (or sometimes the Singing Rambos) after they formed a new trio with their daughter Reba. The group's innovative songs, powered by Reba's strong soprano and Dottie's distinctive alto, offered fans of gospel music an exciting new sound. With original compositions like "He Looked Beyond My Faults," "Tears Will Never Stain the Streets of that City," "We Shall Behold Him," and "If that Isn't Love," the Rambos jumped to the top of the gospel music charts and became regular guests on gospel music television programs. In early 1967, they made a much-advertised tour of Vietnam, performing for the growing number of American troops serving there.[72]

Also especially creative were the Imperials, a new quartet founded in December 1963 by veteran lead singer Jake Hess. Hess wanted a new sound and, as he had often told his peers, longed to form his own quartet composed of performers that "could go out on a stage and flatfooted . . . sing, really sing."[73] He surrounded himself with four of the brightest young men in the gospel music business—old friend Henry Slaughter to play piano and help with arrangements, bass singer Armond Morales from the Weatherfords, baritone Gary McSpadden from the Oak Ridge, and nineteen-year-old tenor singer Sherrill Nielsen, who had recently been singing with the Speers.

From the beginning, the Imperials had a unique sound—one that emphasized smoothness and blend. Under Hess's direction, the group also looked and acted different. For one thing, they dressed unconventionally—often abandoning ties for the more youthful, open-collar look; for another, they refused encores. By 1965, they added backup musicians complete with electric guitars and drums. The changes appealed to young people, and Hess's reputation was enough to give the group credibility. Within just a couple of years of their inaugural performance, few groups could match the high quality of their sound.[74]

Though Hess and all the original members except Morales had left

The World of Southern Gospel

the group by 1970, the Imperials continued to chart a new path in gospel music. In the late 1960s, partly because of a lull in their singing engagements after the retirement of the popular Hess, the group increased their work as backup artists for prominent entertainers like Elvis Presley, Carol Channing, and Jimmy Dean.[75] By the early 1970s, they had oriented themselves solidly behind the new Christian youth movement and the popular contemporary gospel. Even the group's album covers reflected the pop art and symbolism of the period, though promoters were always careful to include a clear Christian message.[76]

In February 1972, the Imperials surprised many in the gospel music world when they hired the talented black stylist Sherman Andrus, becoming the first major interracial group in the industry. Recently a performer in the musical *Show Me*, the newest Imperial had already earned a name for himself as a member of the popular Andrae Crouch and the Disciples.[77] With Andrus singing baritone, Terry Blackwood singing lead, Jim Murray singing tenor, and Morales carrying the bass part, the new Imperials created a powerful sound and approached the edge of the popular market, appearing on successful television programs like *The Mike Douglas Show* and *The Merv Griffin Show*. By the time Blackwood and Andrus left the group in 1976—eventually to form Andrus, Blackwood, and Company, a decidedly contemporary gospel group—few individuals in gospel music doubted either the talent or the modern direction of the Imperials. With Morales remaining as group mentor, the Imperials continued to sing and record primarily for the contemporary market. A promotional contract with Word Records in the late 1970s pushed the group's album sales upwards of 300,000 and 400,000 copies per project.[78]

Other groups were also experimenting with new sounds, although they remained more solidly in the camp of the traditional gospel quartet stylists. From California, the Hinsons, a family group led by brothers Ronny, Kenny, and Larry and sister Yvonne, burst upon the scene largely through appearances on the *Jubilee* television show. Their country feel was unique, but the group also benefited from Kenny and Ronny's songwriting abilities. In 1972, the Ronny Hinson composition "The Lighthouse" became one of the most popular songs in the industry. Both the Hinson version and a cover version by the Goodmans remained on the industry's list of top twenty songs for two years running.[79] Similarly, the Downings also profited from exposure on the *Jubilee*. Paul Downing and his wife, Ann, formerly Ann Sanders of the Speer Family, were joined by an assortment of talented singers and musicians and, over the course of the 1970s, became one of the most innovative-sounding groups in the industry.[80]

A CONSERVATIVE COUNTERACTION—THE INSPIRATIONS

Perhaps not surprisingly, the most successful new group to emerge during the period was the most conservative in appearance and presentation. The Inspirations from Bryson City, North Carolina, were nonetheless unique. Formed in 1964, the group owed its own inspiration to a high school physics and chemistry teacher named Martin Cook. Cook, formerly a piano player for the Kingsmen and a longtime fan of gospel quartet music, taught several of his teenage students at Swain County High School how to sing the various harmony parts. Initially singing gospel songs in Cook's basement, the group included fifteen-year-old Archie Watkins on tenor, fifteen-year-old Ronnie Hutchins on lead, and nineteen-year-old Jack Laws on baritone. A graduate of Swain County High, Dean Robinson, joined the group on the bass part. After a couple of years of rehearsing and singing locally, Robinson dropped out of the group and the three other young men were joined by fourteen-year-old bass singer Troy Burns. Shortly thereafter, the quartet recorded its first album and gradually began expanding its weekend singing schedule.[81]

Over the next few years, the young Inspirations captured the imaginations of the fans of traditional gospel singing. With Watkins often taking a tenor lead throughout an entire song, the group forged a distinctive sound. After the boys graduated from Swain County High, in 1969, Cook retired from teaching and concentrated full time on performing gospel music and coaching the Inspirations. At about the same time, Jack Laws and Troy Burns left the group and two new youngsters, Eddie Deitz and Marlin Shubert, replaced them, anchoring the baritone and bass parts, respectively. Laws and Burns remained on friendly terms with the group, sometimes filling in when needed and eventually returning to take up full-time positions as back-up musicians. By the early 1970s, a string of successful hits, including "Jesus Is Coming Soon," "When I Wake Up to Sleep No More," "Touring that City," and "Jesus Is Mine," had earned the Inspirations a spot alongside the major concert groups in the industry—most significantly, a regular slot with the Florida Boys on the *Gospel Singing Jubilee.* In addition, in December 1970, the group enjoyed an eight-minute feature on the *CBS Weekend News* hosted by veteran newsman Roger Mudd.[82]

The World of Southern Gospel

Significantly, the Inspirations' clean-cut image provided more conservative fans of gospel music with a model for how the next generation might represent the music. From the beginning, Cook, himself a conservative Baptist, recognized the importance of the image he was creating and its value to the traditional sector of the gospel music community. Early on, he communicated clearly the message that the group hoped to convey. "I am proud of our personnel . . . and in more ways than singing. These are good, clean-cut, young Christian men who want to help others have a better way of life. I have confidence in their purpose; it's a heartfelt purpose. . . . I believe there's a place in gospel music for the gentleman Christian approach, and that's exactly the way we go about our work."[83] In the midst of an American culture obsessed with antiestablishment symbolism, the Inspirations drafted a formalized commitment to conservative Christian values. Their 1973 bylaws required not only that each member of the group "be saved and living for God" but also that "when before the public, [he be]clean shaven, freshly bathed, moderately dressed, and above all must always maintain a neat appearance in his hair style."[84]

Aware of their status as the most popular young conservative group in the industry, the Inspirations also remained true to the musical formula that brought them success. Few groups ever created a more unique sound. Having contracted with Canaan Records by the early 1970s, their projects proved durable, as did their annual gospel music celebration, "Singing in the Smokies," which was begun in 1968 and held during Fourth of July celebrations near their home in Bryson City. Remarkably, the Inspirations incurred few personnel changes over the remainder of the century, most notably the replacement of Shubert by bass singer Mike Holcomb in 1972. By the late 1990s, "Singing in the Smokies" had been expanded to take place over nine days around the July 4 holiday and an additional four days over the Labor Day weekend. After more than thirty years, it endured as one of the most successful gospel quartet events of the year.[85]

QUARTET EVANGELISM—FROM ENTERTAINMENT TO MUSIC MINISTRY

In addition to experimenting with new sounds in the late 1960s, gospel quartets also embraced a new emphasis on evangelism. Given gospel music's roots in a southern culture closely tied to American evangelical thought, this new trend was not surprising. Up to this point, the de-

veloping quartet industry had emphasized the performance and entertainment value of gospel singing—perhaps taking for granted that the
spiritual nuances were already understood and shared by listeners. In the
1960s, however, the growing belief among evangelicals that American
culture was out of step with Christian values led many to believe that the
true goal of all Christian efforts needed to be evangelism. At the same
time, the newer contemporary artists—shaped by the Jesus movement
and a sincere desire to change the lives of their listeners—also focused
on evangelical efforts.

Prominent in the increased attention given to evangelism was an Indiana songwriter named Bill Gaither. Gaither, whose songs came to include quartet staples like "He Touched Me," "The King Is Coming," and
"Because He Lives," grew up with an abiding love of the quartet music
made famous in the South. As an adult, he recalled driving out to the
highest point near his Alexandria, Indiana, home in order to tune in radio
programs featuring groups such as the Rangers, the Homeland Harmony
Quartet, the Blackwoods, and the Statesmen. His earliest ambitions were
to sing in a quartet, and though he would ultimately achieve that goal,
his greatest contribution would come as an innovator in gospel music.[86]

The Gaither Trio—Bill Gaither, his younger brother, Danny, and his
younger sister Mary Ann, began as a family group in the early 1960s. In
the mid-1960s, Mary Ann married and decided to retire from the group.
Bill's wife, Gloria, ultimately took her place. On the strength of Bill and
Gloria Gaither's songwriting ability and Danny Gaither's strong lead
voice, the group soared to the top of the gospel music charts in the late
1960s and early 1970s. Their 1968 album *Alleluia*, widely considered the
beginning of a new genre of "praise and inspirational" music, enjoyed
phenomenal success within the gospel music market, selling in excess of
250,000 copies.[87]

Although there had been other popular trios, most notably the Sons
of Song, the Goss Brothers, the Rangers Trio, and the Rambos, the Gaithers were different because they refused to compete head-to-head with
the other groups in the industry. Though their concerts consistently
filled auditoriums with an average crowd size of 10,000, Bill Gaither
never believed his group had a powerful stage presence, at least compared to the industry standard set years before by the Statesmen and
the Blackwoods, whom he had so admired and idolized. Believing that
he lacked the established groups' power to captivate an audience with a
polished presentation or a silky-smooth rendition of a spiritual or one of

The World of Southern Gospel

the old convention songs, Gaither focused on simple tunes that stressed a worshipful evangelical message. Deeply committed members of the Church of God of Anderson, Indiana, the Gaithers were comfortable performing in church services where worship and praise time served as the ultimate goal of their music. In hindsight, their example was considerably more influential because they did not follow a previously marked trail. The Gaithers' songs were customarily recorded by the established quartets, but, more important, the group was expanding into the church market, which southern quartets had routinely avoided. As the contemporary gospel sound of the decade flourished, the Gaithers and their compositions popularized gospel music in churches and homes where the older entertainment format had failed to secure a foothold.[88]

During the 1980s, Bill Gaither formed a quartet known as the Gaither Vocal Band, and, true to form, his group proved anything but traditional. Comfortable with a variety of gospel styles, the Vocal Band built bridges between fans of differing types of gospel music—they were as comfortable with an old-style hymn or gospel quartet favorite as they were with the newer contemporary material. Choosing singers from traditional quartet circles as well as from the world of black gospel and of the newer contemporary music, Gaither—perhaps more than any other gospel artist—served as a conduit for the various styles of religious music that had emerged by the late decades of the century. By the 1990s, Gaither's influence was such that he was able to mix much of the music of the traditional white quartets together with both contemporary and black gospel in a series of phenomenally successful concerts and videotapes marketed under the title *Homecoming.*[89]

Even before the Gaithers began to popularize the evangelical side of gospel quartet music, several other groups had introduced their music as a distinct Christian ministry. The Couriers Quartet, which had settled in western Pennsylvania by the early 1960s, was unique in that the members of the group had actually trained for the ministry when they began singing together at a Bible college in Springfield, Missouri. Self-conscious about their inability to reproduce the "big sound" of some of the more popular quartets, they settled north of the Mason-Dixon line and contented themselves with spreading a new style to a new audience. In doing so, they also shared their unique commitment to be ambassadors of the Christian Gospel. In a 1996 interview, Duane Nicholson recalled overhearing other groups that sang with them in concert appearances remarking sarcastically, "Here come the preacher boys."[90] Though technically their comments were true, at least in part—Dave Kyllonen, the bass singer, was an ordained minister—Nicholson understood the remarks to be criticism and feared that other quartets resented his group's resolve to use their music specifically as ministry. Still, he and the other Couriers believed strongly that their gift for entertainment represented a call to Christian evangelism. Years after he began his career, Nicholson explained his own commitment to that mission: "There's nothing wrong with entertainment. Jesus was always entertaining with his message. He wasn't boring; the crowds came around Him. And you've got to entertain the people before they even listen to you. You've got to make a friend of them, you've got to make them laugh; you've got to have a good time with them. Then you punch home the message."[91]

By the early 1970s, the Couriers had made an even greater commitment to spread the gospel through their music. When baritone singer Don Baldwin left the group in the mid-1960s to pursue a studio recording business, Nicholson, Kyllonen, and Neil Enloe hired a series of individuals, including Enloe's brother, Phil, to round out the quartet and to provide accompaniment. However, by 1968, the three men decided to reorganize the Couriers as a trio. Since the group also lacked a regular pianist at the time, they decided to improvise. On recently added material, Enloe could accompany the trio on piano, but elsewhere the Couriers became the first major gospel group to travel and perform on stage backed completely by sound track recordings. Even though the sound quality of their tracks was impeccable—they ultimately paid for the services of the London Symphony Orchestra—the decision to scale back their operation was nevertheless surprising in an industry in which groups had typically added more instruments and singers rather than removed them.[92]

Important in their decision to scale back was the three men's shared commitment to promote their music as a gospel ministry, complete with evangelical altar calls, in which non-Christians were invited to walk to the front of the church and accept Christ. Though they still worked some major concerts, their bread-and-butter performances shifted more and more to church services, often in the North, where audiences were not accustomed to the more vibrant performances of southern quartets at the all-night sings. They also found much success in Canada, where a thriving evangelical movement relished their combination of vocal harmony and heart-felt testimony. Nicholson later recalled the freedom that the three men felt when they embarked on a clear evangelical emphasis. "We shared from the Word. This is not to put anyone else down. This

The World of Southern Gospel

was just us. We felt we had to give out the Word. . . . We felt a tremendous responsibility that what we said, although we had a lot of fun, we wanted to make sure that those people knew where we were coming from, that we had an obligation to share Jesus Christ with them. And they had to make some kind of decision in our services whether to accept Christ or reject Him again."[93]

More comfortable than most with contemporary gospel music, the Couriers found major success during the 1970s—in part through the songwriting ability of Neil Enloe, who penned the Dove Award–winning "Statue of Liberty," among other Courier favorites. By 1975, they had pioneered a unique form of gospel music ministry, one that entertained but also enabled each member to testify and share his personal faith. Enloe candidly noted that the evangelical aspect of their work was all that really mattered. "We live for the altar call each evening. We judge the success of our program only by the response of that altar call. We might have sung well and received standing ovations, but this means nothing if we do not see people come to Christ. This is the whole message of our music."[94] As a result, the group invested a growing percentage of their budget into foreign missions—literally traveling at their own expense to overseas mission stations operated by American churches and singing their brand of gospel music.[95]

Another group that foreshadowed the move of gospel quartets toward an emphasis on ministry was the Cathedral Quartet, a group formed in Akron, Ohio, in the mid-1960s. The Cathedrals were an offshoot of the Weatherford Quartet, the members of which had spent time on the staff of Reverend Rex Humbard's Cathedral of Tomorrow. When, in 1963, Earl Weatherford and his wife, Lily Fern, took their group back on the full-time traveling circuit, they became, in effect, a new group. Left behind in Akron were several former members of the quartet— Glen Payne, Danny Koker, and Bobby Clark. With Koker accompanying on piano, the three men formed the Cathedral Trio and continued to work for the Humbard ministry. A year and a half later, they were joined by George Younce—another ex-Weatherford who had most recently served nine years with the Blue Ridge Quartet. Now with Payne singing lead; Koker, baritone; Clark, tenor; and Younce, bass, the Cathedrals began promoting themselves in the gospel music community.[96]

For the next half decade, the group remained tied to Humbard's church—giving them a level of security but also limiting their ability to experiment on the quartet circuit. The association, however, gave them radio and television exposure that served them well in establishing name recognition. More important, the association forced the group to examine its own relationship within the Christian community. Reflecting on the group's history decades later, George Younce acknowledged that the Cathedrals consciously sought to find the ideal mix between entertainment and evangelism:

> We don't exactly call what we do . . . we feel like it's a ministry but we don't go out saying, "This is our ministry." God has called us to what we do and we're proud of it. But what we do . . . we get paid for what we do . . . so we are brought in there to entertain. We are Christian entertainers, you know, but not just that. What we do is we sing; we entertain; we have fun. The first part of our program is entertaining. But it's not just that. If we were there just to entertain, what a vain group of men we would be. The second part of our program, we get into praise time. So we feel that if you can get people to laugh with you, you can get them to cry with you. And if you can get them to cry with you, then you can present the Lord Jesus Christ in such a manner and in such a way that men, women, and boys and girls will want to know the Jesus that we sing about. So, everything that we do boils down to that last twenty minutes that we're on stage that we give people a chance to accept the Jesus that we know . . . whether it's in a church or an auditorium.[97]

With this approach, the Cathedrals gradually established themselves in the gospel music marketplace. As members of the group left to pursue other activities, Payne and Younce retained ownership of the group. Over the years, they hired a succession of talented singers and musicians — serving in many respects as a training ground for future performers of note, among them George Amon Webster, Mack Taunton, Roy Tremble, Mark Trammell, Danny Funderburk, Kirk Talley, Gerald Wolfe, Roger Bennett, Scott Fowler, and Ernie Haase.[98]

Gospel quartets encountered new obstacles when they increased the evangelical aspect of and the emphasis on worship in their concert appearances. Savvy quartet men and songwriters had always known that, within the world of American evangelicalism, it was wise to walk as wide a path as possible in order to prevent bringing up the many fine points of theological debate that might arise among Protestants. Now they also faced the potential ire of Protestant pastors whose livelihood and Christian vision depended upon the faithfulness of devoted supporters in their

The World of Southern Gospel

communities. Gospel music as entertainment was clearly an expense far removed from parishioners' obligations to their local churches and Christian missions, but, once gospel groups touted their work as ministry, some feared that limited funds churches acquired from members would be diluted by gospel singers. No doubt more than a few Protestant ministers would have been chagrined to read a reader's comments to the *Singing News* in the fall of 1969 admitting that the *"Gospel Jubilee* program on television each Sunday morning is my inspiration more than the church I attend on Sunday nowadays."[99] The fear that gospel music programming and concert presentations might lessen some participants' devotion to local church outreach programs provided an interesting omen for the coming volatile relationship between Protestant churches and an expanding number of televangelists who appeared on American TV stations by the 1980s.

GROWING DISCORD

The simultaneous expansion of gospel music into the contemporary market and growth of congregations of evangelical churches caused tremendous conflict within the industry. Gospel quartets, born in the competition to sell convention songbooks, often continued to gauge their own success by the level of success they perceived their counterparts enjoyed. The result was an almost continuous behind-the-scenes battle played out in endless bickering and rivalry.

Part of the problem was the lack of a uniform vision among those who now sang gospel music. For those groups with roots in the Depression, gospel music had been a way off the farm and a route to a better life. Though many gospel musicians believed in the message of the Christian gospel, preaching and reaching their audiences with that message was not the goal of their work. At best, gospel music might aid ministers and church workers. Surely the message of gospel music was better, they thought, than the message sometimes dispensed through secular music. But music was not ministry. Rather, it was hard work and it was entertainment. Most of all, music was to earlier generations of gospel singers an opportunity to make a living doing something they enjoyed.

Contemporary artists, however, joined the gospel music family with a sense of urgency and mission. Born in the spirit of idealism that characterized the 1960s, their music seemed more appropriately sung in church or, better yet, during youth retreats and campfire prayer meetings. Characteristically, some artists refused money for their compositions—arguing that, as a work of inspiration, it properly should be offered free of charge as the Lord's work.[100] As contemporary gospel grew in popularity, the idealism of some of the early artists faded and marketplace savvy replaced it. Still, in the music born in the Jesus movement of the late 1960s and nourished in the expanding evangelical revival of the 1970s, there would remain a sense of ministry that was largely absent from older gospel quartet circles. Many older singers ultimately adapted to the new environment, although privately plenty of skepticism emerged about the frequent attempts to inject worship into concerts for which admission had been charged.[101]

The continued pushing of musical limits also created discord among gospel music artists and their fans. Within the growing conservative evangelical subset of 1970s American Christianity, some believers reacted against any sound that seemed to accommodate Christian values to those of the dominant culture. The increased use of drums, electric guitars, and brass instruments on gospel recordings seemed to cater to a stratum of American society that was specifically non-Christian. For staunch conservatives, true Christian music ought to sound different from popular music and evoke a particular image.

Rising drug use among America's youth also worried these conservatives. In their opinion, gospel musicians should set a high standard of behavior—and one that unequivocally communicated the message of salvation and separation from the secular culture. At the height of the Oak Ridge Boys' success in gospel music in the early 1970s, for example, conservative Christian audiences were questioning the type of music they played and their stage presentation. The dilemma for conservatives seemed confirmed when, in 1975, the group, one of the most popular in the industry, left gospel music for the larger economic draw of the country music world. Though years were lean until their 1977 hit "Ya'll Come Back Saloon" catapulted them onto the country charts, the Oaks persevered and became successful country music artists. Their ties with the gospel music community, however, were almost completely broken.[102]

Backbiting and jealousy were common features of the gospel quartet world of the early 1970s, but, as the renegade look and sound of the Oaks was taking shape, the banter turned unusually ugly. Groups moving rapidly in the direction of a gospel music ministry registered alarm at rumors of alcohol and drug use by members of the Oaks as well as some other quartets. Conservative singers feared that such a tainted image

The World of Southern Gospel

cast a bad light on all quartets and destroyed the credibility of the entire industry before Protestant evangelicals.

Animosity ran particularly high between the Oaks and the Kingsmen. In fact, according to Oak Ridge tenor Joe Bonsall, on one occasion Kingsmen lead singer Jim Hamill (himself a former baritone with the Oaks) made a disparaging remark as his group walked out onto a darkened stage in a stand immediately before the Oak Ridge were scheduled to perform: "Wait!" Hamill reportedly said, "Turn these lights up. We're no nightclub act. They're coming out later."[103] At a 1975 concert held in Roanoke, Virginia—significantly, the last event booked for the Oaks by an all-gospel promoter—some two hundred members of the audience marched out in protest. Members of the Oak Ridge blamed the Kingsmen for orchestrating the embarrassing event, though Kingsmen manager Eldridge Fox staunchly insisted that his group had nothing to do with it. Nevertheless, the die now cast, the Oaks parted company with the gospel music world that had birthed the group three decades earlier.[104]

By the late 1970s, the stage was set for even further division in the world of gospel music. Contemporary gospel music, and the powerful marketing behind it, threatened the popularity of both traditional black and traditional white gospel music. With Americans becoming more conservative in the post-Watergate era, the time was ripe for a much stronger alliance between gospel music and evangelical Christian ministry. In the 1976 presidential campaign, the media seemed caught off guard by Democratic candidate Jimmy Carter's open discussion of his evangelical "born again" experience. The scope and substance of reporters' questions symbolized the degree to which the mainstream press remained largely out of touch with the religious convictions of American evangelicals. As the 1980s dawned, conservative gospel musicians stood poised to reap the benefits of a religious awakening that had been brewing since the 1950s.

The Singing Americans, mid-1980s. Left to right: Danny Funderburk (tenor), Ivan Parker (lead), Ed Hill (baritone), and Dwayne Burke (bass). Courtesy Southern Gospel Music Hall of Fame and Museum, Sevierville, Tenn.

The Hoppers, early 1990s. Left to right, standing: *Shannon Childress (piano), Dean Hopper (lead), and Claude Hopper (bass);* left to right, seated: *Kim Greene Hopper (soprano), Mike Hopper (drums), and Connie Hopper (alto). Courtesy Southern Gospel Music Hall of Fame and Museum, Sevierville, Tenn.*

The Talleys, late 1980s. Left to right: *Kirk Talley (tenor), Roger Talley (lead), and Deborah Talley (alto). Courtesy Southern Gospel Music Hall of Fame and Museum, Sevierville, Tenn.*

Gold City, ca. 1990. Left to right: *Garry Jones (piano), Mark Fain (bass), Steve Lacey (baritone), Doug Riley (drums), Ivan Parker (lead), Tim Riley (bass), and Brian Free (tenor). Courtesy of* Singing News *magazine, Boone, N.C.*

Charles Johnson and the Revivers, early 1990s. Left to right: *Ricky Luster (tenor), Charles Johnson (lead), and Darrell Luster (baritone).* Courtesy of Singing News magazine, Boone, N.C.

The Bishops, 1999. Left to right: *Carl Williams Jr. (instrumentalist), Kenny Bishop (tenor), Kenneth Bishop (baritone), Mark Bishop (lead), and Chris Key (instrumentalist). Courtesy of* Singing News *magazine, Boone, N.C.*

The Greenes, 2001. Left to right: *Tim Greene (tenor), Taranda Kiser Greene (soprano), and Tony Greene (baritone). Courtesy of* Singing News *magazine, Boone, N.C.*

The Kingdom Heirs, Dollywood's resident southern gospel quartet, late 1990s. Top row, left to right: Eric Bennett (bass) and Jamie Graves (piano); middle row, left to right: Steve French (baritone), David Sutton (tenor), and Arthur Rice (lead); bottom row, left to right: Dennis Murphy (drums) and Kreis French (bass guitar). Courtesy of Singing News magazine, Boone, N.C.

Greater Vision in concert, 2000. Left to right: Gerald Wolfe (lead), Rodney Griffin (baritone), and Jason Waldroup (tenor). Courtesy of Singing News magazine, Boone, N.C.

The Perrys, 2000. Left to right, standing: *David Hill (lead), Libbi Perry Stuffle (alto), and Tracy Stuffle (bass).* Left to right, seated: *Dennis Horton (piano) and Nicole Watts (soprano). Courtesy of* Singing News *magazine, Boone, N.C.*

The SGMA Hall of Fame and Museum, Dollywood Theme Park, Pigeon Forge, Tennessee. Courtesy Southern Gospel Music Hall of Fame and Museum, Sevierville, Tenn.

Belfast, North Carolina, December 24, 1960, and
Louisville, Kentucky, September 25, 1998

I'm a couple of weeks shy of my fourth birthday in the Christmas photo. There I am with the first of half of what eventually would be the eighteen grandchildren on my mother's side of the family. And there in that room at Granny and Granddaddy's is where they were. Those trophies . . . a whole line of them ranging from two-feet-high ones sporting the title "Grand Trophy" to smaller cups announcing "First Place—Trio Division." The Harmony Trio—composed of three of the Forehand kids, my Uncle Loyd, Uncle Charles, and Aunt Carolyn—competed in singing contests during the 1950s, when most of that first set of us grandkids were born. We all heard them sing on Sundays at church, but we knew that other people heard them as well. That's where the trophies came from . . . from places like Benson, North Carolina, where an annual singing affair drew groups from all over the state and a few from out of state. They competed along with the others—some in the quartet division, others in trio or duet, and a handful in the soloist division. There was also a trophy for "Best Overall," and some of those sat in Granny's living room, where each Christmas and sometimes on Sunday afternoons I would read each one, imagining the details and the thrill of winning. What was sung? How many people were there? How loud did the audience clap?

Now, the scene shifts. It's thirty-eight years later and my wife, Connie, and I are seated in the audience at Freedom Hall in Louisville, Kentucky, on Friday night. The place is packed . . . 20,000 fans are seated to hear southern gospel's finest. One after the other, singers appear on stage, each for a twenty-to-thirty-minute stand, with groups ranging from the youth-oriented, contemporary-sounding Martins, to the smooth trio harmony of Greater Vision, to the classic quartet sound of the Kingsmen and the Cathedrals. From 6:00 P.M. to midnight, the concert continues . . . and the audience hangs on. They can't seem to get enough. Adjacent to the main arena, an exhibit area full of individual group products and recording company displays stretches to the size of a small mall . . . and it is crowded too. In all respects, southern gospel has made it. Another group is now on stage . . . another song. The 1990s are years of prosperity for America and they are the flush times for southern gospel.

9
THE EMERGENCE OF SOUTHERN GOSPEL

As Americans entered the Christmas season of 1980, major changes loomed on the horizon—changes that for many evangelicals promised hope for their vision of the nation's future. The recent national election resulted in the overwhelming victory of Republican Ronald Reagan to the presidency—spurred in part by the increasing strength of conservative Christian organizations. For the first time, issues like military support for Israel, a return of prayer and Bible reading to the public school classroom, and the addition of an anti-abortion, right-to-life amendment to the nation's Constitution were discussed with a degree of plausibility.

Though the Reagan revolution ultimately succeeded more on the economic and military front than in stimulating quantifiable social and cultural change, the confidence of the nation's evangelical Christians grew by leaps and bounds. Represented by the financial success of major television evangelists and commentators like Pat Robertson, James Robison, Jim Bakker, Jerry Falwell, and Jimmy Swaggart, the political clout of "born-again conservatives" became a force to be taken seriously in national policy matters. In 1983, and again in the campaign year of 1984, Reagan acknowledged the importance of America's evangelicals with a speaking engagement at the annual meeting of the National Association of Evangelicals—an organization that, despite steady growth, had received little national attention since its origins in 1942. Estimated in the mid-1980s as a force representing as much as a third of the nation's population, evangelical Christians had undeniably come into their own and were targeted increasingly as an untapped economic niche.[1]

Reflecting the expanding importance of Christians in America, gospel music—presented in a diverse assortment of styles—stood poised for growth as well. Shortly after Reagan's election, PBS aired a second installment of a program focusing on the nation's gospel music talent, hosted by the popular singer and emcee Tennessee Ernie Ford. Ford's first special, "That Great American Gospel Sound," aired the previous year, "surprised TV professionals and audiences alike" when it pulled an unexpected share of the viewing audience on its way to becoming the tenth highest ranked program in the history of public television. Ford's second special, "More of that Great American Gospel," showcased the music again, featuring an assortment of styles ranging from the contemporary talent of Andrae Crouch and the Disciples to the traditional gospel sound of the Happy Goodmans.[2]

Network executives should have known better than to question the power of gospel music before the nation's viewing audience. Less than a decade before, CBS had axed *Hee Haw*, a country music version of the unorthodox but popular variety program *Laugh-In*. Despite *Hee Haw*'s high ratings, executives at CBS wanted to changed the network's image, so they cut the show. The producers of the offbeat variety show, however, recognized the growing appeal of country music and immediately launched the show into local syndication. Close to 99 percent of the local affiliates that had originally carried the show picked up the syndicated version, and, with additional local stations now available, the program actually increased its viewing audience by a third.[3]

Significantly, the show had already endured a fight over the inclusion of a weekly gospel music segment introduced by veteran country performer Louis Marshall "Grandpa" Jones. Network executives had questioned whether a gospel quartet number sung by the Hee Haw Gospel Quartet, composed of Jones, Buck Owens, Roy Clark, and Kenny Price, might offend national viewers. Jones, who was a seasoned star of country music radio since the 1920s and had been a gospel performer with the Brown's Ferry Four back in the 1940s, stuck to his native sense of the audience's taste and the segment survived. Clark, one of the co-hosts of the successful program's more than twenty-year run, noted later that "the weekly gospel number became one of the most popular and enduring segments of the show."[4]

Though gospel music was clearly popular, gospel music groups still lacked the celebrity that most popular musicians enjoyed. Known intimately within the world of gospel music fans, they went virtually unrecognized in the larger secular market. In early 1971, few gospel groups enjoyed the success of the Oak Ridge Boys. Their release of "Jesus Is Coming Soon" had won the Dove Award the previous year as the top gospel song of the year, and the group's songs consistently appeared on the new *Singing News* Top Forty charts. With a fresh, energetic sound, they reached out to the new contemporary gospel audience, appealing to young people most of all. They also benefited by a name that had been familiar to gospel music fans since the late 1940s. Still, the Oaks remained obscure outside the world of gospel music, a fact demonstrated in the spring of 1971 by a humorous event in which the quartet's bus was attacked "by hundreds of anti-war demonstrators" just outside Washington, D.C. With none of the quartet members onboard the bus at the time, the job of explaining that the bus was not the property of the Oak Ridge Atomic Energy Defense Plant in Oak Ridge, Tennessee, fell to the group's bus driver, Darrell Jones, and the manager of their Silverline Music Company, Aaron Brown. Despite the two men's "pleas that the Oak Ridge Boys was a gospel quartet and was in no way affiliated with the government defense plant," protesters opened a cargo bin on one side of the bus in an attempt to destroy what they believed to be defense department property. Only when Jones and Brown "began passing out copies of the Oak Ridge Boys' latest Heartwarming single recording, 'Jesus Christ, What A Man,' like they were going out of style" did the demonstrators realize their error and allow the bus to continue on its way.[5]

Despite the relative anonymity of the nation's top gospel groups, the growing evangelical revival combined with television and recording promotions to enhance the visibility of gospel music over the next decade. By the early 1980s, the potential in the larger marketplace of the four-part-harmony style of singing appeared significant. The Oaks themselves had made the successful transition into country music, and newer artists such as the group Alabama flirted with harmonic sounds long enjoyed by gospel audiences. Even earlier, crossover gospel artists like the Swanee River Boys, the Jordanaires, and the Sunshine Boys had proven not only that talented gospel quartets could make their mark singing popular music but also that gospel material held a strong appeal for much of the American audience. Elvis Presley's use of the Jordanaires, the Imperials,

The World of Southern Gospel

and the Stamps as stage and recording backup artists during segments of his meteoric career had also showcased the style of the quartets as well as his own innovative presentation of gospel music.

By far, the most enduring and successful gospel quartet in the secular arena was the Statler Brothers, a group of high school friends who began their career in 1955 singing gospel on weekends in and around their hometown of Staunton, Virginia. Originally known as the Four Star Quartet, they consciously modeled themselves after groups like the Statesmen and Blackwood Brothers. By 1961, the group was composed of brothers Don and Harold Reid, along with Phil Balsley and Lew DeWitt, and they were calling themselves the Kingsmen. Their repertoire included gospel, country, and pop tunes. When the Portland, Oregon–based rock 'n' roll band known as the Kingsmen gained notoriety with the release of their smash single "Louie, Louie," the four young men from Staunton renamed themselves the Statlers—choosing the name from a local tissue product. The group teamed with country music performer Johnny Cash in 1964, and the 1965 release "Flowers on the Wall" became their first secular hit. By the late 1970s, a string of hits—many written by the Reid brothers—propelled the Statlers to the top of the country music profession. With only one personnel change, tenor singer Jimmy Fortune replacing an ailing Lew DeWitt in 1982, the group continued their phenomenal run through the rest of the century, which included the production of the successful *Statler Brothers Show* on The Nashville Network in the 1990s. Nevertheless, the quartet often recalled their gospel roots, paying homage to the legends in the industry that had first inspired them and frequently including gospel numbers in concerts and on recording projects.[6]

Their early accomplishments in country and their lack of any prior celebrity within the gospel field combined to shield the Statlers from the kind of criticism that the Oak Ridge Boys faced when they made their celebrated crossover in the mid-1970s. Just as crucial, and perhaps more so, was the fact that the members of the Statler Brothers retained a decidedly conservative image and message. With songs that celebrated family and the nostalgic roots of the American past, they found a warm reception in country without alienating the traditional gospel audience. Eldridge Fox of the Kingsmen remembered fondly that, after joining the country music circuit, the Statlers "sounded, dressed, acted . . . everything, just like they did [before]." And recalling the controversy that accompanied the more flamboyant Oaks' exit from the gospel arena,

Les Beasley of the Florida Boys reasoned, "On top of that, we're talking about some class guys. They're not Oak Ridge–type people. They're good Christian people [who] go to church [and] have families. They're upstanding citizens."[7]

The popularity of gospel music in the late 1970s was also enhanced by President Jimmy Carter, the first man from the Deep South to be elected to the nation's highest office since before the Civil War. Carter wore his evangelical faith on his sleeve, forcing the media ultimately to recognize "the estimated 90 million Americans who identify with the born-again experience" as "the nation's largest single subculture."[8] In early September 1979, Carter single-handedly bolstered public awareness of the contribution of gospel music to American culture by inviting groups from across the broad spectrum of the gospel music community to perform on the White House lawn in what was dubbed "An Old Fashioned Gospel Singin.'" Black gospel legends Shirley Caesar and Reverend James Cleveland joined stalwart white gospel performers like James Blackwood and Doug Oldham. Likewise, group singing ranged from the traditional black quartet sound of the Mighty Clouds of Joy to the traditional white sound perfected by the Kingsmen. Contemporary artists like Larry Norman and Reba Rambo also performed at the celebrated event.[9]

Despite the growing exposure, gospel music revenues remained small when compared to the total wealth generated by the nation's music industry in the early 1980s. Estimates suggested that gospel music represented no more than 120 million of the total 2.5 billion dollars of retail sales generated in 1980. Still, executives were enthusiastic that the percentage was only a small part of what gospel could eventually draw in the marketplace. Pointing to the growing country music market, one publicist predicted in 1982 that "in the next couple of years, gospel music will be where country music is today."[10]

Yet the defeat of President Carter by the more conservative Reagan in 1980 should have been an indicator of troubled waters for the larger gospel music industry. The optimistic projections for the growth of gospel revolved primarily around the continued expansion of the contemporary Christian wing of the market. Product sales by the new artists had frankly dwarfed that of the more traditional quartets. A few pop artists, most notably B. J. Thomas, had even crossed over into the Christian market. Their captivating testimonies of personal conversion from the alluring snare of rock 'n' roll stardom were partly responsible for spurring their substantial appeal. Contemporary Christian music seemed to

The World of Southern Gospel

offer the best of both worlds—an opportunity for musicians to continue applying their talents, now to the glory of God, without the problems so often encountered as a consequence of life in the fast lane.[11]

The cheerful accounts of conversion no less than the buoyant outlook of market analysts, however, hid the depth of contention that lay beneath the surface within the gospel music community. By the 1980s, the GMA represented a diverse collection of artists and styles held together by little more than the optimistic growth of recent decades. Organization leaders attempted to put the best face possible on the diversity within their ranks. As late as 1987, Executive Director Don Butler—himself a former performer in the traditional camp—was promoting gospel music's wide appeal: "I often tell people there's no such thing as gospel music and they look at me like I'm crazy. . . . Music is music. The unique thing about the gospel music area is that we take any style of music, be it classical, jazz, rhythm and blues, rock, country or pop, and we take that style of music that appeals to a certain demographic and we couch the lyrics of Good News—the positive-message lyric with those styles of music, and we reach all areas."[12] And the broadening definition of gospel music had, in fact, paralleled higher record sales and presumably a much larger audience. By the late 1980s, industry representatives were claiming more than $300 million in annual sales of gospel records and tapes. Yet, even as Butler attempted to widen the scope of gospel music enough to encompass the many divergent styles now operating within his camp, warning signs began to appear on the fringes of his organization.[13]

One of the biggest sources of contention surfaced over organizational expectation. Older, established artists remained firmly committed to the establishment of a Hall of Fame complex to recognize their many years of service in the industry. Younger artists were understandably more interested in promotional ventures that might improve their opportunities in the current marketplace. On several occasions, the GMA publicly announced plans for a Hall of Fame building and began fund-raising campaigns to accomplish this goal. Yet, despite annual elections that resulted in more than twenty-five members of the Hall of Fame by 1978, no building was constructed and various pieces of donated memorabilia simply languished in storage or were placed on limited display at the GMA offices in Nashville.[14]

Even more significant, turmoil brewed within the organization as a result of a debate over the image and presentation of gospel music. The

Singing News chronicled a running feud between fans tolerant of the in-clusion of more contemporary styles and those who believed that the changes signified the end of gospel music itself. In a reference to Mar-joe Gortner, the former Pentecostal boy-preacher-turned-actor who shocked religious conservatives with an exposé of evangelism in 1972, Rev. Gene Adkins opined in his "Parson to Person" column, "I predict that some group, or groups will keep playing footsie with the world until they will, thankfully, drop the word 'Gospel' from their title, move to Helliwood, and make a Gospel-music version of 'Marjoe.'"[15] In a similar vein of criticism, a fan wrote the editor to complain, "I love my Lord and I love Gospel music but not from the hippie, long hair, worldly groups you see today."[16] Other fans focused their complaints on a variety of per-ceived ills, including "swiveling contortions" on stage, "open shirtfronts," the appearance of groups at Las Vegas clubs, the increased volume of sound systems, and the widespread use of drums.[17] Though many gospel music fans took the approach of the *Singing News* reader who concluded, sagelike, "I am not sure that any of us have the only correct method or style in how to worship God," others became convinced that there were indeed concrete limits to what gospel music fans could stomach.[18]

Also controversial was the association of some gospel groups with popular entertainers. J. D. Sumner's September 1971 decision to enter his Stamps Quartet into a permanent arrangement with Elvis Presley's traveling concert show promised him financial security but also jeopar-dized his own standing in the gospel music community. Never one to back down in the face of public criticism, Sumner maintained an unwaver-ing stance against those who felt that a group's rock 'n' roll superstar image or its performance of secular material compromised its commit-ment to Christian music.[19] When the Happy Goodmans publicized their September 17, 1971, departure from the GMA in the *Singing News*, it was undoubtedly Sumner and the Stamps to whom they referred. The Goodmans alerted readers, "[W]e have a personal conviction and re-sponsibility to God and to singing of the gospel that compels us to take the stand we now take." Angered that the GMA-produced *Good News* had been used "to promote and advertise night club acts in Las Vegas"— a not-so-veiled reference to the Stampses' association with the Presley show, which at the time was the biggest act in the history of the famous Nevada resort town—the group accused the organization of catering to "the more hippie oriented crowd, and night club acts."[20]

Despite the criticism, Sumner continued to flaunt his association with the famous pop singer and, in the process, challenged the bounds of gospel music performance. Five years after Presley's premature death in 1977, Sumner defended his actions in an editorial in the *Singing News*, explaining that they were a way of spreading the overall appeal of gospel music. "I sang with Elvis for seven years," he wrote. We opened his programs with gospel musiuc [*sic*], plus, because we were there, he sang three or four gospel songs on his program. . . . I have tried all kinds of music and there is nothing wrong with country music. I am not ashamed of having sung with Elvis, I am proud because I sang my music — 'Gospel Music' — to millions of people who would never had [*sic*] heard it."[21]

The legendary bass, now with the Masters Five, also took the occasion to blast gospel music fans for their lack of support and insinuated that such was the reason that talented quartets like the Oak Ridge Boys had found their way into the larger country music market:

> We were in a church in Florida recently. We sang up to offering. James and Hovie were taking up our offering. Begging you might say! Jake, Rosie, and I were at the record table, and two men came out of the church so they would miss the offering plate. One man ran down the Oak Ridge, and asked me if the Thrashers were going country. I said yes. He said why? I said people like you. They are taking up our offering now and you are out here so you will not have to give. You are a free loader and it's people like you that ran the Oaks and Thrashers to country music, by not supporting them in gospel music.[22]

Obviously not known for mincing words or straddling an issue, Sumner went on to express his deep love for gospel music and his hope that fans would show their appreciation of performers by recognizing their talents appropriately. Long one of the industry's best-loved personalities, he absorbed criticism better than most, and there was little doubt that publicizing such controversial positions would quickly put a lesser known artist out of work in the gospel music business.

Despite his relative openness on the merits of secular music, Sumner soon became embroiled in a bitter debate over the lack of traditional or southern gospel exposure in the GMA and, ironically, helped establish a more restrictive view of the proper bounds of gospel music. As did fellow icon James Blackwood, he published an open letter in the April 1984 *Singing News* objecting to the image the organization was portraying. He criticized the most recent GMA-sponsored Dove Awards and the Grammy Awards telecast sponsored by the National Academy of

Recording Arts and Sciences (NARAS) for all but ignoring traditional gospel groups in favor of the more heavily marketed contemporary and "Jesus Rock" categories. The result, for Sumner, was a spectacle that was "a poor representation for Gospel Music and a disgrace for Southern Gospel Music."[23] Sumner noted of the Grammys, "[I]f you are Southern Gospel, I hope you kept a bucket nearby in case you wanted to puke as I did."[24]

For Blackwood, the Grammy show had been particularly offensive. Distressed that both "country music and gospel music" had been "treated like unwanted stepchildren," the popular gospel legend reacted most strongly to the performance of a number from the French film *La Cage Aux Folles* and the appearance of British pop star Boy George. Both performances, Blackwood believed, portrayed an immoral lifestyle inconsistent with modern Christianity. He argued that the "video clips that were shown plus the homosexual act that was performed, in my opinion, should not have been shown on prime time TV." The elder statesman of quartet gospel felt compelled to "apologize to our concert crowds that I asked to watch this year's telecast."[25]

At the heart of the conflict lay the fact that much of modern rock 'n' roll offended the sensibilities of conservative evangelical Americans. For both Sumner and Blackwood, the GMA had moved dangerously close to an alliance with the enemy in its promotion of newer styles in gospel music. Many individuals in the industry were also upset that traditional artists now faced head-to-head competition for awards with contemporary performers as a result of the NARAS lumping various types of gospel music into generic categories.

Obvious to the casual observer was the fact that southern gospel artists were angered by their loss of influence within an industry they had helped pioneer. As Blackwood complained bitterly in a follow-up letter to the *Singing News*, neither the black gospel songwriter Cleavant Derricks nor Hovie Lister—both GMA Hall of Fame inductees at the 1984 awards banquet—had been given more than a brief introduction preceding the actual telecast. Most offensive to Blackwood, and no doubt other pioneers, was the fact that Lister—who only two decades earlier had stood as a pivotal force in the industry—had been introduced as "Hoover Lester."[26]

For the pioneers and aficionados of traditional gospel, the GMA seemed to be taking advantage of an industry inherited from decades of others' backbreaking service. From their perspective, that they be remembered and honored was only a small favor. In the end, it was Sumner who threw down the gauntlet, noting, "[W]e in Southern Gospel Music will not take this lying down because we will fan the flames into a fire and you will be able to see it."[27] The controversy over the Doves and Grammys received national attention when the May 12 issue of *Billboard* magazine mentioned Sumner's and Blackwood's *Singing News* letters. Pushed to explain himself, Blackwood refused to back down, noting that "if we continue to be completely shut out of the GMA, we'll have to form a completely separate organization or work with a group like the Southern Gospel Association. That idea has a lot of merit."[28]

A humorous parody written by veteran pianist Henry Slaughter put some perspective on the growing conflict between different types of gospel music. Published in the *Singing News* as a two-part story in the summer of 1984, the engaging tale explained to readers that "Sweet Thing (The Gospel Music Association)" had, over time, come to have three suitors. Her first beau, "Country Boy (Southern Gospel Music)," had met her back "in the late 60's" and "it was love at first sight for both of them." Then, the two lovers had "decided to invite some friends to their party." The result was that Sweet Thing began to spend an increasing amount of time with "Ordinary Guy (Middle of the Road Gospel Music)." Since "sometimes it was difficult to distinguish them one from another," Country Boy and Ordinary Guy tended to get along well even after "Sweet Thing was dancing more and more with Ordinary Guy and less and less with Country Boy." But an invitation by "a good looking, strong, healthy, talented and exciting young man" named "Now (Contemporary Gospel Music)" created tension with Country Boy. Sweet Thing was understandably "turned on" by the "popular and successful" Now. Since "he was 'with it, right on' and knew what was happening in the music world of today," he "brought a lot of excitement to Sweet Thing's party."[29]

Trouble erupted, Slaughter continued, because "Now didn't know Ordinary Guy very well" and knew "Country Boy hardly at all." Most of the resentment stemmed from Country Boy, who "was rather suspicious" of Now. Sweet Thing, human and thus "not without faults," nonetheless had good intentions, though she "sometimes made wrong decisions." "Guilty of shunning the good ole boy who brought her to the party," she had nonetheless created "a very successful party" and "had caused a lot of different people to become interested and involved in her work." Now was young and inexperienced but "was growing and needed the patience that Country Boy and Ordinary Guy needed when they were growing up." Though the conflict between the three suitors had brought much opposition and conflict, God was now reminding all three of the commandment to "love one another." Consequently, "the Lord began to work mightily through them all, more than ever before."[30]

Despite Slaughter's charitable manner and optimistic forecast, the growing diversity in gospel music proved to be more than some individuals in the industry could handle. The first important break within the GMA had already come with the establishment of the Southern Gospel Music Association in the spring of 1982. An Albany, Georgia–based organization founded by promoter Charles Waller, the SGMA existed essentially to recognize groups with annual awards. Fueled by the lack of attention certain kinds of gospel music were getting from the GMA, the new organization's annual GEM Awards focused only on traditional gospel groups. In Waller's words, "Southern Gospel Music deserves the best, and we mean business."[31]

By this time, the term "southern gospel" was becoming widely accepted as the preferred description for traditional white gospel quartet music, and Waller's new organization appropriately advanced the term. In June 1985, SGMA president Les Beasley—himself a former two-term president of the GMA—abruptly announced that the new organization had been "able to raise enough money to . . . buy the SGMA from Waller." Though the Georgia promoter remained executive director and was appropriately recognized with the organization's Pioneer Award, the action proved to be the first step toward dissolving the SGMA. The following year, a neutral organization that fit more neatly under the GMA umbrella was established.[32] By the middle of 1986, the Nashville-based Southern Gospel Music Guild had been formed as a way specifically to promote the spread of the traditional music. The guild, for instance, would not initially sponsor an annual awards banquet but would work more generally throughout the music industry to address the needs of its membership.[33] Though many guild members remained affiliated with the larger GMA, the message nevertheless was clear that—for many musicians within the industry—the needs and desires of conservative, traditional elements were not being met.[34]

In the 1980s, a number of new groups entered the scene to carry the banner now identified as southern gospel. Joining the ranks of the Kingsmen, Cathedrals, and Inspirations in the tradition of the four-part-harmony male quartet came the Singing Americans, Gold City, the Dixie Melody Boys, Heaven Bound, and the Kingdom Heirs. The Singing Americans originated as a part-time group, but, under the direction of Maiden, North Carolina–based promoter Charles Burke, the name became associated with some of the finest young voices in quartet music. Gold City, originally from Dahlonega, Georgia, but by the mid-1980s under the direction of bass singer Tim Riley, from Gadsden, Alabama, scored tremendous success in the late 1980s and early 1990s only to see most of the individual members of the quartet branch out into solo and separate quartet ventures. Nevertheless, Riley always seemed able to regroup and hire a batch of talented singers in order to maintain the group's popularity. The Dixie Melody Boys, who were based in Kinston, North Carolina, under the direction of bass singer Ed O'Neal, moved from part-time status during the 1960s to score big with audiences on the full-time circuit by the early 1980s. After a brief unsuccessful venture into Christian country music under the name The DMB Band, O'Neal returned the group to its southern gospel origins in the late 1980s and again found a ready audience. Also from Kinston was Heaven Bound, a quartet that flourished in the 1980s on the strength of baritone singer Jeff Gibson's songwriting talent. The Kingdom Heirs followed perhaps the most unusual route to success. Relatively unknown in the early 1980s, the group became a regular performer at the Dollywood theme park in Pigeon Forge, Tennessee, in 1986. The constant appearances gave the group an opportunity to build its name as well as introduce southern gospel to an array of fans that attended the park in search of more traditional country tunes.[35]

Also popular in the 1980s were a host of family groups, continuing the tradition begun by the Speers, the LeFevres, the Blackwoods, and the Carters more than half a century before. The Nelons enjoyed the stability of their founder and namesake Rex Nelon, the longtime bass singer for the LeFevres. Likewise, the Dixie Echoes, with roots dating back to the early 1960s, entered the decade under the direction of talented lead singer Dale Shelnut. Upon Shelnut's untimely death in 1983 at the age of forty-seven, his son Randy assumed the group's reins and continued to travel and promote their sound. The Hopper Brothers and Connie shortened their moniker to the Hoppers after bass singer Claude Hopper and his talented wife, Connie, took full control of the group and began adding their children on harmony parts. Also popular in the decade were the Hemphills, a Nashville-based family group that scored big with several of Joel Hemphill's gospel compositions, especially "He's Still Working on Me," which made it to the top of the annual *Singing*

News chart at the end of 1981. From the rural confines of Waco, Kentucky, emerged the Bishops, a father-and-son trio that featured close harmony and a touch of country. Even more closely related to country music were the McKameys, family members from Clinton, Tennessee, who had been singing together since the late 1960s. The group's warmth and unpretentious style scored big with southern gospel fans, who appreciated the rural origins of its music.[36]

More polished were the Talleys, the combination of former Cathedral Kirk Talley and his brother and sister-in-law, Roger and Deborah Talley. The Talleys' successful technique mixed elements of contemporary with traditional gospel music, serving as proof of the fact that southern gospel as a genre had begun to expand. Also making headway by the late 1980s were the Perrys, from Dahlonega, Georgia; the Greenes, from Boone, North Carolina; the Paynes, from Grafton, Ohio; and the Perry Sisters, from Ceredo, West Virginia. Continuing the bluegrass gospel tradition were the Primitive Quartet, from Candler, North Carolina, and Jeff and Sheri Easter, from Lincolnton, Georgia. Almost all of the new groups existed within the tight-knit world of industry executives and concert promoters that had defined southern gospel since the 1980s. With the exception of Bill Gaither's quartet, with the unique name the Gaither Vocal Band, few groups enjoyed the luxury of being able to cross over into the larger world of contemporary Christian music.[37]

Even as southern gospel became recognized as a separate genre within gospel music, the music itself ironically moved down new avenues of diversity. A handful of notable black artists found some success by tailoring their music to predominantly white southern gospel audiences. The first group to have a major impact in this regard was Teddy Huffam and the Gems, from Richmond, Virginia. Huffam, a talented stylist and pianist, surrounded himself with a lineup of young black singers and performed a unique mix that combined traditional black vocals with well-known white arrangements. His recording of the Eldridge Fox classic "Gone" rose to the top of the *Singing News* Top Forty chart early in 1979 and remained there as one of the top twenty songs for the next three years.[38]

In many ways, Huffam paved the way for later black artists in the southern gospel marketplace—most notably Charles Johnson and the Revivers in the late 1980s and early 1990s. Johnson, a former member of the legendary black gospel Nightingales, consciously wove the two styles together seeking a sound that might be appreciated by a more diverse audience.[39] Inspired by his success, other artists, including Don Degrate and Strong Tower, from Charlotte; the Gospel Enforcers, from Morganton, North Carolina; soloist Willis Canada, from Richmond, Virginia; the Scotts, from Franklin, Virginia; and the Reggie Saddler Family, from Vale, North Carolina, continued to provide an important minority presence within the southern gospel industry at the close of the twentieth century. Although audiences remained predominantly white, the acceptance of blacks on stage stood as a hopeful sign of southern gospel's move to reach out to a broader evangelical coalition.[40]

As southern gospel expanded, it became more ambitious. In 1995, forces within the industry led by *Singing News* owner Maurice Templeton founded a new Southern Gospel Music Association. In some ways, the move had been foreshadowed some years earlier when, shortly after his 1986 purchase of *Singing News*, Templeton made the decision to cover southern gospel only. The change proved crucial in giving traditional artists a forum for both promoting and defining their place within the larger gospel music industry. A decade later, the time seemed right for a more comprehensive statement. Adopting the same name and logo used earlier by Waller's now-defunct fraternity, southern gospel industry leaders created an organization specifically chartered to establish a Hall of Fame and to build a museum complex.[41] Resolving the Hall of Fame issue, long a bone of contention for the aging performers in traditional gospel music, more than anything else energized elements within southern gospel. Selecting from GMA Hall of Fame members deemed to be distinctly southern gospel, the new association inducted thirty-seven recipients initially and began an annual election process and awards banquet in 1997.[42] Now obviously a parallel organization to the GMA, the SGMA forged ahead to build the long-awaited hall of fame complex. Through a partnership with Dollywood, the popular vacation theme park in Pigeon Forge, Tennessee, the organization opened a museum and Hall of Fame building in April 1999.[43]

An even more obvious sign of the health of southern gospel was the phenomenal growth of the National Quartet Convention. Purchased by a board of eight investors in 1982, the week-long annual convention moved from Nashville to Louisville, Kentucky's Freedom Hall in 1994. Within two years, weekend concerts drew sellout crowds of more than 20,000—double the capacity of the War Memorial Auditorium in Nashville. With a permanent headquarters in Louisville, the NQC also established branch events, inaugurating the Great Western Quartet Convention in Fresno, California, in 1997; the Canadian Quartet Convention in Red Deer, Alberta, Canada, in 1999; and the Central Canada Gospel Quartet Convention in Hamilton, Ontario, Canada, in 2000.[44]

Instrumental in the growth of southern gospel during the 1990s was the advent of Bill Gaither's *Homecoming* series. Inspired by Charles Waller's Grand Ole Gospel Reunion, begun in Greenville, South Carolina, in 1988, Gaither soon constructed a veritable empire based on nostalgia. In a succession of video recordings—accompanied by tapes, CDs, and songbooks—he featured the older style of four-part-harmony quartet singing. Gaither's innovative pairing of aging gospel performers with younger artists provided an opportunity for fans both to remember the glory days of gospel concerts in schoolhouses and churches across rural America and to meet current southern gospel performers. The *Homecoming* series proved successful beyond Gaither's wildest dreams. Individual titles in the series sold well over 100,000 copies apiece, and total sales topped three million by the middle of the decade.[45]

As the final years of the twentieth century approached, southern gospel found itself more than ever wedded to the fortunes of American evangelicalism. Conservative Christianity attracted attention in the nation's media, particularly during national elections, when issues associated with the traditional family were raised. Yet, it was in the trenches far from the observation of the media that conservative evangelicalism made its greatest impact. Alarmed by a series of trends in American life that they associated with a "politically correct" agenda, particularly the call for gay and lesbian rights, the pro-choice position on abortion, and the increased secularization of America's schools and civic culture, conservative evangelicals sought to build a bulwark upon which they could maintain the cultural values of the past. Gospel music, and specifically the traditional world of southern gospel, provided an attractive niche within which like-minded believers could find solace and strength. Statistics gleaned from performance schedules listed by the *Singing News* suggest that southern gospel performers responded accordingly by focusing more of their own energy on church audiences. Throughout the 1970s, southern gospel performers had conducted on average only 17 percent of their annual personal appearances inside the walls of churches. Remarkably, by the mid-1990s, that average had soared to 65 percent.[46]

Southern gospel's tie to a more conservative agenda had been detectable since the 1970s. Beginning with the Blackwood Brothers' "God and

The World of Southern Gospel

Country" petition in the spring of 1969, conventional-minded quartets demonstrated a willingness to stand up and speak out when matters of faith seemed threatened by a changing political and cultural landscape. Others in the industry followed suit. In February 1970, Gene Adkins reported in the *Singing News'* "Parson to Person" column, "SOMETHING'S HAPPENING . . . Have you noticed[?] Something's happening in the world of politics and government. Good old-fashioned conservatism is being heard."[47] Little more than a decade later, the monthly magazine took a strong stand in support of President's Reagan's conservative agenda, particularly the proposed prayer-in-school amendment and efforts to make abortions illegal.[48]

More significantly, southern gospel singers and songwriters echoed the trend with songs that supported these positions. Particularly successful by the 1990s were several compositions predicated on issues that seemed to cross the line between civic and sacred duty. The Inspirations' "Cry for the Children" dramatically demonstrated conservative evangelicals' despair at contemporary society's condonation of abortion:

Values of this world are twisted and evil.
And in our minds, we cannot find right or wrong anymore.
We spend to recycle, keep our highways clear
We're concerned about things like the earth's atmosphere
And some even cry because the whales may not always be here.

But we're killing our children
It's time to cry for the children.
For their blood flows like a river in the name of women's rights.
But God knows each heartbeat
He knows when every birthday should have been.
America, please get back on your knees
For the sake of our children.

Eyes that never saw mother now gaze on the Saviour.
Cries never made are now cries of praise to the Lamb they adore.
Little hands that in death were torn apart
Are held by a hand that's been nail scarred.
Heaven now welcomes innocent children we daily destroy.[49]

The Nelons' 1994 release "We've Got to Get America Back to God" made a similar appeal. The song pointed to a larger array of problems that could only be combated by Christians in the voting booth.

Whatever happened to "In God We Trust"
Prayer has been banned and taken from us.
When will we say, "Enough is enough,"
And get our country back to God.

We've got to get America back to God.
We've got to rule the world with a staff and rod.
We've got to fight the devil everywhere he trods
We've got to get America back to God.

Millions of babies we've lost each year
What have we done to stop their tears?
Christians, rise up, let America hear.
We will take our country back to God.[50]

However influential, neither tune matched the commercial success of
the 1996 release "We Want America Back." Written and recorded by the
Steeles, a relatively new group that originated in southern Mississippi in
the mid-1980s, the song caught the attention of the gospel music world as
a result of an aggressive marketing campaign by Daywind Music Group.
Mailing copies via certified mail to every member of Congress, as well
as to President Bill Clinton and Vice President Al Gore, Daywind propelled the group and their song to the top of the southern gospel market.[51] Blasting much of what evangelicals feared in modern American life,
the stirring lyrics plainly touched a nerve. By the end of 1997, the song
ranked as the year's top-rated recording in southern gospel according
to *Singing News* charting statistics.

Something is wrong with America.
She once held the Bible as her conscience and guide.
But we've allowed those who hold nothing to be sacred,
Like Sodom of old, to push morals aside.
Where are the men who once stood for right
And the women who championed their cause?
We must return to the values we left
Before this country we love is totally lost.

We want America back, We want America back.
From those who have no self control,
We want America back.
This nation is like a runaway train,

Headed down the wrong track.
It's time for the army of God to arise
And say we want America back.[52]

Southern gospel's conservative social and political agenda brought new direction to an industry that had long survived by following the path of least resistance. The older generation of southern gospel singers remembered the controversy of years past when Christian artists were criticized for performing at paid concerts or for singing in too wide a circle of evangelical churches. It had always seemed prudent to chart a wide course—avoiding the perils of theological divisions and personal convictions whenever possible in order to appeal to as large an audience as possible. After all, Baptists and Pentecostals sat side by side at concerts in high school auditoriums and fairgrounds. So did a growing assortment of Methodists, Presbyterians, Holiness, Amish, and Mennonite fans. Always it had seemed best to find common ground to avoid the risk of alienating potential fans.

But changes had taken place in America by the late decades of the twentieth century. After the tumultuous 1960s and 1970s, a loose alliance of conservative Christians found in southern gospel a type of music that spoke to their fears and reassured their faith. Likewise, southern gospel artists—many as dismayed by recent trends in the nation as their fans—became emboldened to speak out for traditional values and to proclaim an unadorned message of salvation in Jesus Christ. In an attack on the "watered-down" lyrics of contemporary Christian music, longtime *Singing News* editor Jerry Kirksey spoke for many in the industry when he noted in 1995 that "promoters of this so-called market expansion have duped many good groups, record labels, radio stations and other entities in our industry into playing down the Gospel in order to reach new markets. If we play down the Gospel, we have no reason to reach broader markets because it was the Gospel we wanted to reach these people with in the first place." The result was, for Kirksey, a clear evolution of the meaning of southern gospel. "Southern Gospel is not just four guys singing four-part harmony. Southern Gospel is any style of music sung by any number of people. What makes it Southern Gospel is not the style and not the number of people; it is that the lyrics contain the Gospel of Jesus Christ. What makes it Southern Gospel is a message as bold as the messages written by the apostle Paul, proclaiming Jesus Christ is Lord, Jesus Christ is Salvation, Jesus Christ is the way, the only way. No one comes unto the Father except through Jesus. That is the message of Southern Gospel Music."[53] Kirksey's attitude reflected in-your-face Christianity, and it played well to the new audience.

As southern gospel anchored itself to conservative evangelicalism in American life, it continued to diversify. Minority artists made marginally successful inroads. In addition, by the late 1990s, an array of soloists, most prominently Squire Parsons, Janet Paschal, Kirk Talley, Brian Free, Amy Lambert, Michael Combs, Quinton Mills, Carroll Roberson, and Ivan Parker, appeared regularly in concerts alongside southern gospel groups. They also received considerable airplay on southern gospel radio stations, and their songs frequently ranked at the top of gospel music charts.

At the close of the twentieth century, southern gospel, forged almost a hundred years earlier as an arm of the publishing business, stood more firmly than ever as a form of Christian entertainment. Along the way to becoming a popular genre in its own right, it had both influenced and been influenced by the larger music culture in America. Similarly, southern gospel had maintained a symbiotic relationship with conservative evangelicalism. Now it stood to benefit from the continued strength of evangelical Christianity in American life and culture precisely because it found itself in closer harmony than ever before.

CONCLUSION

By century's end, the commercial success of southern gospel as a separate wing of the gospel music industry remained difficult to gauge. Overall annual sales of "Christian music" recordings weighed in at $550 million according to an early 1997 *Forbes* magazine analysis.[1] Three years later, wire service reports disclosed that GMA figures for 1999 revealed a 21 percent increase in music sales over the previous year, with Christian pop artists such as dc Talk, Michael W. Smith, Amy Grant, Steven Curtis Chapman, CeCe Winans, and Jars of Clay responsible for much of the growth. Other industry analysts judged Christian music sales at 6.8 percent of the total market, fifth "behind R&B, rap, country and soundtracks and bigger than metal, jazz, classical, Latin, and new age."[2]

Southern gospel music undoubtedly made up only a small percentage of the total Christian-related music sales boasted by the GMA, but exactly how small a percentage was anyone's guess. Enhanced by the continued visibility of conservative evangelicals in American life, the southern gospel industry—even with the growth of the guild and the SGMA —still did not have a clearinghouse with the capacity to measure its specific growth rate. Outside of the *Singing News*, which boasted more than 200,000 regular subscribers by the year 2000, and the enterprises run by Bill Gaither, few individuals in the industry could claim more than modest success.[3]

Nevertheless, southern gospel seemed poised for continued, if limited, prosperity in the new century. Evidence of this was the phenomenal growth of the *Singing News*—the magazine's circulation rate literally doubled during the 1990s—and the strong performance of other monthly publications that focused exclusively on southern gospel. In the summer of 2000, Jonesboro, Arkansas, promoter Paul R. Boden's *U.S. Gospel News*, formed in the late 1980s, enjoyed a monthly circulation rate of approximately 75,000. At the same time, the circulation rate of *The Gospel Voice*, originally established as a separate division of *Music City News* in 1988 and then purchased in the mid-1990s by Gottem Entertainment, Inc., was almost 30,000.[4] Despite the fact that *The Gospel Voice* struggled to increase its subscriber base and, as a result, ceased publi-

cation in the spring of 2001, the health of the other major monthlies revealed the passionate interest in southern gospel. And these publications
reflected only a percentage of the total interest in southern gospel. At the
local and regional level lurked a number of lesser tabloids—often distributed free at concerts—printed at remote shops or newspaper offices,
each bearing the advertising logos of a multitude of homegrown business
interests.

At the other end of the spectrum, southern gospel took advantage
of an expanding web of technological advances. Bill Gaither's *Homecoming* series translated well into the cable television market, finding tremendous success on The Nashville Network as well as some
smaller cable outlets. By the conclusion of the decade, the innovative
singer-songwriter had produced several new televised specials in addition to promoting ambitious concert tours, which he called "Gaither and
Friends." Most promising for future expansion seemed Gospel Music
Television, a cable network offering southern gospel music twenty-four
hours a day. Though it struggled to sell its product in the larger market,
GMT represented the optimism that a decade of growth had brought.

Radio remained a crucial cog in the industry's wheel of success. Paul
Heil's two-hour weekly program *The Gospel Greats*, which had originated in Lancaster, Pennsylvania, in February 1980, chronicled the world
of southern gospel with artist interviews, inside stories, and a monthly
countdown of the twenty most popular songs in the industry. Highly
polished and accessible, the syndicated show entered its twentieth year
of existence on more than two hundred radio stations across North
America.[5] In 1990, the Nashville-based Reach Satellite Network began
offering daily southern gospel programming to radio stations across the
nation. By the late 1990s, under the direction of former Disney executive
James Cumbee, Reach—renamed the Solid Gospel Radio Network—
provided a signal to more than one hundred stations that carried it during all or part of the broadcast day.[6]

On other fronts at the end of the century, southern gospel appeared
energized. With the explosion of the Internet, a host of industry and fan-
based sites surfaced.[7] And, in addition to the phenomenal success of the
NQC and a handful of other annual events that drew numbers in excess of
10,000, smaller concerts were being put on by the hundreds. The entertainment industry in general benefited from the economic prosperity
of the 1990s, and southern gospel enjoyed its share of the abundance.
On literally every weekend of the spring, summer, and fall months, sev-

eral southern gospel events, with attendance ranging from 500 to 5,000, took place in communities across the nation. The *Singing News*'s state-by-state "Concert Billboard" for July 2000 included listings for sixty-nine such upcoming performances in twenty-three different states from Florida to Washington. A half-dozen major events were to take place in Georgia, a southern gospel stronghold, in the month of July alone. With ticket prices ranging from $5.00 to $15.00, depending on the mix of local and national talent, these local and regional music festivals breathed life into rural towns. A good number—almost a fourth—charged no admission, publicizing simply that "a freewill offering will be received."[8]

These major community events were simply the icing on the cake. Well over a hundred southern gospel groups advertised in the "Personal Appearances" section of the *Singing News*. Individual groups performed from a handful to as many as twenty concerts a month in a range of venues that included churches, high school auditoriums, local fairgrounds and rodeo arenas, and elaborate civic centers. Moreover, not all promoters or groups chose to advertise in the pages of the *Singing News*. Small concerts could be just as successfully advertised in local newspapers and on radio or, in the case of a large suburban church, through word of mouth or newsletter.[9]

Though no southern gospel group captured the national attention or claimed the popularity that Amy Grant, Michael W. Smith, Jars of Clay, or CeCe Winans did, as a collective body they packed an impressive punch. By the early 1990s, a phenomenal 446 groups loosely affiliated with the genre counted themselves as "full-time quartets . . . who derive 100% of their income from their Quartet." Even more astounding, 938 additional groups categorized themselves as "part-time quartets" with members earning at least a share of their regular income from weekend touring.[10]

Virtually unknown remained the number of local performing church quartets that did not rely on singing as a substantial part of their livelihood. Only 250 categorized themselves this way in a 1990 *Singing News* survey based on groups listed in the magazine's business files. However, groups of this type were surely underrepresented in the survey results. Few would have had the advertising relationship with the magazine necessary for receiving a questionnaire in the first place. Another piece of data drawn from a later survey of *Singing News* readers proved more revealing. In late 1998, 28 percent of the magazine's 200,000 subscribers reported that they "belong[ed] to informal singing groups" other than their church choirs. If each respondent represented a different local group, that would mean that there were more than 55,000 indigenous quartets among magazine subscribers alone. Although this conclusion is hardly scientific, by the end of the twentieth century, regardless of how one computed the local interest in the southern gospel genre, the figures came up big.[11]

Singing News survey statistics also demonstrated that the typical southern gospel fan represented the backbone of middle-aged, mainstream evangelical America. The 1998 survey results revealed an average subscriber age of fifty-six, fairly evenly split between male and female readers. Over 70 percent lived "in a small town or rural area," more than three-quarters were married, and 85 percent had children—most over the age of eighteen. A third had already retired, and the average subscriber household income was just over $44,000 per year.

Consistent with those findings, 92 percent owned their own homes and almost that same percentage had "attended 1 or more Southern Gospel concerts in the past year." Not surprisingly, 90 percent reported that southern gospel was "their favorite type of music" and only 6 percent showed any interest in contemporary Christian music. Forty-six percent identified their religious preference as "Baptist." Following that designation gushed forth an assortment of Pentecostal denominations that suggested that a full 70 percent of southern gospel devotees represented an uncommon alliance of Baptists and their more expressive neighbors. As might be expected, more than 90 percent attended weekly services at their church and almost half also attended "weekday evening services" and "participated in a Bible study program."[12]

The travails of southern gospel by the year 2000 revealed an industry still in search of its own identity. Despite positive reviews from fans who visited the SGMA Hall of Fame and Museum during the inaugural year of 1999, the organization still drew criticism from some quarters for having partnered with Dollywood in order to build and maintain the complex. Some fans resented having to attend the theme park—and pay the admission price—in order to visit the shrine for their southern gospel heroes, even as organization leaders optimistically pointed out the publicity that came from the attraction being linked to the popular vacation mecca.[13] More distressing, the SGMA still drew a very small minority of the industry into its active membership pool and, despite the successful opening of the museum, had yet to establish itself as the accepted umbrella organization to showcase southern gospel artists.

In addition, the industry began losing many of its tried and true celebrities. The acerbic but tender-hearted J. D. Sumner died of heart failure late in 1998 while on tour in South Carolina, and a graceful, but aging Brock Speer passed away from complications associated with Alzheimer's in the spring of 1999. The seemingly ageless Glen Payne lost a very brief bout with cancer late in 1999, and the universally regarded and admired Rex Nelon stunned the industry when he died suddenly in January 2000 after suffering a heart attack while on tour with Bill Gaither in the British Isles. Even before the death of Payne, the Cathedral Quartet—by far the most popular southern gospel group of the decade—had already announced its farewell as of the end of 1999. Ironically, the declining health of the group's heralded bass singer, George Younce, had hastened the decision to bring a close to the quartet's successful run. But, as it turned out, Younce would conclude the concert schedule while Payne, his longtime partner and seemingly the more fit of the two popular performers, would not. With each sobering announcement, fans grieved to see a generation of giants pass from the gospel stage.[14]

As a result, some questions lingered. Much of the recent growth in southern gospel had been fueled by the nostalgic force of Bill Gaither's *Homecoming*-style reunions, combining the quartet stars of the past with newer singers in a celebration of the power of the music on a century of American life. Though many competent and enthusiastic young singers stood ready to fill the shoes of these musical pioneers, it remained to be seen exactly how well and how long audiences would respond to their new mix of music and ministry. More significantly, southern gospel faced an ever-changing American social milieu. As in the past, its fortunes remained tied to the success of American evangelicalism, with all the pitfalls and advantages that such a marriage implied. The music thrived in the past because it spoke to the faith of those who both embraced its message and welcomed its joyous presentation. As that combination persisted, so would southern gospel.

NOTES

Introduction

1. Jerry Kirksey, "A Very Special Night," *Singing News* 28 (July 1997): 10.

2. Some of the more recent work in these fields are Paul Oliver, Max Harrison, and William Bolcom, *The New Grove: Gospel, Blues, and Jazz* (New York: W. W. Norton and Company, 1986); Robert Cantwell, *Bluegrass Breakdown: The Making of the Old Southern Sound* (Urbana: University of Illinois Press, 1984); Jeff Todd Titon, *Early Downhome Blues: A Musical and Cultural Analysis* (Chapel Hill: University of North Carolina Press, 1994); Cecelia Tichi, *High Lonesome: The American Culture of Country Music* (Chapel Hill: University of North Carolina Press, 1994); and Paul Friedlander, *Rock and Roll: A Social History* (Boulder, Colo.: Westview Press, Inc., 1996).

3. The pioneering work on *Sacred Harp* and shape notes is George Pullen Jackson's *White Spirituals in the Southern Uplands* (Chapel Hill: University of North Carolina Press, 1933; reprint, New York: Dover Publications, 1965).

4. Bill C. Malone's major contributions have come in his *Country Music, U.S.A.*, rev. ed. (Austin: University of Texas Press, 1985)—the first edition in 1968 gave only limited coverage to gospel music—and *Southern Music, American Music* (Lexington: University Press of Kentucky, 1979), 67–69, 113–19, and 166–67. Charles K. Wolfe's contributions have been in articles, many of which are cited below, and in his excellent analysis "Gospel Music, White," in William Ferris and Charles Reagan Wilson, eds., *Encyclopedia of Southern Culture* (Chapel Hill: University of North Carolina Press, 1989), 1013–14.

5. Among the more important doctoral dissertations are Stanley Heard Brobston's "A Brief History of White Southern Gospel Music and a Study of Selected Amateur Family Gospel Music Singing Groups in Rural Georgia" (Ph.D. diss., New York University, 1977) and Jo Lee Fleming's "James D. Vaughan, Music Publisher, Lawrenceburg, Tennessee, 1912–1964" (S.M.D. diss., Union Theological Seminary, 1972). Don Cusic's *The Sound of Light: A History of Gospel Music* (Bowling Green, Ohio: Bowling Green State University Popular Press, 1990) is one of the few works available to the general public. Although sensitive to the genre of southern gospel, his work is too general—covering the broad spectrum of gospel music from "Music in the Bible" to the twentieth-century maze of contemporary and traditional black and white gospel.

6. See William Lynwood Montell, *Singing the Glory Down: Amateur Gospel*

Music in South Central Kentucky, 1900–1990 (Lexington: University Press of Kentucky, 1991). See also Paul M. Hall, "The *Musical Million:* A Study and Analysis of the Periodical Promoting Music Reading through Shape-Notes in North America from 1870 to 1914" (D.M.A. diss., Catholic University of America, 1970).

7. The best of these accounts are Bob Terrell's *The Music Men: The Story of Professional Gospel Quartet Singing* (Asheville, N.C.: Bob Terrell Publisher, 1990); Lois Blackwell's *The Wings of the Dove: The Story of Gospel Music in America* (Norfolk, Va.: Donning Co., 1978); and Duane Allen and Jesse Burt, *The History of Gospel Music* (Nashville: Silverline Music, Inc., 1971).

8. The best treatments of black gospel quartets are Kip Lornell's *Happy in the Service of the Lord: Afro-American Gospel Quartets in Memphis* (Urbana: University of Illinois Press, 1988) and Ray Allen's *Singing in the Spirit: African American Sacred Quartets in New York City* (Philadelphia: University of Pennsylvania Press, 1991). A more general treatment of all of black gospel is found in Anthony Heilbut's *The Gospel Sound: Good News and Bad Times*, rev. ed. (New York: Limelight Editions, 1985).

9. Salvatore Caputo, "Gospel Singers Continue a Rich Tradition," *Charlotte Observer*, November 28, 1995, sec. E, p. 6.

10. See Talmadge W. Dean, *A Survey of Twentieth-Century Protestant Music in America* (Nashville: Broadman Press, 1988), 1–23.

11. The best example of this kind of concern appeared in William Ernest Denham, "The Gospel Song Movement" (Th.D. diss., Southern Baptist Theological Seminary, 1916).

12. Charles K. Wolfe, "Frank Smith, Andrew Jenkins, and Early Commercial Gospel Music," *American Music* (Spring 1983): 49–59. There is a sense in which white gospel music in the early years—prior to the 1950s—was always an arm of country music. Thus, as Wolfe suggests in this article, the "center" of gospel music shifted along with that of country from Atlanta to Nashville.

13. Malone, *Country Music*, 10.

14. Jerry Kirksey, "Watering Down the Message, It's Not Gospel Music," *Singing News* 26 (August 1995): 10. On the importance of the marketplace as a vehicle for religious products, see R. Laurence Moore, *Selling God: American Religion in the Marketplace of Culture* (New York: Oxford University Press, 1994).

15. An example of this tendency is Mancel Warrick, Joan R. Hillsman, and Anthony Manno, *The Progress of Gospel Music: From Spirituals to Contemporary Gospel* (New York: Vantage Press, 1977). The authors virtually discount white gospel, proclaiming that "gospel music is primarily a black artists' field." The lack of understanding is demonstrated further in the acknowledgment that "the only white artist I know who came from gospel is Elvis Presley" (50). Though Presley was clearly influenced by both black and white gospel, he was by no means the only white artist to have gospel music roots. No doubt much of the misunderstanding comes from the fact that, unlike Presley, who

was influenced by both white and black gospel, most white artists—particularly in country music—had their exposure within the confines of white gospel music circles. Similar is the proclamation of another music historian that "no one would disagree that the black church created and owns the gospel song." See Horace Clarence Boyer, "Contemporary Gospel Music," *Black Perspective in Music* 7 (Spring 1979): 11. Despite the long existence of white gospel groups, Boyer argues that gospel music "became multi-racial" after its acceptance in the 1940s (22). On the other end of the spectrum is the work by Lois Blackwell, which rejects the idea that gospel music evolved from the Negro spiritual and argues that it evolved from the optimistic religious folk songs of revivals and camp meetings. In fact, gospel music is indebted to contributions from both, and any attempt to try to separate the mix is futile. See Eileen Southern, *The Music of Black Americans: A History*, 2nd ed. (New York: W. W. Norton and Company, 1983), 82–88, 444–45, and Dean, *Survey of Twentieth-Century Protestant Music*, 61–62, for a better balance on the interracial nature of gospel music.

16. On the dynamics of race and religion in the churches of the Old South, see John B. Boles, ed., *Masters and Servants in the House of the Lord: Race and Religion in the American South, 1740–1870* (Lexington: University Press of Kentucky, 1988).

17. See Malone, *Country Music*, 13–14, and Oliver, Harrison, and Bolcom, *New Grove*, 195–97. Ironically, Boyer, in "Contemporary Gospel Music" (5), notes the importance of Pentecostalism to black gospel but then fails to acknowledge that white Pentecostals have had precisely the same influence on white gospel.

18. This assumption is made in Oliver, Harrison, and Bolcom, *New Grove*, 191, where the white gospel tradition is traced to a suppression by "Sankey and Moody's gospel song" at the same time that "black gospel assumed a character of its own." The failure here is not recognizing the dynamic impact that the interracial Holiness-Pentecostal movement would have on both races and their worship style.

19. Many writers have focused on the importance of the migration of black and white southerners northward. See Joyce Marie Jackson, "The Changing Nature of Gospel Music: A Southern Case Study," *African American Review* 29 (Summer 1995): 185–200. Jackson also correctly acknowledges the importance of Holiness and Pentecostal churches in this transition.

20. For an example of an early secular artist who became associated with gospel songs, see Charles K. Wolfe, "Uncle Dave Macon: The Birth of Country Gospel," *Precious Memories* (March–April 1989): 17–22.

21. On the origins of the term "gospel music," see Edward Ayers, *The Promise of the New South: Life after Reconstruction* (New York: Oxford University Press, 1992), 396–98. See also Michael W. Harris, *The Rise of Gospel Blues: The Music of Thomas Andrew Dorsey in the Urban Church* (New York: Oxford University Press, 1992), 151. Harris notes that Ira Sankey, the musical arm

of Dwight L. Moody's urban-based revival campaigns in the late nineteenth century, first heard the phrase "to sing the gospel" in Sunderland, England, in 1873.

22. Sales of the first few volumes of the video series begun in 1991 topped 100,000 each, and, by 1996, total video sales had exceeded three million (personal interview with Bill and Gloria Gaither, Louisville, Ky., September 19, 1996). On the success of Gaither's projects, see also Deborah Evans, "Southern Gospel: Selling the Sound," *Billboard* 108 (October 5, 1996): 1, 107.

23. The uniqueness of white gospel musicians in this regard was noted in 1979 by Betsy Farlow in "The Untouchables: Aspects of White Gospel Music" (paper presentation at the meeting of the Popular Culture Society in the South, Louisville, Ky., October 19, 1979). Farlow concludes that this is the dominant reason that black gospel has exceeded white gospel in carving out an identifiable niche and suggests that "white gospel music appears destined to remain on a treadmill that goes nowhere" (10). However, the continued growth of evangelicalism in American society, in my opinion, has radically changed the face of white gospel music.

24. After achieving success with the comic rendition of "Here Come the Rattlesnakes" in 1971, Wendy Bagwell reportedly "received myriad offers to cross over into pop music"—all of which he refused. See Robert Anderson and Gail North, *Gospel Music Encyclopedia* (New York: Sterling Publishing Company, 1979), 25.

25. Popular bluegrass and country gospel groups today include the Primitives, the Lewis Family, the Isaacs, and Jeff and Sheri Easter. On the peculiarities of bluegrass and country gospel, see Wayde Powell, "The Primitive Quartet," *Precious Memories* (July–August 1988): 25–29, and Wayne W. Daniel, "Making a Joyful Noise unto the Lord—the Gospel Roots of Bluegrass," *Bluegrass Unlimited* 19 (March 1985): 58–62.

Chapter One

1. On the development of American culture and its interaction with religious belief during the early years of the nineteenth century, see Nathan O. Hatch's excellent discussion in *The Democratization of American Christianity* (New Haven: Yale University Press, 1989). Also helpful as a broad overview of all of American history is George M. Marsden, *Religion and American Culture* (Fort Worth, Tex.: Harcourt Brace Jovanovich, 1990).

2. Irving Lowens, *Music and Musicians in Early America* (New York: W. W. Norton and Company, 1964), 25. In this classic account, Lowens identifies the Pilgrim Psalter as the "Ainsworth psalter" adopted from the Pilgrims short-lived stay in Holland; the Puritan version was the "Sternhold and Hopkins psalter" used by most members of the Church of England. The concern over translation seems to have developed with the growth of Puritan sus-

picions about the direction of the English church and was reflected in the Psalm book's proper title, *The Whole Booke of Psalmes Faithfully Translated into English Metre.*

3. Ibid., 17–22. Lowens concludes that musical ability had actually been high during the earliest years of colonial settlement and that the increase in "lining out" by the mid-seventeenth century indicates the degree to which such ability was lost by successive generations.

4. Ibid., 281.

5. Robert Stevenson, *Protestant Church Music in America* (New York: W. W. Norton and Company, 1966), 21–31. Also on the development of a separate American music tradition, see Talmadge W. Dean, *A Survey of Twentieth-Century Protestant Music in America* (Nashville: Broadman Press, 1988), 23–33.

6. Most writers credit Rev. Thomas Symmes with inaugurating the better-music movement. Symmes, a Harvard graduate and pastor of a Congregational church in Bradford, Massachusetts, published a booklet in 1720 titled *The Reasonableness of Regular Singing* to promote and defend the singing societies. On Symmes, the singing societies, and opposition, see Lowens, *Music and Musicians,* 19–20, and William Ernest Denham, "The Gospel Song Movement" (Th.D. diss., Southern Baptist Theological Seminary, 1916), 25. Another popular innovator was William Billings, a tanner whose popular tunes and work as a singing school master contributed to the spirit of American independence during the late eighteenth century. See Gilbert Chase, *America's Music: From the Pilgrims to the Present,* 3rd ed. (Urbana: University of Illinois Press, 1987), 115–20. For evidence that twentieth-century gospel music publishers recognized Billings's contribution, see *Vaughan's Family Visitor* 21 (January 1932): 4.

7. The earliest reference in the South was apparently William Byrd II's note of singing school activity in the Virginia colony in 1710. See Stevenson, *Protestant Church Music,* 53–58. The best study of early musical activity in a southern colony is Ron Byrnside, *Music in Eighteenth-Century Georgia* (Athens: University of Georgia Press, 1997). For an overview of religious and secular music among rural southerners, see Bill C. Malone, "Neither Anglo-Saxon nor Celtic: The Music of the Southern Plain Folk," in *Plain Folk of the South Revisited,* ed. Samuel C. Hyde Jr. (Baton Rouge: Louisiana State University Press, 1997), 21–45.

8. On Watts's influence, see James Sallee, *A History of Evangelistic Hymnody* (Grand Rapids, Mich.: Baker Book House, 1978), 11–12; Chase, *America's Music,* 38–40; and William J. Reynolds and Milburn Price, *A Joyful Sound: Christian Hymnody,* 2nd ed. (New York: Rinehart and Winston, 1978), 42–44. Sallee also credits Watts with a shift from a general emphasis on God's majesty to "a personal expression of the gospel" and thus a focus that would be consistent with Evangelicalism in the century to come. Also see Don Cusic, *The Sound of Light: A History of Gospel Music* (Bowling Green, Ohio: Bowling Green State University Popular Press, 1990), 26–31.

9. On the influence of the Wesleys, see Chase, *America's Music*, 40–43; Sallee, *History of Evangelistic Hymnody*, 13–17; Reynolds and Price, *Joyful Sound*, 44–50; and Cusic, *Sound of Light*, 32–39.

10. The revival spirit of the early nineteenth century is categorized by some historians as "The Second Great Awakening" to distinguish the outbreak from the celebrated revivals of the 1740s. Southern historians have tended to specify the southern phenomenon as "The Great Revival" in part because of its unique character. For a general account of the nationwide emphasis on spiritual renewal, see Edwin S. Gaustad, *A Religious History of America*, rev. ed. (New York: Harper Collins, 1990), 128–34; Marsden, *Religion and American Culture*, 47–93; Mark A. Noll, *A History of Christianity in the United States and Canada* (Grand Rapids, Mich.: William B. Eerdmans Publishing Company, 1992), 165–90; and Winthrop S. Hudson and John Corrigan, *Religion in America*, 5th ed. (New York: Macmillan Publishing Company, 1992), 131–54. The classic work by Sydney E. Ahlstrom, *A Religious History of the American People* (New Haven: Yale University Press, 1972), covers the entire revival period but restricts the designation "Second Great Awakening" to events in New England while referring to other revival outbreaks as "The Great Revival in the West." see ibid., 415–54.

11. For a discussion of the reform movements of early-nineteenth-century America, see Ronald G. Walters, *American Reformers, 1815–1860* (New York: Hill and Wang, 1978), and Ernest J. Tuveson, *Redeemer Nation: The Idea of America's Millennial Role* (Chicago: University of Chicago Press, 1968). Still valuable is Alice Felt Tyler's classic account of reform in antebellum America, *Freedom's Ferment: Phases of American Social History from the Colonial Period to the Outbreak of the Civil War* (Minneapolis: University of Minnesota Press, 1944).

12. On the importance of the Great Revival, see John Boles, *The Great Revival, 1787–1805: The Origins of the Southern Evangelical Mind* (Lexington: University Press of Kentucky, 1972, 1996).

13. Christine Leigh Heyrman, *Southern Cross: The Beginnings of the Bible Belt* (Chapel Hill: University of North Carolina Press, 1997), 263–66, and Ahlstrom, *Religious History*, 718–26. Methodism's rise in prominence was based in part on its adherents' adaptability to the frontier experience, providing ministers regularly through parish appointments of itinerant, circuit-riding preachers. On the relative merits of Methodists, Baptists, and Presbyterians in capitalizing on the frontier revival spirit, see Ahlstrom, *Religious History*, 431–32. On the Methodist experience specifically and the dramatic growth rate as compared to that of Methodists in Great Britain, see Richard Carwardine, *Transatlantic Revivalism: Popular Evangelicalism in Britain and America, 1790–1865* (Westport, Conn.: Greenwood Press, 1978), 45–52.

14. Estimates at Cane Ridge reported the attendance at this unusually large camp meeting to be as high as 25,000. However, scholars generally believe that those figures were inflated and that actual attendance was likely

to have been somewhere closer to half that number. Boles estimates that attendance at the camp meetings of the early nineteenth century "seemed to average between four and ten thousand" (*Great Revival*, 184). For a general discussion of activity at Cane Ridge, see ibid., 63–69, and Paul K. Conkin's excellent detailed description in *Cane Ridge: America's Pentecost* (Madison: University of Wisconsin Press, 1990).

15. For a description of a typical day at an 1817 camp meeting, recorded by a black Methodist woman, Zilpha Elaw, see Gaustad, *Religious History*, 134. Gaustad notes that the revival spirit in Kentucky extended even to recently arrived Catholics.

16. On this development, see Sallee, *History of Evangelistic Hymnody*, 28–37. Two examples of the camp meeting chorus are those that are attached in popular Protestant hymnbooks today to the classic Isaac Watts hymn "Alas and Did My Saviour Bleed." The original song can be found as the verses for both "At the Cross" and "He Loves Me." Some hymnbooks even include both "songs." Compare *Church Hymnal* (Cleveland, Tenn.: Tennessee Music and Printing Company, 1951), nos. 264 and 355; *All-American Church Hymnal* (Nashville: John T. Benson Publishing Company, 1957), nos. 79 and 130; *The American Service Hymnal* (Nashville: John T. Benson Publishing Company, 1968), nos. 19 and 211; and *The Gospel Hymnal* (Franklin Springs, Ga.: Advocate Press, 1973), nos. 169 and 192.

17. On the impact of songsters and the transfer of theology through the early improvised singing, see Boles, *Great Revival*, 121–24. Nathan Hatch contends that, musically, the camp meeting period is unparalleled in Christian history. He notes that "never has the Christian church been blessed with such a furious and creative outpouring of vernacular song" (*Democratization of American Christianity*, 160).

18. Adam Rankin, *A Review of the Noted Revival in Kentucky, 1801* (Lexington: N.p., 1803), 10. Also quoted in Ellen Jane Lorenz, *Glory Hallelujah! The Story of the Campmeeting Spiritual* (Nashville: Abingdon Press, 1978), 29. For a general discussion of camp meeting songs and singing, see Dickson D. Bruce Jr., *And They All Sang Hallelujah: Plain-Folk Camp-Meeting Religion, 1800–1845* (Knoxville: University of Tennessee Press, 1974), 90–122.

19. On the theological divisions that erupted following Cane Ridge, especially among Presbyterians, see Conkin, *Cane Ridge*, 115–63.

20. On improved camp meeting grounds, the protracted meeting, and the general differences in revival patterns among denominations in the South, see Anne C. Loveland, *Southern Evangelicals and the Social Order, 1800–1860* (Baton Rouge: Louisiana State University Press, 1980), 74–84.

21. Luther Lee, *The Revival Manual* (New York: Wesleyan Methodist Book Room, 1850), 98–99. Also quoted in Lorenz, *Glory Hallelujah!*, 38. Lee contended that "though frequent singing may be useful, long singing by all means should be avoided; it cannot fail to be hurtful. From one to four verses is all that should be sung at a time in revival meetings" (99).

22. Orson Parker, *The Fire and the Hammer: Revivals and How to Promote Them* (Boston: James H. Earle, Publisher, 1877), 47–48. Also quoted in Lorenz, *Glory Hallelujah!*, 39.

23. Many historians have established the degree to which blacks and whites worshiped together during the antebellum period. In general, integrated worship activity was much greater then than in the post-Reconstruction South. For a discussion of the role of race in worship patterns in various southern states during this period, see John B. Boles, ed., *Masters and Slaves in the House of the Lord: Race and Religion in the American South, 1740–1870* (Lexington: University Press of Kentucky, 1988). See also Conkin, *Cane Ridge*, 174–77.

24. G. W. Henry, *Trials and Triumphs in the Life of G. W. Henry* (Oneida: G. W. Henry, 1861), 176–77; also quoted in Lorenz, *Glory Hallelujah!*, 31. See also Presbyterian minister Samuel Davies's recollection of interracial singing at Cane Ridge as quoted in Conkin, *Cane Ridge*, 38–39.

25. For a discussion of this phenomenon, see Paul Oliver, Max Harrison, and William Bolcom, *The New Grove: Gospel, Blues, and Jazz* (New York: W. W. Norton and Company, 1986), 6–14 (which refers to the phenomenon as "leader-and-chorus antiphonal singing"), and Eileen Southern, *The Music of Black Americans: A History*, 2nd ed. (New York: W. W. Norton and Company, 1983), 93–104, 446–47. Southern notes that blacks played an integral part in the shape-note singing schools at least as early as the 1780s through the work of Newport Gardner (1746–1826) and others. see ibid., 69–70 and Lois Blackwell, *The Wings of the Dove: The Story of Gospel Music in America* (Norfolk, Va.: Donning Co., 1978), 103–6.

26. The question of black versus white origins in gospel music has been unnecessarily contentious. My study supports the conclusions of those who have found a tradition of mutual influence and continued development despite elements of segregation within the industry. For a look at some of the most balanced approaches to the question, see Ray Allen, *Singing in the Spirit: African-American Sacred Quartets in New York City* (Philadelphia: University of Pennsylvania Press, 1991), 4–5; Oliver, Harrison, and Bolcom, *New Grove*, 1–22, 189–91; Cusic, *Sound of Light*, 81–92; and Southern, *Music of Black Americans*, 82–88, 444–56.

27. James B. Finley, *Sketches of Western Methodism* (Cincinnati: Methodist Book Concern, 1856), 518, quoted in Lorenz, *Glory Hallelujah!*, 31. There are accounts of Cherokee participation in shape-note singing as early as the middle decades of the nineteenth century as well as a separate "Indian Singing Convention" as late as 1921. See Max R. Williams, ed., *The History of Jackson County* (Sylva, N.C.: Jackson County Historical Association, 1987), 358–60. For a broader discussion of the musical interaction between Indians and English colonists, see Byrnside, *Music in Eighteenth-Century Georgia*, 17–19.

28. For a listing of English and American hymnbooks popular during the

Great Revival, see Enos Everett Dowling, *Hymn and Gospel Song Books of the Restoration Movement: A Preliminary Bibliography* (Lincoln, Ill.: Dowling, 1975; 2nd ed., 1988).

29. On Tufts and the publication of similar instruction books in the early eighteenth century, see Chase, *America's Music*, 32–34, and Lowens, *Music and Musicians*, 39–57. Also on the transition from Puritan psalters to more popular music books, see Cusic, *Sound of Light*, 19–25.

30. Lowens argues that Tufts's publication marked "the beginning of organized music education in America" (*Music and Musicians*, 39).

31. The exact credit for publication of *The Easy Instructor* has been a matter of some scholarly debate. For an explanation of the evidence and a synopsis of the various theories, see Lowens, *Music and Musicians*, 115–37, and Irving Lowens and Allen P. Britton, "The Easy Instructor (1798–1831): A History and Bibliography of the First Shape Note Tune Book," *Journal of Research in Music Education* 1 (Spring 1953): 31–55.

32. Although the shape-note system was resisted at the time by traditionalists, historians of early American music have acknowledged its ingeniousness. Lowens paid a compliment to the system while blasting the inferred snobbery of those who resisted its advantages when he noted in 1964: "No one who has witnessed the astonishing sight-singing virtuosity exhibited by the shape-note singers of the rural South today, trained with what is basically the *Easy Instructor* method, can possibly doubt the effectiveness of the device. Had this pedagogical tool been accepted by 'the father of singing among the children,' Lowell Mason, and others who shaped the patterns of American music education, we might have been more successful in developing skilled music readers and enthusiastic amateur choral singers in the public school" (*Music and Musicians*, 117).

33. On the importance of Aikin's *Christian Minstrel*, which was subsequently published in an amazing 171 editions, see Chase, *America's Music*, 182, and Jo Lee Fleming, "James D. Vaughan, Music Publisher, Lawrenceburg, Tennessee, 1912–1964" (S.M.D. diss., Union Theological Seminary, 1972), 6–7.

34. The quote is ascribed to William Walker, a notable shape-note publisher, in 1866. Quoted in Chase, *America's Music*, 184.

35. The fervency of the shape-note movement is indicated by its considerable success despite the opposition by the urban musical establishment. An example of how devoted the professional gospel music industry has been to the concept is a fairly detailed article on the basics of music theory presented in both traditional and shape-note methods printed in a popular gospel music publication as recently as 1980. See *Singing News* 11 (January 1980): 21–22A.

36. Lowens, *Music and Musicians*, 116–17. See also Lowens and Britton, "Easy Instructor," 32. Hastings's most enduring contribution to American gospel music was the classic hymn "Rock of Ages." On his overall contribution to American music, see Chase, *America's Music*, 138–42.

37. On Mason, see Chase, *America's Music*, 131–38, and J. H. Hall, *Biography*

of Gospel Song and Hymn Writers (New York: Fleming H. Revell Company, 1914), 16–21.

38. On the class divisions represented by the promoters and detractors of shape notes, see Stevenson, *Protestant Church Music*, 85–91; Lowens, *Music and Musicians*, 116–18; and Doug Allison, "Shape Note Music in America," *Precious Memories* (November–December 1988): 26–27. On the emergence of folk tunes from popular involvement in early-nineteenth-century music, see George Pullen Jackson, ed., *Spiritual Folk-Songs of Early America* (Gloucester, Mass.: Peter Smith, 1975).

39. Recent decades have witnessed an increase in academic interest in shape-note music, particularly of the older four-note variety. By the 1980s, researchers, fascinated by the small though devoted following still evident among both white and black southerners, stepped up their efforts to preserve and understand shape-note music. See Doris J. Dyen, "New Directions in Sacred Harp Singing," in William Ferris and Mary L. Hart, eds., *Folk Music and Modern Sound* (Jackson: University Press of Mississippi, 1982), 73–79.

40. George Pullen Jackson, *The Story of the Sacred Harp: 1844–1944* (Nashville: Vanderbilt University Press, 1944), 7. Jackson's first and most comprehensive investigation of early shape-note music appeared in *White Spirituals in the Southern Uplands* (Chapel Hill: University of North Carolina Press, 1933). On the relative importance of the *Sacred Harp*, see also Doug Allison, "Shape Note Music in America," *Precious Memories* (November–December 1988): 26–31; Charles Linwood Ellington, "The Sacred Harp Tradition: Its Origin and Evolution" (Ph.D. diss., Florida State University, 1969); and Buell E. Cobb Jr., *The Sacred Harp: A Tradition and Its Music* (Athens: University of Georgia Press, 1978, 1989).

41. On White, Walker, and Davisson and the fortunes of their respective songbooks, see Bruce, *They All Sang Hallelujah*, 92–95. Bruce notes that Walker's *Southern Harmony* sold over 600,000 copies from 1835 to 1860. Brothers-in-law Walker and Benjamin White engaged in a bitter feud over their early music work together. White claimed that Walker cheated him out of his share of credit for *Southern Harmony*, and, as a result, the two men never spoke to each other again. For an early account of the dispute, see Joseph S. James, *A Brief History of the Sacred Harp and Its Author, B. F. White, Sr., and Contributors* (Douglasville, Ga.: New South Book and Job Print, 1904), 29–31. Also see Cobb, *Sacred Harp*, 74–75. On Davisson, see Rachel Augusta Harley, "Ananias Davisson: Southern Tunebook Compiler" (Ph.D. diss., University of Michigan, 1972). On Walker, see Glenn C. Wilcox, "Southern Harmony," *Rural Kentuckian* (October 1987): 17–21, and Jackson, *White Spirituals*, 55–69. On Funk, see John Walter Wayland, *Joseph Funk, Father of Song in Northern Virginia* (Dayton, Va.: Ruebush-Kieffer Co., 1911), reprinted and distributed from the *Pennsylvania German* 12 (October 1911): 580–94.

42. Quoted in Chase, *America's Music*, 184. For some discussion of Walker's conversion to the seven-note system and its impact on his business, see

Glenn C. Wilcox's introduction to William Walker, comp., *The Southern Harmony and Musical Companion* (1854; Lexington: University of Kentucky Press, 1987). On Swan, see Chase, *America's Music*, 182–84, and Sidney Robertson Cowell's introduction to *Old Harp Singing* (New York: Folkways Records Album No. FP 56, 1951).

43. On Funk's decision to switch to the seven-note system, see Chase, *America's Music*, 184–86. Funk's decision was critical given the importance of his grandson, Aldine Kieffer, in late-nineteenth-century shape-note publishing.

44. On the work of the southern reformers, see Lawrence A. Cremin, *American Education: The National Experience, 1783–1876* (New York: Harper and Row, 1980), 174–77. On the work of Horace Mann, see ibid., 133–42.

45. On educational reform in general, see Walters, *American Reformers*, 206–11. Walters notes that evangelical Protestants supported the reform movement toward public education since it "would be . . . morally sound and an ally for their own Sunday schools and Bible and tract societies" (208). On literacy during this period, see Cremin, *American Education: The National Experience*, 490–95. For a relative discussion of advances in literacy prior to and after this period, see Cremin's *American Education: The Colonial Experience, 1607–1783* (New York: Harper and Row, 1970), 546–51, and *American Education: The Metropolitan Experience, 1876–1980* (New York: Harper and Row, 1988), 653–57.

46. Funk and his heirs championed their journal as the first of its kind in the South (*Southern Musical Advocate and Singer's Friend* 1 (July 1859): 3). See Jackson, *White Spirituals*, 388–89.

47. On the Civil War and American religion, see Gardiner H. Shattuck's *A Shield and Hiding Place: The Religious Life of the Civil War Armies* (Macon, Ga.: Mercer University Press, 1987). For a brief analysis, see Noll, *History of Christianity*, 313–34.

48. On Moody, see James F. Findlay Jr., *Dwight L. Moody: American Evangelist, 1837–1899* (Chicago: University of Chicago Press, 1969).

49. On the relationship between Moody and Sankey, see Findlay, *Dwight L. Moody*, 122–24, 176–77, 209–19, and William R. Moody, *The Life of Dwight L. Moody* (New York: Fleming H. Revell Company, 1900), 125–27, 170–81. A particularly enlightening account of Moody and Sankey as "educators" of the public is included in Cremin, *American Education: The Metropolitan Experience*, 29–39.

50. The significance of Sankey's "singing the gospel" was reported in one of the earliest scholarly works on popular religious music. See Denham, "Gospel Song Movement," 2. However, according to William Moody, Phillip Bliss's publication *Gospel Songs* actually inspired the Sankey collection and appeared approximately two years earlier. See Moody, *Life of Dwight L. Moody*, 172. Nevertheless, it is likely that too much has been made of the term "gospel," given that the music would have flourished regardless of the name.

The greater significance lies in the association of the music to the evangelical movement.

51. Quite a few books have appeared over the years devoted to hymn writers and the stories behind popular songs. For an example of this type of literature, see Ace Collins, *Turn Your Radio On: The Stories behind Gospel Music's All-Time Greatest Songs* (Grand Rapids, Mich.: Zondervan Publishing House, 1999); Lindsay L. Terry, *Stories behind Popular Songs and Hymns* (Grand Rapids, Mich.: Baker Book House, 1990); Haldor Lillenas, *Modern Gospel Song Stories* (Kansas City, Mo.: Lillenas Publishing, 1952); George W. Sanville, *Forty Gospel Hymn Stories* (Winona Lake, Ind.: Rodeheaver-Hall Mack Company, 1943); and George C. Stebbins, *Reminiscences and Gospel Hymn Stories* (New York: George H. Doran Co., 1924). Rev. Barry Flanagan, an evangelist from Poteau, Oklahoma, has aided me in my search for this type of literature. Flanagan actively researches popular gospel songs and "the story behind them" in order to use this information as a backdrop for many of his sermons.

52. Findlay, *Dwight L. Moody*, 121–22.

53. On Bliss, see David Smucker, "Philip Paul Bliss and the Musical, Cultural, and Religious Sources of the Gospel Music Tradition in the United States, 1850–1876" (Ph.D. diss., Boston University, 1981), 33–64. See also Mrs. J. R. [Clarice Howard] "Ma" Baxter and Videt Polk, comps., *Gospel Song Writers Biography* (Dallas: Stamps-Baxter Music and Printing Company, 1971), 104–5, and Hall, *Biography of Gospel Song*, 176–83. Many writers work hard at drawing a distinction between gospel hymns and gospel songs. The difference, however, is difficult to pin down and there is no general consensus. As a result, Smucker's decision to treat the two as virtually synonymous, that is, songs with a religious text, makes the most sense. For Smucker's rationalization and excellent historiography up to about 1980, see "Philip Paul Bliss," 3 and 9–24. For a variant approach, see Sallee, *History of Evangelistic Hymnody*, 77–98.

54. Stella Vaughan, "History of the James D. Vaughan Publishing Company," *Vaughan's Family Visitor* 49 (July 1960): 4. Also on Rowe, see Fleming, "James D. Vaughan," 19, and his obituary in *Vaughan's Family Visitor* 22 (November 1933): 8–9.

55. On Kirkpatrick, Bradbury, and the importance of Sunday school songs, see Sallee, *History of Evangelistic Hymnody*, 43–54. See also Baxter and Polk, comps., *Gospel Song Writers*, 152–53, and Hall, *Biography of Gospel Song*, 22–27, 154–61.

56. On Bradbury, see Blackwell, *Wings of the Dove*, 36–37. The early gospel music pioneers, most notably those associated with the James D. Vaughan Publishing Company, considered Bradbury "one of the great trio to which the church and vocal music of this country owe much, the other two being Drs. Lowell Mason and George F. Root." See *Vaughan's Family Visitor* 23 (October 1934): 2.

57. On Crosby, see James I. Warren Jr., *O for a Thousand Tongues: The History, Nature, and Influence of Music in the Methodist Tradition* (Grand Rapids, Mich.: Francis Asbury Press, 1988), 131–38. See also Baxter and Polk, comps., *Gospel Song Writers*, 149–50.

58. B. C. Unseld, "Fanny J. Crosby: Biographical Sketch," *Musical Visitor* 4 (March 1915): 3.

59. On the influence of Gabriel, see Terry Wayne York, "Charles Hutchinson Gabriel (1856–1932): Composer, Author, and Editor in the Gospel Tradition" (D.M.A. thesis, New Orleans Baptist Theological Seminary, 1985). On Doane, see Baxter and Polk, comps., *Gospel Song Writers*, 167–68.

60. On Tindley, see Ralph H. Jones, *Charles Albert Tindley: Prince of Preachers* (Nashville: Abingdon Press, 1982). One of Tindley's standards, "I'll Overcome Some Day" (1901), is generally credited with being the genesis for the theme song of the civil rights movement beginning in the 1950s. See also Oliver, Harrison, and Bolcom, *New Grove*, 190, and Warren, *O for a Thousand Tongues*, 252–55.

61. Dorsey is regarded as the "Father of Gospel Music" within the black gospel music community. On Dorsey's life and contributions, see Michael W. Harris, *The Rise of Gospel Blues: The Music of Thomas Andrew Dorsey in the Urban Church* (New York: Oxford University Press, 1992); Anthony Heilbut, *The Gospel Sound: Good News and Bad Times*, rev. ed. (New York: Limelight Editions, 1985), 21–35; and Cusic, *Sound of Light*, 88–92. The importance of Dorsey and the popularity of his music in both white and black gospel music illustrates the degree to which racial barriers were liquid in the segregated South. Dorsey's songs have undoubtedly been sung by many who had no knowledge of his ethnic background. The "story behind the song" collection by Lindsay Terry includes Dorsey's "Take My Hand, Precious Lord" but never alludes to the writer's race, though there is a note that he was once "a blues entertainer." See Terry, *Stories behind Popular Songs*, 47–48. On the other hand, the influence was also sometimes missed when songs by white writers were adapted and made popular by black artists. "O Happy Day," a song originally composed by Philip Doddridge around 1751, became an international hit in 1969 via a recording by the Edwin Hawkins Singers. The song was subsequently referred to by some authors as simply "an old Black Baptist hymn." See Terry, *Stories behind Popular Songs*, 23–25, with Horace Clarence Boyer, "Contemporary Gospel Music: Sacred or Secular," *First World* 1 (January–February 1977): 48.

62. For a discussion of the distinction between hymns and gospel songs, see Everett Peach Jr., "The Gospel Song: Its Influences on Christian Hymnody" (master's thesis, Wayne State University, 1960), 57–65.

63. Smucker, "Philip Paul Bliss," 257. On the secular influences on gospel music, see also Paul Gaarder Kaatrud, "Revivalism and the Popular Spiritual Song in Mid-Nineteenth Century America: 1830–1870" (Ph.D. diss., University of Minnesota, 1977), 98–106.

64. Smucker, "Philip Paul Bliss," 94–96. See also Findlay, *Dwight L. Moody,* 213–16. On the use of such songs by labor and political organizations, see James C. Downey, "The Gospel Hymn, 1875–1930" (master's thesis, University of Southern Mississippi, 1963), 103–8. Downey contends that late-nineteenth-century gospel hymns had three major influences: "the military band music of the Civil War, the sentimental songs of the genteel tradition, and the hymns used by the Sunday School movement in the United States" (55). Smucker focuses on the combination of rural forces (i.e., the early-nineteenth-century revival songs) and urban forces (devotional hymns and white minstrel songs) that created a gospel style that "could evoke both the rural life which people saw disappearing before their eyes and the urban life which they partially accepted" (315).

65. On Luther's contribution, see Cusic, *Sound of Light,* 15–18. On this general philosophy, see Bill C. Malone, *Country Music, U.S.A.,* rev. ed. (Austin: University of Texas Press, 1985), 11. The quote has also been attributed, without direct evidence, to John and Charles Wesley. See Bill C. Malone, "Music, Religious, of the Protestant South," in Samuel S. Hill, ed., *Encyclopedia of Religion in the South* (Macon, Ga.: Mercer University Press, 1984), 517.

66. Quoted in Ted Ownby, *Subduing Satan: Religion, Recreation, and Manhood in the Rural South, 1865–1920* (Chapel Hill: University of North Carolina Press, 1990), 120. For a brief discussion of the popularity of the tune "Sweet Barbara Allan" in the early American colonies, see Byrnside, *Music in Eighteenth-Century Georgia,* 9–10.

67. Denham noted in his 1916 study that, even then, barely a year after Fanny Crosby's death, even that revered songwriter was controversial in some circles of Protestantism. In time, of course, Crosby's works would be classified among the standards of almost all American Protestant organizations. See Denham, "Gospel Song Movement," 41.

68. Kaatrud, "Revivalism and the Popular Spiritual Song," 155. Kaatrud contends that "the extreme simplicity of song texts and tunes was not due to any literary and musical inability, but rather to a deliberate rational choice" (327). For an excellent discussion of the many elements that merged to form the gospel songs by late in the nineteenth century, see ibid., 285–333.

69. Smucker, "Philip Paul Bliss," 259–63. According to Smucker, the original tune was published in New York by W. L. Bloomfield in 1853. The Watts hymn "Alas! And Did My Savior Bleed?" was one of the most popular and actually provided for the creation of another such song, "He Loves Me," with an alternate melody and chorus lyrics. Both "At the Cross" and "He Loves Me" appeared simultaneously in many Protestant hymnals during the early twentieth century. Similarly, the popular gospel song "I Love Him" was modeled on the secular rendition of "Old Black Joe." See Vernon M. Whaley, "Trends in Gospel Music Publishing: 1940 to 1960" (Ph.D. diss., University of Oklahoma, 1992), 33–38.

70. Much of the evangelical fear of urbanization included a suspicion of

immigrants who filled America's cities in the late nineteenth century. On this suspicion, see George M. Marsden, *Understanding Fundamentalism and Evangelicalism* (Grand Rapids, Mich.: William B. Eerdmans Publishing Co., 1991), 13–17. On the considerable diversity represented within evangelicalism, see Donald W. Dayton and Robert K. Johnston, *The Variety of American Evangelicalism* (Downers Grove, Ill.: Intervarsity Press, 1991).

71. On the American concept of manifest destiny and divine guidance, see Tuveson, *Redeemer Nation*, 91–136. For a good discussion of the impact of postmillennial hopes on the development of late-nineteenth-century hymnody, see Kaatrud, "Revivalism and the Popular Spiritual Song," 1–17.

72. On the historical development of premillennialism, see Timothy P. Weber, *Living in the Shadow of the Second Coming: American Premillennialism, 1875–1982*, rev. ed. (Chicago: University of Chicago Press, 1987).

73. On Pentecostalism and its growth over the course of the twentieth century, see Vinson Synan, *The Holiness-Pentecostal Tradition: Charismatic Movements in the Twentieth Century* (Grand Rapids, Mich.: William B. Eerdmans Publishing Co., 1997); Walter J. Hollenweger, *Pentecostalism: Origins and Developments Worldwide* (Peabody, Mass.: Hendrickson Publishers, Inc., 1997); and Robert Mapes Anderson, *Vision of the Disinherited* (New York: Oxford University Press, 1979).

Chapter Two

1. For a reference to the avid debate and the lingo used, see B. C. Unseld's "Question Box" in *The Musical Visitor* 4 (March 1915): 3.

2. Few remnants of this tradition linger in the southern gospel music industry. The 1966 program for the Stamps Conservatory of Music made no specific mention of shape notes, and its "Department of Theory" advertised that the student course of study included "rudiments—scales—major, minor, chromatic" (*Stamps Conservatory of Music Summer Session Program* [Dallas: Stamps Quartet Music Company, 1966]). The closest successor to the annual Stamps school, the Stamps-Baxter School of Music, now owned and operated by Ben Speer Music, Nashville, Tennessee, also survives without any dependence on the art of shape notes. Rather, the school's promotional literature notes that "theory, harmony, song writing, sight reading, ear training, performance training, conducting, voice, piano, guitar, bass and drums are taught." See "Ben Speer's Stamps-Baxter School of Music 1996 Brochure" (Nashville: Ben Speer Music, 1996). An exception is a video by Janet Burton, which teaches students the "do-re-mi" method of shape-note singing. See "The Do Re Mi's of Music with Janet Wisner Burton," videocassette recording, produced and directed by Charles Waller, Rainsville, Ala., n.d. Also, as late as 1980, an article in the *Singing News* explained the rudiments of music to readers in both traditional and shape-note theory. See *Singing News* 11

(January 1980): 21–22A. The Church of God Music and Printing Company continues to print a well-known church hymnal in shape notes, and there are a handful of annual convention books also published across the South.

3. On Steele, see Irving Lowens and Allen P. Britton, "The Easy Instructor (1798–1831): A History and Bibliography of the First Shape Note Tune Book," *Journal of Research in Music Education* 1 (Spring 1953): 39.

4. On the retention of shape notes in the rural South, see Buell E. Cobb Jr., *The Sacred Harp: A Tradition and Its Music* (Athens: University of Georgia Press, 1989), 63.

5. The prospect of leaving the hard work of farming would be a consistent theme for many individuals moving into music in the late nineteenth and early twentieth centuries. On the difficulties of southern agriculture and especially the perilous cotton market, see Charles W. Calomiris and Christopher Hanes, "Consistent Output Series for the Antebellum and Postbellum Periods: Issues and Preliminary Results," *Journal of Economic History* 54 (June 1994): 409–22.

6. *Musical Visitor* 4 (February 1915): 2.

7. Ibid.

8. The quote comes from Irving Lowens, *Music and Musicians in Early America* (New York: W. W. Norton and Company, 1964), 282, and is from a letter written by a Yale student to Simeon Baldwin, who later became a Connecticut attorney.

9. Schools could last from ten days to three weeks, depending on the desires, finances, and schedules of both the teacher and all available students. For excellent descriptions of rural singing schools, see Jo Lee Fleming, "James D. Vaughan, Music Publisher, Lawrenceburg, Tennessee, 1912–1964" (S.M.D. diss., Union Theological Seminary, 1972), 36–41, and Lois S. Blackwell, *The Wings of the Dove: The Story of Gospel Music in America* (Norfolk, Va.: Donning Co., 1978), 65–68.

10. Personal interview with James Blackwood, Anderson, Ind., April 3, 1996. On the popularity of singing schools and singing conventions in the rural South, see the collection of interviews included in " 'I Love to Sing,'" *Foxfire* 12 (Spring 1978): 74–100.

11. Jenny Lynn Smith, " 'It Just Comes on Down': T. B. Mosley and Sand Mountain's Gospel Music," pt. 2, *Alabama Baptist Historian* 24 (January 1988): 16. Also on Mosley, see Vernon W. Lackey, "A Biography of T. B. Mosley," *Vaughan's Family Visitor* 75 (November 1975): 8, 11.

12. For a listing of rules established by prominent teachers for a successful singing school, see Jack Spruiell Bottoms, "The Singing School in Texas" (Ph.D. diss., University of Colorado, 1972), 51–60. Bottoms's research in the early 1970s revealed the cost of a three-week singing school to be in the range of $300–500 with each student paying $3 to $4 each (p. 35). That, of course, would assume an average class of at least a hundred students. On the same

information with a slightly earlier time frame, see Paul M. Hall, "The *Musical Million:* A Study and Analysis of the Periodical Promoting Music Reading through Shape-Notes in North America from 1870 to 1914" (D.M.A. diss., Catholic University of America, 1970), 57–59. On the distinction of a music normal, see Bottoms's explanation on 42–43.

13. Cobb, *Sacred Harp,* 129–30.

14. William Lynwood Montell, *Singing the Glory Down: Amateur Gospel Music in South Central Kentucky* (Lexington: University Press of Kentucky, 1991), 32–35. For a good description of the differences between local singings, singing conventions, and gospel concerts, see Fleming, "James D. Vaughan," 22–36.

15. Cobb, *Sacred Harp,* 128–35.

16. Ted Ownby, *Subduing Satan: Religion, Recreation, and Manhood in the Rural South, 1865–1920* (Chapel Hill: University of North Carolina Press, 1990), 141–42.

17. An excellent compilation of minutes and news reports from various conventions in Arkansas is *Gospel Music Scrapbook, 1921–1949,* 3 vols., comp. Harry M. Wakefield (Troy, Mich.: Lee Marks, 1996).

18. For an example of the early tie between singing conventions and the music publishers, compare the coverage given in one of the early issues of James Vaughan's monthly magazine of conventions in Texas, Tennessee, and Alabama, *Musical Visitor* 4 (March 1915): 7. Vaughan himself supported the establishment of such conventions, understanding their importance in spreading music throughout the rural South and also in building his own music business. See the photo of Vaughan at the 1912 formation of the Allen County Singing Convention in Kentucky in Montell, *Singing the Glory Down,* 37.

19. Stella Benton Vaughan, "History of the Twenty-five Years of the National Singing Convention, 1936–1961," *Vaughan's Family Visitor* 50 (October–November 1961): 4–12. According to Vaughan, each publisher held one vote in convention matters. The list of charter members included the Morris-Henson Company, the Vaughan Quartet, James D. Vaughan Music Publishers, the Hartford Music Company, A. J. Showalter Company, Denson Music Company, Theodore Sisk Music Company, Tennessee Music and Printing Company, George W. Sebren, W. P. Ganus, and the Stamps-Baxter Music and Printing Company. All these companies were supporters of the seven-note system popularized by Jesse Aikin almost a century earlier.

20. William Ernest Denham, "The Gospel Song Movement" (Th.D. diss., Southern Baptist Theological Seminary, 1916), 71–72.

21. Ibid., 50–63. Given their concern for educating the masses, Aldine Kieffer and other shape-note advocates would have no doubt sensed some achievement in Denham's objection that the newer gospel songs were too easy to learn. For Denham's analysis of the differences between hymns and gospel songs, see ibid., 3–11.

22. Ibid., 87. For Denham's recommendations, see ibid., 73–87.

23. Quoted in Arthur L. Stevenson, *The Story of Southern Hymnology* (Salem, Va.: Arthur L. Stevenson, 1931), 86–87.

24. Stevenson, *Story of Southern Hymnology*, 86. Given the reference to singing conventions, it is likely that at least part of Poteat's scathing attack was against shape notation in general. As late as 1966, a *Billboard* article linked entertainment with shape notes and church worship with round notes. See Norvell Slater, "Shaped Notes and Round Notes," *Billboard* 78 (October 22, 1966): 36.

25. Stevenson, *Story of Southern Hymnology*, 89–90. Poteat's critique, which appeared as part of his *Practical Hymnology* (1921), was given widely across the South in lecture form throughout the 1920s. George Pullen Jackson even referred to it in his 1933 study *White Spirituals in the Southern Uplands* (Chapel Hill: University of North Carolina Press, 1933; reprint, New York: Dover Publications, 1965), 432–33. Despite Poteat's criticism, shape-note publishers continued to include many of the traditional hymns in their collections. See Talmadge W. Dean, *A Survey of Twentieth-Century Protestant Music in America* (Nashville: Broadman Press, 1988), 59–60.

26. For references to these claims, see *Apostolic Faith* (Los Angeles) 1 (September 1906): 1, 4.

27. Calvin M. Johansson, "Trends in Music and the Arts in the Assemblies of God" (unpublished manuscript in the Assemblies of God Archives, Springfield, Mo., January 1992), 3. One of the more interesting connections between early gospel music and Pentecostalism is the visit by noted gospel songwriter Herbert Buffum to Charles Parham's Bethel Bible School in Topeka, Kansas. The visit seems to have come at about the time of the initial outbreak of Pentecostal glossolalia. See Herbert Buffum and Lillie Buffum, "Warsaw, Mo.," *Nazarene Messenger* 6 (July 18, 1901): 5.

28. Many scholars have noted the degree to which Holiness, and especially Pentecostal, audiences were receptive to gospel singing. See Delton L. Alford, *Music in the Pentecostal Church* (Cleveland, Tenn.: Pathway Press, 1967), 17–21, 48–56; Bill C. Malone, "Albert E. Brumley: Folk Composer," *Bluegrass Unlimited* 21 (July 1986): 72–73; Bill C. Malone, *Country Music, U.S.A.*, rev. ed. (Austin: University of Texas Press, 1985), 13–14; and Ellen Jane Lorenz, *Glory Hallelujah! The Story of the Campmeeting Spiritual* (Nashville: Abingdon Press, 1978), 82–86.

29. See D. L. Alford's "Pentecostal and Charismatic Music," in Stanley M. Burgess and Gary B. McGee, eds., *Dictionary of Pentecostal and Charismatic Movements* (Grand Rapids, Mich.: Zondervan Publishing House, 1988), 688–95.

30. Robert Brown, "Jazz," *Glad Tidings Herald* (February 1937): 3. Brown's article was reprinted in the wider denominational organ almost twenty years later. See R. A. Brown, "Jazz at Church," *Pentecostal Evangel* (March 4, 1956): 29. For an early reference to the debate over hymns and choruses among

Pentecostals, see Donald Gee, "Pentecostal Singing," *Latter Rain Evangel* (May 1929): 22–23.

31. Jenny Lynn Smith, "'It Just Comes on Down'—T. B. Mosley and Sand Mountain's Gospel Music," pt. 1, *Alabama Baptist Historian* 23 (April 1987): 14. Also see Blackwell, *Wings of the Dove*, 27, and John W. Wayland, *Joseph Funk: Father of Song in Northern Virginia* (Dayton, Va.: Ruebush-Kieffer Company, 1911), 3.

32. Blackwell (*Wings of the Dove*, 27) insinuates that Funk left the Mennonite Church because of its opposition to his use of instruments and that he led the family into Baptist circles. Funk remained essentially Mennonite, however, publishing a theological defense of the Mennonite tradition as late as 1837. See Wayland, *Joseph Funk*, 4.

33. Wayland, *Joseph Funk*, 8. Funk was writing to his daughter, Mary Kieffer, in Missouri. Wayland quotes extensively from the correspondence.

34. *Southern Musical Advocate and Singer's Friend* 1 (July 1859): 2.

35. Funk rather awkwardly suggested that his publication was first, noting, "This is probably almost the first effort that has ever been made south of *Mason & Dixon's* Line, to establish a musical journal" (ibid., 3). George Jackson's study seems to confirm the claim, dating only A. D. Fillmore's *Musician and the General Intelligencer* earlier. Jackson admitted, however, that his list was not complete. Fillmore's journal, though marketed in the South, was published in the border town of Cincinnati beginning in the late 1840s. See Jackson, *White Spirituals*, 388–89.

36. *Southern Musical Advocate and Singer's Friend* 1 (July 1859): 2.

37. Ibid., 4. As indicated, an alternate name for shape notes was "patent notes," supposedly because various publishers sought to obtain a government patent for their inventions. The issue of a patent was a controversial one throughout most of the nineteenth century and was apparently one of the reasons that a Boston music publisher bothered to issue an early "history" of shape-note use. See F. H. Gilson, *The History of Shaped or Character Notes* (Boston: F. H. Gilson, 1889). Another derivative was "buckwheat note," also derisive and supposedly named from the diamond shape of the character note "mi." See Gilbert Chase, *America's Music: From the Pilgrims to the Present*, rev. 3rd ed. (Urbana: University of Illinois Press, 1987), 170–72, and Hall, "*Musical Million*," 5–7. Hall also notes that Aldine Kieffer's opponents referred to him sarcastically as "the Don Quixote of Buckwheat Notes" while proponents dubbed him "the apostle of musical democracy" (13). See also Jackson, *White Spirituals*, 348.

38. On Funk, also see Chase, *America's Music*, 184–86. Wayland (*Joseph Funk*, 10) contends that Funk's *Harmonia Sacra* sold a minimum of 80,000 copies in ten separate editions. Detractors—and sometimes supporters— called it the "Hominy Soaker." See William J. Reynolds and Milburn Price, *A Joyful Sound: Christian Hymnody*, 2nd ed. (New York: Holt, Rinehart, and Winston, 1978), 102, and Don Cusic, *The Sound of Light: A History of Gospel*

Music (Bowling Green, Ohio: Bowling Green State University Popular Press, 1990), 94.

39. Hall, *"Musical Million,"* 14–17.

40. Ibid.

41. Weldon T. Myers, "Aldine S. Kieffer, the Valley Poet, and His Work," *Musical Million* 39 (August 1908): 230. Ephraim Ruebush almost always played a secondary public role to that of Kieffer. Researchers have suggested that his primary work involved the routine of company business. It is also possible that his position as an in-law and his service to the Union during the war were factors in downplaying his services. For a brief account of his life, see Hall, *"Musical Million,"* 53–54. Jackson lists Ruebush's wife as Lucilla Kieffer (*White Spirituals*, 360).

42. *Musical Million* 21 (March 1890): 40; Hall, *"Musical Million,"* 18.

43. *Musical Million* 21 (April 1890): 56. Buell Cobb (*Sacred Harp*, 76–77) notes evidence of the use of the *Sacred Harp* by soldiers during the war as well.

44. Kieffer also enjoyed other educational opportunities while in the Civil War POW camp. C. J. Miller, a music teacher and a contemporary of Kieffer, reported that Kieffer had "received instruction in Latin, Algebra, and Geometry from a university graduate who was also in prison." See *Vaughan's Family Visitor* 26 (September 1937): 8.

45. *Musical Million* 21 (March 1890): 40 and 21 (May 1890): 73. See also Hall, *"Musical Million,"* 17–19, 53–54. There is some speculation, apparently handed down through family lore, that Ruebush, who rose to the rank of captain in the Union army, intervened and secured his brother-in-law's release. The account was included in Jackson's *White Spirituals* (346) and was repeated by various others. Bob Terrell's account, for instance, simply notes that Ruebush "rescued" Kieffer "from a Union camp for prisoners-of-war." See Bob Terrell, *The Music Men: The Story of Professional Gospel Quartet Singing* (Asheville, N.C.: Bob Terrell Publisher, 1990), 14. While it is likely that Ruebush wrote a letter and perhaps even made a personal visit, the major reason for Kieffer's release in April 1865 was undoubtedly the impending fate of the Confederate army demonstrated by Lee's surrender.

46. Ruebush's role in the war is less certain than that of Kieffer, though sources indicate without a doubt that he was a Union officer throughout much of the conflict. Not surprisingly, it was a topic rarely mentioned in print over the last half of the nineteenth century, perhaps because both men feared it would be a deterrent to their business interests. On Ruebush's war service, see Hall, *"Musical Million,"* 18–19.

47. Ibid., 8–14.

48. Ibid., 19, 96–98. William Blake, who came to work for the Ruebush-Kieffer firm around 1872, estimated in 1908 that the journal had reached a subscription rate of 5,000 by the late 1870s. See William B. Blake, "Aldine S. Kieffer," *Musical Million* 39 (August 1908): 237–38.

49. *Musical Million* 39 (August 1908): 240. The quote is from a Kieffer editorial published first in the journal in 1883.

50. Kieffer's concern for a single notation system foreshadowed the similar concerns brewing within the emerging industrial world of the late nineteenth century. During the 1880s both railroad track gauges and time zones would be standardized because of concerns for efficient commerce.

51. Kieffer noted in the preface to the *Temple Star*, published two years later, that "the union of certain publishers and authors upon one set of characters, representing the scale names, is a great event in the history of this reform. Professor Aiken's [*sic*] characters have been chosen. Whilst he should have preferred Funk's, yet for the ultimate good of the reform, the editor of these pages acquiesced in their adoption." See Joel F. Reed, "Anthony J. Showalter (1858–1924): Southern Educator, Publisher, Composer" (Ed.D. diss., New Orleans Baptist Theological Seminary, 1975), 4.

52. For the best discussion of this meeting, see Hall, "*Musical Million*," 39–42. See also Hall's account in "The Shape-Note Hymnals and Tune Books of Ruebush-Kieffer Company," *The Hymn* 22 (July 1971): 71. The information about a potential lawsuit was reported in Jackson, *White Spirituals*, 352, though Jackson listed the year of the visit as 1877.

53. The reference to Kieffer's moodiness comes from Blake, "Aldine S. Kieffer," 239.

54. *Musical Million* 39 (August 1908): 240–41. The quote is from an editorial originally published in 1885. The words also demonstrate, of course, the degree to which the comparison with Jefferson is not valid. Influenced by a century of evangelicalism, Kieffer equated deism and universalism with atheism, a connection Jefferson would not have made.

55. The idea was one that Kieffer had been promoting since 1867 (Hall, "*Musical Million*," 43–44). The Virginia Normal also provided an opportunity to diversify the musical training prospects of the *Musical Million*. School administrators and faculty, like B. C. Unseld, were solicited to contribute occasional articles.

56. On Unseld's misgivings, see Hall, "*Musical Million*," 43, and Jackson, *White Spirituals*, 355–58. The tradition of requiring music teachers to know standard notation continued: as late as 1956, W. B. Walbert at the Vaughan School of Music explained that sight-reading classes were conducted in round notes, since "to be a musician, one must know the round notes." See W. B. Walbert, "Why Is the South a Great Singing Country?" *Vaughan's Family Visitor* 45 (September 1956): 3.

57. See Hall, "*Musical Million*," 42–49. The Shenandoah Seminary became known as Shenandoah College by the mid-1880s and ultimately became the Shenandoah Conservatory of Music, which relocated to Winchester, Virginia. Hall notes that, by the early decades of the twentieth century, the school was getting requests for longer and more involved music courses. It is likely, then, that the summer normal curriculum was ultimately absorbed into the over-

all program of the school. On the evolution of the school, see ibid., 37–38. See also Robert J. Miller, *A History of Shenandoah College* (Winchester, Va.: Shenandoah College, 1950).

58. On Hildebrand, see A. J. Showalter, *The Best Gospel Songs and Their Composers* (Dalton, Ga.: A. J. Showalter Company and Dallas: The Showalter-Patton Company, 1904), 23. Showalter notes that Hildebrand (spelled Hilderbrand in various sources) was the "principal of the Dayton Music School" from 1894 to 1899. He also notes that Hildebrand "does normal work during the summer months," which seems to be when he taught Vaughan.

59. On Showalter's early years, see Reed, "Anthony J. Showalter," 9–24.

60. Showalter, *Best Gospel Songs*, 4.

61. Exactly what precipitated Showalter's break is unclear, though it is likely that his success on the road convinced him that he could do better financially out from under the family enclave in Dayton, Virginia. See Reed, "Anthony J. Showalter," 25–28, 34–36. Also see Hall, "Shape-Note Hymnals," 72, and "*Musical Million*," 98–99.

62. Reed, "Anthony J. Showalter," 36. In 1884, Showalter also published collections with the Ruebush-Kieffer Company, the John Church Company of Cincinnati, and the Root and Sons Music Company of New York. Reed mistakenly identifies one of Showalter's coeditors, James B. Vaughan, as James D. Vaughan. Compare p. 47 with *Good Tidings* (Dalton, Ga.: A. J. Showalter, 1884).

63. Hall reports that the renaming came as a result of a request from the John Church Company, which published a similar monthly titled *The Musical Visitor* ("*Musical Million*," 99).

64. Reed, "Anthony J. Showalter," 6. On Showalter's importance, see also William J. Northen, ed., *Advance Sheets of Men of Mark in Georgia* (Atlanta: A. B. Caldwell, ca. 1906), 5–9.

65. Reed, "Anthony J. Showalter," 36–37.

66. Ibid., 109–11. For a list of Showalter's advertised rates, see p. 110.

67. Ibid., 28–31. The significance of Showalter's decision to resign from the First Presbyterian Church and whether it was connected to his divorce and remarriage is not clear. He and his first wife divorced in 1908 on a trip to Reno, Nevada. Showalter maintained his ties to the church until July of 1912, when he withdrew amidst an investigation into his membership qualifications. Despite his strained relationship with the Dalton church, Showalter's funeral was nonetheless held there after his death in Chattanooga on September 15, 1924.

68. The quote is attributed to T. S. Shope in Jackson, *White Spirituals*, 363.

69. Reed, "Anthony J. Showalter," 94–95.

70. Ibid., 110–25.

71. Ibid., 124–25.

72. Smith, "It Just Comes on Down," pt. 1, 13.

73. Myers, "Aldine S. Kieffer," 231–32. Arthur Stevenson's 1931 study of southern gospel hymn publishers (*Story of Southern Hymnology*, 69) reported the Ruebush-Kieffer Company claim that, by that date, the book "had a sale of over a million." See also Hall, "Shape-Note Hymnals," 69–75, and Grace I. Showalter, *The Music Books of Ruebush & Kieffer, 1866–1942: A Bibliography* (Richmond: Virginia State Library, 1975). In the forward to her book, Grace Showalter claims that, counting updated editions, the number of Ruebush-Kieffer publications topped 200.

74. Jackson, *White Spirituals*, 348. This phenomenon was noted in Smith, "It Just Comes On Down," pt. 1, 15.

75. Hall, "*Musical Million*," 101.

76. The Ruebush-Kieffer Company's decision in 1891 to begin printing music books in both shape- and round-note editions has led some scholars to conclude that, even before his death in 1904, Kieffer had lost his optimism about the future of shape-note notation. See Showalter, *Music Books*, ix, and Hall, "*Musical Million*," 100–105.

Chapter Three

1. On Jones, see Kathleen Minnix, *Laughter in the Amen Corner: The Life of Evangelist Sam Jones* (Athens: University of Georgia Press, 1993). On Sunday, see Roger A. Bruns, *Preacher: Billy Sunday and Big-Time American Evangelism* (New York: W. W. Norton and Company, 1992), and Lyle W. Dorsett, *Billy Sunday and the Redemption of Urban America* (Grand Rapids, Mich.: William B. Eerdmans Publishing Company, 1991).

2. Though an Iowan by birth and the son of a Union soldier killed in the Civil War, Sunday was a popular speaker in the turn-of-the-century South. His acquiescence on matters of race and segregation did nothing to deter that popularity. See Bruns, *Preacher*, 225–47.

3. Minnix, *Laughter in the Amen Corner*, 81. On Jones's emphasis on music and a comparison of his popularity with that of Dwight Moody, see ibid., 92–99. A brief profile of E. O. Excell is included in *Vaughan's Family Visitor* 32 (August 1943): 24 and in J. H. Hall, *Biography of Gospel Song and Hymn Writers* (New York: Fleming H. Revell Company, 1914), 298–303.

4. *Vaughan's Family Visitor* 26 (April 1937): 6.

5. Bruns, *Preacher*, 103. On Rodeheaver's overall importance to Sunday's work, see 103–5. See also Dorsett, *Billy Sunday*, 101–2.

6. Bruns, *Preacher*, 104–5. On Rodeheaver's importance in music promotion, see Thomas Henry Porter, "Homer Alvan Rodeheaver (1880–1955): Evangelistic Musician and Publisher" (Ed.D. diss., New Orleans Baptist Theological Seminary, 1981). On Gabriel, see Hall, *Biography of Gospel Song*, 348–53.

7. Rodeheaver responded to criticism of the song's catchy tune by noting:

"It was never intended for a Sunday morning service, nor for a devotional meeting—its purpose was to bridge that gap between the popular song of the day and the great hymns and gospel songs" (William G. McLoughlin Jr., *Billy Sunday Was His Real Name* [Chicago: University of Chicago Press, 1955], 85). Also quoted in James C. Downey, "The Gospel Hymn, 1875–1930" (master's thesis, University of Southern Mississippi, 1963), 93–94, and Don Cusic, *The Sound of Light: A History of Gospel Music* (Bowling Green, Ohio: Bowling Green State University Popular Press, 1990), 72. Downey argues that Sunday and Rodeheaver represented an important shift in revival music, mixing "sacred and secular compositions without attempting to distinguish between musical style or content" (110). For an explanation of Sunday's open-mindedness regarding religious music, see the contemporary account by William T. Ellis, *"Billy" Sunday: The Man and His Message* (Philadelphia: John C. Winston Company, 1914), 261–66.

8. On the uniqueness of Tennessee during the decades after the Civil War, see Roger L. Hart, *Redeemers, Bourbons, and Populists: Tennessee, 1870–1896* (Baton Rouge: Louisiana State University Press, 1975).

9. *Vaughan's Family Visitor* 49 (May 1960): 4. Most of the details of Vaughan's career are preserved in a series of articles contributed to *Vaughan's Family Visitor* by his daughter-in-law, Stella B. Vaughan. Stella Vaughan's eleven articles, titled "History of the James D. Vaughan Publishing Company," first appeared from May 1960 through June 1961. They were reprinted in the *Visitor* from August through December 1975. Another version appeared in pamphlet form as Stella B. Vaughan, *A Heritage to Keep: History of James D. Vaughan, Music Publisher*, edited by Connor B. Hall (Cleveland, Tenn.: James D. Vaughan, Music Publisher, ca. 1976). This same account serves as the introductory history in the *"Vaughan's Family Visitor* Microfilm Collection" (Murfreesboro, Tenn.: Center for Popular Music, 1988). A good brief account of Vaughan's life and career can be found in Karen M. McDearman, "James D. Vaughan," in *Encyclopedia of Southern Culture*, ed. Charles Reagan Wilson and William Ferris (Chapel Hill: University of North Carolina Press, 1989), 1087–88. See also Jo Lee Fleming, "James D. Vaughan, Music Publisher, Lawrenceburg, Tennessee, 1912–1964" (S.M.D. diss., Union Theological Seminary, 1972), 48–67.

10. *Vaughan's Family Visitor* 18 (August 1929): 9 and 30 (February 1941): 23–24. Vaughan's early religious ties are difficult to ascertain. By adulthood, he affiliated with the Church of the Nazarene and is credited with financing much of the building of the Nazarene Church in Lawrenceburg, Tennessee. The church is today named Vaughan Memorial Nazarene Church (personal interview with Brock Speer, Nashville, Tenn., May 23, 1996). Evidence suggests that Vaughan's early church connection in Giles County was Methodist, given that James Vaughan's uncle, Richard B. Vaughan, was a Methodist minister and that, upon moving to Lawrenceburg in the early 1900s, Vaughan joined the local Methodist church. Ottis Knippers, a young acquaintance of

Vaughan's beginning about 1930, recalled hearing that Vaughan left Methodism "around 1926" because the Methodists refused to use his songbooks in any of their worship activities (personal interview with Ottis J. Knippers, Lawrenceburg, Tenn., March 25, 1998).

11. The best account of the early family quartet is found in Charles W. Vaughan, "Reminiscences of the First Vaughan Quartet and the Second Vaughan Quartet," *Vaughan's Family Visitor* 14 (May 1927): 7. Depending on the octave range, the alto part is sometimes referred to as baritone, though that term is occasionally used to refer to the melody or lead as well. In this case, young Charles Vaughan sang in the alto range normally associated with females. In time, a male singer taking this part as written would be designated first tenor. See also *Vaughan's Family Visitor* 32 (August 1943): 8–9, where Charles Vaughan refers to the early group specifically as "the Vaughan Boys Quartet."

12. On the business implications of the Vaughan brothers' singing, see Fleming, "James D. Vaughan," 49–50.

13. Another factor in the move to Texas was the illness of another brother of George Vaughan's. According to Stella Vaughan's account, John Vaughan suffered from tuberculosis and died from the disease in April of 1891. That date seems to place both James Vaughan and his parents in Texas a year or so earlier. Ironically, George Vaughan also died in Cisco the following year in May 1892—also of tuberculosis. See *Vaughan's Family Visitor* 49 (May 1960): 4.

14. My chronology here differs from others who have attempted to interpret Stella Vaughan's rather vague sequence of events. Fleming ("James D. Vaughan") assumed that James Vaughan attended a Hildebrand-directed normal in Tennessee prior to moving to Texas in 1890. However, my reading of the evidence suggests that the meeting would have had to come no earlier than 1892, since Showalter's account of Hildebrand notes that the young teacher "did his first normal work in 1892." See A. J. Showalter, *The Best Gospel Songs and Their Composers* (Dalton, Ga.: A. J. Showalter Company, 1904), 23. This date would also be consistent with Hildebrand's age and would explain Stella Vaughan's contention that James Vaughan became interested in composing following a normal taught by Hildebrand in Cisco, Texas. I am suggesting that this normal was actually the first encounter between the two men. This assertion is consistent with the memory of James Vaughan's younger brother Charles. See *Vaughan's Family Visitor* 18 (August 1929): 9.

15. *Vaughan's Family Visitor* 30 (February 1941): 22.

16. The most interesting work in the collection is no. 218, "The Open Fountain," a song for which James Vaughan contributed both words and music. Clearly excited by his first published composition, the young writer noted in the top margin "my first song published 1896" and changed the abbreviation "Jas." in "Jas. D. Vaughan" to "James." See J. H. Hall, J. H. Ruebush, and A. S. Kieffer, *Crowning Day, No. 2* (Dayton, Va.: Ruebush-Kieffer Company, 1896), 219, personal copy of Mr. James D. Walbert, Birmingham, Ala.

17. *Vaughan's Family Visitor* 30 (February 1941): 24. A letter from W. Henry Quillen on p. 8 ("Love and Friendship") indicates that at least one of these volumes was being compiled in 1898. The preface of the first of these early songbooks clearly indicates Vaughan's importance as coauthor. Vaughan's contribution to the volume was extensive. He both composed and wrote the lyrics to five songs; four others were numbers for which he had written the lyrics; and one other selection included his music to someone else's lyrics. See E. T. Hildebrand and James D. Vaughan, *Onward and Upward* (Logansport, Ind.: Home Music Company, 1898).

18. *Vaughan's Family Visitor* 49 (May 1960): 4; Showalter, *Best Gospel Songs*, 23.

19. Family members recalled that James Vaughan remained terrified of sudden storms to the extent that he had a "concrete storm cellar" built at his home in Lawrenceburg. Ottis Knippers recalled that, as a young man, he would watch Vaughan emerge from his office, stand under a small tree beside the street, and scan the horizon for the early signs of a threatening storm (Knippers interview and *Vaughan's Family Visitor* 49 [May 1960]: 4).

20. *Vaughan's Family Visitor* 49 (August 1960): 4.

21. Ibid., 30 (February 1941): 22. Vaughan's first edition of *Gospel Chimes* listed a Minor Hill, Tennessee, address as Vaughan's rural residence in Giles County, where he served as principal of the public school in Elkmont Springs. See Bobby Alford, *History of Lawrence County, Tennessee*, vol. 3 (Lawrenceburg, Tenn.: Bobby Alford, 1997), 59.

22. Fleming, "James D. Vaughan," 51–52.

23. Vaughan revised *Gospel Chimes* in 1903, published a new songbook each year from 1905 through 1908, skipped 1909, and then began the string of at least one book per year in 1910. In 1915, 1921, 1928, and 1933, the company published two books; for each of the five years from 1935 through 1939, three books were issued. See *Vaughan's Family Visitor* 30 (February 1941): 24.

24. "Male Quartets 25 Years Ago and Now," ibid., 21 (December 1932): 4. It is likely that the "Texas company" was the Trio Music Company of Waco, Texas. Owned by F. L. Eiland, the company was one of the first important shape-note establishments in Texas and was one of the most prosperous of the pre-Vaughan era. George Sebren, lead singer in Vaughan's first quartet, had previously worked for the Trio Company. See ibid., 19 (November 1930): 7–8 and 29 (January 1940): 15.

25. Charles W. Vaughan, "Reminiscences," 7. Terms used for part assignments have varied over the course of the history of gospel quartet singing. Most recent male quartets use the terms lead, tenor, baritone, and bass. The early Vaughan quartets often stuck with the traditional designations of soprano, alto, tenor, and bass. As quartets developed, terms were used to distinguish between male and female voices. A man singing the soprano line was often designated baritone or lead. Alto was sometimes designated first tenor, with the term "second tenor" referring to the lead part. Baritone also

became associated with the alto part sung an octave below what was written. The confusion in terms was less a problem in the early days of the quartet movement when most fans of the groups were themselves amateur musicians who could read music (at least via shape notes) and understood the basics of the musical scale. Later fans followed quartets only for the entertainment value and would have more difficulty with the designations. From a practical standpoint, in any musical quartet, someone will sing the melody or lead and usually there will be a harmony part both above (usually tenor) and below (baritone) that lead part. The bass part is oftentimes covering one of the other parts albeit at a lower octave. A common nineteenth-century term for the lead part was "the air." For a brief explanation of the switching of terms and the confusion that could result, see Benjamin Unseld's article in *Vaughan's Family Visitor* 11 (December 1922): 8.

26. This scenario is the one recorded by Charles Vaughan seventeen years later in "Reminiscences," 7.

27. Ibid. A similar recounting by Charles Vaughan, printed as "Retrospective" in *Vaughan's Family Visitor* 31 (February 1942): 4, notes that the tent used for the assembly had "a seating capacity of 5000 people." Elsewhere, Charles Vaughan confirmed that he had quit his job after this 1910 meeting because his brother "wanted me to manage his first quartet" (*Vaughan's Family Visitor* 30 [February 1941]: 25).

28. William Lynwood Montell, *Singing the Glory Down: Amateur Gospel Music in South Central Kentucky* (Lexington: University Press of Kentucky, 1991), 18.

29. See *Vaughan's Family Visitor* 6 (June 1917): 23. The Greenville operation and a later Texas base at Jacksonville survived into the mid-1920s.

30. Ibid., 49 (May 1960): 5, and Fleming, "James D. Vaughan," 54–56.

31. *Vaughan's Family Visitor* 49 (June 1960): 5. Reports in the magazine suggest that the permanent association with Unseld began in 1911, with Unseld relocating to Lawrenceburg two years later. See ibid., 12 (November 1923): 3 and 28 (March 1939): 4. Also on Unseld, see Hall, *Biography of Gospel Song*, 238–45.

32. *Vaughan's Family Visitor* 12 (November 1923): 3; *Stamps Quartet News* 4 (February 1948): 6. On the influence of Seward and Mason, see Gilbert Chase, *America's Music: From the Pilgrims to the Present*, rev. 3rd ed. (Urbana: University of Illinois Press, 1987), 226–27, 341–45, and Hall, *Biography of Gospel Song*, 134–38. On Tourjee, see Eben Tourjee, *Reminiscences and Reflections of a Tourist of Tourjee's Musical and Educational Excursion of the Summer of 1883* (United States: s.n., ca. 1883; reproduced for the Cooperative Preservation Microfilming Project, Research Libraries Group, Andover, Mass.: Northeast Document Conservation Center, 1986).

33. *Vaughan's Family Visitor* 49 (June 1960): 5. On the Fisk Jubilee Singers, see Chase, *America's Music*, 226–28.

34. Even before the arrival of Unseld, Vaughan had begun to offer his

songbooks in both round- and shaped-note editions. The 1910 book *Voices for Jesus* ([Lawrenceburg, Tenn.: James D. Vaughan, 1910], opening fly page) noted, "Published in Round and Shaped Notes . . . Always state the kind of Notes wanted." This trend seems to have prevailed through the 1920s, although, by the late 1930s, Vaughan books were advertised as "Shaped Notes Only." See the opening fly pages of *Temple Bells* (Lawrenceburg, Tenn.: James D. Vaughan, 1921) and *Happy Praises* (Lawrenceburg, Tenn.: James D. Vaughan, 1938).

35. *Vaughan's Family Visitor* 12 (November 1923): 3. See also ibid., 49 (June 1960): 5, and Fleming, "James D. Vaughan," 61–62. Unseld was one of the most loved individuals associated with shape-note singing in the South. When he died, former students and associates immediately expressed their love by the creation of a fund to care for his widow. See *Vaughan's Family Visitor* 12 (December 1923): 3. Also on Unseld, see ibid., 44 (September 1955): 7.

36. Dating the original Vaughan normal is difficult. Stella Vaughan believed the first normal was held in 1911 (*Vaughan's Family Visitor* 49 [June 1960]: 5), but an article in the *Musical Visitor* 4 (January 1915): 22 ("Opening of the Normal") implies that the sessions had been going on for seven years. It is likely that 1911 was the first year of the winter normal held in Lawrenceburg but that other Vaughan-sponsored normals were held in earlier years. This also seems confirmed by a 1933 reference that James Vaughan "about twenty-five years ago had the first session of a Vaughan school taught at Lawrenceburg and twenty-two years ago established the Vaughan School of Music with one session annually" (*Vaughan's Family Visitor* 22 [November 1933]: 3).

37. *Vaughan's Family Visitor* 30 (February 1941): 25. For a specific example, see ibid., 11 (December 1922): 5, where Adger M. Pace reports on his recent study in New York with "Dr. Richardson . . . considered one of the leading musicians of America." See also ibid., 12 (July 1923): 18, where reference is made of Kieffer Vaughan and W. W. Combs studying with "the great voice teacher Oscar Saenger."

38. Even after the establishment of the Lawrenceburg Normal, the company sponsored other short-term schools around the South to promote the company. Vaughan's schools focused on individual training and never sought to be degree-granting institutions. Even with experience at a Vaughan school, singing-school teachers were expected to build a reputation by word of mouth. Only in the 1930s was the suggestion made to issue certificates as a way of verifying an individual's credentials as a singing-school teacher. See ibid., 25 (January 1936): 4.

39. George W. Sebren served as the journal's initial editor from the first issue in January 1912 until January 1914, when Unseld took over the duties. Following Unseld's death in 1923, Charles Vaughan became editor.

40. Vaughan's decision to have the songbooks printed in Cincinnati was

not unusual given the peculiarities of music publishing. The Armstrong Printing Company was one of the few publishing companies that specialized in shape-note publishing for distribution throughout the South. See *Vaughan's Family Visitor* 11 (December 1922): 17–18, which reprints a *Cincinnati Enquirer* article detailing the work of the Armstrong operation. On the printing capacities in Lawrenceburg, see *Musical Visitor* 4 (December 1915): 7, which includes a sketch of the company's new "Merganthaler Linotype."

41. *Musical Visitor* 4 (May 1915): 15; *Vaughan's Family Visitor* 12 (October 1923): 10. Charles Wolfe estimated that, at its height in the 1920s, the *Visitor* enjoyed a circulation of between twenty and thirty thousand ("Introduction to the *Vaughan Family Visitor* Microfilm Collection" [Murfreesboro, Tenn.: Center for Popular Music, 1988], reel 1, p. 5).

42. Stella Vaughan, *Heritage to Keep*, 2.

43. A photo of the 1917 normal shows eighty-two students—seventy-five males and seven females. See *Musical Visitor* 6 (November 1917): 8–9. One of the last normals before Vaughan's death drew 182 students. See *Vaughan's Family Visitor* 29 (June 1940): 4.

44. On Vaughan's relationship with the privately sponsored summer normals, see "Texas Normal, Comanche, Texas" and "Vaughan Modern Normal School of Music," *Musical Visitor* 4 (April 1915): 5 and 4 (May 1915): 6.

45. "The Country People," ibid., 4 (January 1915): 7.

46. James D. Vaughan, ed., *Voices for Jesus* (Lawrenceburg, Tenn.: James D. Vaughan, 1910), fly page.

47. For the reference to females attending with a tuition waiver, see "Comments of W. W. Davis" in *Vaughan's Family Visitor* 4 (January 1915): 14. Also see ibid., 4 (August 1915): 7 and 4 (November 1915): 4. The tuition cost for the six-week 1915 term was $8.50. On Vaughan's Bible sessions, see ibid., 49 (July 1960): 5.

48. Ibid., 21 (January 1932): 7. The article is a reprint of a Vaughan piece published originally in the *Musical Million and Fireside Friend* around 1900. The reference to Grady is to the *Atlanta Constitution* editor Henry Grady, who in the 1880s popularized the concept of a progressive, industrial "New South."

49. Ibid., 12 (January 1923): 8 and *Vaughan Conservatory of Music and Bible Institute: Session of 1923* (Lawrenceburg, Tenn.: James D. Vaughan, 1922). By the early 1930s, the length of the annual school had returned to six weeks. On the varying lengths of the normal term, see *Vaughan's Family Visitor* 21 (January 1932): 8. One of the most unusual testaments to Vaughan's religious devotion was the testimony of the undertaker who cared for his body at the time of his death in 1941. The undertaker noted that "Mr. Vaughan's knees were thickened with callouses [*sic*]—where he had knelt in prayer" (Stella Vaughan, *Heritage to Keep*, 7).

50. *Musical Visitor* 4 (April 1915): ad page between the cover and page 1.

51. See "Editorial: The 1915 Normal," ibid., 4 (February 1915): 12. Unseld

contrasted the success of the 1915 normal with the difficulty some of Vaughan's competitors encountered—the "almost total failure of four of the best and strongest schools of the south."

52. See "Our Hustlers," ibid., 4 (February 1915): 15. Issues typically included letters from music teachers who were using the Vaughan books in singing schools across the rural South. For a representative sample, see ibid., 4 (March 1915): 17–24.

53. "A Correction," ibid., 4 (July 1915): 15. Also see "Our Hustlers" in ibid., 4 (May 1915): 15.

54. Most of the Vaughan sources have claimed that WOAN was the first radio station in the state of Tennessee. However, at least three stations received Commerce Department licenses before Vaughan. WKN, Memphis, owned by the Riechman-Crosby Company, was licensed on March 23, 1922, and its cross-town rival, WPO, owned by the United Equipment Company, was licensed five days later. In addition, WDAA, Nashville, owned by the Ward-Belmont School, was awarded a license on May 15, 1922. However, none of these stations survived beyond one year, and it is quite likely that, in mid-1923, Vaughan's station was the only "functioning" station in the state. By the time the Federal Radio Commission was created in February of 1923, there were 732 American radio stations on the air. The FRC was succeeded by the Federal Communications Commission in 1934. See "The Broadcast FAQ List," *The Broadcast Archive*, n.d. See also <http://www.oldradio.com/current/bc_faq.htm> (April 10, 1998). This site, ably managed by Barry Mishkind, the "Eclectic Engineer," is a marvelous source for information on early radio and the various disputes relating to which station came first.

55. See *Nashville Tennessean*, December 14, 1924, sec. A, p. 11, and "Radio Station WOAN," *Vaughan's Family Visitor* 84 (November 1983): 8–9. On the station, also see *Vaughan's Family Visitor* 49 (July 1960): 5 and Gordon H. Turner, "Only One Brother Left of Vaughan Family Singers" (miscellaneous news clippings, 1946, James D. Walbert files, Birmingham, Ala.). According to Turner, WOAN and WSM, Nashville, worked out an agreement to share a band setting by alternating broadcast times.

56. Most accounts have assumed that WOAN was always at the 600 setting; however, over its eight-year history, the station actually spent time at eight different locations on the AM dial: 833, 1090, 1060, 840, 790, 1050, 1250, and 600 (Barry Mishkind, *barry@broadcast.net*, "Re: TN station WOAN," April 26, 1998, personal e-mail [April 30, 1998]).

57. *Vaughan's Family Visitor* 12 (February 1923): 24. For a sampling of letters received by the station from across the country, see page 8 and ibid., 49 (July 1960): 5–6.

58. Vaughan's foray into radio broadcasting came during a time of unprecedented change in the communications industry. In 1922, 100,000 radios were sold across the United States and, by the end of the decade, half of all

American households owned one. See Steven Lubar, *Infoculture: The Smith-sonian Book of Information Age Inventions* (Boston: Houghton Mifflin Company, 1993), 216. For a complete discussion of the impact of radio in the twentieth century, see 213–41.

59. Vaughan introduced the station in the program for the 1923 normal, noting, "If a sufficient number are interested, a class in Radio will be orga-nized and placed in [the] charge of a competent instructor" (*Vaughan Conser-vatory of Music, 1923*, 30). Also on the station, see Alford, *History of Lawrence County*, 62–65.

60. *Vaughan's Family Visitor* 49 (July 1960): 6.

61. It appears that the decision to make recordings was made in 1921 and that most of the early songs were cut in 1922. The first songbook to publicize the new recordings was *Awakening Praises*, which appeared in January 1923. The 1924 book, *His Voice of Love*, listed seventeen different 78-rpm record-ings at a price of $1.00 each. See James D. Vaughan, comp., *Awakening Praises* (Lawrenceburg, Tenn.: James D. Vaughan, 1923), back cover, and James D. Vaughan, comp., *His Voice of Love* (Lawrenceburg, Tenn.: James D. Vaughan, 1924), inside back cover. For early ads in *Vaughan's Family Visitor*, see the back covers of the April through August 1923 issues.

62. The best source of information on the specifics of the early Vaughan records is Charles K. Wolfe, "The Vaughan Quartets: Original 1927–1947 Recordings" (liner notes to TFS-110, Murfreesboro, Tenn.: Tennessee Folk-lore Society, 1992). The Wisconsin company was undoubtedly the Wisconsin Chair Company, which began making recordings at the end of World War I under the name New York Recording Laboratories. See Norm Cohen, "Intro-duction to a Label, a Series, a Reissue," supplement to *Paramount Old-Time Tunes: An Album of Recordings Originally Made in the 1920s and 1930s*, John Edwards Memorial Foundation 103, [1970s]. Ironically, Vaughan's venture into the phonograph industry was accompanied by a sharp decline in sales nationwide, due in large part to the popularity of radio and player pianos. Phonograph sales in 1920 topped $100 million; by 1930, wracked by both the Depression and the growing popularity of radio, sales had dropped to $46 million. See Lubar, *Infoculture*, 174–75.

63. Stella Vaughan, "History of the James D. Vaughan Publishing Com-pany," *Vaughan's Family Visitor* 49 (August 1960): 6. Stella Vaughan's article places the quartet there on August 25, 1921, specifically at the time of Rode-heaver's brother Jack's fatal plane crash. See "Two Dead in Aeroplane Acci-dent," *Warsaw (Ind.) Daily Times*, August 26, 1921, 1.

64. Although not official, the name helps distinguish Kieffer Vaughan's quartet from the many other quartets that took the Vaughan name. The dis-tinction was suggested to me by Ottis Knippers, who recalled that locals used it in conversation (Knippers interview).

65. Wolfe, "Vaughan Quartets," 2.

66. Ibid., 2–3. The records were advertised occasionally in the pages of

the *Visitor*, but Vaughan seems to have been reluctant to give them too much coverage. This was probably because only a small percentage of his customers would have as yet owned phonograph players. The ads were more aggressive on the back covers of his annual songbooks, where recordings were listed by order number alongside both song titles and names of performers. For early ads, see James D. Vaughan, ed., *Heavenly Praises* (Lawrenceburg, Tenn.: James D. Vaughan, 1925), and James D. Vaughan, ed., *Millennial Praise* (Lawrenceburg, Tenn.: James D. Vaughan, 1927).

67. *Nashville Tennessean*, December 14, 1924, sec. A, p. 11. See also *Vaughan's Family Visitor* 49 (July 1960): 5.

68. James D. Vaughan, ed., *Millennial Revival* (Lawrenceburg, Tenn.: James D. Vaughan, 1928), back cover.

69. *Vaughan's Family Visitor* 12 (February 1923): 14.

70. Ibid. The reference to "Mr. Stamps" is to V. O. Stamps, at the time the head of Vaughan's branch office in Jacksonville, Texas.

71. Ibid., 49 (July 1960): 4–5.

72. Ibid., 30 (February 1941): 24. One county history notes that Lawrence County boasted a more vibrant two-party system than most areas of southern Tennessee and the surrounding region. See Edward M. Lindsey, ed., *Lawrence County, Tennessee: Pictorial History* (Paducah, Ky.: Turner Publishing Company, 1994), 88. The Vaughan family proved very influential in Lawrenceburg politics. In addition to James D. Vaughan, Charles Vaughan and Kieffer Vaughan also served terms as mayor. See *Vaughan's Family Visitor* 50 (April 1961): 4–5.

73. See Charles K. Wolfe, "Uncle Dave Macon: The Birth of Country Gospel," *Precious Memories* (March–April 1989): 22. Macon's son, Esten, wrote a regular column for *Vaughan's Family Visitor* beginning in 1935. See "Views of Life," *Vaughan's Family Visitor* 30 (February 1941): 27.

74. Alford, *History of Lawrence County*, 65. For a partly personal account of the excitement of the 1920s and 1930s in Lawrenceburg, see the recollections of Vaughan's grandson, James D. Walbert, in "James D. Vaughan and the Vaughan School of Music," *Rejoice!* 2 (Summer 1990): 12–15.

75. On the sale of WOAN for $9,000, see Alford, *History of Lawrence County*, 65. The phonograph company was reorganized for a brief period after World War II and produced additional recordings, but the Vaughan company did not become a major distributor. On the phonograph company, see Wolfe, "Vaughan Quartets," 3, and Turner, "Only One Brother Left." On Lawrenceburg's early potential to be a music capital, see Carl Swafford, "'Music City USA': Could Lawrenceburg Have Captured This Title?" *Wayne County (Tenn.) News*, September 26, 1975, 12, news clipping files of James D. Walbert, Birmingham, Ala. On the recording industry in the 1920s and 1930s, see Bill Malone, *Country Music, U.S.A.*, rev. ed. (Austin: University of Texas Press, 1985), 34–39, 65–67, 94–95.

76. For a brief sketch, see John W. Rumble, "Music Industry," and

Charles K. Wolfe, "Ralph Peer," in Wilson and Ferris, ed., *Encyclopedia of Southern Culture*, 746–47 and 1075–76, respectively.

77. See James D. Vaughan, ed., *Millennial Revival*, back cover, with Vaughan's obituary in *Vaughan's Family Visitor* 30 (February 1941): 5. It is estimated that Vaughan sold an average of 117,000 copies each of his 105 known publications between 1900, when the company began, and 1964, when it moved out of Lawrenceburg. That figure places the total sales of Vaughan songbooks in excess of twelve million. See McDearman, "James D. Vaughan," 1088, and Charles K. Wolfe, *Tennessee Strings: The Story of Country Music in Tennessee* (Knoxville: University of Tennessee Press, 1977), 53.

78. James D. Vaughan, *Vaughan's School Songs* (Lawrenceburg, Tenn.: James D. Vaughan, 1931).

Chapter Four

1. V. O. Stamps also worked briefly for the Trio Music Company and the Quartet Music Company, both Texas competitors of James D. Vaughan. See Emma Lee Hogg, "The Stamps Story," *Gospel Singing World* 3 (August 1956): 4.

2. On Jordan as head of the Vaughan Texas office, see *Vaughan's Family Visitor* 16 (December 1927): 5–6 and 18 (April 1929): 5. Jordan noted in the April 1929 article that "I have been with Mr. Vaughan's Branch House at Wills Point, Texas, for almost five years and have failed to have an article in only two issues."

3. Mrs. J. R. [Clarice Howard] "Ma" Baxter and Videt Polk, comps., *Gospel Song Writers Biography* (Dallas: Stamps-Baxter Music and Printing Company, 1971), 5; Mrs. Frank (Sally) Stamps, "In Loving Memory: Frank H. Stamps," in *Give the World a Smile* (Wesson, Miss.: M. Lynwood Smith, 1969), 5. The reference to William Stamps as postmaster is from a report by V. O. Stamps in *Musical Visitor* 4 (March 1915): 17.

4. It is possible that Virgil attended Morgan's singing school a year earlier and that Virgil and Frank Stamps are the "Stamps brothers" who attended a singing school near Center City, Texas, during the first six weeks of 1907. This school was conducted by Will M. Ramsey of the Central Music Company, Hartford, Arkansas. See *Central Musical Advocate* 3 (March 1907): 4. On Morgan, see *Virgil O. Stamps' Radio Song Album* (Dallas: Stamps-Baxter Music Company, 1937), 36.

5. Shirley L. Beary, "The Stamps-Baxter Music and Printing Company: A Continuing American Tradition, 1926–1976" (D.M.A. diss., Southwestern Baptist Theological Seminary, 1977), 84.

6. Mrs. V. O. [Trueman] Stamps, *Precious Memories of Virgil O. Stamps* (Dallas: Stamps-Baxter Music and Printing Company, 1941), v. Much of this

account was reprinted in a 1974 memorial by C. C. Stafford in "Virgil Oliver Stamps," *Vaughan's Family Visitor* 73 (March 1974): 6–7. See also D. T. Loyd, "Upshur County History," in Charles T. Stamps and William T. Stamps, *The Stamps Family History and Lineage* (Clinton, Utah: William T. Stamps, 1986), and Sally Stamps, "In Loving Memory," 5–6.

7. Beary, "Stamps-Baxter Music and Printing," 84. This song was also advertised in the pages of Vaughan's *Musical Visitor* in late 1915. See *Musical Visitor* 4 (November 1915): 15. Lyrics and music were later published in the pages of the *Vaughan's Family Visitor* 12 (February 1923): 22–23.

8. Beary, "Stamps-Baxter Music and Printing," 85. See also [Trueman] Stamps, *Precious Memories*, vi. One account of Stamps's life that corroborates this scenario is "The Story of a Man and a Book" (pamphlet in *Gospel Music Scrapbook: 1939–1949*, vol. 3, comp. Harry M. Wakefield [Troy, Mich.: Lee Marks, 1996], 26–28). It is also likely that the statement refers to Virgil Stamps's early and brief association with two other music companies, the Trio Music Company of Waco, Texas, and the Quartet Music Company of Fort Worth. See *Memories and Modern Songs* (Dallas: Stamps Quartet Music Company, 1955), 5.

9. *Musical Visitor* 4 (January 1915): 15.

10. For the earliest reports of Stamps's association with the Vaughan School of Music and then as a representative of the Vaughan songbooks, see ibid., 4 (January 1915): 13, 15, and 17; 4 (February 1915): 15; 4 (March 1915): 17; 4 (May 1915): 14; and 4 (June 1915): 13 and 18–19.

11. "Personal Mention," ibid., 4 (February 1915): 14.

12. "Personal Mention," ibid., 4 (October 1915): 14. On the song, see ibid., 4 (November 1915): 15. Significantly, the song was advertised from January 1917 through April 1917 without Stamps's name. The reason for the omission is unclear and is odd given that other songwriters' names were generally included. It might have been that, as publisher, Vaughan held rights to the song and simply omitted Stamps's name when he left the company.

13. Ibid., 6 (June 1917): 14.

14. Beary, "Stamps-Baxter Music and Printing," 85.

15. "Personal Mention," *Musical Visitor* 6 (June 1917): 14. Stamps's own letter admits that he considered his ill-fated move to Atlanta "the greatest mistake of my life." See ibid., 6 (July 1917): 17.

16. "V. O. Stamps Passes On," *Vaughan's Family Visitor* 29 (August 1940): 12. This is one of the few references anywhere to Stamps's personal life. Since his marriage to Addie ended in divorce, probably in the mid-1920s, it is likely that Stamps preferred to keep much of his personal life private. Divorce would have been a potential stumbling block for him among the church audiences associated with the gospel music business. V. O. married Trueman Bussey in the early 1930s but had no children from this second union (telephone interview with Marion Snider, Dallas, Tex., July 1, 1999). Snider, who played piano

for the V. O. Stamps Old Original Quartet in the mid-1930s, was married to Trueman Bussey's sister.

17. *Musical Visitor* 6 (July 1917): 15. The selection of individuals to sing with Stamps was perhaps by design. Walbert, Allen, and Foust all had long ties with the Vaughan company. Until Stamps joined, the three men had been traveling with Adger Pace as the Vaughan Saxophone Quartet. Several months after Stamps's arrival, Hilman Barnard and T. R. Shaw replaced Walbert and Foust. See ibid., 6 (October 1917): 10.

18. Beary, "Stamps-Baxter Music and Printing," 85–86.

19. By February 1923, Stamps claimed to have "the largest business west of the Mississippi river [*sic*] at Jacksonville and possibly the largest in the south with the exception of the home office at Lawrenceburg." See *Vaughan's Family Visitor* 12 (February 1923): 6.

20. Ibid., 12 (February 1923): 14. The quip was frequently used by the Vaughan company in advertising the records. See Charles K. Wolfe, "The Vaughan Quartets: Original 1927–1947 Recordings" (liner notes to TFS-110, Murfreesboro, Tenn.: Tennessee Folklore Society, 1992), 2. Stamps's younger brother, Frank, was also representing the Vaughan company by 1922 as a member of a Texas-based Vaughan quartet. See *Vaughan's Family Visitor* 11 (December 1922): 6, 13–14; and 12 (February 1923): 13.

21. *Vaughan's Family Visitor* 12 (August 1923): 5.

22. The number of students attending the Lawrenceburg Normal in January 1923 is not known. The Vaughan company paper simply noted that numbers were smaller than in previous sessions because of an outbreak of influenza. It is likely that Stamps's 119 total was actually larger than the number of students who arrived in Lawrenceburg two months later. See ibid., 12 (January 1923): 8.

23. *Vaughan Conservatory of Music and Bible Institute: Session of 1923* (Lawrenceburg, Tenn.: James D. Vaughan, 1922), 15.

24. For Stamps's report of the Lawrenceburg school in progress, see *Vaughan's Family Visitor* 12 (February 1923): 6.

25. Ibid., 12 (September 1923): 5. On the branch of the Vaughan Normal School, see 24 and ibid., 12 (December 1923): 4.

26. Ibid., 12 (November 1923): 4–5.

27. Ibid., 12 (June 1923): 7.

28. Ibid., 12 (July 1923): 5.

29. Ibid., 12 (August 1923): 6. Evidence suggests that Stamps and Ramsey patched up whatever differences they had in the intervening years. Stamps noted later in 1923 that the misunderstanding had been cleared up. See ibid., 12 (October 1923): 6. Also, the 1937 publication of *Stamps' Radio Song Album*, a collection of songs and short biographies of gospel singers and songwriters, included a preface by Ramsey with a glowing assessment of V. O. Stamps.

30. See "Photo Index" of *Stamps' Radio Song Album*.

31. Compare ibid. with Ottis J. Knippers, *Who's Who among Southern Singers and Composers* (Lawrenceburg, Tenn.: James D. Vaughan Music Publisher, 1937). There was much crossover between the Vaughan and Stamps fraternities during the 1930s, so some recognition of the other side was unavoidable. Examples of notables prominently displayed in both books were G. T. Speer and Adger M. Pace, long associated with Vaughan, and Frank Stamps and Luther G. Presley, Stamps-Baxter stalwarts.

32. Personal interview with Ottis J. Knippers, Lawrenceburg, Tenn., March 25, 1998. The mutual silence was broken only occasionally in the records I have seen. The November 1933 issue of *Vaughan's Family Visitor* focused on key individuals throughout the company's history. Along with biographies of Vaughan, W. B. Walbert, A. M. Pace, B. C. Unseld, and others was a brief profile and photo of V. O. Stamps. Not surprisingly, the photo was an old one and the article noted that "we haven't seen him in some time." Nevertheless, the writer's comments were complimentary, noting that Stamps "is still considered as one of the 'Vaughan boys' although he is in business for himself" (*Vaughan's Family Visitor* 22 [November 1933]: 6). In addition, a later issue included coverage of Stamps's untimely death in August 1940, and the Stamps-Baxter publication covered Vaughan's passing several months later. See *Vaughan's Family Visitor* 29 (August 1940): 12 and *Gospel Music News* 7 (February 1941): 8–9. Other than that, there were only passing references to the two men while they were alive. An example is *Vaughan's Family Visitor* 18 (May 1929): 9.

33. Robin Clayton interview with Otis L. McCoy, July 6, 1987, and August 10, 1988. Personal copy compliments of Robin Clayton, WLRC-AM, Walnut, Miss. See also Bob Terrell, *The Music Men: The Story of Professional Gospel Quartet Singing* (Asheville, N.C.: Bob Terrell Publisher, 1990), 36–37.

34. [Trueman] Stamps, *Precious Memories*, vi.

35. Beary, "Stamps-Baxter Music and Printing," 87.

36. The details of Stamps's personal life are murky, but, sometime between the death of his son in 1917 and the late 1920s, he and Addie Stamps divorced. Addie is not mentioned in any of the Vaughan publications following V. O. Stamps's return to the company after the tragic death. Unfortunately, few copies of the *Musical Visitor* survive from this pivotal period. In any event, it is highly likely that Stamps's business decisions, particularly the travel and perhaps even the gamble to form his own company, played at least some role in the breakup of the marriage. By 1932, Stamps had married again. Unlike his first wife, Trueman Bussey took an active role in the day-to-day affairs of the music business. See Loyd, "Upshur County History," and Mrs. V. O. [Trueman] Stamps Pankey, "News and Views," *Gospel Music News* 17 (September 1951): 3.

37. J. R. Baxter Jr., "V. O. Stamps as I Knew Him," *Gospel Music News* 7 (September 1940): 6; Beary, "Stamps-Baxter Music and Printing," 87–88 and 100–101. It was Baxter's ultimate success as a part of Stamps-Baxter that

led Joel Reed to dub him "the most successful and widely known musician to graduate from a Showalter normal school." See Joel F. Reed, "Anthony J. Showalter (1858–1924): Southern Educator, Publisher, Composer" (Ed.D. diss., New Orleans Baptist Theological Seminary, 1975), 124. Also on Baxter, see Lois Blackwell, *The Wings of the Dove: The Story of Gospel Music in America* (Norfolk, Va.: Donning Co., 1978), 53, and Jenny Lynn Smith, "'It Just Comes On Down'—T. B. Mosley and Sand Mountain's Gospel Music," pt. 2, *Alabama Baptist Historian* 24 (January 1988): 17.

38. It is likely that Vaughan began publishing songbooks in Lawrenceburg in the mid-1930s, which is when his books cease acknowledging the work of the Armstrong Printing Company. Vaughan's decision to change printers was possibly influenced by the Stamps-Baxter Music Company's purchase of the shape-note music plate equipment from Armstrong in 1936. See Beary, "Stamps-Baxter Music and Printing," 64–65.

39. On the growth of the Stamps-Baxter company, see ibid., 87–88. Also see Blackwell, *Wings of the Dove*, 49–50, and Doc Horsley, *Gospel Quartet Music: Then and Now, Music on the "Old Gospel Ship"* (Carbondale, Ill.: Cultural Press, 1995), 11–12. On Presley, see Knippers, *Who's Who among Southern Singers and Composers*, 111.

40. [Trueman] Stamps, *Precious Memories*, vi–vii.

41. The last ad V. O. Stamps wrote for his *Gospel Music News* advertised that new songbooks would be produced four times each year and outlined a plan in which subscribers could receive all four at a cost of $1 annually. By 1940, the Dallas plant employed around thirty people. See *Gospel Music Scrapbook*, vol. 3, 25, 63.

42. Frank Stamps served in the navy during World War I and, shortly after the war ended, began his career in gospel music helping V. O. Stamps conduct several singing schools near Sand Mountain, Alabama. By 1920, he was traveling with his first quartet, representing the Vaughan company. The other singers were Carl Jordan and Bill and Zeke Kitts. See *Memories and Modern Songs*, 6–7.

43. In time, Frank Stamps dubbed his quartet the Frank Stamps All-Star Quartet to distinguish the group from others using the Stamps name. See Sally Stamps, "In Loving Memory," 5–11. According to this article, Frank Stamps's quartet first cut recordings with the Dixie Phonograph Company around 1926 (see p. 7). On the group, see also *Memories and Modern Songs*, 5–7, and Rebecca L. Folsom, "A Brief History of White Southern Gospel Music as Seen through the Career of Dwight Moody Brock" (D.M.A. diss., University of Missouri–Kansas City, 1997), 43–53.

44. Competition between Stamps-Baxter and Vaughan was fierce during the 1930s with legendary exploits of oneupmanship at the annual singing conventions. See Terrell, *Music Men*, 32–34, and Jo Lee Fleming, "James D. Vaughan, Music Publisher, Lawrenceburg, Tennessee, 1912–1964" (S.M.D. diss., Union Theological Seminary, 1972), 58–59.

45. Blackwell, *Wings of the Dove*, 49–50; Terrell, *Music Men*, 43–44.

46. J. I. Ayres, "From Now on . . . Gospel Music News," *Gospel Music News* 6 (March 1940): 2.

47. *Gospel Music News* 6 (March 1940): 1.

48. On Stamps-Baxter, see [Trueman] Stamps, *Precious Memories*, vii, and Beary, "Stamps-Baxter Music and Printing," 237–45. On *Vaughan's Family Visitor*, see Charles K. Wolfe, "Introduction to the *Vaughan Family Visitor* Microfilm Collection" (Murfreesboro, Tenn.: Center for Popular Music, 1988), reel 1, p. 5.

49. Beary, "Stamps-Baxter Music and Printing," 144–47. By the late 1940s, the Chattanooga school was being held in January. See "Stamps-Baxter Annual School," *Gospel Music News* 15 (November–December 1948): 16–17.

50. The particulars of Combs's arrangement with Stamps and Baxter are not clear. He purchased stock in the company around 1929, apparently as a part of his agreement to move to Dallas and head up the annual school there. He sold his stock back to Stamps and Baxter in 1937. See Mrs. Ma [Clarice Howard] Baxter, "Opportune Observations," *Gospel Music News* 28 (October 1962): 2; Luther G. Presley, "Arkansas," *Gospel Music News* 29 (November 1962): 3; and Beary, "Stamps-Baxter Music and Printing," 166. His association with Stamps and Baxter probably dated to the summer of 1927, when he had suddenly disappeared from the pages of *Vaughan's Family Visitor*. He had headed up the Vaughan School of Music from January to May 1927. See "News from Headquarters," *Vaughan's Family Visitor* 14 (May 1927): 5, and "The Lawrenceburg School," *Vaughan's Family Visitor* 14 (December 1927): 4. See also W. W. Combs, "An Interesting Story Remeniscent [*sic*] of W. W. Combs," *Gospel Music News* 25 (October 1959): 18, 30; Dwight Brock, "Great Music Master Passes to His Reward," *Gospel Music News* 42 (February 1974): 2; and J. R. Baxter Jr., introduction to William Walker Combs, *The Voice in Singing: Its Care and Development* (Dallas: W. W. Combs, 1938), 2–3. See also James D. Walbert, "James D. Vaughan and the Vaughan School of Music," *Rejoice!* 2 (Summer 1990): 13, and Baxter and Polk, comps., *Gospel Song Writers*, 73–75.

51. [Trueman] Stamps, *Precious Memories*, vii. There is evidence that Stamps's school in Dallas and Baxter's in Chattanooga quickly had an adverse effect on the numbers attending the Vaughan school, which, by the late 1920s, enrolled as few as fifty students in the main winter session. See *Vaughan's Family Visitor* 17 (February 1928): 5 and 18 (January 1929): 7.

52. On V. O. Stamps's association with KRLD, see [Trueman] Stamps, *Precious Memories*, vii–ix.

53. Telephone interview with Marion Snider, Dallas, Tex., July 23, 1998. See also Terrell, *Music Men*, 46–47. Shortly before V. O. Stamps's death, the company was advertising its connections with twenty-eight different radio stations in the South, noting that this was only a "Partial List." See *Gospel Music News* 6 (July–August 1940): 26.

54. *Gospel Music News* 6 (July–August 1940): 14–18. See also Beary, "Stamps-Baxter Music and Printing," 92–93, 181–82, and *Gospel Singing World* 1 (October–December 1996): 8.

55. For a wealth of personal reminiscences on the two men, see *Gospel Music News* 7 (September 1940) and 26 (February 1960).

56. Personal interview with James Blackwood, Anderson, Ind., April 3, 1996. On Baxter, see *Gospel Music News* 26 (February 1960): 11. On the working relationship between the two men, see also Terrell, *Music Men*, 37.

57. George Pullen Jackson, *White Spirituals in the Southern Uplands* (Chapel Hill: University of North Carolina Press, 1933; reprint, New York: Dover Publications, 1965), 366–67. On the Teachers' Music Publishing Company, see *In His Name* (Hudson, N.C.: Teachers' Music Publishing Company, 1916), and *Telling Jesus, No. 2* (Hudson, N.C.: Teachers' Music Publishing Company, 1923). On the Athens Music Company, see C. A. Brock, comp., *Songs of Love* (Athens, Ala.: Athens Music Company, 1925). On the John Benson Publishing Company, see Blackwell, *Wings of the Dove*, 54. On the Trio Music Company, see F. L. Eiland, Emmett S. Dean, and J. F. Mayfield, *Happy News! No. 1* (Waco, Tex.: Trio Music Company, 1900).

58. On the loyalty of people in rural areas to specific shape-note publishers, see Smith, "It Just Comes on Down," pt. 2, 16–17.

59. Norma Michael, "Hartford. . . . Days of Past Glory and Its Future," *The Citizen*, September 12, 1974, 3, in files of the Hartford Museum, Hartford, Ark.

60. Ramsey seems to have been the major force behind the Central Music Company. He was listed as president of the company and was editor of its monthly publication, the *Central Musical Advocate*. David Moore and G. L. Lindsey were listed as associate editors. Like the other shape-note companies, the Central Music Company also operated an annual normal school. Like Vaughan, Ramsey had studied under E. T. Hildebrand of Roanoke, Virginia. On Ramsey, see Baxter and Polk, comps., *Gospel Song Writers*, 116–17. Bartlett was affiliated with the company as a singing-school teacher by at least early 1907. See *Central Musical Advocate* 3 (March 1907): 8.

61. On Hartford, Arkansas, see Michael, "Hartford. . . . Days of Past Glory," 3, and Jean Winkler, "Singing by Shape Note," [Little Rock] *Arkansas Gazette*, December 15, 1940, 3, 6, in files of the Hartford Museum, Hartford, Ark.

62. Both Ramsey and Bartlett ultimately had some association with the Vaughan company. Before his death in January 1941, Bartlett had spent some time aligned with both Vaughan and Stamps-Baxter. See *Vaughan's Family Visitor* 27 (November 1938): 3 and 30 (March 1941): 4. Ramsey contributed occasional articles to Vaughan's magazine during the ten years leading up to his death in March 1939. See ibid., 18 (October 1929): 5; 20 (September 1931): 5–6; 24 (June 1935): 4; and 28 (March 1939): 8.

63. *Gospel Music Scrapbook*, vol. 1, 67.

64. Kay Hively and Albert E. Brumley Jr., *I'll Fly Away: The Life Story of*

Albert E. Brumley (Branson, Mo.: Mountaineer Books, 1990), 30. On Bartlett
and the origins of the Hartford company, see Mary L. Couch, "Music From
the Hills and Valley" (xeroxed copy, files of the Hartford Museum), and E. M.
(Gene) Bartlett, "Bartletts and the Hartford Music Company," *The Key* (Summer 1986): 42, as reprinted in *First Annual Gospel Songfest Program*, May 12,
1991, files of the Hartford Museum.

65. Hively and Brumley, *I'll Fly Away*, 18. Albert's father, William, arrived
in Oklahoma Territory in 1899, "staking a homestead claim in one of the
many land runs that opened up Indian Territory." Apparently, by 1905, the
claim was forfeited in favor of a tenant farming arrangement and eventual
land purchase. See ibid., 9–10. I am also indebted to Albert Brumley's son for
sharing glimpses into his father's life (personal interview with Bob Brumley,
Springdale, Ark., August 1, 1996).

66. Hively and Brumley, *I'll Fly Away*, 19. The best overall account of
Brumley's life and influence is Bill C. Malone, "Albert E. Brumley: Folk Com-
poser," *Bluegrass Unlimited* 21 (July 1986): 69–77. See also Charles K. Wolfe,
"'I'd Rather Be an Old-Time Christian': The Music of Albert E. Brumley,"
Precious Memories (May–June 1991): 15–18, and Paul Stubblefield, "Brumley
Is Ozark's Country/Gospel Songmaster," *Music City News* 14 (April 1977):
25, 40.

67. The six-month schedule for traveling groups corresponded with
singing conventions held from spring through early fall. Bell served as the
group's principal pianist, and McNinch took care of the managerial respon-
sibilities. In time, Dalton became a noted songwriter, composing gospel
favorites like "What a Savior" and "Looking for a City." Brumley also played
piano briefly for the Hartford-sponsored Melody Four Quartet of Harrison,
Arkansas. See Hively and Brumley, *I'll Fly Away*, 26–27.

68. The song was ultimately made into a hit by famed country singer
Little Jimmy Dickens. See ibid., 29, and Bill C. Malone, *Country Music, U.S.A.*,
rev. ed. (Austin: University of Texas Press, 1985), 225.

69. "Their Music Spreads the Word," *Billboard* 78 (October 22, 1966): 23.

70. *Music City News* 3 (July 1965): 18.

71. The dates used here reflect the original copyright. Brumley's best-
known songs are compiled in *The Best of Albert E. Brumley* (Powell, Mo.:
Albert E. Brumley and Sons, 1966).

72. See Wolfe, "I'd Rather Be an Old-Time Christian," 15.

73. The quote is attributed to Gene Gideon, a music writer from Branson,
Missouri, and a promoter of Brumley publications in the 1970s. See *Albert E.
Brumley's Songs of the Pioneers* (Powell, Mo.: Albert E. Brumley and Sons,
1970), insert between songs 29 and 30.

74. *Singing News* 1 (December 1, 1969): 2. For similar comments, see the
Brumley segment in the documentary *The History of Southern Gospel Music*,
videocassette recording, Greystone Communications, 1997. On the simplicity

of Brumley's style, also see *Singing News* 1 (December 1, 1969): 1–2, and Blackwell, *Wings of the Dove*, 58–59.

75. Hively and Brumley, *I'll Fly Away*, 116–21. See also Robert K. Oermann, "Gospel Dynasty Keeps Father's Music Alive," [Nashville] *Tennessean*, April 9, 1987, sec. D, p. 12.

Chapter Five

1. As with the Vaughan company, Showalter's quartet men were involved in a variety of enterprises connected with the firm and it is difficult to separate their work as a quartet from other aspects of their association. On the Big Quartet, see Joel F. Reed, "Anthony J. Showalter (1858–1924): Southern Educator, Publisher, Composer" (Ed.D. diss., New Orleans Baptist Theological Seminary, 1975), 103–5. Showalter's emphasis on a specific quartet seems to have come with the 1912 publication of *The Sunny South Quartet Book* (Dalton, Ga.: A. J. Showalter Company, 1912). Even earlier, his company had published the more generically titled *Showalter's Men's Quartet and Chorus Book* (Dalton, Ga.: A. J. Showalter Company, 1895).

2. The Jenkins Family ultimately made records with Okeh. See Charles K. Wolfe, "Frank Smith, Andrew Jenkins, and Early Commercial Gospel Music," *American Music* (Spring 1983): 50–53. Also on Jenkins, see Zell Miller, *They Heard Georgia Singing* (Macon, Ga.: Mercer University Press, 1996), 160–61.

3. Wolfe, "Early Commercial Gospel Music," 53–59.

4. Ibid., 58.

5. Ibid. Wolfe notes that Smith's success prompted music publishers like Vaughan and Stamps-Baxter to contact him in an effort to promote their own songs but that Smith refused to align with any particular company.

6. Other scholars have also noted the connection between secular artists and older, tested gospel material. See, for example, Charles K. Wolfe, "Uncle Dave Macon: The Birth of Country Gospel," *Precious Memories* (March–April 1989): 21. An exception to this trend of secular artists singing only traditional gospel tunes, as Wolfe points out, was a song coming out of an unusual event, such as Uncle Dave Macon's "The Bible's True," written in response to the 1925 Scopes trial in Dayton, Tennessee.

7. See William Lynwood Montell, *Singing the Glory Down: Amateur Gospel Music in South Central Kentucky* (Lexington: University Press of Kentucky, 1991), 52. The strain of the quartet presence at conventions was clear by the summer of 1923 when Charles Vaughan felt compelled to express his own view that quartets had helped conventions. See *Vaughan's Family Visitor* 12 (June 1923): 14.

8. J. H., "County Singers, No. 4" (1925), in *Gospel Music Scrapbook, 1921–1934*, vol. 1, comp. Harry M. Wakefield (Troy, Mich.: Lee Marks, 1996), 33.

For a similar criticism leveled by Adger M. Pace, one of James Vaughan's most valuable employees, see "Give Us More Chorus Singing," *Vaughan's Family Visitor* 23 (November 1934): 9–10.

9. Will M. Ramsay, "Too Much Levity in Singing Conventions," *Vaughan's Family Visitor* 24 (August 1935): 14.

10. Escaping the farm has been a consistent theme in gospel and country music. See Pete Daniel, "Rhythm of the Land," *Agricultural History* 68, no. 4 (1994): 1–22. This theme of wanting to escape farm or mill work came up consistently in my interviews with gospel singers.

11. "Reminiscences from J. M. Allen," *Vaughan's Family Visitor* 18 (January 1929): 9.

12. Ibid.

13. Many early groups changed members almost annually with little concern. In fact, changes were probably viewed as a strength since they would offer the singing convention audiences something new on a regular basis. Only in the 1920s, when family groups began to represent the music companies and radio established the permanent identity of certain groups, was there any degree of regularity in group personnel. Even then, frequent turnover remained a part of the quartet business.

14. Both Allen and Foust continued to travel for the company and were in and out of Vaughan quartets over the next few years. In 1915, Allen reported that "as general field man for the James D. Vaughan song book concern . . . I was in eleven different states, attended fourteen county singing conventions, sang in 6 revival meetings, secured 454 subscriptions for the *Visitor*, sold approximately 3,600 *Glorious Refrain* song books and traveled by rail 10,600 miles" (*Musical Visitor* 4 [January 1915]: 19). See also Foust's report in ibid., 21.

15. On the origins of first tenors, see *Vaughan's Family Visitor* 18 (April 1929): 8–9; 49 (April 1960): 5; and Edward M. Lindsey, ed., *Lawrence County, Tennessee: Pictorial History* (Paducah, Ky.: Turner Publishing Company, 1994), 204–6.

16. On Charles Vaughan's importance beginning with his brother's earliest business days, see Gordon H. Turner, "Only One Brother Left of Vaughan Family Singers" (miscellaneous news clippings, 1946, James D. Walbert files, Birmingham, Ala.).

17. Lindsey, *Lawrence County*, 207; *Vaughan's Family Visitor* 21 (August 1932): 8; *Musical Visitor* 4 (May 1915): 16, 22; 4 (June 1915): 17; 6 (May 1917): 19; and 6 (June 1917): 3, 19–21. Also on early quartet transportation, see Elton Whisenhunt, "From Model T to Highway Pullman . . . From Gravel Roads to Super Highways: Gospel Quartets Take to the Roads," *Billboard* 77 (October 23, 1965): 10–11.

18. For early reports of Vaughan quartets' travel in Tennessee, Kentucky, and Florida, see *Musical Visitor* 4 (March 1915): 16; 4 (April 1915): 17–18; 4 (May 1915): 16; and 4 (June 1915): 17.

19. Ibid., 6 (April 1917): 20–21. The Vaughan Saxophone Quartet was revived in the 1920s as a part of the programming on Lawrenceburg's WOAN. At that time, the personnel included Walbert and Pace, along with two newcomers, Theodore Shaw and Claude Sharp. See Lindsey, *Lawrence County,* 211, and Bob Terrell, *The Music Men: The Story of Professional Gospel Quartet Singing* (Asheville, N.C.: Bob Terrell, 1990), 25. In the late 1930s, a similarly talented arrangement included guitar, saxophone, accordion, ukulele, and piano. See *Vaughan's Family Visitor* 27 (February 1938): 11.

20. On the impact of the war on Vaughan employees, see *Vaughan's Family Visitor* 19 (November 1930): 7–8. This article confirms that business boomed in the early 1920s and leveled off with increased competition from Stamps-Baxter by the late 1920s.

21. On the variety of radio presentations, see *Vaughan's Family Visitor* 29 (October 1940): 4.

22. The group was using this name at least as early as February 1929 to distinguish it from other prominent Vaughan quartets. See *Vaughan's Family Visitor* 18 (February 1929): 8. Given their popularity and extensive travel, this is probably the quartet to which George Pullen Jackson referred in *White Spirituals in the Southern Uplands* (Chapel Hill: University of North Carolina Press, 1933; reprint, New York: Dover Publications, 1965), 430. On the origins of the quartet, established in 1923, see *Vaughan's Family Visitor* 49 (October 1960): 4–5, 14 and 50 (May 1961): 8.

23. *Vaughan's Family Visitor* 21 (August 1932): 8.

24. The only major personnel change, other than short-term temporary replacements, was the addition of Albert A. Roberson in place of Otis McCoy in October 1930. See ibid., 19 (October 1930): 9.

25. On the Vaughan Radio Quartet, see James D. Walbert, "James D. Vaughan and the Vaughan School of Music," *Rejoice!* 2 (Summer 1990): 13. By the late 1930s, James Walbert was billed as the "wizard of the piano." See *Gospel Music Scrapbook*, vol. 3, 31. Also on the Vaughan Radio Quartet, see Bobby Alford, *History of Lawrence County, Tennessee*, vol. 3 (Lawrenceburg, Tenn.: Bobby Alford, 1997), 74–76, and Stella B. Vaughan, *A Heritage to Keep: History of the James D. Vaughan, Music Publisher*, edited by Connor B. Hall (Cleveland, Tenn.: James D. Vaughan, Music Publisher, ca. 1976), 3. On the extent of their travels, particularly outside the South, see their itinerary posted in *Vaughan's Family Visitor* 20 (September 1931): 13, 16. Cecil and Ottis Knippers had traveled briefly with Cullie Wilson as the Vaughan Trio until Wilson's untimely death in 1932 (personal interview with Ottis J. Knippers, Lawrenceburg, Tenn., March 25, 1998).

26. Personnel in this group included Walbert, LeRoy Carver, Luther Drummond, and George Schnake. Walbert's son, James, again served as pianist. The group, as the name indicates, was made up of staff members at the Vaughan publishing concern in Lawrenceburg and reflected Walbert's increasing duties as coeditor of the monthly journal (personal interview with

James D. Walbert, Birmingham, Ala., July 27, 1996). On the Vaughan Office Quartet, see *Vaughan's Family Visitor* 28 (May 1939): 9 and 28 (August 1939): 8.

27. The quartet was usually known as simply Kieffer's Quartet, though insiders apparently remembered it as the "Recording Quartet" because of Kieffer Vaughan's early prominence on the recordings (Knippers interview).

28. *Vaughan's Family Visitor* 12 (May 1923): 13. An early photo of the group with this personnel also showed Ted Shaw as group pianist. However, it is likely that Shaw accompanied the group only in studio sessions. See ibid., 49 (July 1960): 14.

29. This quartet began as a separate traveling unit in March 1928, though it seems to have been performing on radio as early as 1925. See ibid., 17 (April 1928): 8 and 49 (October 1960): 4–5, 14.

30. Ibid., 17 (August 1928): 8.

31. Ibid., 29 (October 1940): 4. See also Charles K. Wolfe, "The Opry's Hidden Wellsprings," as quoted in "Lawrence County History: James D. Vaughan—Father of Modern Gospel Music," *Murray (Ohio) Horizon* (February 1990): 31. Wolfe has also compiled an unpublished "Vaughan Discography" (private copy, personal files of Bruce Johnston, Lawrenceburg, Tenn.).

32. On Kieffer Vaughan's reorganized group, see *Vaughan's Family Visitor* 49 (November 1960): 4, 10; Lindsey, *Lawrence County*, 208; and Terrell, *Music Men*, 43–45. On the daily program on WSM, see *Vaughan's Family Visitor* 24 (January 1935): 9 and 24 (October 1935): 15. In the October article, Alphus LeFevre was listed as accompanist.

33. For the earliest references to Kieffer Vaughan's group as the Vaughan Radio Quartet, see *Vaughan's Family Visitor* 25 (March 1936): 8 and 26 (January 1937): 8. By 1938, the name was used always to refer to the latter group, though there was sometimes confusion. See ibid., 27 (February 1938): 8 and 28 (August 1939): 8–9 with *Gospel Music Scrapbook*, vol. 3, 17. On the overall history of this Kieffer Vaughan group, see Rebecca L. Folsom, "A Brief History of White Southern Gospel Music as Seen through the Career of Dwight Moody Brock" (D.M.A. diss., University of Missouri–Kansas City, 1997), 58–74.

34. *Gospel Music Scrapbook*, vol. 1, 49.

35. *Vaughan's Family Visitor* 14 (May 1927): 9.

36. Walbert, "James D. Vaughan," 13, and Charles K. Wolfe, "The Vaughan Quartets: Original 1927–1947 Recordings" (liner notes to TFS-110, Murfreesboro, Tenn.: The Tennessee Folklore Society, 1992), 3. See also *Vaughan's Family Visitor* 18 (October 1929): 10. The Happy Two originated in the summer of 1924 with Sebren and Joseph M. Allen. After a year, Wilson replaced Allen and the group soon gained its greatest acclaim. The group disbanded in January 1932, when the Depression forced James Vaughan to remove them as salaried employees. See *Vaughan's Family Visitor* 21 (January 1932): 11.

37. The number of full-time quartets is sometimes listed as sixteen. See *Vaughan's Family Visitor* 14 (October 1927): 9 and Stella Vaughan, *Heritage to*

Keep, 2. This entire year of the *Vaughan's Family Visitor* journal was incorrectly labeled as volume 14 instead of 16.

38. Walbert, "James D. Vaughan," 13–14; *Vaughan's Family Visitor* 49 (November 1960): 4, 10. Several singers who would achieve prominence in southern gospel circles were represented in these quartets, including Fred Maples, Aycel Soward, and Erman Slater. On the Victory Four, Melody Girls, and Sand Mountain Quartet, see *Vaughan's Family Visitor* 25 (October 1936): 6; 26 (March 1937): 4; and 26 (September 1937): 13.

39. *Vaughan's Family Visitor* 14 (October 1927): 9.

40. Ibid., 17 (March 1928): 10.

41. Mrs. Frank (Sally) Stamps, "In Loving Memory: Frank H. Stamps (1896–1965)," in *Give the World a Smile* (Wesson, Miss.: M. Lynwood Smith, 1969), 7. For various references to this personnel with the Vaughan company during 1923, see *Vaughan's Family Visitor* 12 (April 1923): 11; 12 (October 1923): 5–6, 12; and 12 (November 1923): 18. A slightly different account of the chronology is contained in a letter from Johnny Wheeler published in *Gospel Music Hi-Lites* (May 1965): 7.

42. *Gospel Music News* 7 (September 1940): 19. On Bill and Zeke Kitts, see Virgil O. Stamps, *Radio Song Album* (Dallas: Stamps-Baxter Music Company, 1937), 201. A later source claims that the Kitts brothers had sung with Frank Stamps, Carl Jordan, and Otis Deaton earlier in what comprised the first "Stamps" quartet—though presumably this would have been a Stamps "Vaughan" quartet since both V. O. and Frank Stamps were working for the James D. Vaughan Music Company. See Emma Lee Hogg, "The Stamps Story," *Gospel Singing World* 3 (August 1956): 18.

43. Shirley L. Beary, "The Stamps-Baxter Music and Printing Company: A Continuing American Tradition, 1926–1976" (D.M.A. diss., Southwestern Baptist Theological Seminary, 1977), 87–88. On Baxter, see ibid., 96–102, and the entire memorial issue of *Gospel Music News* 26 (February 1960).

44. Information on these earliest Stamps recordings is scarce. According to one source, V. O.'s quartet recorded a custom version of "Give the World a Smile" two years before the song would be made famous by Frank's quartet in a recording session for Victor (telephone interview with Robin Clayton, WLRC, Walnut, Miss., July 22, 1998). The reference to the Dixie Phonograph Company is from Sally Stamps, "In Loving Memory," 7.

45. Telephone interview with Tommy Wheeler, son of Palmer Wheeler, DeSoto, Tex., June 23, 1998. See also Tommy Wheeler, "The History of the Stamps Quartet" (unpublished manuscript, Tommy Wheeler, DeSoto, Tex.), and "J. E. Wheeler—Porterville, Calif.," *Gospel Music Hi-Lites* (May 1965): 7. My version of events is a composite of these two accounts, some portions of which are irreconcilable.

46. Stamps Quartet Reunion tape, April 11, 1973, personal files of Tommy Wheeler, DeSoto, Tex.

47. On Dwight Brock, see Folsom, "Brief History," 43–47; Terrell, *Music*

Men, 38–39; Lois Blackwell, *The Wings of the Dove: The Story of Gospel Music in America* (Norfolk, Va.: Donning Co., 1978), 51; Mrs. J. R. [Clarice Howard] "Ma" Baxter and Videt Polk, comps., *Gospel Song Writers Biography* (Dallas: Stamps-Baxter Music and Printing Company, 1971), 47–48; Jenny Lynn Smith, "'It Just Comes on Down'—T. B. Mosley and Sand Mountain's Gospel Music," pt. 2, *Alabama Baptist Historian* 24 (January 1988): 19; and Charles Novell, "Gospel Roots: Tapping America's Heritage," *Billboard* 64 (July 4, 1976): MR78.

48. Stamps Quartet Reunion tape.

49. Echols is variously referred to as "Odis" and "Otis." His proper name was apparently "Odis" since that is the spelling used in the program for a memorial sing held several months after his death in 1974. See "Third Annual Odis 'Pop' Echols Gospel Music Spectacular, First Memorial" (Program, Leon Williams Stadium, Clovis, New Mexico, July 6, 1974).

50. The song is often referred to as the first "million seller" in gospel music, though others also claim that hard-to-confirm honor. On the origins of the song, see Otis Deaton, "The Origin of 'Give the World a Smile,'" *Stamps Quartet News* 7 (October 1951): 8, and Folsom, "Brief History," 48–49.

51. Though Johnny Wheeler left the group in 1927, he returned sporadically as a replacement for Odis Echols and appeared on several of the group's recordings. Though Echols ordinarily sang baritone, lead singer Roy Wheeler switched to baritone in favor of his brother's lead vocal on those recordings. See copies of "RCA Victor Recording Ledgers," no. 039-1938 (Atlanta, Ga., October 20, 1927; Memphis, Tenn., February 10, 1928; Bristol, Tenn., November 1–2, 1928) and Tommy Wheeler, "Stamps Quartet—Discography," personal files of Tommy Wheeler, DeSoto, Tex. For a brief history of the Frank Stamps' All-Stars, see Folsom, "Brief History," 43–57.

52. *Memories and Modern Songs* (Dallas: Stamps Quartet Music Company, 1955), 6; *Gospel Music News* 7 (September 1940): 10.

53. In the summer of 1940, the Frank Stamps Quartet and the Blackwood Brothers switched territories. The Frank Stamps group began appearing on KWKH, Shreveport, in August, and the Blackwoods made their debut on KMA, Shenandoah, Iowa. See *Gospel Music News* 6 (July–August 1940): 12.

54. Personal interview with Mary "Sally" Stamps Dearman, Dallas, Tex., July 28, 1996. See also Charles K. Wolfe, "Gospel Goes Uptown: White Gospel Music, 1945–1955," in William Ferris and Mary L. Hart, eds., *Folk Music and Modern Sound* (Jackson: University Press of Mississippi, 1982), 83.

55. The Beulah Girls Quartet and the Pennington Quartet noted specifically that they had male managers. For Stamps-Baxter publicity on these groups, see *Gospel Music News* 6 (March 1940): 25; 6 (May 1940): 8, 13; and 6 (July–August 1940): 5, 7. The Vaughan company had publicized an all-female group, the Gaines Quartet, as early as 1915. See *Musical Visitor* 4 (June 1915): 15. From the beginning, both the Vaughan and Stamps-Baxter music schools enrolled women as well as men.

Notes to Pages 121–23

56. On the origins of V. O. Stamps's annual sing, see *Gospel Notes* 1 (Christmas 1966): 2.

57. On Frank Stamps's decision to leave the company, see Beary, "Stamps-Baxter Music and Printing," 72–75, 152–56. For a listing of groups affiliated with the new company by late 1947, see *Stamps Quartet News* 3 (September 1947): 10; 3 (October 1947): 10; and 3 (November 1947): 10.

58. Kay Hively and Albert E. Brumley Jr., *I'll Fly Away: The Life Story of Albert E. Brumley* (Branson, Mo.: Mountaineer Books, 1990), 26–42.

59. On Utley and his group, see *Gospel Music Scrapbook*, vol. 3, 13, and Terrell, *Music Men*, 46, 189.

60. Personal interview with Robert S. Arnold, Springdale, Ark., August 3, 1996. Arnold recalled having taught a singing school every single year from 1924 until the early 1990s. In 1937, he helped form the National Music Company, one of a handful of shape-note convention companies still in existence.

61. The best account of the Speer family is Paula Becker, *Let the Song Go On: Fifty Years of Gospel Singing with the Speer Family* (Nashville: Impact Books, 1971). Also valuable is the short account in Terrell, *Music Men*, 64–69. For updates on the group's development since Becker's account, see *Singing News* 6 (December 1, 1974): 2–3B; and 15 (January 1985): 8–9; and *Gospel Voice* 2 (November 1989): 8–9. The Speers retired in 1997 as the longest continuing group in gospel music.

62. Becker, *Let the Song Go On*, 35.

63. Family members remember the account fondly. Noting that his father also tried selling insurance for a living during this period, Brock Speer commented that "Daddy never did anything that was a success except gospel music" (personal interview with Brock Speer, Nashville, Tenn., May 23, 1996).

64. Ibid.

65. Personal interview with Rosa Nell Powell, Mary Tom Reid, and Ben Speer, Nashville, Tenn., May 22, 1996.

66. For the earliest references to Tom Speer (known professionally as G. T. Speer) and his singing schools, see *Vaughan's Family Visitor* 20 (November 1931): 7; 21 (May 1932): 9; 21 (September 1932): 7; and 21 (December 1932): 2. The December 1932 issue noted, "He is one of the best in the business and always makes good."

67. Ibid., 23 (November 1934): 4.

68. Ibid., 24 (April 1935): 6.

69. Ibid., 27 (February 1938): 8; Becker, *Let the Song Go On*, 51–64; Powell-Reid-Speer interview. For a photo of the Speers with their instruments, see *Vaughan's Family Visitor* 27 (February 1938): 12.

70. Becker, *Let the Song Go On*, 73–88; Brock Speer interview. The last reference to the Speers as employees of the Vaughan company came in *Vaughan's Family Visitor* 30 (April 1941): 8.

71. Personal interview with Eva Mae LeFevre, Louisville, Ky., September 21, 1996. See also Terrell, *Music Men*, 69–72, and Jesse Burt and Duane

Allen, *The History of Gospel Music* (Nashville, Tenn.: K & S Press, Inc., 1971), 160–62. Other brief accounts of the LeFevres are Blackwell, *Wings of the Dove*, 77–81; Miller, *They Heard Georgia Singing*, 180–83; and Wayne W. Daniel, "The LeFevres: Gospel Music Pioneers," *Rejoice!* (August–September 1991): 3–8. Daniel suggests that a religious experience at the Church of God's Bible Training School (BTS) convinced the LeFevre brothers "to switch their musical allegiance from country to gospel" (p. 4). However, their decision to attend BTS in 1930 as well as earlier church performances suggests that they had already contemplated this move. It is probable that their experience at the Church of God school deepened their commitment to focus on gospel music.

72. Wayne W. Daniel, "LeFevres," 4; Eva Mae LeFevre interview; Lucy Justus, *Travel with the LeFevres* (Atlanta: The LeFevres, ca. 1960), 3. There is some discrepancy in my sources on parts and personnel. *Vaughan's Family Visitor* 23 (October 1934): 8 noted that the group included McCoy singing lead, Urias LeFevre singing baritone, Alphus LeFevre singing tenor, and B. C. Robinson singing bass. This assertion, combined with similar comments from other sources, indicates that it is likely that Yates sang in an early grouping and was then succeeded by B. C. Robinson. Similarly, Urias LeFevre and James McCoy likely alternated on the lead part.

73. *Vaughan's Family Visitor* 23 (November 1934): 8. Alphus LeFevre taught "mandolin, violin and guitar" at the January 1935 Vaughan normal (ibid., 24 [January 1935]: 8–9).

74. *Singing News* 14 (November 1982): 16.

75. Ibid., 8 (August 1976): 9A.

76. Eva Mae LeFevre interview.

77. *Vaughan's Family Visitor* 24 (April 1935): 7.

78. The Vaughan association, which included Vaughan's son-in-law, William Walbert, as a "manager" for the group, lasted most of 1935. See ibid., 24 (February 1935): 5 and 24 (April 1935): 6–7. By the end of 1935, references to the group disappear.

79. The Hemphill Church of God eventually became Mt. Paran Church of God, one of the denomination's most influential churches and still a regular stop on many southern gospel quartets' annual schedules.

80. Eva Mae LeFevre interview; Wayne W. Daniel, "LeFevres," 5; Miller, *They Heard Georgia Singing*, 181.

81. On the degree of commercialization that had affected southern music in general by the early 1930s, see Bill C. Malone, "Writing the History of Southern Music: A Review Essay," *Mississippi Quarterly* 45, no. 4 (1992): 387. Like country music, gospel songs often glorified the new technology of the twentieth century. Two of the best-known examples are Albert Brumley's "Turn Your Radio On" and Charles Wycuff's "My Non-Stop Flight to Glory" (personal interview with Martin Cook, Louisville, Ky., September 17, 1996). On the connection between the Great Depression and the growing acceptance of and adaptation to the new technology, see Bill Malone, *Southern*

Music, American Music (Lexington: University Press of Kentucky, 1979), 70–87.

82. One important gospel music promoter acknowledged that, by the 1930s and 1940s, a weekly radio program would give each member of a quartet the equivalent of a week's salary in a southern mill. In addition to this income, quartet members could earn money from gospel concerts. Although successful gospel group members were not wealthy entertainers, their positions did give them substantially improved financial positions over those of their peers (personal interview with Charles Burke, Boone, N.C., February 8, 1996).

83. See Blackwell, *Wings of the Dove*, 75–77. On the direction of other forms of southern music during the same period, see John Egerton, *Speak Now against the Day: The Generation before the Civil Rights Movement in the South* (Chapel Hill: University of North Carolina Press, 1994), 241–48.

84. On the difficulty of the Depression and its effect on traveling gospel groups, see Blackwell, *Wings of the Dove*, 88–91.

85. *Vaughan's Family Visitor* 21 (December 1932): 4. On the impact of the Depression on country music and American entertainment in general, see Bob Coltman, "Across the Chasm," *Old Time Music* 23 (Winter 1976–77): 6–12.

86. E. M. Bartlett's Hartford Music Company claimed to be surviving the Depression well as late as 1932. See "Arkansas Music Publishing Company Finds Depression Has No Depressing Effect upon Demand for Religious Song Books," in *Gospel Music Scrapbook*, vol. 2, 11.

87. See "Editorial," *Vaughan's Family Visitor* 30 (February 1941): 24, and Beary, "Stamps-Baxter Music and Printing," 314–16. Beary distinguishes annual "convention books" from the slightly more expensive "special books" that appeared on a regular basis. See pp. 67–68.

88. Robin Clayton interview with Otis L. McCoy, August 10, 1988, personal recorded copy compliments of Robin Clayton, WLRC-AM, Walnut, Miss.

89. The most extensive treatment of the Chuck Wagon Gang is Bob Terrell's *The Chuck Wagon Gang: A Legend Lives On* (Goodlettsville, Tenn.: Roy Carter, 1990). A short account that contains an accurate analysis of the group's place in music history is found in Bill Malone, "The Chuck Wagon Gang: God's Gentle People," *Journal of Country Music* 10 (Spring 1985): 2–12. See also a brief biographical account in *Singing News* 17 (March 1987): 10–11.

90. Malone, "Chuck Wagon Gang," 5.

91. Terrell, *Chuck Wagon Gang*, 12–14.

92. Bob Terrell, "Member of the Legendary Chuck Wagon Gang Passes Away," *Singing News* 28 (July 1997): 82. See also Terrell, *Chuck Wagon Gang*, 14–23.

93. Personal interview with Roy Carter, Bedford, Tex., July 29, 1996.

94. Terrell, *Chuck Wagon Gang*, 24–25.

95. Ibid., 27–29; Roy Carter interview.

96. In later years, the original members of the quartet recalled dressing in cowboy garb only once, though their sponsor, Bewley Mills, did distribute photos of the group in western dress around a chuck wagon (Malone, "Chuck Wagon Gang," 7, and Terrell, *Chuck Wagon Gang*, 32).

97. The name changes were significant in part because all three of the Carter children involved in the original group became better known through-out the rest of their lives by the new stage names. The changes also created some confusion since another sibling already had the name Anna.

98. Roy Carter interview. For a discography of the group's songs, see Ter-rell, *Chuck Wagon Gang*, 205–48. Many groups have claimed the mantle of having been "all gospel" first, but the fact is that most groups, even those formed by the publishing companies, tended to sing secular music as well as gospel in nonchurch settings and on early radio programs. The trend toward gospel-only programs seems to have begun in the late 1930s and was probably inspired by the Depression as well as the talents of new gospel songwriters like Albert E. Brumley.

99. Malone, "Chuck Wagon Gang," 4.

100. Roy Carter interview.

101. Ibid.

102. James Blackwood and Dan Martin, *The James Blackwood Story* (Monroeville, Pa.: Whitaker House, 1975), 28. On the influence of the Black-woods in the industry, see Don Cusic, *The Sound of Light: A History of Gospel Music* (Bowling Green, Ohio: Bowling Green State University Popular Press, 1990), 102–7, and Terrell, *Music Men*, 99–108.

103. Blackwood and Martin, *James Blackwood Story*, 15–31; Kree Jack Racine, *Above All: The Fascinating and True Story of the Lives and Careers of the Famous Blackwood Brothers Quartet* (Memphis: Jarodoce Publications, 1967), 19–35. During this period, Doyle even learned to play a Russian balalaika, which the family referred to as "a tater bug." See Blackwood and Martin, *James Blackwood Story*, 44–45. On the success of the Delmore Brothers during the 1930s and 1940s, see Mike Leadbitter, "Wayne Raney and the Delmore Brothers on King," *Old Time Music* 10 (Autumn 1973): 19–23, and Charles K. Wolfe, "The Brown's Ferry Four: Country's First All-Star Quartet," *Precious Memories* (November–December 1988): 6–12. For another example of the Delmore Brothers' tie to gospel music, see Bob Brumley and Sharon Boles, comps., *Albert E. Brumley's America's Memory Valley* (Powell, Mo.: Albert E. Brumley and Sons, 1992), 32.

104. Racine, *Above All*, 55–57; Blackwood and Martin, *James Blackwood Story*, 33–39; personal interview with James Blackwood, Anderson, Ind., April 3, 1996.

105. R. W. Blackwood's name was literally "R. W." (James Blackwood interview).

106. Racine, *Above All*, 61–64; Blackwood and Martin, *James Blackwood*

Story, 43–44. James Blackwood recalls that he initially sang the baritone part an octave high and adjusted as his voice changed.

107. Racine, *Above All*, 63; Blackwood and Martin, *James Blackwood Story*, 43. Blackwood and Martin erroneously imply that Doyle Blackwood sang with the Homeland Harmony in the early 1930s and then again in 1935–36. See pp. 43–44 and 49.

108. Blackwood and Martin, *James Blackwood Story*, 52–57; Racine, *Above All*, 69–72. See also James Blackwood interview.

109. James Blackwood interview.

110. Blackwood and Martin, *James Blackwood Story*, 57. This general scenario of having to prove the commercial appeal of gospel songs is a common one among early southern gospel groups, with parallels extending at least to the V. O. Stamps Old Original Quartet as well as the Chuck Wagon Gang. Although the stories focus on the reluctance of stations to play gospel music, they also reflect a self-conscious attempt to explain away gospel groups' early secular performances. See *Gospel Music News* 7 (September 1940): 10 and Terrell, *Chuck Wagon Gang*, 32.

111. James Blackwood interview. On the influence of Stamps on the group, see also Wolfe, "Gospel Goes Uptown," 84; Racine, *Above All*, 81–82; and Blackwood and Martin, *James Blackwood Story*, 63–64. Roper's length of service with the group was about three months. He was followed by Wallace Milligan and Marion Snider, who also played during the group's Shreveport era.

112. James Blackwood interview. On the move, see also Blackwood and Martin, *James Blackwood Story*, 73–77, and Racine, *Above All*, 85–86. Frank Stamps's quartet had only recently moved to Des Moines, and it is likely that the reception there had been less enthusiastic than expected, thus the decision to have the Blackwood's home base in Shenandoah. See "Moves to WHO . . ." and "Frank Stamps Speaking," *Gospel Music News* 6 (May 1940): 1, 10.

113. Blackwood and Martin, *James Blackwood Story*, 73–77; Racine, *Above All*, 88–90; James Blackwood interview. In order to allow for concerts, the group performed live broadcasts at 7:30 A.M. and 12:30 P.M. and then recorded a program for the 5:30 A.M. slot that would air the following morning. With travel to concerts, the group would oftentimes not arrive back in town until 4:00 or 5:00 A.M., catch a couple of hours of sleep, and then perform the first live broadcast at 7:30.

114. Racine, *Above All*, 90–93. See also Blackwood and Martin, *James Blackwood Story*, 76–77, and James Blackwood interview.

115. Robin Clayton interview with Otis L. McCoy, July 6, 1987. The origins and exact personnel of Homeland Harmony are obscure. It seems to have been one of many groups that emerged in the 1930s from the school, one of which was comprised of McCoy (tenor), J. H. Walker (lead), B. C. Robinson (bass), and Lloyd McClain (baritone). This is probably the foursome that recorded on Okeh Records in the early 1930s under the name Tennessee Music

and Printing Quartet. McCoy later sang lead in a version of the BTS Quartet that included Aycel Soward (bass), Fred C. Maples (baritone), Eugene Whitt (tenor), and Frances Johnson (piano). McCoy credited Alphus LeFevre with the origins of the name in the mid-1930s. LeFevre provided the title and the cover art for the songbook *Homeland Harmony* (Cleveland, Tenn.: Tennessee Music and Printing, 1936), and the popularity of the collection led to the use of the name. The group, in addition to its unique name, would become more widely known after Connor Hall reorganized it during World War II. See Terrell, *Music Men*, 31–32 and 180–85.

116. *Vaughan's Family Visitor* 26 (August 1937): 8. Daniel should not be confused with John Daniels, who briefly sang with Kieffer Vaughan's quartet in 1937. Compare this reference with *Vaughan's Family Visitor* 24 (April 1935): 5. The best overall account of the Daniel Quartet is Wayne W. Daniel, "The John Daniel Quartet: Country Gospel Pioneers," *Precious Memories* (September–October 1990): 21–27.

117. Wayne W. Daniel, "John Daniel Quartet," 22–23.

118. Jack Callaway, "The First Decade," *Precious Memories* (September–October 1989): 5.

119. On the Rangers, see Mrs. Vernon Hyles, "I Married a Gospel Singer," *The Rangers Quartet: Book of Memories* (Dallas: Rangers Quartet, ca. 1955), 20–26, and Terrell, *Music Men*, 76–85. On the use of the image of the American cowboy in religious music, see the introductory essay in Austin Fife and Alta Fife, *Heaven on Horseback: Revivalist Songs and Verse in the Cowboy Idiom* (Logan: Utah State University Press, 1970), 1–7.

120. For a sample of news reports during this period, see *Gospel Music Scrapbook*, vol. 2, 34 and 42.

121. Hyles, "I Married a Gospel Singer," 21.

122. Callaway, "First Decade," 6; Hyles, "Gospel Singer," 21–22.

123. Callaway, "First Decade," 6–7; Hyles, "Gospel Singer," 22–23. Charles Wolfe notes that the Rangers, the Chuck Wagon Gang, and the MacDonald Brothers Quartet from Missouri were all unique with respect to avoiding a link with the publishing companies. In some ways this forced them into other areas, and, consequently, they "were the only white gospel groups to be heard on major record labels on the eve of the war" (Wolfe, "Gospel Goes Uptown," 83). The Rangers did occasionally make the rounds of singing conventions, however. See *Vaughan's Family Visitor* 29 (September 1940): 16. The Johnson Family Singers survived for several years as "vagabonds of song" until they secured regular employment as staff musicians at WBT in 1942. They left WBT in 1951. See Kenneth M. Johnson, *The Johnson Family Singers: We Sang for Our Supper* (Jackson: University Press of Mississippi, 1997), 30–47.

124. It is likely that the group intended its name to be the "Suwannee" River Boys after the famed southern river but, given rural pronunciations, simply shortened the spelling.

125. Terrell, *Music Men*, 150–53. See also Wayne W. Daniel, *Pickin' on*

Peachtree: A History of Country Music in Atlanta, Georgia (Urbana University of Illinois Press, 1990), 199–200.

126. For an account of Stamps's death and the reaction of the gospel music community, see the memorial issue of *Gospel Music News* 7 (September 1940). On Vaughan's death and reactions to it, see *Vaughan's Family Visitor* 30 (February 1941).

Chapter Six

1. Quoted in "Singing Schools of Today," *Arkansas Gazette*, June 15, 1941, news clipping in *Gospel Music Scrapbook, 1939–1949*, comp. Harry M. Wakefield, vol. 3 (Troy, Mich.: Lee Marks, 1996), 72. The best articles on the "professionalization" of the southern gospel quartets during this period are Charles K. Wolfe, "Gospel Goes Uptown: White Gospel Music, 1945–1955," in William Ferris and Mary L. Hart, eds., *Folk Music and Modern Sound* (Jackson: University Press of Mississippi, 1982), 80–100; Charles K. Wolfe, "'Gospel Boogie': White Southern Gospel Music in Transition, 1945–55," *Popular Music* 1 (1981): 73–82; and David Crawford, "Gospel Songs in Court: From Rural Music to Urban Industry in the 1950s," *Journal of Popular Culture* 11 (Winter 1977): 551–67.

2. On the success of Tennessee Music and Printing as a church press, see Charles W. Conn, *Like a Mighty Army: A History of the Church of God, 1886–1976*, rev. ed. (Cleveland, Tenn.: Pathway Press, 1977), 225–26. Stamps-Baxter Music and Printing survived until 1974, when it was purchased by Zondervan Publishing House. See *Singing News* 6 (January 1975): 3 and Shirley L. Beary, "The Stamps-Baxter Music and Printing Company: A Continuing American Tradition, 1926–1976" (D.M.A. diss., Southwestern Baptist Theological Seminary, 1977), 131–35. For a focus on gospel music publishing outside the South during this same period, see Vernon M. Whaley, "Trends in Gospel Music Publishing: 1940–1960" (Ph.D. diss., University of Oklahoma, 1992), 62–96.

3. On Otis McCoy's influence, see *Vaughan's Family Visitor* 76 (April 1976): 3, 9 and Mrs. J. R. [Clarice Howard] "Ma" Baxter and Videt Polk, comps., *Gospel Song Writers Biography* (Dallas: Stamps-Baxter Music and Printing, 1971), 100–102.

4. Telephone interview with Charles Towler, an employee of Tennessee Music and Printing Company who began there in 1965 and retired as director of music in 1997, Cleveland, Tenn., March 24, 1998. On the A. J. Showalter Company, see Joel F. Reed, "Anthony J. Showalter (1858–1924): Southern Educator, Publisher, Composer" (Ed.D. diss., New Orleans Baptist Theological Seminary, 1975), 38–46.

5. Personal interview with Mary "Sally" Stamps Dearman, Dallas, Tex., July 28, 1996. On the formation of the Stamps Quartet Music Company, see Beary, "Stamps-Baxter Music and Printing," 72–73, 152–54, 193–96. By 1946,

Frank Stamps's school boasted more than a thousand students. See *Stamps Quartet Souvenir Album* (Dallas: Stamps Quartet Music Company, 1962), 16–17. By 1970, the Frank Stamps School was still in operation under the control of Stamps Quartet owner J. D. Sumner. See *Singing News 2* (June 1, 1970): 1, 15, and *Stamps Conservatory of Music Program* (Dallas: Stamps Quartet Music Company, 1966).

6. As late as 1946, the Vaughan company claimed more than sixty "Vaughan-affiliated singing groups currently appearing on regular radio programs throughout the country." Yet, by the 1960s, the tie between professional quartets and the publishing companies was almost nonexistent. On the Vaughan claim, see Gordon H. Turner, "Only One Brother Left of Vaughan Family Singers" (miscellaneous news clippings, 1946, James D. Walbert files, Birmingham, Ala.). Frank Stamps noted in 1957 that his Stamps Quartet Music Company "owned three quartets and 'indirectly' sponsored about 200 more." However, the Stamps Quartet company was unique, in part because Frank Stamps himself had always identified foremost with the quartet men on the road. See Crawford, "Gospel Songs in Court," 561.

7. On Truman's executive order to desegregate the military and the federal Civil Service, see David McCullough, *Truman* (New York: Simon and Schuster, 1992), 651 and 915. On the larger motivations undergirding Truman's action, see Harvard Sitkoff, "Harry Truman and the Election of 1948: The Coming of Age of Civil Rights in American Politics," *Journal of Southern History* 37 (1971): 597–616, and Monroe Billington, "Civil Rights, President Truman and the South," *Journal of Negro History* 58 (April 1973): 127–39.

8. For a good firsthand look at the world of the quartets in the years before and after World War II, see Mac Bruington, *The Rest of the Story: An Autobiography* (Richmond, Va.: F. M. Bruington, 1989), 177–262.

9. On the military considerations of the 1956 Federal Aid Highway Act, see Chester J. Pach Jr. and Elmo Richardson, *The Presidency of Dwight D. Eisenhower*, rev. ed. (Lawrence: University Press of Kansas, 1991), 123–24. For an overall look at the dramatic impact of the Interstate Highway System, see Tom Lewis, *Divided Highways: Building the Interstate Highways, Transforming American Life* (New York: Viking Penguin, 1997).

10. *Vaughan's Family Visitor* 27 (February 1938): 8.

11. Ibid., 29 (March 1940): 21. As if to illustrate Barnard's point, a radio gospel group was formed in the next few years with the unlikely name Brown's Ferry Four. The quartet, made up of the Delmore brothers (Alton and Rabon), Merle Travis, and Louis Marshall Jones, chose the name from one of Alton Delmore's earlier songs titled "Brown's Ferry Blues." The song, which Travis later described as "Alton's bawdy 'Two old maids layin' in the sand' song," was originally suggested as a name for the group only in jest but then was used anyway, "and nobody ever connected it." The Delmores were already recognized country artists as would be Travis and Jones (better

known as "Grandpa Jones"). See "Interview: Merle Travis Talking to Mark Humphrey, Part 2," *Old Time Music* 37 (Autumn 1981–Spring 1982): 21. Also see Alana White, "Grandpa Jones and the Hee Haw Gospel Quartet," *Bluegrass Unlimited* 22 (June 1988): 24, and Charles K. Wolfe, "The Brown's Ferry Four: Country's First All-Star Quartet," *Precious Memories* (November–December 1988): 6–8.

12. A 1952 advertisement for the New York–based Bibletone Records listed the LeFevre Trio, the Homeland Harmony Quartet, the Harmoneers, and the Crusaders as "Bibletone Exclusive Artists." See *Sing: A Magazine about Happy Rhythm* (Tallahassee, Fla., Fall 1952): 29.

13. Wolfe, "Gospel Goes Uptown," 80–86. On the growing popularity of gospel music, see also Bob Rolontz, "Sacred Songs Close Kin to C&W Music," *Billboard* 65 (December 1953): 42, 62.

14. On reasons for the decline of the conventions, see William Lynwood Montell, *Singing the Glory Down: Amateur Gospel Music in South Central Kentucky* (Lexington: University Press of Kentucky, 1991), 39–45. Also see Max R. Williams, ed., *The History of Jackson County* (Sylva, N.C.: Jackson County Historical Association, 1987), 358–60.

15. On the incompatibility of the conventions and the professional quartets, see Jack Spruiell Bottoms, "The Singing School in Texas" (Ph.D. diss., University of Colorado, 1972), 30–31, and Montell, *Singing the Glory Down*, 30. The link between shape notes and gospel artists' training is evident in the identification of the Stamps Quartet Conservatory of Music by 1969 as a "gospel-music-oriented school." See "Stamps Music School Enters 45th Year," *Singing News* 1 (May 15, 1969): 1.

16. See *Vaughan's Family Visitor* 24 (June 1935): 6.

17. Crawford, "Gospel Songs in Court," 563.

18. *Affiliated Music Enterprises, Inc., Plaintiff, v. SESAC, Inc., Defendant*, trial transcript from the Federal Archives and Record Center, Building 22, MOT, Bayonne, N.J., 1239–40, as quoted in ibid., 564.

19. This was the case mostly during the early years of the movement when Pentecostal evangelists like Charles Parham sponsored parades with colorful flags in order to attract media attention. The tradition continued with the evangelistic antics of "Sister" Aimee Semple McPherson, the movement's best-known figure during the pre–World War II period. On Parham, see James R. Goff Jr., *Fields White unto Harvest: Charles Fox Parham and the Missionary Origins of Pentecostalism* (Fayetteville: University of Arkansas Press, 1988), 90–105. On McPherson's life and contribution, see Edith Blumhofer, *Aimee Semple McPherson: Everybody's Sister* (Grand Rapids, Mich.: William B. Eerdman's, 1993). There is no definitive work on the tie between Pentecostalism and popular gospel music. The most comprehensive study to date is Delton L. Alford, *Music in the Pentecostal Church* (Cleveland, Tenn.: Pathway Press, 1967).

20. James Blackwood and Dan Martin, *The James Blackwood Story*

(Monroeville, Pa.: Whitaker House, 1975), 46–47. Pentecostals were not "a denomination." Rather, they formed a core of denominations that eagerly supported the development of the gospel music industry. Among predominantly white Pentecostal churches, the Assemblies of God, the Church of God of Cleveland, Tennessee, the Pentecostal Holiness Church, and the United Pentecostal Church were the largest. Among predominantly black Pentecostal organizations, the largest were the Church of God in Christ and the Pentecostal Assemblies of the World.

21. Blackwood and Martin, *James Blackwood Story*, 46–47. On the Blackwoods' initial connection to Pentecostalism, see ibid., 24–26.

22. Winsett actually attended the Assemblies' founding convention in Hot Springs, Arkansas, in 1914. See "Letter from Benjamin A. Baur to R. E. Winsett, Drawer 248, Dayton, Tennessee, May 20, 1935," Assemblies of God Archives, Springfield, Mo. The letter includes Winsett's handwritten reply, dated May 25, 1925, at the bottom of the original.

23. The connection between gospel music and Pentecostalism has been noted by others, including Stephen R. Tucker, "Pentecostalism and Popular Culture in the South: A Study of Four Musicians," *Journal of Popular Culture* 16 (Winter 1982): 68–80, and Bill C. Malone, *Southern Music, American Music* (Lexington: University Press of Kentucky, 1979), 77. On specific songwriters with Pentecostal connections, see Stanley M. Burgess and Gary B. McGee, eds., *Dictionary of Pentecostal and Charismatic Movements* (Grand Rapids, Mich.: Zondervan Publishing House, 1988), 101, 230, 260–61, 604, and 810; Edith Blumhofer, "'Jesus Only': The Ministry of Charles Price Jones," *Motif* (January 1986): 11–12; and Wayne Warner, "Herbert Buffum," *Assemblies of God Heritage* 6 (Fall 1986): 11–14, 16.

24. On Dottie Rambo's career in gospel music, see Buck Rambo and Bob Terrell, *The Legacy of Buck and Dottie Rambo* (Nashville: Star Song Publishing, 1992). The Pentecostal connection is also evident among black gospel songwriters and performers. On this connection, see Horace Clarence Boyer, *How Sweet the Sound: The Golden Age of Gospel* (Washington, D.C.: Elliott and Clark Publishing, 1995), 12–26, and Paul Oliver, Max Harrison, and William Bolcom, *The New Grove: Gospel, Blues, and Jazz* (New York: W. W. Norton and Company, 1986), 196–99.

25. Personal interviews with Brock Speer, Nashville, Tenn., May 23, 1996, and Bill and Gloria Gaither, Louisville, Ky., September 19, 1996.

26. James C. Downey, "Mississippi Music—That Gospel Sound" (unpublished manuscript, William Carey College, Hattiesburg, Miss., October 1978), 3.

27. J. J. Mueller, "Making Melody unto the Lord," *Pentecostal Evangel*, January 10, 1954: 13. For similar support, see Clinton H. Patterson, "Why, How, and What Shall We Sing?" ibid., May 15, 1937, 2–3; Donald Gee, "Pentecostal Singing," *Latter Rain Evangel* (May 1929): 22–23; Cameron Wesley Wilson, "We Serve a God of Song," *Pentecostal Evangel*, March 17, 1957, 4–5;

and Arnold B. Cheyney, "Why Christians Love to Sing," *Pentecostal Evangel,* July 15, 1956, 19.

28. *Pentecostal Evangel,* March 20, 1955, 2.

29. James E. Hamill, "Praising the Lord in Song," ibid., November 24, 1963, 2. For similar views on the importance of dedicated singers, see "God-Anointed Music," ibid., July 8, 1956, 2, and F. J. Lindquist, "Ministering in Music," ibid., March 16, 1958, 5, 21.

30. Hamill, "Praising the Lord in Song," 13. The minister's son, Jim, became one of the best-known lead voices in the industry in a career that stretched from 1953 to his retirement in 1996 and included stints with the Melody Men, the Foggy River Boys, the Weatherfords, the Blue Ridge Quartet, the Oak Ridge Quartet, the Rebels, and the Kingsmen (personal interview with Jim Hamill, Alexandria, Ind., April 2, 1996).

31. On Nowlin, see "Most Colorful GM Promoter in Texas: W. B. Nowlin," *Gospel Notes* (Christmas 1966): 5–6; Bob Terrell, "W. B. Nowlin," *Singing News* 19 (April 1989): 48–49; and Jimmy Mass, "Wilmer Nowlin, 89, former DeLeon Mayor, Promoter," *Fort Worth Star-Telegram,* December 12, 1994, sec. A, p. 15. On Fowler as a promoter, see Bob Terrell, *The Music Men: The Story of Professional Gospel Quartet Singing* (Asheville, N.C.: Bob Terrell Publisher, 1990), 121–27.

32. "Most Colorful GM Promoter," 5.

33. On the Blackwoods' work with Snow, see Hank Snow, *The Hank Snow Story* (Urbana: University of Illinois Press, 1994), 372, and Wayne Hilliard, John W. Crenshaw Jr., and Jim Guild, *The Blackwood Brothers Quartet: The Complete Discography, 1934–1986* (Portland, Ore.: Silver Star Publishing, 1996), 11. In the late 1960s, the quartet also recorded a series of three albums with country star Porter Wagoner (Hilliard, Crenshaw, and Guild, *Blackwood Brothers Quartet,* 23, 25–26). On the Blackwoods' influence on Presley's youth in the Memphis area, see Peter Guralnick, *Last Train to Memphis: The Rise of Elvis Presley* (Boston: Little, Brown, and Company, 1994), 46–48. On the Jordanaires and their work with Presley, see Patricia Jobe Pierce, *The Ultimate Elvis: Elvis Presley Day by Day* (New York: Simon and Schuster, 1994), 69, 103–6. On the phenomenon of gospel singers collaborating with popular musicians in general, see Malone, *Southern Music, American Music,* 117–18.

34. On Nowlin's many promotional exploits, see Terrell, *Music Men,* 236–52. For coverage of the Battle of Songs, see Emma Lee Hogg, "Battle of Songs in Texas," *Gospel Singing World* 3 (January 1956): 7, 11, 13. Nowlin retired on January 2, 1993, and died on December 10, 1994. See *Singing News* 23 (January 1993): 14 and Mass, "Wilmer Nowlin, 89."

35. On the initial Ryman sing, see "Spirituals Swing through Long Night," *Nashville Tennessean,* November 6, 1948, 1. Extensive coverage of Fowler's all-night sings came several years later in national magazines like *Colliers.*

36. Allen Rankin, "They're Singin' All-Nite in Dixie," *Colliers* 136 (August 19, 1955): 26–27. On Fowler's accomplishments, see Wayne W.

Daniel, "Wally Fowler: The All-Night Singing Man," *Precious Memories* (September–October 1991): 21–27, and Dave Taylor, "Wally Fowler: Pioneer Promoter," *Gospel Singing World* (Greenville, S.C.) 1 (October–December 1996): 6–7, 10–11.

37. On Orrell, see Joan Orrell, "Lloyd Orrell—Gospel Music Past and Present," *Singing News* 11 (November 1979): 6B, 19B, and "Lloyd Orrell: 'His Steps Were Ordered by God,'" *Singing News* 14 (May 1983): 42–43. On McCormick, see *Sing: A Magazine about Happy Rhythm* (Tallahassee, Fla., Fall 1952): 22–23. See also personal interview with Jerry Kirksey, editor in chief, *Singing News Magazine*, Inc., Boone, N.C., August 10, 1995.

38. Jerry Kirksey interview with W. B. Nowlin, November 1992, cassette tape in the files of the *Singing News* Offices, Boone, N.C. Editorials written by Pierce LeFevre in 1964 provide illuminating insight into the volatile relationship between groups and promoters. The son of Urias and Eva Mae LeFevre praised Nowlin's conduct and operational practices while blasting those of Fowler. See *Sing* (Atlanta, Ga.) 4 (March 1964): 6 and 4 (December 1964–January 1965): 3.

39. For an example of singing convention coverage, see *Gospel Singing World* 2 (August 1955): 8–9, 11. Even when Batson's publication did report on the singing conventions, it was clearly from the perspective of an outsider. The Neches Valley Singing Convention in Lufkin, Texas, was "the first one for *Gospel Singing World* to report on." Though Batson promised that "we do not intend for it to be the last," the emphasis on conventions was clearly secondary, in contrast to company publications like *Vaughan's Family Visitor* and *Gospel Music News*, which had always kept them as their primary focus. The difference between the two kinds of publications was easy to understand. Batson reported on quartet activity as a fan; shape-note companies reported on the conventions that made up the major market for their annual songbooks.

40. Batson's *Gospel Singing World* seems to have existed primarily on individual subscriptions and was never able to build a strong advertising base. That may well have contributed to its demise at the end of the 1950s, when it was combined with another Batson publication, *Gospel Singing Guide*. See *Gospel Singing Guide* (April 1959): 1–2. Nonetheless, no publication focusing on all the quartets within the industry would survive longer until the *Singing News* was formed in 1969. Even then, the *Singing News* would not feature stock and photo quality comparable to that of *Gospel Singing World* until the 1980s. In 1996, Batson's publication was revived briefly by promoter Charles Waller, who republished the 1950s coverage to help promote his annual Grand Ole Gospel Reunion. See *Gospel Singing World* (Greenville, S.C.) 1 (January–March 1996): 2.

41. Brock Speer interview. Three of the Chuck Wagon Gang's Carter family served in the war, but the group was only temporarily off the air. See Bob Terrell, *The Chuck Wagon Gang: A Legend Lives On* (Goodlettsville, Tenn.: Roy Carter, 1990), 48–49.

42. Personal interview with James Blackwood, Anderson, Ind., April 3, 1996. Also on the Blackwoods' wartime struggles, see Kree Jack Racine, *Above All: The Fascinating and True Story of the Lives and Careers of the Famous Blackwood Brothers Quartet* (Memphis: Jarodoce Publications, 1967), 96–103, and Blackwood and Martin, *James Blackwood Story*, 79–97.

43. Wayne W. Daniel, "The LeFevres: Gospel Music Pioneers," *Rejoice!* 3 (August–September 1991): 8.

44. *Stamps Quartet News* 3 (November 1947): 1.

45. On Payne's career, see Van Payne, "50 Years of Memories with a Gospel Music Legend," *Singing News* 24 (January 1994): 40–43.

46. Bill Malone, "The Chuck Wagon Gang: God's Gentle People," *Journal of Country Music* 10 (Spring 1985): 9–10.

47. Terrell, *Chuck Wagon Gang*, 48–55, 64–73.

48. Paula Becker, *Let the Song Go On: Fifty Years of Gospel Singing with the Speer Family* (Nashville: Impact Books, 1971), 89–107, and Ken Apple, "Ken Apple Turns the Spotlight on the Singing Speer Family," *Gospel Singing World* 2 (November–December 1955): 10–11, 18–19, 29.

49. Wayne W. Daniel, "LeFevres," 5.

50. Zell Miller, *They Heard Georgia Singing* (Macon, Ga.: Mercer University Press, 1996), 283. Miller erroneously insinuates that the group stopped performing in late 1952. In fact, led by Buford Abner, the Swanee River Boys continued to perform a mixture of popular and gospel music through the 1960s. As did groups like the Blackwoods and the Chuck Wagon Gang, the Swanee River Boys seem to have chosen their direction strictly from the standpoint of fan appeal.

51. Personal interview with Glenn Sessions and Cecil Pollock, Springdale, Ark., August 3, 1996. On the accident that killed Slater and injured Arnold Hyles, see *Gospel Music News* 17 (January 1951): 14 and Terrell, *Music Men*, 90–91.

52. See Jack Callaway, "The Rangers Quartet: The First Decade (1936–1946)," *Precious Memories* (September–October 1989): 9, and "The Rangers Quartet: Their Second Decade," *Precious Memories* (November–December 1989): 5–12.

53. For a photo and a brief notice of the Lister Brothers as "South Carolina Friends" of the Stamps-Baxter organization, see *Gospel Music News* 7 (February 1941): 7.

54. Personal interview with Hovie Lister, Alexandria, Ind., April 2, 1996. The best synopsis of Lister's early years is in David L. Taylor's *Happy Rhythm: A Biography of Hovie Lister and the Statesmen Quartet* (Lexington, Ind.: TaylorMade Write, 1994), 9–17. See also Terrell, *Music Men*, 109–20.

55. By 1947, when Lister began his stint at WEAS, some stations were experimenting with playing recordings on the air, a practice that had been avoided in earlier decades because of fierce competition between the radio and recording industries. Lister claims to have been "the first gospel disc

jockey in America" since his program played gospel recordings exclusively. See *Gospel Music Hi-Lites* (April 1966): 15 and Taylor, *Happy Rhythm*, 13.

56. Hovie Lister interview.

57. Ibid. See also Taylor, *Happy Rhythm*, 14–15.

58. Personal interview with Mosie Lister, Odessa, Fla., June 13, 1996. See also Terrell, *Music Men*, 112–13, and Taylor, *Happy Rhythm*, 15–17.

59. One of the earliest photos of the new quartet published in a gospel music publication appeared in *Vaughan's Family Visitor* 38 (January 1949): 5. Personnel at that time included Hovie Lister, along with Hess, Strickland, Kendrick, and Hill. By November 1948, Jake Hess had become a permanent member of the quartet. Mosie Lister, however, did continue to have an important influence on the group—writing many songs exclusively for them during the next decade (Hovie Lister interview; Mosie Lister interview; and personal interview with Jake Hess, Alexandria, Ind., April 2, 1996).

60. Ott originally came to the group in 1951 to play piano for Hovie Lister, who was serving in the Korean War. When Lister returned shortly thereafter, Kendrick decided to leave and join former Statesman Bobby Strickland with the Crusaders Quartet. Ott then assumed the position as the group's permanent baritone singer. See Taylor, *Happy Rhythm*, 30.

61. On the frequent personnel changes in quartets during the late 1940s and early 1950s, see Taylor, *Happy Rhythm*, 24–31.

62. In a 1969 interview, Lister, an ordained Baptist minister since 1950, acknowledged the degree to which his stage work had always been loose and impromptu: "I never have a prepared sermon or list of songs to go by—I play each concert by feeling and a sense of what the people want" (*Singing News* 1 [August 15, 1969]: 5).

63. Lister acknowledged that the Gospel Harmonettes even taught the group the famous step included as choreography in the Statesmen's version of the song (Hovie Lister interview). See also the perspective of Anthony Heilbut in *The Gospel Sound: Good News and Bad Times*, rev. ed. (New York: Limelight Editions, 1985), 163. Heilbut incorrectly classifies the Statesmen and the Blackwood Brothers as "hillbilly quartets" (40).

64. On Crumpler's contribution to the group, see Taylor, *Happy Rhythm*, 40–41 and 62–65.

65. Ibid., 37–39.

66. James Blackwood interview. See also Hovie Lister's recollections in Allen Dennis, ed., *James Blackwood Memories* (Brandon, Miss.: Quail Ridge Press, 1997), 85–88.

67. On the Blackwoods' extensive recording career, see Hilliard, Crenshaw, and Guild, *Blackwood Brothers Quartet*. For a brief period in the late 1940s, the Blackwoods operated two traveling quartets. See Blackwood and Martin, *James Blackwood Story*, 102–3.

68. On the Statesmen's recording ties, see Taylor, *Happy Rhythm*, 28 and 46–49.

69. Blackwood and Martin, *James Blackwood Story*, 113; *Gospel Singing World* 4 (July 1957): 8–9. For an analysis of the rich musical heritage of Memphis, see Peter Guralnick's *Last Train to Memphis: The Rise of Elvis Presley* (Boston: Little, Brown, and Company, 1994), 38–65, and Pete Daniel, "Rhythm of the Land," *Agricultural History* 68 (Fall 1994): 4–5.

70. On the Statesmen's radio program, see *Gospel Singing World* 4 (July 1957): 5. See also Taylor, *Happy Rhythm*, 39–40.

71. On the Nabisco show, see *Statesmen Quartet Picture Album* (Atlanta: Statesmen Quartet, ca. 1956), 9–11, and Taylor, *Happy Rhythm*, 50–56.

72. On the Blackwoods' appearance, see newspaper coverage reprinted in *The Blackwood Brothers Memorial Picture Album* (Memphis, Tenn.: Blackwood Brothers, 1955) and the accounts in Racine, *Above All*, 125–29, and Blackwood and Martin, *James Blackwood Story*, 125–27. Both Racine and Blackwood and Martin erroneously report their appearance date as June 12. On the Statesmen, see Taylor, *Happy Rhythm*, 45–46, and *Gospel Singing World* 1 (November 1954): 14–15, 34.

73. A third passenger, John Ogburn Jr., the son of the Clanton, Alabama, banker who had founded the Peach Festival eight years earlier, also perished in the crash (personal interview with James Blackwood, Springdale, Ark., August 3, 1996). On the plane crash and the difficult decision to rebuild the quartet, see Racine, *Above All*, 130–60; Blackwood and Martin, *James Blackwood Story*, 127–43; *Gospel Singing World* 1 (November 1954): 6–7; and Jake Hess's account in Dennis, ed., *James Blackwood Memories*, 77–79. For an account of the accident by fans, see "Sixteen Year Old Plane Crash Story Told," *Singing News* 2 (June 1, 1970): 2. See also the accounts in contemporary industry publications: *Vaughan's Family Visitor* 43 (July 1954): 11 and *Gospel Music News* 20 (July 1954): 1, 6, and the anniversary coverage in *Gospel Singing World* 2 (July 1955): 4–5, 10. More than 5,000 people attended the funeral in Memphis for Blackwood and Lyles. For contemporary newspaper accounts, see [Memphis] *Commercial Appeal*, July 1, 1954, 1, 10; July 2, 1954, 1, 5; and July 3, 1954, 1, 2. For recent retrospectives, see Ken Horn, "The Blackwoods: A Gospel Music Tradition," *Pentecostal Evangel* (March 26, 2000): 8–12, and Tim Gardner, "June 30, 1954: Gospel Music's Darkest Day," *Singing News* 32 (June 2000): 110–12.

74. On Sumner's career, see J. D. Sumner and Bob Terrell, *Gospel Music Is My Life* (Nashville: Impact Books, 1971), as well as the revised version, titled *The Life and Times of J. D. Sumner* (Nashville: J. D. Sumner, 1994).

75. The winning selection in this appearance was "That's What the Good Book Says." See "Blackwoods Score Again on Talent Scouts," *Gospel Singing World* 3 (October 1956): 5, 19–20. Also see Blackwood and Martin, *James Blackwood Story*, 153, and Racine, *Above All*, 162.

76. In 1959 the National Quartet Convention (NQC) was held in Birmingham, Alabama, and the following year, in Atlanta, Georgia. Other than those years, it was held in Memphis until Sumner purchased it in 1971 and moved

it to Nashville. From 1980 to 1982, the convention continued to be held in Nashville, although at that time it was owned by J. G. Whitfield. In 1982, the enterprise was purchased and reorganized by a collection of eight investors. It remained in Nashville through 1993, then moved to Louisville, Kentucky, the following year. On the origins of the NQC, see Taylor, *Happy Rhythm*, 57, and Racine, *Above All*, 162–64, though both sources mistakenly date the first convention to 1956 rather than 1957. For publicity on the first gathering, see the convention issue of *Gospel Singing World* 4 (October 1957) and the coverage in 4 (November 1957): 2–6. See also Sumner's reflections in Calvin McGuyrt, "The NQC—The Untold Story," *Southern Gospel Music News* 2 (October 1983): 8.

77. Personal interview with J. D. Sumner, Sevierville, Tenn., May 20, 1996. See also *Gospel Singing World* 2 (June 1955): 10; Sumner and Terrell, *Gospel Music Is My Life*, 98–109; Sumner and Terrell, *Life and Times of J. D. Sumner*, 88–97; and Blackwood and Martin, *James Blackwood Story*, 157–70.

78. Fowler's considerable talent as a country music songwriter helped forge the tie between the Oak Ridge Boys and the southern music industry. By the age of twenty-seven, he had already published seventy-five songs (both gospel and country) and appeared on the cover of *Billboard*. See "Wally Fowler: Gospel Singer at Six," *Billboard* 58 (September 14, 1946): 17; Don Cusic, *Eddy Arnold: I'll Hold You in My Heart* (Nashville: Rutledge Hill Press, 1997), 32–33, 54–55; and Miller, *They Heard Georgia Singing*, 113–14. Miller erroneously dates the first Ryman sing to 1946.

79. On the founding of the group, see Ellis Widner and Walter Carter, *The Oak Ridge Boys: Our Story* (Chicago: Contemporary Books, 1987), 9–33. See also Walter Carter, "Wally Fowler's Big Idea: The Origins of the Oak Ridge Boys," *Journal of Country Music* 12 (Spring 1987): 34–42.

80. Widner and Carter, *Oak Ridge Boys*, 18–20.

81. Personal interview with Glen Allred, Live Oak, Fla., June 14, 1996. Allred, no relation to Joe Allred (the group's tenor in the early 1950s), still carries a picture of Jesus given to him by a fan in October 1951. On the back of the photo is the date October 4, 1951, along with the note "Oak Ridge Boys." Widner and Carter acknowledge the photo's origins but note that "it would be more than a decade before they would officially call themselves 'Boys.'" See *Oak Ridge Boys*, 20. For information on the personnel of this group shortly after the return of Johnny New in 1950, see *Wally Fowler and His Famous Oak Ridge Quartet: Gospel and Spirituals Song Book of Nation Wide Hit Songs* (Nashville: Wally Fowler, 1950).

82. Although controversy still exists over the nature of the arrangement, Weber insisted that he accepted Fowler's offer (i.e., the group name in exchange for a no-interest loan) but that he was never repaid the $10,000 (Widner and Carter, *Oak Ridge Boys*, 20).

83. For some of the original publicity on this version of the Oaks, see *Gospel Singing World* 4 (February 1957): 19. On Gatlin, see Claude Hall, "Gospel

Music's Missionary to the Masses," *Billboard: The World of Religious Music* (1965–66 Special Edition), 50–51; *GMA Good News* 4 (April 1972): 1; and *Singing News* 2 (January 1971): 11.

84. Widner and Carter, *Oak Ridge Boys*, 29. For information on the Oaks and their members during this period, see *Sing Along with the Oak Ridge Quartet* (Nashville: Oak Ridge Quartet, n.d.).

85. Personal interview with Willie Wynn, Greenville, S.C., August 9, 1996; Widner and Carter, *Oak Ridge Boys*, 31–32.

86. Golden had joined the Oaks as baritone singer in 1964, following tenures in that position by Gary McSpadden and Jim Hamill (Widner and Carter, *Oak Ridge Boys*, 39–40). For coverage of the Oak Ridge Boys at a time when they were at the top of the gospel music industry, see *Singing News* 1 (September 15, 1969): 13.

87. Terrell, *Music Men*, 180–85. On Hall's influence, see also Lois Blackwell, *The Wings of the Dove: The Story of Gospel Music in America* (Norfolk, Va.: Donning Co., 1978), 68–69; *Vaughan's Family Visitor* 80 (April 1980): 7; and *Cumberland Valley Newsletter* (Dresden, Tenn.) 3 (July–September 1992): 3–6.

88. Wolfe, "'Gospel Boogie,'" 75–77.

89. Blackwell, *Wings of the Dove*, 68–69. See also "Homeland Harmony," *Gospel Music World* 1 (October 1950): 5, 14, and "One of the Oldest — 'Homeland Harmony,'" *Gospel Singing World* 2 (May 1955): 10.

90. The best source on the Sunshine Boys is Wayne Daniel's "The Sunshine Boys: A Study in Versatility," *Precious Memories* (January–February 1989): 24–28. See also Daniel's *Pickin' on Peachtree: A History of Country Music in Atlanta, Georgia* (Urbana: University of Illinois Press, 1990), 200–201, and Terrell, *Music Men*, 188–92.

91. Wayne Daniel, "Sunshine Boys," 25.

92. The number of films the Sunshine Boys appeared in is disputed. Wayne Daniel ("Sunshine Boys," 26) concludes "about 25"; Terrell (*Music Men*, 191) concludes that they appeared in nineteen, from 1945 to 1949, and several more in the early 1950s; and Sumner and Terrell, in *Life and Times of J. D. Sumner*, 68, indicate that the group was featured in "seventeen Westerns." The Sunshine Boys' versatility led Terrell (*Music Men*, 192) to compare them to the popular country-and-western group the Sons of the Pioneers.

93. Wayne Daniel, "Sunshine Boys," 27–28.

94. Telephone interview with Kenny Gates, Greenville, S.C., January 23, 2001. On the Blue Ridge Quartet, see *Gospel Singing World* 2 (March 1955): 14; 3 (May 1956): 19, 23; and 3 (September 1956): 7. See also Terrell, *Music Men*, 215–18.

95. Telephone interview with Marion Snider, Dallas, Tex., July 23, 1998. See also "Whatever Happened to the Imperial Quartet?" *Imperial Crown* (Sugar Land, Tex.) 33 (August 1985): 1–2; "Texas Quartet Rings Bell with SESAC Music," *SESAC Music* 9 (December 1950): 5; and *Gospel Music News* 15 (March 1949): 1.

96. Telephone interview with Jack Pittman, Boone, N.C., January 19, 1999. On the Palmetto State Quartet, see Terrell, *Music Men*, 178–79.

97. On Jones and the Deep South, see Montell, *Singing the Glory Down*, 66–68, and *Gospel Singing World* 3 (January 1956): 19, 31.

98. On the Melody Boys, see Henrietta Brown, "The Melody Boys: Quartetting for More than Half a Century!" *Gospel Voice* 13 (August 2000): 35–38. See also Williams's autobiographical account in Gerald Williams, *Mighty Lot of Singin'* (Little Rock: TMBQ Publishing, 1999).

99. Personal interview with Bob Crews, Alexandria, Ind., April 2, 1996.

100. On Strickland and the Crusaders, see *Gospel Singing World* 2 (July 1955): 12–13, 16. On the Harvesters, see "The Harvesters Quartet of WBT-TV," ibid., 2 (August 1955): 28–29.

101. On the Crossroads Quartet, see *Gospel Singing Guide* (May–June 1959): 13.

102. Mosie Lister interview. On the brief history of the Sunny South, see Jake Hess, *Nothin' but Fine* (Columbus, Ga.: Buckland Press, 1995), 45–52, and Terrell and Sumner, *Life and Times of J. D. Sumner*, 48–57.

103. On the Melody Masters, see Terrell, *Music Men*, 114–16; Hess, *Nothin' but Fine*, 52–65; and Taylor, *Happy Rhythm*, 18–23. See also personal interview with Wally Varner, Greenville, S.C., August 10, 1996.

104. Terrell and Sumner, *Life and Times of J. D. Sumner*, 49–52.

105. On the Rebels, see *Gospel Singing World* 2 (June 1955): 11; *Singing News* 1 (June 15, 1969): 13; and *Gospel Singing Guide* (May–June 1959): 20.

106. "Behind the Scene," *Singing News* 1 (May 15, 1969): 2.

107. Ibid., 1. Also on Whitfield, see "J. G. and Hazel Whitfield," *Singing News* 16 (May 1985): 15. On the origins of the Florida Boys, see Don Cusic, *The Sound of Light: A History of Gospel Music* (Bowling Green, Ohio: Bowling Green State University Popular Press, 1990), 153–55, and Terrell, *Music Men*, 259–62.

108. For a loving account of Whitfield's life and contribution to southern gospel, see Debbie Fleming, *J. G. Whitfield: A Tribute in Essence* (Alexander, N.C.: Mountain Church, 2000).

109. Jerry Kirksey, "Les Beasley: One of Southern Gospel Music's Most Powerful Men," *Singing News* 27 (May 1996): 57.

110. Personal interviews with J. G. Whitfield, Live Oak, Fla., June 15, 1996, and Les Beasley, Live Oak, Fla., June 14, 1996. The story is also recounted in Cusic, *Sound of Light*, 153, and Terrell, *Music Men*, 260. For original press on the name change, see *Gospel Singing World* 2 (June 1955): 14.

111. Les Beasley interview.

112. Personal interview with Eldridge Fox, Boone, N.C., June 18, 1996. On the Kingsmen, see Cusic, *Sound of Light*, 155–57; Terrell, *Music Men*, 217–23; and Deana Surles, "And the Beat Goes on Even after 40 Years—The Kingsmen," *Singing News* 26 (September 1995): 30–36.

113. The earliest photo of the group appeared in 1957 in *The Cup*, the year-

book of the Central Bible Institute in Springfield, Missouri. Personnel at the time included Dave Kyllonen, Don Baldwin, Duane Nicholson, Lemuel Boyles, and Bob Casebeer. The following year, Neil Enloe and Eddie Reece joined the group, replacing Boyles and Casebeer. See "That's Life," *Concert Life* 5 (July–August 1977): 34.

114. The best source on the early years of the Couriers is Charles R. Hembree, *They Sing the Mighty Power: The Unique and Inspiring Story of the Couriers* (Stow, Ohio: New Hope Press, 1975), 11–30.

115. Personal interview with Neil Enloe, Alexandria, Ind., April 3, 1996.

116. Hembree, *They Sing the Mighty Power*, 19–21.

117. Works on the significant growth of conservative churches in the postwar period appeared in the mid-1970s. See Dean R. Hoge and David A. Roozen, eds., *Understanding Church Growth and Decline, 1950–1978* (New York: Pilgrim Press, 1979), and Dean M. Kelley, *Why Conservative Churches Are Growing: A Study in Sociology of Religion*, updated ed. (New York: Harper and Row, Publishers, 1977). Also see David E. Harrell Jr., *All Things Are Possible: The Healing and Charismatic Revivals in Modern America* (Bloomington: Indiana University Press, 1975).

118. Personal interview with Duane Nicholson, Alexandria, Ind., April 3, 1996. See also Hembree, *They Sing the Mighty Power*, 23–30.
end notes chs. five and six

Chapter Seven

1. Personal interview with James Blackwood, Anderson, Ind., April 3, 1996; Kree Jack Racine, *Above All: The Fascinating and True Story of the Lives and Careers of the Famous Blackwood Brothers Quartet* (Memphis: Jarodoce Publications, 1967), 100. See also personal interview with Mary "Sally" Stamps Dearman, Dallas, Tex., July 28, 1996.

2. Personal interview with Lily Fern Weatherford, Alexandria, Ind., April 3, 1996. On the Stamps connection, see *Stamps Quartet News* 3 (March 1948): 1 and 10 (February 1955): 1.

3. Lily Fern Weatherford interview. On the Weatherfords, see also Lily Fern Weatherford and Gail Shadwell, *With All My Heart: A Life in Gospel Music* (Carrollton, Tex.: Alliance Press, 1999), and *The Weatherfords: Thru the Years* (promotional photo collection, privately printed, ca. 1995).

4. On the origins of the Segos, see James Sego, *Sego* (Plainfield, N.J.: Logos International, 1977), 59–64, and Richard L. Bennett and J. Edgar Renfroe, *Naomi, Gospel Singer: The Authorized Biography of the First Lady of Gospel Music* (Fitzgerald, Ga.: Bennett Renfroe Associates, 1988), 54–59.

5. On Naomi Sego's inclusion in the group and the importance of "Sorry, I Never Knew You," see Sego, *Sego*, 65–77, and Bennett and Renfroe, *Naomi, Gospel Singer*, 59–62. Sego notes that the song ultimately attained "sales of

one million records—the most ever by a single gospel tune" (71). Although it is likely he meant aggregate sales of one million dollars rather than one million units, there is no independent verification for the claim. Sales of gospel records in the 1950s and 1960s were not consistently tracked. A similar claim has been made regarding Wendy Bagwell and the Sunliters' "Here Come the Rattlesnakes" in 1971. On Bagwell's hit, see John Pugh, "For Heavens' Snakes: A Man Named Wendy Is Gospel's Hottest Act," *Nashville Gospel* 1 (October 1977): 60–61.

6. Alan Rikmann, "The Lesters: Generation to Generation," *Singing News* 27 (March 1997): 20–24.

7. Personal interview with Dwayne Friend, former guitarist for the Happy Goodmans, Springfield, Mo., July 16, 1995. The best account of the Goodman story is Jamie Buckingham's *O Happy Day: The Happy Goodman Story* (Waco: Word Books, 1973). See also the more personalized account in Vestal Goodman, *Vestal!* (Colorado Springs, Colo.: Waterbrook Press, 1998). For an account of the Goodmans at the height of their popularity, see "Hottest Gospel Group of the Year," in *Billboard: The World of Religious Music* (1965–66 Special Edition), 56.

8. The four Lewis sons performed bluegrass briefly in the late 1940s as the Lewis Brothers. It was not until the addition of Roy Sr. and the sisters in the early 1950s that the group became exclusively gospel. The oldest son, Esley, had dropped out of the group by the mid-1950s, and Talmadge retired in 1972. By the late 1970s, grandsons Travis Lewis and Lewis Phillips had joined the group. On the Lewis family, see *The Lewis Family: A Retrospective* (Hendersonville, Tenn.: Lewis Family, 1996); Wayne W. Daniel, "The Lewis Family: First Family of Bluegrass Gospel Music," *Precious Memories* (March–April 1989): 4–9; Don Rhodes, "On the Hallelujah Turnpike with the Lewis Family," *Bluegrass Unlimited* 14 (June 1980): 18–24; and Zell Miller, *They Heard Georgia Singing* (Macon, Ga.: Mercer University Press, 1996), 187–89.

9. On the Porters, see *Vaughan's Family Visitor* 25 (February 1936): 7 and 25 (November 1936): 3. In the 1970s, the popular Galileans were the Hispanic equivalent. On the Galileans, see *Singing News* 4 (March 1973): 13; 5 (September 1973): 9; and 7 (November 1975): 19A.

10. Personal interview with Vernon Klaudt, Greenville, S.C., August 10, 1996. See also *Klaudt Family: Gospel Specials No. 2* (Cleveland, Tenn.: Tennessee Music and Printing, 1950); *Gospel World of Songs and Singers* 1 (October 1964): 3–4; "The Klaudt Indian Family of the Dakota Badlands," *Sing* 3 (September 1963): 4–5; and "Klaudt Indian Family Is Talented and Smart," *Singing News* 1 (December 1, 1969): 13.

11. On the Plainsmen, see *National Quartet Convention Souvenir Program* (Birmingham, Ala., July 3–5, 1959), 12.

12. On Davis's career, see Gus Weill, *You Are My Sunshine: The Jimmie Davis Story* (Gretna, La.: Pelican Publishing Company, 1987). For insight into Davis's affection for gospel music, see Peter Mikelbank, "Places in the Sun:

The Many Splendored Careers of Jimmie Davis," *Journal of Country Music* 10 (Fall 1985): 28–32, 49–56; Toru Mitsui, "Music, Politics, and Popular Song: An Interview with Jimmie Davis," *Old-Time Country* 7 (Spring 1990): 4–13 and 7 (Summer 1990): 16–24; and Gerald Smith Jr., "The Legendary Jimmie Davis," *Rejoice!* 2 (Summer 1990): 3–7.

13. *Gospel Singing World* 5 (August 1958): 15.

14. Personal interview with "Little David" Young, Boone, N.C., August 22, 1997. On the Sons of Song, see Bob Terrell, *The Music Men: The Story of Professional Gospel Quartet Singing* (Asheville, N.C.: Bob Terrell, 1990), 289–91.

15. Personal interview with Mary Wise, Judy Johnson, and Anna Reece (the Johnson Sisters), Greenville, S.C., August 10, 1996. See also *Gospel Singing Guide* (May–June 1959): 21. In the early 1960s, Margaret retired from the group and the trio continued with Mary rounding out the three-part vocal harmony.

16. Jerry Kirksey, "Wendy Bagwell: A Legend in His Own Time," *Singing News* 27 (August 1996): 30–33. Also on the Sunliters, see Miller, *They Heard Georgia Singing*, 31–32.

17. On the importance of the convention for young groups seeking to make it in the gospel music profession, see Buck Rambo and Bob Terrell, *The Legacy of Buck and Dottie Rambo* (Nashville: Star Song Publishing, 1992), 98–100.

18. Personal interview with Claude Hopper, Steve Hopper, and Will Hopper, Boone, N.C., June 23, 1999. On the Hoppers, see Danny Jones, "40 Years and They're Still Shoutin'," *Singing News* 28 (September 1997): 62–68.

19. For a discussion of the changes that came as a result of the reduced ties with the publishing companies, see Charles K. Wolfe's analysis in "'Gospel Boogie': White Southern Gospel Music in Transition, 1945–55," in *Popular Music I: Folk or Popular? Distinctions, Influences, Continuities*, ed. Richard Middleton and David Horn (Cambridge: Cambridge University Press, 1981), 73–82, and "Gospel Goes Uptown: White Gospel Music, 1945–1955," in *Folk Music and Modern Sound*, ed. William Ferris and Mary L. Hart (Jackson: University Press of Mississippi, 1982), 80–100.

20. Both Robert Arnold and Ottis Knippers remembered at least some black participants in shape-note schools as early as the 1920s. Given economic constraints, it is likely that music leaders in black southern churches learned the technique and then passed on that knowledge orally (personal interviews with Robert S. Arnold, Springdale, Ark., August 3, 1996, and Ottis J. Knippers, Lawrenceburg, Tenn., March 25, 1998). For evidence of the shape-note tradition within the southern black community, see Doris J. Dyen, "New Directions in Sacred Harp Singing," in Ferris and Hart, eds., *Folk Music and Modern Sound*, 73–79; Eileen Southern, *The Music of Black Americans: A History*, 2nd ed. (New York: W. W. Norton and Company, 1983), 69–70, 447–48; *Gospel Music Hi-Lites* (July 1965): 1; and *Gospel Music Scrapbook, 1921–1934*, vol. 1, comp. Harry M. Wakefield (Troy, Mich.: Lee Marks, 1996), 48.

21. As with white gospel, black gospel was indebted to the influence of Holiness and Pentecostal churches. See Joyce Marie Jackson, "The Changing Nature of Gospel Music: A Southern Case Study," *African American Review* 29 (Summer 1995): 185–200.

22. The literature on black gospel is extensive. For a broad overview and introduction to available material, see Horace C. Boyer, *How Sweet the Sound: The Golden Age of Gospel* (Washington: Elliott and Clark Publishing, 1995); Bernice Johnson Reagan, ed., *We'll Understand It Better By and By: Pioneering African American Gospel Composers* (Washington: Smithsonian Institution Press, 1992); Michael W. Harris, *The Rise of Gospel Blues: The Music of Thomas Andrew Dorsey in the Urban Church* (New York: Oxford University Press, 1992); Paul Oliver, Max Harrison, and William Bolcom, *The New Grove: Gospel, Blues, and Jazz* (New York: W. W. Norton and Company, 1986), 189–222; Viv Broughton, *Black Gospel* (New York: Poole, Dorset, Blandford Press, 1985); Anthony Heilbut, *The Gospel Sound: Good News and Bad Times*, rev. ed. (New York: Limelight Editions, 1985); Wyatt T. Walker, *"Somebody's Calling My Name": Black Sacred Music and Social Change* (Valley Forge, Pa.: Judson Press, 1979); and Irene V. Jackson, *Afro-American Religious Music: A Bibliography and a Catalogue of Gospel Music* (Westport, Conn.: Greenwood Press, 1979). On the black gospel quartet tradition specifically, see Ray Allen, *Singing in the Spirit: African American Sacred Quartets in New York City* (Philadelphia: University of Pennsylvania Press, 1991); Kip Lornell, *Happy in the Service of the Lord* (Urbana: University of Illinois Press, 1988); and Kerill Leslie Rubman, *From "Jubilee" to "Gospel" in Black Male Quartet Singing* (Chapel Hill, N.C.: K. L. Rubman, 1980). On the importance of race records, see Paul Oliver, *Songsters and Saints: Vocal Traditions on Race Records* (Cambridge: Cambridge University Press, 1984), 274, and Joyce Marie Jackson, "The Performing Black Sacred Quartet: An Expression of Cultural Values and Aesthetics" (Ph.D. diss., Indiana University, March 1988), 71–85.

23. "We'll Soon Be Done with Troubles and Trials" was first published by Stamps-Baxter in 1934 and was followed three years later by "Just a Little Talk with Jesus." "When God Dips His Love in My Heart" was published by Tennessee Music and Printing Company in 1944. When the three songs appeared in the popular *Church Hymnal* (Cleveland, Tenn.: Tennessee Music and Printing, 1951), the perennial favorite known as the "red-back hymnal," only "Just a Little Talk with Jesus" carried the notation "Spiritual." Compare nos. 30, 92, and 138. On black songwriters within the shape-note tradition, see also *Gospel Music News* 7 (February 1941): 15.

24. Derricks, a 1984 inductee into the GMA Hall of Fame, became a 2001 inductee into the corresponding SGMA Hall of Fame. His selection made him the first black to be honored specifically as a pioneer of the southern gospel tradition. On Derricks, see Cleavant Derricks, "A Personal Testimony," in *Melodious Messengers* (Knoxville, Tenn.: Derricks Music House,

ca. 1948), 10–11; Boyer, *How Sweet the Sound*, 150–52; LaWayne Satterfield, "Famous Composer Cleavant Derricks Rediscovered," *Singing News* 7 (October 1, 1975): 11A, 23A; and "Death Claims Derricks," *Singing News* 9 (June 1, 1977): 1. Although the 1970s coverage noted that Derricks "had never received a penny" in royalties for his early songs, it is likely that he received songbooks from Stamps-Baxter in exchange for both "Just a Little Talk with Jesus" and "We'll Soon Be Done with Troubles and Trials." Such was the common practice of shape-note publishers, who almost always retained copyrights during the 1930s and early 1940s (personal interview with Mosie Lister, Odessa, Fla., June 13, 1996).

25. On the attractiveness of black spirituals because of copyright absences, see David Crawford, "Gospel Songs in Court: From Rural Music to Urban Industry in the 1950s," *Journal of Popular Culture* 11 (Winter 1977): 559. On the parallel growth of professionalism within the black quartet industry, see Anthony Heilbut, "The Secularization of Black Gospel Music," in Ferris and Hart, eds., *Folk Music and Modern Sound*, 101–15, and Horace Clarence Boyer, "Contemporary Gospel Music: Sacred or Secular?" *First World* 1 (January–February 1977): 46–49.

26. All three of these spirituals were recorded numerous times by the Blackwoods over the next two decades. See Wayne Hilliard, John W. Crenshaw Jr., and Jim Guild, *The Blackwood Brothers Quartet: The Complete Discography, 1934–1986* (Portland, Ore.: Silver Star Publishing, 1996), 104–6.

27. On the musical interchange between southern blacks and whites in the era of segregation, see Pete Daniel, "Rhythm of the Land," *Agricultural History* 68 (Fall 1994): 1–22. My interviews with white southern gospel artists of the 1950s, most notably James Blackwood, Hovie Lister, and Rex Nelon, revealed this kind of influence from black groups (James Blackwood interview and personal interviews with Hovie Lister, Alexandria, Ind., April 2, 1996, and Rex Nelon, Boone, N.C., June 18, 1996). In addition, my interview with Charles Johnson and Joseph Wallace (Durham, N.C., August 12, 1996), who were both prominent black gospel artists in the 1960s, although less conclusive, suggested that there was at least an awareness on the part of black groups of what white gospel groups were recording. It is likely that further study of surviving artists of the period will reveal that a significant number of white and black quartet members were influenced to some degree by each other.

28. On the Golden Gate Quartet, see Billy Altman, "Liner notes for *The Golden Gate Quartet: Traveling Shoes*" (New York: RCA Heritage Series, BMG Recording Studios, 1992); Boyer, *How Sweet the Sound*, 44–45; and Allen, *Singing in the Spirit*, 5–6, 28–29. For examples of other influential black quartets of the period, see *Rejoice!* 3 (Winter 1990): 7–12; 3 (December 1991–January 1992): 3–11; and 4 (October–November 1992), 7–12.

29. James Blackwood interviews, April 3, 1996, and Springdale, Ark.,

August 3, 1996. See also Hovie Lister interview. On the popularity of the Golden Gate with predominantly white audiences, see Joyce Marie Jackson, "Performing Black Sacred Quartet," 80–81.

30. Evidence of the group's appeal was their inclusion in a promotional picture album for W. B. Nowlin's 1952 "Battle of Songs" concerts (*First Anniversary: The Battle of Songs 1951* [Fort Worth, Tex.: W. B. Nowlin, 1951; Archives of the Southern Gospel Music Association, Pigeon Forge, Tenn.]). Of the nineteen groups pictured in the album, they were the only black one. All nineteen groups, plus the Statesmen, who were not pictured, had appeared in the previous year's concerts.

31. Possibly influenced by the racial strife as well as competition from rhythm-and-blues performers, the Golden Gate Quartet made a European tour in 1955. Their success was so overwhelming that, by the early 1960s, they relocated to Europe, where they continued to perform for the next three decades.

32. That group, Andrae Crouch and the Disciples, was a distinctly contemporary gospel group. Black groups would not appeal to the traditional "southern gospel" audience until the late 1970s, when Teddy Huffam and the Gems pulled off the feat. On the popularity of Crouch, see Andrae Crouch and Nina Ball, *Through It All* (Waco, Tex.: Word Books, 1974); "Nashville Awaits Conventioneers," *Good News* 3 (September 1971): 1; and Gary Archer, "Andrae Crouch and Disciples Movin' On," *Gospel West* 1 (October 1972): 1, 3. On Teddy Huffam and the Gems, see "Black Gospel Spanning New Horizons," *Concert Life* 5 (January–February 1978): 16, and *The Gospel Trade* 4 (March 1977): 38.

33. On Brumley and his ability to buy his own copyrights, see Kay Hively and Albert E. Brumley Jr., *I'll Fly Away: The Life Story of Albert E. Brumley* (Branson, Mo.: Mountaineer Books, 1990), 113–21.

34. A collection of Lee Roy Abernathy's work and views on gospel music is found in Lee Roy Abernathy, *"It": Modern Gospel Music* (Canton, Ga.: Abernathy Publishing, 1948). For a brief sketch of his early years, see ibid., 5.

35. Wayne W. Daniel, "Gospel Music Entrepreneur . . . Lee Roy Abernathy," *Precious Memories* (September–October 1989): 22.

36. According to Abernathy, the group recorded fifty songs on either the Bluebird or the Decca label (ibid., 23).

37. See Miller, *They Heard Georgia Singing*, 4–8, and Jesse Burt and Duane Allen, *The History of Gospel Music* (Nashville: K & S Press, 1971), 43–49. An earlier edition of Miller's work was published as *They Heard Georgia Singing: Great Georgians*, vol. 2 (Franklin Springs, Ga.: Advocate Press, 1984).

38. According to Miller (*They Heard Georgia Singing*, 5), the FDR song (titled "Good Times Are Coming Soon") "had to be shelved after the NRA was declared unconstitutional." On Abernathy's move to sheet music, see Wayne W. Daniel, "Gospel Music Entrepreneur," 24–25.

39. "Lee Roy Abernathy, 79, Gospel Musician Who Ran for Governor," *Atlanta Constitution*, May 27, 1993 (copy in the files of Gaither Studios, Alexandria, Ind.).

40. Miller, *They Heard Georgia Singing*, 5–6.

41. Abernathy claimed to have spent nine years working out the details for his piano-by-mail course, which he put into action immediately after the war in 1945. By 1947, others were copying his idea. See Miller, *They Heard Georgia Singing*, 6, and *Gospel Music Scrapbook*, vol. 3, 106.

42. Miller, *They Heard Georgia Singing*, 6. On the song and the controversy it generated, see Abernathy, "*It*," 53–57.

43. Wolfe, "Gospel Boogie," 77–79. For publicity on the song, see *Billboard* 60 (April 10, 1948): 2. On the Chicago origins of the boogie-woogie beat, see Southern, *Music of Black Americans*, 372. Elements of the style can also be traced to tavern music in mid-nineteenth-century southern lumber camps. See Timothy Michael Kalil, "The Role of the Great Migration of African Americans to Chicago in the Development of Traditional Black Gospel Piano by Thomas A. Dorsey, circa 1930" (Ph.D. diss., Kent State University, 1993), 56–59, 175–76.

44. Abernathy, "*It*," 48. See also ibid., 49–51, and Wolfe, "Gospel Boogie," 79.

45. Wolfe, "Gospel Boogie," 78; Wayne W. Daniel, "Gospel Music Entrepreneur," 23.

46. Abernathy printed four thousand copies of "*It*" and sold them each for $12.95. Copies today are difficult to locate. Copy on file at Gaither Studios, Alexandria, Ind.

47. Wolfe, "Gospel Boogie," 81.

48. For evidence of the growing popularity and commercialism of gospel music by the 1950s, see Bob Rolontz, "Sacred Songs Close Kin to C&W Music," *Billboard* 65 (December 5, 1953): 42, 62. Note also the inclusion of "Sacred Artists" (the Blackwood Brothers and George Beverly Shea) in the RCA Victor ad on ibid., 50–51.

49. Rupert Cravens, "Path of Light," *Vaughan's Family Visitor* 39 (April 1950): 2. See also Wolfe, "Gospel Boogie," 80.

50. Rupert Cravens, "Path of Light," *Vaughan's Family Visitor* 39 (May 1950): 2. See also Wolfe, "Gospel Boogie," 81. On Cravens's opposition to all-night sings, see an even more direct assault in "Path of Light," *Vaughan's Family Visitor* 39 (April 1950): 2–3. In spite of the opposition, references to popular quartets were carried in occasional issues of the journal and Blackwood Brothers Quartet recordings could be purchased through the Vaughan office alongside those of the Vaughan Quartet (compare p. 22 of April 1950 with p. 14 of May 1950). See also *Vaughan's Family Visitor* 39 (November 1950): 15 and 40 (January 1951): 4. The January 1951 article reported the tragic death of the Rangers' baritone Erman Slater.

51. On Stanphill, see Ira Stanphill and Earl Green, *This Side of Heaven* (Fort Worth, Tex.: Hymntime Ministries, 1983). Stanphill noted the difficulty of publishing within the confines of southern shape-note publishing houses and recognized the degree to which he contributed to a new era. See especially ibid., 43–46.

52. On Ellis, see Stanley M. Burgess and Gary B. McGee, eds., *Dictionary of Pentecostal and Charismatic Movements* (Grand Rapids, Mich.: Zondervan Publishing House, 1988), 260–61.

53. On Hamblen, see David L. Taylor, *Happy Rhythm: A Biography of Hovie Lister and the Statesmen Quartet* (Lexington, Ind.: TaylorMade Write, 1994), 34.

54. On Shea and the popularity of "How Great Thou Art," see Don Cusic, *The Sound of Light: A History of Gospel Music* (Bowling Green, Ohio: Bowling Green State University Popular Press, 1990), 164–67. See also *Singing News* 14 (June 1983): 22–23.

55. *Gospel Singing World* 2 (August 1955): 15. For a brief biography of Lister and a collection of his most successful songs, see *Good Ol' Gospel* (Kansas City, Mo.: Lillenas Publishing, 1994). For an account written during the height of his success in composing for the Statesmen, see "The Mosie Lister Story," *Gospel Singing World* 2 (August 1955): 4–5, 15–16, 30.

56. Personal interview with Mosie Lister, Odessa, Fla., June 13, 1996; *Good Ol' Gospel*, 15–16.

57. The album went as high as no. 13 on *Billboard*'s Top LP chart. See Patricia Jobe Pierce, *The Ultimate Elvis: Elvis Presley Day by Day* (New York: Simon and Schuster, 1994), 475.

58. All dates included here are copyright dates.

Chapter Eight

1. By 1969, the annual sing that had been sponsored by the Kiwanis Club in Bonifay, Florida since the mid-1950s, was billed as "the world's largest all-night singing," drawing between fifteen and twenty thousand spectators. See "Bonifay Sing Planned June 28," *Singing News* 1 (May 15, 1969): 1. Also drawing large crowds was the Waycross Singing, another all-night affair held in a football stadium in Waycross, Georgia, for the benefit of Shriner's Crippled Children's Hospital in Greenville, South Carolina. See "Waycross Singing Raises $100,000," ibid., 3 (August 1971): 1.

2. Ella Taylor, *Prime-Time Families: Television Culture in Postwar America* (Berkeley: University of California Press, 1989), 20.

3. On the growth of television and the relative decline of radio, see David Halberstam, *The Fifties* (New York: Villard Books, 1993), 180–87.

4. Lee Roy Abernathy, lyricist and composer, "Television." Lyrics reprinted by permission of Abernathy Publishing Company, Canton, Ga. On

the writing of the song, see Lee Roy Abernathy, *"It": Modern Gospel Music* (Canton, Ga.: Abernathy Publishing, 1948), 75–77.

5. On the transition from radio to television in the late 1940s and early 1950s, see Erik Barnouw, *Tube of Plenty: The Evolution of American Television*, rev. ed. (New York: Oxford University Press, 1982), 99–148, and Mary Ann Watson, *Defining Visions: Television and the American Experience Since 1945* (Fort Worth: Harcourt Brace and Company, 1998), 7–21.

6. "Editorials," *Gospel Music World* 1 (November 1950): 17.

7. On the Sunshine Boys and WSB-TV, see Wayne W. Daniel, *Pickin' on Peachtree: A History of Country Music in Atlanta, Georgia* (Urbana: University of Illinois Press, 1990), 212–13.

8. Lois Blackwell, *The Wings of the Dove: The Story of Gospel Music in America* (Norfolk, Va.: Donning Co., 1978), 51.

9. On the popularity of the barn dance formula and the growth of television in country music, see Bill C. Malone, *Country Music, U.S.A.*, rev. ed. (Austin: University of Texas Press, 1985), 269–74.

10. *Sky-Lite HiLites* (March 1962): 2 and (August 1962): 7. Also on Poole, see Charles Waller, "Gospel Trackdown," *Singing News* 18 (July 1987): 62.

11. The best source on the various gospel programs available across the country by the late 1950s is the *Gospel Singing World*. On Fowler's *Gospel Sing*, the Blue Ridge Quartet program *Songs of Inspiration*, and Arthur Smith's variety show, see "Gospel Singing on Television," *Gospel Singing World* 5 (July 1958): 2–3, 5–6, 15, 18. On the Blackwoods, see "Television Activities of the Blackwood Brothers," ibid., 3 (November–December 1956): 6–7. On the Lewis Family, see "The Lewis Family on WJBF-TV Augusta, Ga.," ibid., 4 (July 1957): 22. On the Harvesters and Crossroads Quartets, see "Double Feature," ibid., 4 (July 1957): 10. On the Rebels, see "Rebels Quartet of Tampa, Fla.," ibid., 2 (September 1955): 7, and "Looking at the Rebels on TV: Tampa-Orlando, Fla.," ibid., 4 (July 1957): 7, 20. On the Speers, see "Speer Family TV Program," ibid., 4 (April 1957): 9, and "Speer Family Now Have Busy TV Schedule," ibid., 4 (July 1957): 18. On *Gospel Jubilee*, see "Atlanta TV Viewers Have Full Hour Gospel Program," ibid., 3 (October 1956): 9, 23.

12. On the importance of the program, see David L. Taylor, *Happy Rhythm: A Biography of Hovie Lister and the Statesmen Quartet* (Lexington, Ind.: Taylor-Made Write, 1994), 50–54. On the origins of the show, see "New TV Program—Statesmen," *Gospel Singing World* 2 (June 1955): 9, 28; "Statesmen Television Programs Now on Network," *Gospel Singing World* 3 (April 1956): 12; and "The Camera Looks at the Statesman TV Productions," *Gospel Singing World* 3 (November–December 1956): 2–3, 12.

13. See "The Gospel Singing Caravan," *Sing* 5 (November 1965): 7–10.

14. Telephone interview with Jim McReynolds, Gallatin, Tenn., September 14, 1999.

15. Personal interviews with Eva Mae LeFevre, Louisville, Ky., September 21, 1996, and Jerry Goff (no relation to author), Boone, N.C., June 19,

1996. On the popularity of the show in the Louisville, Kentucky, market, see *Sing* 5 (April 1965): 3. Page 4 includes a list of forty-four stations, primarily across the South, that carried the program each week. By 1966, Stinson was president of Hal Smith TV Production, Inc., and served as executive producer of the *Wills Family Inspirational Time* (personal interview with Lou Wills Hildreth, Louisville, Ky., September 18, 1996). On Stinson's influence in gospel music, see "A. O. Stinson Is Man of Many Talents, Charms," *Gospel Notes* (December 1966): 1.

16. According to Les Beasley, the *Song Shop* ultimately appeared on thirty-one southern stations and convinced the Chattanooga Medicine Company, as well as Noble Dury, that there was a market for a quartet program with the proper balance of gospel music talent (personal interview with Les Beasley, Live Oak, Fla., June 14, 1996). On the Jubilee, see *Gospel World of Songs and Singers* 1 (October 1964): 1–2 and Don Cusic, *The Sound of Light: A History of Gospel Music* (Bowling Green, Ohio: Bowling Green State University Popular Press, 1990), 154.

17. Les Beasley interview.

18. As did the postwar increase in concerts and group travel, television coverage greatly facilitated the spread of gospel quartet music to other parts of the nation. See Blackwell, *Wings of the Dove*, 128–29. By the 1970s, the southern gospel style had secured a foothold in Canada, the Northeast, and along the West Coast. Evidence of the music's appeal in these regions included touring schedules that stretched across the bulk of the North American continent as well as the establishment of gospel quartet publications outside the traditional South. See *Gospel Music News* (Walnut Creek, Calif.) 1 (April 1964); *Gospel West* (Hollywood, Calif.) 1 (April 1972); and *Gospel Music Speaks Out* (Rockaway, N.J.) 1 (October 1971). Gospel music of the 1970s evidently appealed to international audiences as well. See Janice Cain, "Gospel Music Has Gone International," *Singing News* 1 (April 1, 1970): 4.

19. The number of years the *Jubilee* was on the air has been variously reported; the highest number is twenty-five years. See Cusic, *Sound of Light*, 154. The variation seems to be a result of the lack of distinction between the number of years that new shows were produced and the total number of years the show, including reruns, was on the air. In a 1988 interview, Les Beasley clarified the dates, noting, "It was in production from 1964 to 1975, and it still plays in reruns in a lot of markets. We were in every major market in the U.S." (*Gospel Voice* 1 [January 1988]: 7).

20. Many individuals within the gospel music industry have speculated that the success of the *Jubilee* program was the most important factor in breaking up the power held by the Blackwoods and Statesmen, who were the two most successful groups at that time (Jerry Goff interview). See also Jerry Kirksey, "Les Beasley: One of Southern Gospel Music's Most Powerful Men," *Singing News* 27 (May 1996): 56–62.

21. Lance LeRoy, *The Lewis Family History/Picture Book: 45 Years on the Stages of America—A Retrospective* (Hendersonville, Tenn.: Dulany Printing, 1996), 7–10. On the Presley connection, see J. D. Sumner and Bob Terrell, *The Life and Times of J. D. Sumner*, rev. ed. (Nashville: J. D. Sumner, 1994), 67.

22. Jerry Goff interview.

23. Taylor, *Happy Rhythm*, 96–97, 102.

24. "Gospel as Seen through the Video Tube," *Billboard: The World of Religious Music* 78 (October 22, 1966): 58.

25. Lou Wills Hildreth interview. See also personal interviews with Vernon Klaudt, Greenville, S.C., August 10, 1996; Neil Enloe, Alexandria, Ind., April 3, 1996; and Duane Nicholson, Alexandria, Ind., April 3, 1996. On the Wills family, see "Wills Family Is Gospel Music's King Family," *Gospel Notes* (December 1966): 2. On the Oak Ridge Boys, see *Singing News* 1 (July 15, 1969): 13. On the Couriers, see Charles R. Hembree, *They Sing the Mighty Power* (Stow, Ohio: New Hope Press, 1975), 20–23. Hembree's chronology erroneously insinuates that the Courier television program in Pennsylvania predated their 1964–65 stint on the *Jubilee*.

26. Jerry Goff interview. Goff remembers that the FDA essentially "cut the wheels out from under us" when the agency required a new clinical analysis to prove the medical benefits of Akne-med.

27. Predictably, LeFevre's famous family had not participated in the production of the film (Pierce LeFevre, "The First Gospel Movie Is Bad, Bad, Bad, Bad, Bad!" *Gospel Notes* [December 1966]: 4). Fortunately, LeFevre's advice was not taken and the film survives today as rare footage of some of the more famous groups of the mid-1960s. See *Sing a Song for Heaven's Sake* (videocassette recording, Delray Beach, Fla.: Vic Lewis Video, 1991).

28. *Skylite Hi-Lites* (Atlanta, Ga.) (September 1959): 3 and (December 1959): 3. See also Kree Jack Racine, *Above All: The Fascinating and True Story of the Lives and Careers of the Famous Blackwood Brothers Quartet* (Memphis: Jarodoce Publications, 1967), 173, 185, and Sumner and Terrell, *Life and Times of J. D. Sumner*, 162–63.

29. *Sing* 3 (January 1963): 15; 3 (February 1963): 15; 3 (September 1963): 5; 3 (November 1963): 4, 15; 4 (April 1964): 3; 4 (May 1964): 15; and 4 (October 1964): 14–15.

30. The Blackwood-Statesmen team sold Skylite to an independent group of investors led by Joel Gentry in 1966. By the 1970s, the two groups were once again working separately. See Racine, *Above All*, 185; Sumner and Terrell, *Life and Times of J. D. Sumner*, 163; and Bob Terrell, *The Music Men: The Story of Professional Gospel Quartet Singing* (Asheville: Bob Terrell, 1990), 165. The Caravan team split in the mid-1960s, and, though the LeFevres remained an independent force in gospel music, they gradually declined in influence, with Urias and Alphus LeFevre retiring in the mid-1970s.

31. Cusic, *Sound of Light*, 134–38. Also on Norcross, see Joseph T. Catring,

"In Marvin Norcross There Burned a Special Fire," *Singing News* 19 (June 1987): 14. On the importance of Word, Inc., see Russell Chandler, "The Good News in Gospel Music," *Saturday Evening Post* 254 (April 1982): 19.

32. Personal interview with Nelson Parkerson, Nashville, Tenn., May 23, 1996. On the Benson company, see Sandy Smith, "The Benson Company Has a Strong Past and Its Future Looks Even Stronger," *Gospel Voice* 3 (April 1990): B-2–B-6.

33. "Don Light Talent Agency Is First in Gospel Music," *Gospel Notes* (December 1966): 3.

34. Personal interview with Ed Harper, Goodlettsville, Tenn., May 22, 1996; Sumner and Terrell, *Life and Times of J. D. Sumner,* 163–65. Also on Harper's importance, see "Behind the Scenes," *Concert Life* 5 (July–August 1977): 16; "Herman Harper: Some of Gospel Music's Longest Relationships," *Gospel Voice* 2 (August 1989): 8; and Jerry Kirksey, Deana Surles, and Bob Terrell, "Herman Harper: December 31, 1938–December 17, 1993," *Singing News* 24 (February 1994): 38–39.

35. "The Dove," *Singing News* 1 (November 15, 1969): 6.

36. On the founding of the GMA, see Blackwell, *Wings of the Dove,* 114–15, and "GMA Gains in Stature," *Billboard: The World of Gospel Music* 79 (October 14, 1967): 6–7. On the first awards banquet, in the fall of 1969, see "Gospel Music to Honor Own during Convention," *Singing News* 1 (September 15, 1969): 1; "Awards Banquet Highlights Convention," *Singing News* 1 (November 15, 1969): 1; and J. D. Sumner and Bob Terrell, *Gospel Music Is My Life* (Nashville: Impact Books, 1971), 206–7.

37. Personal interview with J. G. Whitfield, Live Oak, Fla., June 15, 1996. See also Dave Taylor, "The Ole Gospel Man," *Gospel Singing World* 3 (April–June 1998): 20, and James R. Goff Jr., "Looking Back on 30 Years of Singing News," *Singing News* 30 (May 1999): 51–52.

38. "*Singing News* Subscriptions Climb Steadily," *Singing News* 1 (June 15, 1969): 2.

39. Personal interview with Jerry Kirksey, Boone, N.C., March 30, 1999; Goff, "Looking Back," 52–54. See also the articles and editorials explaining the magazine's purpose in *Singing News* 1 (May 15, 1969): 1–2, 6. In addition to the GMA-produced *Good News,* the Nashville-based *Music City News* attempted for a few years to provide coverage of the quartets by including a section titled "MCN Gospel News." See "MCN to Expand Gospel Coverage," *Music City News* 4 (January 1967): 1, and "2nd Gospel Music Publication Bought," *Music City News* 4 (February 1967): 1.

40. "Gospel Hit Parade Established," *Singing News* 1 (January 1, 1970): 1.

41. Jerry Kirksey interview.

42. "Invalidate '71 Dove Awards," *Good News* (Nashville, Tenn.) 3 (November 1971): 1.

43. Personal interviews with James Blackwood, Springdale, Ark., August 3, 1996, and Les Beasley, Live Oak, Fla., June 15, 1996.

44. "Invalidate '71 Dove Awards."

45. "Special Committees Study Dove Awards," *Good News* 3 (December 1971): 1.

46. "Invalidate '71 Dove Awards."

47. On the induction of the first members of the GMA Hall of Fame, see "Name 2 in Hall of Fame Oct. 9," *Good News* 3 (October 1971): 1; "Hall of Fame," *Good News* 3 (December 1971): 1; and "Waites [*sic*], Speer Selected for Hall of Fame," *Singing News* 3 (November 1971): 1.

48. Television remained a powerful force in gospel music through the mid-1970s when, ironically, the syndicated music shows encountered fierce competition from evangelical ministers seeking the Sunday morning air-time to broadcast their own religious programs (Les Beasley interview, June 14, 1996).

49. On the Pentecostal connection to evangelical growth in the 1950s, see David Harrell's *All Things Are Possible: The Healing and Charismatic Revivals in Modern America* (Bloomington: Indiana University Press, 1975).

50. The pioneering work on contemporary gospel is Paul Baker's *Why Should the Devil Have All the Good Music?* (Waco, Tex.: Word Books, 1979). A few years later, Baker (a Christian deejay whose legal name was Frank Edmondson) issued an updated version titled *Contemporary Christian Music: Where It Came From, What It Is, Where It's Going*, rev. ed. (Westchester, Ill.: Crossway Books, 1985). For a brief synopsis of the genre's history, see April Hefner, *CCM* 18 (April 1996): 38–42.

51. Baker, *Why Should the Devil*, 167–71. On Graham's association with celebrity converts, see Marshall Frady, *Billy Graham: A Parable of American Righteousness* (Boston: Little, Brown and Company, 1979), 369–70, and Billy Graham, *Just As I Am: The Autobiography of Billy Graham* (New York: HarperCollins, 1997), 683–97.

52. Elvis Presley's devotion to gospel music is well documented. For a scholarly assessment of its impact on him, see Charles K. Wolfe, "Presley and the Gospel Tradition," in *Elvis: Images and Fancies*, ed. Jac L. Tharpe (Jackson: University Press of Mississippi, 1979), 135–50. A sampling of the many accounts that chronicle Presley's interest are Peter Guralnick's *Last Train to Memphis: The Rise of Elvis Presley* (Boston: Little, Brown, and Company, 1994), 46–48, 77–78, 86–87, and *Careless Love: The Unmaking of Elvis Presley* (Boston: Little, Brown, and Company, 1999), 82–84, 405, 461–62; J. D. Sumner and Bob Terrell, *Elvis: His Love for Gospel Music and J. D. Sumner* (Nashville: Gospel Quartet Music Company, 1991); Sumner and Terrell, *Life and Times of J. D. Sumner*, 123–26; Buck Rambo and Bob Terrell, *The Legacy of Buck and Dottie Rambo* (Nashville: Star Song Publishing, 1992), 142–46; Cusic, *Sound of Light*, 116–20; and Blackwell, *Wings of the Dove*, 153.

53. Elvis auditioned with the Songfellows in July 1953 and was rejected because he had difficulty "hearing harmony" and thus could not easily switch from the lead part to baritone or tenor when needed. Shortly thereafter, he

was actually offered a position with the quartet in part because his ability to switch parts had improved. By then, however, he was under contract with Sun Records. See Bob Terrell, "'Three Chords and a Cloud of Dust': The Jim Hamill Story," *Singing News* 19 (February 1988): 24–26, 32–33; Paul S. Carter, *Heritage of Holiness: An Eye-Witness History, First Assembly of God Church, Memphis, Tennessee* (Memphis: Paul's Press, 1991), 150; Patricia Jobe Pierce, *The Ultimate Elvis: Elvis Presley Day By Day* (New York: Simon and Schuster, 1994), 64–65; and Guralnick, *Last Train*, 67–69, 75–77, 503.

54. The Jordanaires originated in Springfield, Missouri, in the late 1940s and achieved some success by the early 1950s primarily through an association with WSM in Nashville. The group that became associated with Presley was a version of the quartet controlled primarily by tenor singer and pianist Gordon Stoker. On the Jordanaires, see Wayne W. Daniel, "The Jordanaires: Gordon Stoker Talks about His Career in Gospel Music," *Rejoice!* 4 (October–November 1992): 6–9, and Wolfe, "Presley and the Gospel Tradition," 140–44.

55. Cusic, *Sound of Light*, 113–15, 127.

56. George Younce, "Poetry Corner," *Sing* 4 (June 1964): 7.

57. Pierce LeFevre, "One Man's Opinion," ibid., 4 (October 1964): 3. For a similar article associating changes in American life with the threat of communism, see Reverend Kenneth W. Sollitt, "If I Were the Devil," ibid., 5 (October 1965): 4.

58. The quotations are from *Gospel Music Hi-Lites* (December 1965–January 1966): 19 and (February 1966): 2, respectively.

59. Ibid. (March 1966): 25.

60. "Blackwood Petition Growing," *Singing News* 1 (May 15, 1969): 1–2.

61. "The New Ministry: Bringing God Back to Life," *Time* 94 (December 26, 1969): 45. See also ibid., 40–45, and "Toward a Hidden God," *Time* 87 (April 8, 1966): 82–87.

62. By mid-1971, *Time* devoted its cover story to the revival, dubbing the phenomenon "The Jesus Revolution." See "The New Rebel Cry: Jesus Is Coming!" ibid., 96 (June 21, 1971): 56–63.

63. Baker, *Why Should the Devil*, 47.

64. Cusic, *Sound of Light*, 128. See also Zell Miller, *They Heard Georgia Singing* (Macon, Ga.: Mercer University Press, 1996), 179, and "Mylon LeFevre: Ministering Jesus to Kids," *Singing News* 16 (April 1986): 15.

65. Bob Larson, *Hippies, Hindus, and Rock & Roll* (McCook, Nebr.: Bob Larson, 1969), 12–14. See Larson's *Rock and Roll: The Devil's Diversion* (Carol Stream, Ill.: Creation House, 1967) and *Rock & the Church* (Carol Stream, Ill.: Creation House, 1971), in which the author attacks the use of the rock music style by Christian artists. For similar responses to rock 'n' roll, see David Wilkerson, "Rock and Roll—The Devil's Heartbeat," *Pentecostal Evangel* (July 12, 1959): 4–5, and G. B. Robeson, "Beat Music, LSD, and Antichrist," *Pentecostal Evangel* (January 7, 1968): 11. By the late 1970s, Bob Larson had

mellowed his views with respect to at least some forms of contemporary Christian music. See Baker, *Why Should the Devil*, 181–84. For other critiques of Christian rock from the evangelical community, see Dan Peters, Steve Peters, and Cher Merrill, *What about Christian Rock?* (Minneapolis: Bethany House Publishers, 1986); John Blanchard, *Pop Goes the Gospel* (Hertfordshire, England: Evangelical Press, 1983); and Steve Miller, *The Contemporary Christian Music Debate: Worldly Compromise or Agent of Renewal?* (Wheaton, Ill.: Tyndale House Publishers, 1993).

66. Paul Baker, "Explo '72 and Its Fruits," *Harmony* 2 (September–October 1976): 18; Baker, *Why Should the Devil*, 107–11. For advertisements of the various Jesus Festivals, see *Harmony* 1 (June–July 1975): 11 and 1 (August 1975): 13. On Graham's involvement, see Frady, *Billy Graham*, 403–4, and Billy Graham, *The Jesus Generation* (Grand Rapids, Mich.: Zondervan Publishing House, 1971).

67. Baker, *Why Should the Devil*, 65–71; Cusic, *Sound of Light*, 128–29.

68. Paul Baker, "California Dreaming," *Harmony* 2 (July–August 1976): 22; Cusic, *Sound of Light*, 134–38.

69. For a list of stations playing at least some contemporary gospel by the mid-1970s, see *Harmony* 1 (September–November 1975): 14–15, 18. On the difficulty of securing airplay for early contemporary music, see Baker, *Why Should the Devil*, 75–81. John Styll's magazine, eventually known simply as *CCM*, endured to become the standard publication for the devotees of contemporary Christian music.

70. Baker, *Why Should the Devil*, 187. On the phenomenal growth of contemporary Christian music in the 1970s, see Janice D. Terrell, *The Growth of Contemporary Christian Music in the Last Ten Years* (master's thesis, American University, 1984).

71. On the evolution of the Speers during this period, see *Skylite Hi-Lites* (July 1963): 3; *Sing* 3 (November 1963): 6; *Gospel Notes* (December 1966): 8; *Singing News* 2 (March 1971): 16; and *Singing News* 4 (April 1973): 13. See also the explanation of the changes in Paula Becker's *Let the Song Go On: Fifty Years of Gospel Singing with the Speer Family* (Nashville: Impact Books, 1971), 119–75. According to Baker (*Why Should the Devil*, 109), the Speers were one of the few traditional groups to participate in Explo '72.

72. On the Rambos' Vietnam tour, see "Singing Rambos in Vietnam," *Music City News* 4 (March 1967): 18; 4 (April 1967): 24; and 4 (May 1967): 17. See also "Rambos Are in Vietnam," *Gospel Notes* 1 (February 1967): 1, and the follow-up article in 1 (March–April 1967): 5–6. For a contemporary analysis of Dottie Rambo's influence as a songwriter, see "That's Dottie Rambo: Great Song Writer," *Singing News* 2 (January 1971): 6.

73. Jake Hess, *Nothin' but Fine: The Music and the Gospel According to Jake Hess* (Columbus, Ga.: Buckland Press, 1995), 154.

74. On the founding of the Imperials and the uniqueness of their style, see Hess, *Nothin' but Fine*, 137–58; Cusic, *Sound of Light*, 191–94; and William

Lynwood Montell, *Singing the Glory Down: Amateur Gospel Music in South Central Kentucky* (Lexington: University Press of Kentucky, 1991), 116. Accounts vary on gospel music audiences' reaction to the Imperials' introduction of drums to their concerts. Hess recalls that "a scattered few got up and left." Montell claims that one-third of the audience walked out. Compare Hess, *Nothin' but Fine*, 152, with Montell, *Singing the Glory Down*, 116. See also the early industry reaction in "Imperials Make Their Debut in the West," *Gospel Music News* (Walnut Creek, Calif.) 1 (April 1964): 16–17; "Major News of the Year," *Gospel Singing* (1965 Annual Issue published in Kansas City, Mo.): 3; and "One Man's Opinion," *Sing* 4 (April 1964): 4. By late in 1964, the Imperials were publishing their own short monthly promotional titled *The Imperial Times*.

75. See Pierce, *Ultimate Elvis*, 208, 250; Guralnick, *Careless Love*, 343–46; "Imps Booked with Channing," *Singing News* 4 (August 1972): 10; and "Imperials with Dean," *Singing News* 4 (October 1972): 12.

76. Compare the cover of the inaugural Imperials album, *Introducing the Illustrious Imperials*, Nashville, The Benson Company, ca. 1965, with later covers such as *The Imperials Believe It*, Nashville, Vista Records, 1971; *Love Is The Thing!*, Nashville, Impact Records, ca. 1971; and *Imperials: The Song of Love*, Nashville, Impact Records, 1972.

77. "Imperials Hire Sherman Andrus," *Gospel West* 1 (April 1972): 7.

78. Personal interview with Terry Blackwood, Alexandria, Ind., April 3, 1996; Cusic, *Sound of Light*, 193–94. See also "Armond Morales and the Imperials: The First 27 Years," *Rejoice!* 4 (April–May 1992): 18–20, and "The Imperials," *Contemporary Christian Music* 5 (August 1982): 8–12.

79. The Goodman version on Word Records actually scored higher, finishing at number six in 1972 and number three in 1973. The Hinsons' initial recording on Calvary Records placed tenth in 1972 and seventeenth in 1973. See *Southern Gospel Source Book* (Boone, N.C.: Singing News Publishing, 1999), 197. On the Hinsons, see Robert Anderson and Gail North, *Gospel Music Encyclopedia* (New York: Sterling Publishing, 1979), 93–95; "A Conversation with Kenny Hinson," *Singing News* 7 (October 1975): 7A; and Ronnie Joyce, "The Hinsons . . . Young, Charismatic and Energetic," *Singing News* 13 (January 1982): 1–5.

80. On the Downings, see "Up with the Downings," *Singing News* 4 (October 1972): 5, and "The Downings Are Back," ibid., 15 (March 1985): 14.

81. The most extensive treatment of the Inspirations is Bob Terrell's *What a Wonderful Time! The Story of the Inspirations* (Alexander, N.C.: Mountain Church, 2000). On the origins of the group, see ibid., esp. 27–56, 136–38, and 163–65.

82. Personal interviews with Martin Cook, Live Oak, Fla., June 20, 1998, and Louisville, Ky., September 26, 1998. For early coverage of the Inspirations' rise in the industry, see "CBS Praises the Inspirations," *Singing News*

2 (February 1971): 13; "Martin Cook . . . From the Classroom to the Stage," ibid., 4 (December 1972): 3; and "Inspirations Join Jubilee," ibid., 5 (June 1973): 3.

83. Bob Terrell, *The Inspirations* (Asheville, N.C.: Bob Terrell, ca. 1971–72), 2–4.

84. Terrell, *What a Wonderful Time!* 53.

85. Martin Cook interviews. For recent assessments of the Inspirations' impact on gospel music, see Deana Surles, "The Inspirations: Singing the Songs the People Want to Hear," *Singing News* 25 (June 1994): 42–45; Terry Griffin, "Inspirations: A Study in Consistency," ibid., 28 (October 1997): 36–40; and Tim Gardner, "Inspirations: Standing the Test of Time," ibid., 29 (December 1998): 52–56.

86. Personal interview with Bill and Gloria Gaither, Louisville, Ky., September 19, 1996. On Gaither's love of the traditional quartets, see Bill Gaither and Jerry Jenkins, *Homecoming: The Story of Southern Gospel Music through the Eyes of Its Best-Loved Performers* (Grand Rapids, Mich.: Zondervan Publishing House, 1997), 79–83, and Bill Gaither and Jerry Jenkins, *I Almost Missed the Sunset: My Perspectives on Life and Music* (Nashville: Thomas Nelson Publishers, 1992), 41–49.

87. Cusic, *Sound of Light*, 139–41.

88. Ibid. Also on the Gaithers' influence, see Bob Darden, "Song Writers First and Foremost: Bill and Gloria Gaither," *Rejoice!* 2 (Summer 1989): 20–24.

89. Bill and Gloria Gaither interview. On the success of the *Homecoming* series, see Lydia Dixon Harden, "Bill and Gloria Gaither: Memories in the Making," *Gospel Voice* 9 (April 1996): 8–9.

90. Duane Nicholson interview. The behind-the-back comments are alluded to in Charles R. Hembree, *They Sing the Mighty Power* (Stow, Ohio: New Hope Press, 1975), 79–80.

91. Duane Nicholson interview.

92. Neil Enloe interview, April 3, 1996, and in Birmingham, Ala., August 14, 1999. For testimonials on the uniqueness of the Couriers within the industry, see Hembree, *They Sing the Mighty Power*, 93–108 and 123–31.

93. Duane Nicholson interview. On the history of gospel music in Canada, see William E. LaPointe, *Forty Years of Gospel Music: The Gospel Trio and the Gospelaires* (Fredericton, New Brunswick, Canada: Centennial Print and Litho Limited, 1986).

94. The quote is from a promotional newspaper, *The Couriers*, distributed free in the mid-1970s by the group . "Two Decades of Music Ministry," *The Couriers* (Mechanicsburg, Pa.), n.d., 2 (files of the *Singing News* office, Boone, N.C.).

95. Neil Enloe interview, April 3, 1996; Duane Nicholson interview. See also Hembree, *They Sing the Mighty Power*, 109–16.

96. Personal interviews with Glen Payne, Louisville, Ky., September 20, 1996, and Bobby Clark, Greenville, S.C., August 9, 1996. The most complete account of the Cathedrals is Glen Payne and George Younce, *The Cathedrals: The Story of America's Best-Loved Gospel Quartet* (Grand Rapids, Mich.: Zondervan Publishing House, 1998).

97. Personal interview with George Younce, Alexandria, Ind., April 1, 1996.

98. Ibid. Also on the Cathedrals, see "Cathedrals Celebrate 20 Years," *Singing News* 16 (September 1984): 10; Lydia Dixon Harden, "The Cathedrals," *Gospel Voice* 2 (January 1989): 16–18; and Danny Jones, "Cathedrals: A Fond Farewell," *Singing News* 30 (September 1999): 83–89. See also the introductory material in *Cathedral Quartet Souvenir Songbook* (Stow, Ohio: Homeward Bound Music, 1982).

99. *Singing News* 1 (September 15, 1969): 6.

100. The idealism had a foothold in many of America's conservative churches as well. In 1958, the Assemblies of God published an article noting that "paid professional singers with trained voices can never take the place of spirit-filled volunteer singers who love the Lord and who will see the importance of the ministry in music" (F. J. Lindquist, "Ministering in Music," *Pentecostal Evangel* [March 16, 1958]: 5).

101. Gospel music legend J. D. Sumner expressed his skepticism (personal interview with J. D. Sumner, Sevierville, Tenn., May 20, 1996). See also Sumner and Terrell, *Life and Times of J. D. Sumner*, 171–78. A slightly different criticism emerged within traditional black gospel circles. Horace Clarence Boyer argued that the style introduced by contemporary artists "robs the audience of an opportunity to 'participate' in the event. And participation is the essence of gospel." See "A Contemporary Analysis of Traditional and Contemporary Gospel Music," in *More Than Dancing: Essays on Afro-American Music and Musicians*, ed. Irene V. Jackson (Westport, Conn.: Greenwood Press, 1985), 143. Boyer's research also concluded that conflict in the black gospel community revolved around whether or not gospel music could "rock and remain gospel." See "Contemporary Gospel Music," *Black Perspective in Music* 7 (Spring 1979): 10.

102. Personal interview with Willie Wynn, Greenville, S.C., August 9, 1996. On the controversy over the Oaks' exit from gospel, see Ellis Widner and Walter Carter, *The Oak Ridge Boys: Our Story* (Chicago: Contemporary Books, 1987), 133–49. The economic difficulty for the group is also alluded to in Roy Clark, *My Life: In Spite of Myself!* (New York: Simon and Schuster, 1994), 158.

103. Widner and Carter, *Oak Ridge Boys*, 142.

104. Personal interview with Eldridge Fox, Boone, N.C., June 18, 1996. See also Widner and Carter, *Oak Ridge Boys*, 142–43.

Chapter Nine

1. "A Brief History of the National Association of Evangelicals," www. nae.net/about-history.html (July 4, 2000); Edmund Morris, *Dutch: A Memoir of Ronald Reagan* (New York: Random House, 1999), 471–73. On the merits of the Reagan revolution, see John W. Sloan, *The Reagan Effect: Economics and Presidential Leadership* (Lawrence: University Press of Kansas, 1999), and Beth A. Fischer, *The Reagan Reversal: Foreign Policy and the End of the Cold War* (Columbia: University of Missouri Press, 1997). For a more critical evaluation of Reagan's relationship with conservative Christianity, see Haynes Johnson, *Sleepwalking through History: America in the Reagan Years* (New York: W. W. Norton and Company, 1991), 193–214.

2. "Ole Ern's Dream Marches On: 'More of that Great American Gospel,'" *Singing News* 12 (December 1, 1980): 1B.

3. Roy Clark, *My Life: In Spite of Myself!* (New York: Simon and Schuster, 1994), 134. On the entire *Hee Haw* story, see ibid., 118–39. See also Bill C. Malone's analysis in *Country Music, U.S.A.*, rev. ed. (Austin: University of Texas Press, 1985), 273–74.

4. Clark, *My Life*, 133. On Jones's stint with the Brown's Ferry Four and his influence on the Hee Haw Gospel Quartet, see Charles K. Wolfe, "The Brown's Ferry Four," *Precious Memories* (November–December 1988): 6– 12, and Alana White, "Grandpa Jones and the Hee Haw Gospel Quartet," *Bluegrass Unlimited* (June 1988): 22–26. White notes that the Hee Haw Gospel Quartet won seven straight *Music City News* Awards as "favorite gospel act" (22).

5. Jan Cain, "Oak Ridge Bus Attacked by Mob," *Singing News* 3 (June 1971): 14.

6. Similar to *Hee Haw*, the Statler Brothers included a weekly gospel number as the finale of their TNN television show during the 1990s. On the Statlers, see Malone, *Country Music, U.S.A.*, 383–84. See also the historical account included in their three-CD collection, *The Statler Brothers 30th Anniversary Celebration*, written by Colin Escott, December 1993, Mercury Records, a division of Polygram Records, Inc., New York, N.Y., 1994.

7. Personal interview with Eldridge Fox, Boone, N.C., June 18, 1996, and Les Beasley, Live Oak, Fla., June 14, 1996. For insight into the rift between the Oaks and more traditional gospel groups during the early 1970s from the Oaks' perspective, see Betty Hofer, "Bridging a Gap to Entertainment for All," *Country Song Roundup* (January 1973): 38–39.

8. Russell Chandler, "The Good News in Gospel Music," *Saturday Evening Post* 254 (April 1982): 18.

9. For a complete photo spread of the event, see *Singing News* 11 (November 1, 1979): 12–13A.

10. Chandler, "Good News in Gospel Music," 18. Gospel music, and par-

ticularly contemporary gospel, did in fact enjoy phenomenal growth during the 1980s despite a brief downturn in 1986–87. The growth of cable television aided the exposure of gospel, including live television coverage of the annual GMA Dove Awards. See Laura Eipper, "Gospel Awards Show Headed for Prime-Time Television," *Nashville Tennessean,* July 17, 1980, news clipping files of the Country Music Foundation, Nashville, Tenn. For similar optimistic projections in the 1980s, see Bob Millard, "Gospel Music Meet Buoyed by Rising Sales; Execs See Bright Future in New, Upscale Market," *Variety,* April 20, 1983, 179; Michael McCall, "Gospel Music Industry Gears for Aggressive Sales Push," *Nashville Banner,* November 18, 1987, Country Music Foundation files; and Michael McCall, "Gospel Music in High Gear after 2-Year Sales Stall," *Nashville Banner,* April 10, 1988, 1–2.

11. On B. J. Thomas and his conversion to Christianity and gospel music, see "B. J. Thomas: He Just Can't Help Believing," *Concert Life* 4 (May–June 1977): 6–13.

12. Lanella Leigh, "Gospel According to Don Butler," *Nashville Scene,* January 21, 1987, 1.

13. Ibid.

14. Personal interview with J. D. Sumner, Sevierville, Tenn., May 20, 1996. On plans for a Hall of Fame complex and the controversy over its failure to materialize, see Lois Blackwell, *The Wings of the Dove: The Story of Gospel Music in America* (Norfolk, Va.: Donning Co., 1978), 148–50; "Ground Breaking Ceremonies for GMA Hall of Fame Set for Nashville Oct. 9," *Singing News* 8 (October 1976): 1; and "Open Letter from J. D. Sumner," *Singing News* 15 (April 1984): 3. The importance of the issue was demonstrated by individual efforts within gospel music to accomplish a similar goal. See "A Dream Can Come True," *Gospel West* 2 (July 1973): 8, and "Gospel Museum under Construction," *Singing News* 10 (December 1978): 12B.

15. Gene Adkins, "Parson to Person," *Singing News* 4 (January 1973): 15. On Marjoe Gortner, see David Edwin Harrell Jr., *All Things Are Possible: The Healing and Charismatic Revivals in Modern America* (Bloomington: Indiana University Press, 1975), 233–34.

16. C. B. Walker, "Letters to the Editor," *Singing News* 4 (February 1973): 2.

17. "The Mail Bag," ibid., 6 (August 1974): 2. For similar concerns expressed by fans during this period, see ibid., 2 (January 1971): 2; 3 (February 1972): 2; 4 (December 1972): 9; 8 (March 1977): 12B; and 9 (February 1978): 17A. As late as 1987, one reader complained that "Satan is working volume to his advantage" by driving people away from gospel music concerts (ibid., 17 [January 1987]: 4).

18. Interestingly enough, this opinion came from one of gospel music's oldest quartet members, Rev. Roy Blackwood of the original Blackwood Brothers Quartet ("Mailbag," ibid., 2 [February 1971]: 2).

19. On the Stampses' participation in the Presley show, see Peter Gural-

nick, *Careless Love: The Unmaking of Elvis Presley* (Boston: Little, Brown, and Company, 1999), 450. For industry coverage of the Stampses' association with Presley, see "Stamps to Back Up Elvis Presley," *Singing News* 3 (November 1971): 15; "Stamps to Appear in New Presley Movie," ibid., 4 (August 1972): 1; and "Stamps on Worldwide Presley TV Special," ibid., 4 (February 1973): 9. For fan reactions critical of Sumner's actions, see "Your Views," ibid., 14 (November 1982): 4 and 16 (May 1984): 4.

20. "Goodmans Resign GMA," *Singing News* 3 (November 1971): 18. Only one month earlier, the *Singing News* had run a front-page story proclaiming the Goodmans "the highest paid group in Gospel Music today" and "the top Gospel attraction from coast to coast." See "Goodmans Top Paid Gospel Music Group," ibid., 3 (October 1971): 1. Years later, Sumner mused that the Goodmans chose "to criticize [the Stamps] from the stage" at a time when "we sung thirty minutes one night in Pontiac, Michigan, to 68,000 people" while "the Goodmans . . . down the road thirty miles sung to six hundred people. And we sung our music; we sung gospel music" (J. D. Sumner interview).

21. J. D. Sumner, "Guest Editorial," *Singing News* 14 (October 1982): 4.

22. Ibid.

23. J. D. Sumner, "Open Letter from J. D. Sumner," ibid., 15 (April 1984): 3.

24. Ibid., 39.

25. James Blackwood, "Letters to the Editor," ibid., 15 (April 1984): 3.

26. James Blackwood "Your Views," *Singing News* 16 (May 1984): 19. For a look at the controversy from the contemporary camp, see Paul Baker, *Contemporary Christian Music*, rev. ed. (Westchester, Ill.: Crossway Books, 1985), 174–81.

27. Sumner, "Open Letter," 45.

28. Bob Darden, "Blackwood, Sumner on the Warpath," *Billboard* 96 (May 12, 1984): 50. Exacerbating the conflict between traditional and contemporary forces in the GMA was unfavorable publicity, including that on the November 1982 arrest of songwriter Andrae Crouch for possession of cocaine. Though charges were subsequently dropped and Crouch maintained that the drugs belonged to some of his "rowdy friends," the case raised questions among conservatives about the state of contemporary gospel. See "Andrae Crouch Explains Arrest," *Singing News* 14 (May 1983): 23, 25.

29. Henry Slaughter, "A Gospel Music Story," *Singing News* 16 (June 1984): 7 and 16 (July 1984): 27.

30. Ibid. Nowhere in Slaughter's tale was black gospel specifically mentioned, though, since the conflict in question was with the newer, youth-oriented "Jesus Rock," the "Ordinary Guy" probably represented for Slaughter the traditional black gospel genre and the inspirational soloists.

31. "Southern Gospel Music Association Opens New Offices," ibid., 13 (July 1982): 19. Waller had founded the organization originally back in 1980 as the Georgia Gospel Music Association. After two successful awards cere-

monies in 1980 and 1981, he reorganized the group as the SGMA in order to attract a larger audience and represent a larger wing of the industry. Beginning in August 1982, Waller began a regular "SGMA Report," which was published monthly for the next few years in the *Singing News* (Personal interviews with Charles Waller, Greenville, S.C., June 10, 1996, and, via telephone, February 25, 2000).

32. Susan Carrington, "SGMA GEM Awards," *Singing News* 16 (June 1985): 21. Waller interviews.

33. The guild would reverse its position on awards by the mid-1990s, sponsoring the annual Hearts Aflame Awards.

34. Given its nature as an industry organization not open to fan participation, the Southern Gospel Music Guild received only occasional mention in magazines like the *Singing News*. Annual membership was set at $500, and the stated mission of the guild was to promote "the growth and continued advancement of the art form called Southern Gospel." See Bob Crawford, "Down Music Row," *Singing News* 17 (April 1987): 43, and "Southern Gospel Music Guild Sets Next Meeting Site," ibid., 18 (July 1987): 12, 42. See also "SGMG: About Us," www.sgmg.org/About_Us/about_us.html (July 7, 2000).

35. Personal interviews with Charles R. Burke, Boone, N.C., February 8, 1996, and Ed O'Neal, Kinston, N.C., August 13, 1996. For a smattering of publicity on the groups, see "The Singing Americans: Charlie Burke's Dream," *Singing News* 17 (February 1987): 11; "Dixie Melody Boys: After a Hiatus from Southern Gospel Music . . . THEY'RE BACK," *Gospel Voice* 2 (February 1989): 16–17; Teresa Erwin, "Gold City—Still Movin' Up," *Singing News* 18 (December 1987): 8–10; "Heaven Bound: We're a Ministry . . . Make No Mistake," ibid., 18 (March 1988): 27, 30; and Jerry Kirksey, "Gospel Music Part of Dollywood's Daily Entertainment," ibid., 18 (April 1988): 10–12, 43–44.

36. Personal interviews with Rex Nelon, Boone, N.C., June 18, 1996; Randy Shelnut, Live Oak, Fla., June 15, 1996; and Kenneth Bishop, Louisville, Ky., September 20, 1996. See also Joseph T. Catring, "The Nelons Switch to Old-Time Southern Gospel," *Singing News* 17 (February 1987): 32–33; "The Dynamic Dixie Echoes," ibid., 16 (June 1984): 3; Carol Snyder, "Silver Anniversary for Hoppers," ibid., 16 (July 1984): 11, 29; "The Hemphills: Providing an Alternative," ibid., 15 (January 1984): 7–8; and Connie Powell, *The McKameys: Not Afraid to Be Real* (Clinton, Tenn.: McKameys Publishing, 1990).

37. See Kathy Foley and Allen Coleman, "The Talleys: A Heart-Working Trio," *Singing News* 16 (March 1986): 4; Dave Wilcox, "The Perrys . . . Pure Gold," ibid., 17 (January 1987): 12; Deana Surles, "The Greenes: A Family Business," ibid., 20 (September 1989): 44–45; Keith Payne, "From Humble Beginnings: The Paynes," ibid., 15 (March 1985): 19–20; Brook Webster, "The Refreshing Perry Sisters," ibid., 19 (September 1988): 12; Wayde Powell, "The Primitive Quartet," *Precious Memories* (July–August 1988): 25–29; Wayne W. Daniel, "Jeff and Sheri Easter: A Perfect Blend of Bluegrass, Country, and

Southern Gospel," *Bluegrass Unlimited* 22 (May 1988): 24–26; and "The New Gaither Vocal Band," *Singing News* 14 (May 1983): 36–37.

38. On Huffam's success and influence, see Roy Rigdon, "Southern Gospel with a Little Black Flavoring," *Singing News* 18 (October 1987): 22. Huffam had been introduced to southern gospel audiences on the strength of his group's victory in a talent contest in 1973. Their recording of "Gone" charted at no. 14 in 1979, no. 4 in 1980, and no. 19 in 1981 (*Southern Gospel Source Book: 1999* [Boone, N.C.: Singing News, 1999], 199–200).

39. Personal interviews with Charles Johnson, Nashville, Tenn., September 28, 1992, and Durham, N.C., August 12, 1996. The interweaving of white and black gospel clearly had antecedents in the work of the Golden Gate Quartet and in the musical style of Andrae Crouch and the Disciples. On Crouch's appeal to white audiences, see Keith Bernard Jenkins, "The Rhetoric of Gospel Song: A Content Analysis of the Lyrics of Andrae Crouch" (Ph.D. diss., Florida State University, 1990), 90–92.

40. Personal interviews with Don DeGrate, Louisville, Ky., September 19, 1995, and September 20, 1996; with Willis Canada, Louisville, Ky., September 19, 1995; and with Terry Scott, Springdale, Ark., August 1, 1996.

41. Waller's SGMA was purchased as a separate entity in 1985 by a board of directors but survived for only another year. The organization was abandoned in favor of the new SGMG (Charles Waller interviews). The 1986 annual GEM Awards program was the last reported in the *Singing News*. See Susan Carrington, "SGMA GEM Awards," *Singing News* 16 (June 1985): 21, and Charles Waller, "Southern Gospel Music Association GEM Awards," ibid., 17 (July 1986): 25, 52.

42. Added to the Hall of Fame list along with the initial thirty-seven inductees at the May 1997 inaugural banquet was the name of Wendy Bagwell. The recently deceased artist became the first member chosen by the new organization through the election process.

43. James R. Goff Jr., "Looking Back on 30 Years of *Singing News*," *Singing News* 30 (May 1999): 54–56. For coverage of the museum opening, see Jerry Kirksey, "Southern Gospel Music Hall of Fame and Museum: Now Open!" ibid., 30 (May 1999): 112–14, and the photo coverage in ibid., 30 (June 1999): 38–43. See also the organization's website at www.sgma.org.

44. On the evolution of the NQC, See Jerry Kirksey, "New Board Heads National Quartet Convention," *Singing News* 14 (August 1982): 23, 28; Danny Jones, "Pictorial Coverage of the Great Western Quartet Convention," ibid., 28 (July 1997): 52–61; and Danny Jones, "Canadian Quartet Convention," ibid., 30 (September 1999): 52–57. Beginning in April 2000, the Great Western Quartet Convention was held in Sacramento, California.

45. Personal interview with Bill and Gloria Gaither, Louisville, Ky., September 19, 1996.

46. Personal interview with Danny Jones, editor of the *Singing News*, Boone, N.C., March 2, 2000.

47. Gene Adkins, "Something's Happening—Everywhere," *Singing News* 1 (February 1, 1970): 9.

48. Jerry Kirksey, "Prayer Bill Needs Our Prayers . . . and HARD WORK," ibid., 13 (June 1982): 1, 4. See also the May 1984 issue, which, in the middle of the Reagan era, featured well-known conservative evangelist Dr. James Kennedy on the cover; and Bill Faulkner, "God and Government: Freedom of Religion versus Freedom from Religion," ibid., 16 (May 1984): 15–16, 45–46.

49. Lois Gail Sypolt, lyricist and composer, "Cry for the Children." Lyrics reprinted by permission of Tuckaseigee Publishing Co., A Division of Inspirations, Inc., Bryson City, N.C. The song first appeared on The Inspirations' *Cry for the Children*, Inspirations, Inc., 1993. The fact that in 1994 the lyrics were printed on handout cards and were being sold for $1 at the Inspirations' record booth as late as 1996 proved the song's popularity.

50. Jerry Thompson, lyricist and composer, "We've Got to Get America Back to God." Lyrics reprinted by permission of Rex Nelon Music, Brentwood, Tenn. The song first appeared on The Nelons' *A Promised Reunion*, Benson Music Group, 1994.

51. On the phenomenal success of the song, see also Danny Jones, "The Steeles . . . Getting the Attention of America," *Singing News* 28 (July 1997): 46–51.

52. Jeff R. Steele, lyricist and composer, "We Want America Back." Lyrics reprinted by permission of Christian Taylor Music, Hendersonville, Tenn. The song first appeared on The Steeles' *We Want America Back*, Daywind Music Group, 1996.

53. Jerry Kirksey, "Watering Down the Message, It's Not Gospel Music," *Singing News* 26 (August 1995): 10. The lyrics of gospel songs continued to be an issue among members of the GMA. See Steve Rabey, "What Makes Music 'Christian'?" *Contemporary Christian Music* 21 (May 1999): 55–64.

Conclusion

1. Tim W. Ferguson and Josephine Lee, "Spiritual Reality," *Forbes* 159 (January 27, 1997): 70–76.

2. James Lloyd, "Who's Behind the '90s Rise in Christian Pop?" *Charlotte Observer*, January 1, 2000, sec. G, p. 3. See also Daniel Fierman and Gillian Flynn, "The Greatest Story Ever Sold," *Entertainment Weekly*, December 3, 1999, 55–64.

3. For insight into the recent inner workings of the southern gospel recording and music publishing industries, I am indebted especially to Eddie Crook, of the Eddie Crook Company, Goodlettsville, Tenn., whom I interviewed on May 22, 1996; Chris White, of the Reach Satellite Network and Sonlite Records, Nashville, Tenn., whom I interviewed on May 24, 1996; Judy Spencer, of Manna Music, Nashville, Tenn., whom I interviewed on

April 2, 1996; and Johnny Carter, of NRC/Bibletone Video, Rome, Ga., whom I interviewed on August 9, 1996.

4. Telephone interview with Paul R. Boden, publisher/editor in chief, *U.S. Gospel News*, Jonesville, Ark., July 5, 2000, and with Garry Cohn, publisher/editor in chief, *The Gospel Voice*, Nashville, Tenn., July 21, 2000.

5. Telephone interview with Paul Heil, Lancaster, Pa., July 13, 2000. See also "Paul Heil Celebrates His Tenth Anniversary of 'Gospel Greats,'" *Gospel Voice* 3 (February 1990): 21, and *The Gospel Greats 1994 Annual Report to Affiliates* (Lancaster, Pa.: The Gospel Greats, February 1995).

6. Personal interview with Chris White and telephone interview with Jim Cumbee, president, Solid Gospel Radio Network, Nashville, Tenn., July 5, 2000.

7. For an array of links to southern gospel artists and industry organizations, consult www.singingnews.com/links.html and www.gaithermusic.com/links/index.html.

8. "Concert Billboard," *Singing News* 32 (July 2000): 146–52. As of June 2000, listings were also made available at a separate website, www.concertbillboard.com.

9. "Personal Appearances," *Singing News* 32 (July 2000): 122–41.

10. "Southern Gospel Music Quartet Market," in *Singing News Magazine and Southern Gospel Music Rate and Data Information* (Boone, N.C.: Singing News Publishing, 1990), 7–8. This 1990 report was based on a direct-mail survey to 1,830 groups listed in the magazine's files, of which 1,647 responded. For the purposes of this survey, the term "quartet" was interpreted loosely to include any performing group of two or more members.

11. Compare "Southern Gospel Music Quartet Market" with "Singing News Subscriber Survey, November 1998," *Singing News* office records, Boone, N.C., December 15, 1998.

12. "Singing News Subscriber Survey." For a more detailed analysis of the readership of the magazine, see James R. Goff Jr., "The Rise of Southern Gospel Music," *Church History* 67 (December 1998): 741–43.

13. On the controversy, see Roy Pauley, "In My Opinion: More Thoughts on the Hall of Fame," *Singing News* 32 (May 2000): 18, and SGMA Executive Committee, "The SGMA Responds to Roy Pauley," ibid., 32 (June 2000): 20.

14. Jerry Kirksey, "JD," ibid., 30 (January 1999): 26–30; Danny Jones, Bob Terrell, and Rick Francis, "Brock Speer: He Did It Right," ibid., 30 (May 1999): 100–104; Danny Jones, "A Fond Farewell—The Cathedrals," ibid., 30 (September 1999): 83–89; Jim Goff and Danny Jones, "Glen Payne: 1926–1999," ibid., 31 (December 1999): 50–55; Jim Goff, Jerry Kirksey, Larry Ford, and Russ Farrar, "Southern Gospel Mourns the Loss of Rex Nelon," ibid., 31 (March 2000): 44–48; Russ Farrar, "The Cathedrals Say Farewell: The View from the Front Row," ibid., 31 (February 2000): 42–45. Note that the May–October 1999 issues of the magazine were incorrectly cataloged as volume 30 rather than 31.

INDEX

14, 224, 227, 248, 339 (n. 107),
339–40 (n. 115), 343 (n. 12)
Homosexuality: opposition to, 272,
278, 280. *See also* Conservative
Christianity
Hopper, Claude, 256, 275
Hopper, Connie, 256, 275
Hopper, Dean, 256
Hopper, Kim Greene, 256
Hopper Brothers and Connie (Hop-
pers), 208, 256, 275
Hovie Lister and the Statesmen Quartet
(television show), 227
Huffam, Teddy, 196, 276, 375 (n. 38)
Hughes, George, 106, 140–42
Humbard, Rex, 188, 202, 251
Humor: use of within gospel music,
95, 114, 130, 160, 207–8
Hyles, Arnold, 140–41, 147, 168,
206
Hyles, Vernon, 140–41, 147, 168,
206

Impact Records, 232, 242
Imperials, 192, 231, 244–45, 266,
367–68 (n. 74)
Imperial Sugar Quartet, 150, 180
Inspirations, 193, 221, 236, 246–47,
274, 279, 376 (n. 49)
Instruments: controversy over use in
southern gospel, 254
Integration: at camp meetings,
19–20; mutual influence of black
and white gospel music, 210–11,
296 (n. 26), 301 (n. 61); within
southern gospel music groups,
245, 249; in antebellum worship,
296 (n. 23). *See also* Segregation
Isaacs, 292 (n. 25)

Jackson, George Pullen, 23, 54, 92
Jackson, Mahalia, xi, 3
James D. Vaughan Music Publishing

Company, 26, 67, 69, 71–72,
75–78, 81–90, 114–15, 119, 122,
124–29, 131, 139–40, 158–60,
204, 314 (n. 23), 320 (n. 75), 321
(n. 77), 325 (nn. 38, 44), 327
(n. 62), 331 (n. 20), 342 (n. 6)
Jars of Clay, 283, 285
Jazz, 1, 4, 40, 42, 75, 119, 164–65,
214, 269, 283
J. D. Sumner and the Stamps, 13,
197, 231, 233, 267, 270, 373
(n. 20)
Jeff and Sheri Easter, 276, 292
(n. 25)
Jenkins Family, 112, 329 (n. 2)
Jerry and the Singing Goffs, 231
Jesus festivals, 242
Jesus movement, Jesus Rock, 238–
43, 248, 254, 272, 373 (n. 30)
John Benson Publishing Company
(Nashville, Tenn.), 92, 232,
242–43
John Daniel Quartet, 104, 119, 122,
139–40, 170, 226
Johnson, Charles, 199–200, 258, 276
Johnson Sisters, 190, 207, 226, 228,
355 (n. 15)
Jones, Jimmy, 181, 191, 206
Jones, Louis Marshall "Grandpa,"
265, 342 (n. 11)
Jones, Sam, 62–63
Jordanaires, 8, 151, 165, 237, 266,
366 (n. 54)

Kaiser, Kurt, 238
Karnes, Rose Carter. *See* Carter,
Rose
Kendrick, Bervin, 151, 170, 348
(nn. 59, 60)
Kentucky Harmony (songbook), 23
Key, Charles, 148, 181
Kieffer, Aldine Silliman, 44–51,
53–54, 62, 70–73, 299 (n. 43), 307

ern gospel, 5–6, 41–42, 161–64,
286, 291 (nn. 17, 18)
Perrys, 261, 276
Perry Sisters, 276
Petra, 243
Phonograph recording companies,
early, 63, 75–79
Phonograph recordings: as a part
of the growth of southern gospel,
2; early influence on southern
gospel, 82, 85, 89, 109, 111–12,
118, 120–21, 129, 134–35, 142,
319–20 (n. 75), 325 (n. 43), 333
(n. 44); southern gospel groups'
increased use of in the 1940s and
1950s, 157–60, 168–70, 172–74,
179–81, 185, 203–4, 206, 208–9;
of southern gospel in the 1960s
and 1970s, 231–32, 234, 266
Pilgrims, 14–15, 292–93 (n. 2)
Pittman, Jack, 153, 180
Plainsmen, 154, 205–6
Politics, conservative: southern gospel artists' support of, 239–40
Postmillennialism, 30
Poteat, Dr. H. M., 40–41
Praise and Inspirational Music, 248
Premillennialism, 30–31, 161–62,
242
Presbyterians, 17–18, 52, 281
Presley, Elvis, 3, 8, 13, 165, 216, 229,
237–38, 245, 266–67, 270–71,
290–91 (n. 15), 365–66 (n. 53),
366 (n. 54)
Presley, Luther, 80, 89, 324 (n. 31)
Primitive Quartet, 276, 292 (n. 25)
Prohibition, 77
Promoters, southern gospel concert,
164–67
Prophets Quartet, 177, 190, 228,
230–31
Psalters, 14–15
Puritans, 3, 15, 20, 30, 292–93 (n. 2)

Quartet Music Company (Fort
Worth, Tex.), 321 (n. 1), 322
(n. 8)

Race Records, 210–12, 217, 347–48
(n. 55)
Radio: as part of the growth of
southern gospel, 2; early importance of to southern gospel
groups, 74–75, 78–79, 82, 85, 91,
93, 109, 111–12, 117–18, 121–23,
129–30, 132–34, 136–43, 224,
318–19 (n. 58), 319 (n. 59), 326
(n. 53); importance of to southern
gospel in the 1940s and 1950s,
157–61, 164–65, 167–69, 172,
177–82, 184–86, 199, 202–4,
207–12, 217, 224–25, 248, 337
(n. 82), 347–48 (n. 55); continued
importance to southern gospel in
the 1960s, 243, 251–52; advances
of southern gospel on in the
1980s and 1990s, 284
Ragtime, 40, 42
Rains, Carl, 104, 139
Rambo, Buck, 198, 244
Rambo, Dottie, 162, 198, 206, 244
Rambo, Reba, 198, 244, 268
Rambos, 198, 236, 244, 248
Ramsey, Will M., 86, 93, 124, 321
(n. 4), 323 (n. 29), 327 (nn. 60, 62)
Rangers Quartet, 33, 140–42, 147,
158, 160, 168–71, 180, 205–6,
213, 248, 340 (n. 123)
Rangers Trio, 169, 206, 230–31, 248
RCA Records, 156, 172–73, 181, 231
Reach Satellite Network (Solid
Gospel Radio Network), 284
Rebels Quartet, 152, 182–83, 226,
345 (n. 30)
Reconstruction, 20
Reece, David, 147, 169, 206
Reggie Saddler Family, 277

Index

Index

Index

Vaughan Saxophone Quartet, 117, 323 (n. 17)

Vaughan's Family Visitor (The Musical Visitor) (magazine), 27, 71–72, 74–75, 77, 81–86, 90, 116, 118, 126–27, 143, 160, 215, 316 (n. 39), 317 (n. 41), 346 (n. 39), 359 (n. 50)

Victor Records, 118–19, 121, 211

Vietnam War, 223, 239, 244, 266

Virgil O. Stamps Music Company, 82, 86–88

Virginia Normal Music School, 49–51, 70. *See also* Shenandoah Conservatory of Music

V. O. Stamps "Old Original" Quartet, 90–92, 100, 122–23, 142, 180, 339 (n. 110)

V. O. Stamps Quartet, 120

V. O. Stamps School of Music, 90

Waits, James "Big Jim" (also "Pappy"), 99, 118, 140, 147, 152, 177, 183, 206, 235

Walbert, James, D., 99, 117–18, 331 (nn. 25, 26)

Walbert, William B., 57, 84, 97, 99, 116–18, 127, 309 (n. 56), 323 (n. 17), 324 (n. 32), 331 (nn. 19, 26), 336 (n. 78)

Walker, William "Singin' Billy," 24, 64, 298 (n. 41)

Wallace, Eddie, 105, 178–79

Waller, Charles, 274, 277–78, 346 (n. 40), 373–74 (n. 31), 375 (n. 41)

Walter, Thomas, 15

Watkins, Archie, 193, 246

Watts, Isaac, 15–16, 19, 28, 30, 293 (n. 8), 295 (n. 16)

Weatherford, Earl, 188, 202, 251

Weatherford, Lily Fern, 13, 188, 202, 251

Weatherford Quartet (Weather-

fords), 123, 188, 202, 244, 251, 345 (n. 30)

Wendy Bagwell and the Sunliters, 188, 207–8, 230, 232, 353–54 (n. 5)

Wesley, Charles, 16

Wesley, John, 16

Western movies, gospel artists' participation in, 105, 178–79, 206

Wetherington, James "Big Chief," 145, 147, 170, 182, 227

Wheeler, Johnny E., 76, 120–21, 334 (n. 51)

Wheeler, Palmer, 99–101, 118, 120–21

Wheeler, Roy, 100–101, 120–22, 334 (n. 51)

White, Benjamin Franklin, 23, 298 (n. 41)

White Church Records, 160, 172, 214

Whitfield, Jesse Gillis "J. G.," 166, 183–84, 189, 228–29, 233–34, 349–50 (n. 76)

Wills Family, 230

Wilson, Cullie, 331 (n. 25), 332 (n. 36)

Winans, Cece, 283, 285

Winsett, R. E., 162, 344 (n. 22)

WOAN (Lawrenceburg, Tenn.), 57, 74–75, 78–79, 117, 318–19 (n. 58), 318 (nn. 54, 55, 56), 319 (n. 59), 331 (n. 19)

WOAN Orchestra, 57

Wolfe, Gerald, 13, 252, 260

Women: in southern gospel, 73, 122–23, 201–5, 275–76, 334 (n. 55)

Word, Inc., 232, 242–43

Word Records, 245, 368 (n. 79)

World War I, 71–72, 74–75, 82, 84, 117, 120, 325 (n. 42)

World War II, 78, 80, 91, 114, 127,